THE ENDUR... ...ATIONALISM

Aviel Roshwald directly challenges prevalent scholarly orthodoxies about the exclusively modern character of nationalism. He argues that nationalism's enduring power to shape the world we live in arises directly out of its position at the heart of inescapable social and political paradoxes that are not only fundamental to the modern experience, but many of whose roots can be traced back into ancient history. Modern nationalisms, the author contends, cannot be fully understood without first examining their ancient counterparts and archetypes. Deploying a broad array of historical and contemporary case studies, ranging from ancient Jewish nationalism to the contemporary Israeli–Palestinian conflict, from the nationalist politics of ancient Greece to the contested memory of the Alamo, and from the Yugoslav wars to Northern Ireland's Orange Parades, the author argues that a responsible politics of nationalism depends upon a forthright acknowledgment of the deep-seated and intrinsically insoluble dilemmas that inhere in it.

AVIEL ROSHWALD is Professor of History at Georgetown University. His previous publications include *Ethnic Nationalism and the Fall of Empires* (2001) and, as co-editor, *European Culture in the Great War: The Arts, Entertainment, and Propaganda, 1914–1918* (1999).

A

A

A
O

Beszel angolul.

ESE AN_O _O_

MHYI I

THE ENDURANCE OF NATIONALISM

Ancient Roots and Modern Dilemmas

AVIEL ROSHWALD

Georgetown University

CAMBRIDGE
UNIVERSITY PRESS

CAMBRIDGE UNIVERSITY PRESS
Cambridge, New York, Melbourne, Madrid, Cape Town, Singapore, São Paulo

Cambridge University Press
The Edinburgh Building, Cambridge CB2 2RU, UK

Published in the United States of America by Cambridge University Press, New York

www.cambridge.org
Information on this title: www.cambridge.org/9780521603645

First published 2006

Printed in the United Kingdom at the University Press, Cambridge

A catalogue record for this publication is available from the British Library

ISBN-13 978-0-521-84267-9 hardback
ISBN-10 0-521-84267-0 hardback

ISBN-13 978-0-521-60364-5 paperback
ISBN-10 0-521-60364-1 paperback

For Alene

"There are so many inexplicable things in life, but one loses sight of them when singing the national anthem."

Robert Musil, *The Man Without Qualities*, vol. 1, p. 577

Contents

Illustrations

Acknowledgments

I have incurred a large debt of gratitude to many people over the years spent working on this project.

I am thankful to my father, Mordecai Roshwald, who introduced me to the critical, humanistic understanding of the Hebrew Bible and Jewish tradition, and who first showed me how to think and write analytically. My late mother, Miriam Roshwald, also contributed enormously to my fundamental education. Her keen interest in my work and her intellectual and emotional engagement are always missed.

I am grateful to Michael Berkowitz, Steven Grosby, and the anonymous reader for Cambridge University Press for taking the time to read parts or all of this manuscript and for providing me with both constructive criticism and encouraging words.

My deep thanks go to Steven G. Marks, who uncomplainingly plowed through a draft of the entire text and offered me invaluable feedback and advice.

Among my many supportive colleagues, I owe a particular debt to Tommaso Astarita, David Goldfrank, and Richard Stites for their unstinting friendship and encouragement over the years.

Some of the ideas presented in Chapter 1 of this book were first explored in a paper I gave in June 2000 at the conference on "Nationalism, Zionism and Ethnic Mobilisation," organized by Michael Berkowitz at the Institute of Jewish Studies, University College London. I was stimulated to develop these ideas further in the context of my participation in the Georgetown University History Department's Quigley Forum on nationalism, organized by my colleagues Joseph McCartin and Jordan Sand, in November 2000. Erez Manela, Akira Iriye, Ernest R. May, and the other members of the Harvard International History Seminar offered useful criticisms and suggestions in response to my presentation of material from Chapters 1 and 2 in December 2004. In October 2005, I had the opportunity to present material from Chapter 5 at the Second

German–American Frontiers of Humanities (GAFOH) Symposium, co-sponsored by the American Philosophical Society and the Alexander von Humboldt Foundation, in Hamburg, Germany. My thanks go to all the organizers of, and participants in, these events.

An early version of some of my arguments about ancient Jewish nationalism in Chapter 1 appeared in my essay on "Jewish Identity and the Paradox of Nationalism," in Michael Berkowitz, ed., *Nationalism, Zionism and Ethnic Mobilization of the Jews in 1900 and Beyond* (Leiden: E. J. Brill, 2004), 11–24. My thanks go to Brill Academic Publishers for their permission to employ some of this material in revised form here.

Georgetown University's Graduate School of Arts and Sciences provided me with summer research grants and publication fund support that helped further this project, and the university granted me a semester's sabbatical leave that enabled me to make considerable progress on the manuscript. For this valuable combination of time and money, I am most thankful.

David Alan and Lulen Walker of the Special Collections Department at Georgetown University's Lauinger Library provided patient help in my search for illustrations for this book, and David Hagen of Lauinger Library lent his photographic assistance to the production or reproduction of some of these images. I am grateful to all three. I must also express my appreciation for the remarkable online resources made available by the Library of Congress' Prints and Photographs Division. My thanks also go to Sandy Brenner, owner of the website www.JerusalemCoins.com, for providing me with the image of the Bar Kokhba coin that appears in Chapter 1.

For their unflagging enthusiasm for, and encouragement of, this project, I wish to thank William Davies and Michael Watson, the successive history editors at Cambridge University Press. My appreciation also goes to Isabelle Dambricourt, assistant editor at the press, whose professionalism, competence, and courtesy inspire my confidence as this manuscript goes into production.

I tip my hat to the cafés of the greater Washington, DC and Austin, Texas metropolitan areas, for their indulgence and/or indifference in allowing me to spend countless hours drafting this manuscript on their premises. I am particularly indebted in this regard to Café Mayorga in Silver Spring, Maryland.

Finally, my deepest thanks go to my wife Alene, for always being there to sustain my spirits as I have grappled with this undertaking. I dedicate this book to her.

Introduction

Nationalism pervades the modern world, yet its origins, nature, and prospects remain clouded by confusion and controversy. Identified as a quintessentially modern phenomenon by many scholars, it is seen as rooted in pre-modern traditions by a dissenting minority. Embraced as a vital framework for democratic self-determination by some, it is decried as the mortal enemy of tolerance and liberalism by others. Commonly dismissed as a thing of the past by post-1945 observers, nationalism has been the object of renewed fascination since the end of the Cold War, as events such as the break-up of the Soviet Union, the Yugoslav wars, China's growing preoccupation with the Taiwan question, and the surge of collective emotion in the United States following the September 11 attacks have highlighted nationalism's enduring power to shape history.

Although nationalism is routinely described as complex and paradoxical, there remains a strong tendency to fit it into rigid typological categories. Many theorists of nationalism have drawn useful, yet overly sharp, distinctions between national and religious identities, between ethnic and civic forms of nationalism, and between nationalism's linear conception of history and the non-linear temporal sensibilities of pre-modern eras, to take just a few examples. Such compartmentalized analytical approaches have begun to come under increasing critical scrutiny on the part of some social scientists. But there remains a wide gap between the most influential conceptual approaches to nationalism and the scores of historical monographs and studies of individual cases of nationalism that have appeared in recent years. The flow of new information and novel analytical perspectives emerging from these studies has exceeded the carrying capacity of many of the existing theoretical paradigms – particularly those that adhere to the view that nationalism can only be understood as a strictly modern, fundamentally secular phenomenon.[1]

This book places the paradoxical qualities of nationalism at the focal point of its analytical endeavor. I contend that the very contradictions and dilemmas that inhere in nationalism play a central – if often unacknowledged – role in the development of national identities and the historical evolution of nationalist ideologies and institutions. It is precisely its position at the intersection of conflicting principles and sentiments – and the abiding appeal of its unrealizable promise to reconcile these clashing elements – that lends nationalism much of its endurance. Nationalists and the nation-state hold forth hope for a resolution of the tensions between the inescapable reality of historical change and the persistent thirst for continuity of tradition, between the clashing interests of complex societies and the aspiration to a solidarity transcending all classes and parties, between the sense of the nation's uniqueness in the world and the belief that it has a mission to humanity. Like the rabbit in a greyhound race, the harmonization of such divergent impulses always remains just out of reach, yet all the more mesmerizing an objective for that. Rival parties and movements often claim to hold the key to resolving such dilemmas if only they are entrusted with power; the resultant debates and struggles among proponents of competing nationalist agendas have dominated the political and cultural histories of many countries. Nationalism is a dynamic force fueled by competing visions of an idealized, static community.

This study commences with a chapter in which I develop the claim that nationalism existed in the ancient world. This may strike some readers as an odd way to begin a book focused on the dilemmas of nationalism in the modern world. But it is my sense that many of the critical paradoxes of modern nationalism have pre-modern antecedents. Specifically, in the cases of the ancient Jews and Greeks, not only did some of the dilemmas they faced in defining and demarcating their identities *anticipate* modern problems of nationalism; the ways in which they thought about these issues (e.g. the relationship between national particularism and ethical/ religious universalism, or between kinship and citizenship) served as influential paradigms that *helped shape* modern constructions of national identity. By the same token, the elements that distinguish modern nationalism from its pre-modern forms cannot be discussed in an informed and coherent manner unless one places the phenomenon of nationalism in a deep diachronic context, rather than assuming that its contemporary incarnation bears no relation to anything that happened prior to the dawn of the modern age.

The rest of the book is organized thematically around a selection of ostensibly opposing forces and ideas whose intimate interaction has played a vital role in the shaping of national identities and ideologies.

Each chapter will focus on a particular dilemma faced by many if not most nationalisms, employing an assortment of examples and case-studies to explore in concrete, historical terms some of the various ways in which the issue has played out. It is my hope that this comparative, synthetic method will contribute to refining some of our conceptual approaches to nationalism. At the same time, I must acknowledge my enormous debt to the countless scholars on whose research and analysis this study relies; I make no claim to having uncovered new information about any individual example of nationalism. I should also make it clear that in criticizing certain theories of nationalism I do not mean to dismiss the value of these works or to disparage their authors' contributions. On the contrary, the clarity and incisiveness of many of these scholars' arguments has contributed enormously to our very capacity to discuss nationalism in a coherent manner and at an analytically useful level of abstraction. In the absence of such powerfully developed theses to disagree with, I would not have been able to write this book.

* * *

Before embarking on the substance of this study, some definitions are in order. I will use the term "nation" to refer to any community larger than one of mutual acquaintance that claims some form of collective, bounded, territorial sovereignty *in the name of its distinctive identity*, or any population in its capacity as a society on whose behalf such claims are asserted.[2] "Nationalism" refers to any ideology or set of attitudes, emotions, and mentalities based on the assertion of such claims (regardless of whether or not those claims have been fulfilled). "Nation-state" will signify a sovereign polity that claims to embody or represent the identity and will of one particular nation (however disputed and problematic such a claim may be). "Ethnic group" and "nationality" will be used interchangeably to refer to a population larger than an actual kinship group that considers itself – or is considered by a significant proportion of its members – to be bound together by common ancestry and historical experience, as manifested in shared cultural characteristics (including emotional attachment to a specific territory) that mark it apart from the rest of humanity. It should be noted that, on the basis of these definitions, an ethnic group need not have a fully developed sense of nationalism; conversely, a nation can employ criteria other than shared ethnicity in defining itself. For instance, a distinctive political culture might be stressed instead as the source of national identity, as in the case of Americans' shared reverence for their Constitution. (See Chapter 5.)

The term "nation-state" is used advisedly in this volume. As many scholars have pointed out, the uncritical conflation of the terms "nation" and "nation-state" has led to tremendous analytical confusion.[3] The relationship between nation and nation-state is certainly a complicated and often inconsistent one. The legal structures and official policies of the nation-state may be at odds with popular conceptions of national identity and interest. Disaffected minorities may resist the nation-state by establishing separatist movements designed to create nation-states of their own, while xenophobic majorities may claim that the nation-state is not worthy of the name unless it cracks down on aliens within and/or enemies without. Some nationalists may claim that the nation-state's laws and principles of government embody the essence of the nation's identity while others may insist that those institutions serve merely to protect the culture and tradition that constitute the essence of the nation's soul. Yet to recognize such complications does not justify simply doing away with the term "nation-state." After all, insofar as aspiration to independent statehood is one of the defining characteristics of nationalism, it is impossible to have a coherent discussion of nationalism unless it is juxtaposed with both the idealized image and the practical manifestation of the nation-state. It is precisely the tension between how nationalists envision the nation-state and how it functions once their dream of independence has been fulfilled that contributes to many of the dilemmas that this book proposes to examine.

I should also point out that the way in which I employ the term "nation-state" is not so undiscriminating as to encompass all territorially sovereign entities. Polities based on ideals and institutions such as universal religious community, the patrimonial state, the lord–vassal relationship, multi-ethnic empire, or international class solidarity, are not nation-states insofar as their claims to legitimacy are not directly dependent on a particularistic identity ascribed to the governed.

Finally, it is a common practice to distinguish between "patriotism" and "nationalism," such that the former term refers to selfless loyalty to a polity and its governing institutions while the latter describes prior attachment to a nation rather than a state.[4] "Patriotism" is widely used to mean devotion to an already existing, independent state, with "nationalism" then used in a restricted way to depict the attitude and ideology associated with the struggle for the establishment of a sovereign nation-state. Such terminological usage may be appropriate for some analytical purposes. It is not useful in the context of this book. In effect, the terminological territory covered by "patriotism" overlaps extensively with that embraced by the term "civic nationalism" (see Chapter 5), and it is one of the points of this study to explore how civic and ethnic, political and cultural, classical and modern, conceptions of identity interact and shape one another. Treating "patriotism" as a discrete category, conceptually segregated from "nationalism," would impoverish our understanding of the dialectical phenomena – including the tangled relationship between nation and state – whose analysis lies at the heart of this book.[5]

All of these definitions and distinctions are necessarily, yet sometimes frustratingly, abstract. The cut-and-dried categories of human identity and experience that form the basis for many nationalist claims are themselves belied by the complexities of socio-cultural bonds and loyalties. In practice, human identities are more intricate and multidimensional than any typological pigeon-hole or nationalist slogan can adequately convey. The unavoidable oversimplifications of theoretical discussions of nationalism and nationalist rhetoric alike make matters very confusing to thoughtful observers, who will note that no single instance of alleged nationhood appears to conform perfectly to any abstract definition of nationhood. Particularly troubling is the apparent disjuncture between the widely prevalent claim that the nation is a culturally and socially homogeneous collectivity and the kaleidoscopic reality of human loyalties and affections. Such conundrums give rise to perplexing questions. Is a Bavarian or a Texan still a German or an American if s/he feels a strong sense of regional as distinct from national loyalty? Why do Ulster's Protestants define themselves as British rather than Irish, whereas England's Catholics today generally see themselves – and are seen – as loyal Britons? Why did Yugoslavia break apart amidst horrific ethnic warfare even though members of many of the opposing forces spoke mutually intelligible versions of the same language?

The general response to these sorts of questions is that there is no one set of objective socio-cultural criteria that defines national identity. Identity is by its very nature a subjective experience, and national identity is no exception to this pattern. People may latch onto any set of shared characteristics as a basis for claiming nationhood and the right to territorial self-determination associated with it.

Furthermore, no matter what criteria for nationhood become established as social or political norms, in practice, within any given nation, people's loyalties and cultural attributes will fall along an ever-fluctuating gradient ranging from very close correlation with an idealized set of national identity markers to complete non-conformity with, and alienation from, the "official version" of nationhood.[6] Divergences from a dominant conception of national identity may result in conflict and may spawn separatist movements that espouse nationalist claims in their own right. Alternatively, they may be accommodated within the fold of an overarching nationalism that treats regional or sectarian loyalties and minority cultures as building-blocks of the nation rather than as threats to its unity.[7] It is one of the central challenges of any nationalist movement or regime to find ways of marginalizing, assimilating, co-opting, and/or harmonizing those aspects of individual and social identities that appear to threaten the homogeneity and cohesiveness of the nation. How developments unfold depends on a variety of specific circumstances and choices. Texan and Bavarian identities can be seen as taking the form of sub-nationalism, insofar as – for a variety of historical, cultural, and institutional reasons – they are comfortably nested within the overarching frameworks of American and German national identities, respectively. Were a significant proportion of Texans or Bavarians to decide that their right to self-determination was no longer adequately served by their countries' federal systems of government, and that full sovereignty was the only remedy for their grievances, one could speak of a full-fledged Texan or Bavarian nationalism.

To point out the tension between the simplistic ideal of national identity and the complexities that lie beneath its surface is not to diminish nationalism's importance. The fact that people disagree and change their minds about which nation they belong to and what belonging to it means does not make the desire to belong to a nation any the weaker. On the contrary, it is its confrontation with such inescapable, existential dilemmas that lends nationalism much of its emotional force, historical significance, and continued political salience, as the rest of this book will attempt to show.

END NOTES

1 For a critical discussion of these and other problems in the literature on nationalism, see Robert Wiebe, "*Imagined Communities*, Nationalist Experiences," *Journal of the Historical Society*, vol. 1, no. 1 (Spring 2000), 33–63. My thanks to Richard Kuisel for this reference. See also Peter Stearns, "Nationalisms: An Invitation to Comparative Analysis," *Journal of World History*, vol. 8, no. 1 (1997), 57–74.

2 I am influenced here by Benedict Anderson's definition in *Imagined Communities: Reflections on the Origin and Spread of Nationalism*, 2nd edn (London: Verso, 1991), 6. This paragraph as a whole paraphrases and slightly revises the definitions I employed in Aviel Roshwald, *Ethnic Nationalism and*

the *Fall of Empires: Central Europe, Russia and the Middle East, 1914–1923* (London: Routledge, 2001), 6.

3 Walker Connor, *Ethnonationalism: The Quest for Understanding* (Princeton: Princeton University Press, 1994), ch. 4.

4 See John Emerich Edward Dalberg-Acton (Lord Acton), "Nationality" (essay first published in 1862) in Dalberg-Acton, *The History of Freedom and other Essays* (London: Macmillan, 1919), 292; Connor, *Ethnonationalism*, 196; Andrew Vincent, *Nationalism and Particularity* (Cambridge: Cambridge University Press, 2002), ch. 5. For a trenchant critique of the widespread distinction between what are seen as virtuous patriotism and nasty nationalism, see Michael Billig, *Banal Nationalism* (London: Sage Publications, 1995), 55–59.

5 See Billig, *Banal Nationalism*, 5.

6 For a useful case study, see Jeremy King, *Budweisers into Czechs and Germans: A Local History of Bohemian Politics, 1848–1948* (Princeton: Princeton University Press, 2002). King demonstrates that not a few residents of early-to-mid-nineteenth-century Bohemia straddled the Czech–German ethno-cultural/linguistic boundary before the rise of modern nationalism forced them to affiliate themselves exclusively with one group or the other. However, I am not convinced by his inference that applying the very concept of ethnicity to earlier historical periods is anachronistic.

7 Cf. Celia Applegate, *A Nation of Provincials: The German Idea of Heimat* (Berkeley: University of California Press, 1990); Alon Confino, *The Nation as a Local Metaphor: Württemberg, Imperial Germany, and National Memory, 1871–1918* (Chapel Hill: University of North Carolina Press, 1997).

CHAPTER I

Nationalism in antiquity

Precisely because mythmaking is such an essential feature of human belief systems, social scientists have made the debunking of myths one of the essential tools of their trade.[1] The stories peoples, communities, and movements tell about themselves are seen as masks that must be pulled away if their true faces are to be revealed. This approach has been particularly apparent in the recent study of nationalism. As an ideology that seeks to create a broad yet cohesive framework for collective and individual identities alike, nationalism relies heavily upon the simplification and distortion of history, the propagation of beliefs about all-encompassing ties of blood and sentiment, and the disavowal of social, economic, and cultural differences that contradict the all-important themes of unity and fraternity. One of the distinguishing characteristics of nationalism as an ideology has been its attempt to portray itself as a manifestation of what already exists – the political expression of an identity and culture that has been around since time immemorial. Scholars of nationalism have accordingly focused their efforts on exposing how nationalist movements have shaped the very social and cultural conditions and invented the very traditions upon which they stake their claims to legitimacy.[2]

Like any successful methodology, this approach can be taken too far. In their zealous effort to gain critical distance from nationalists' propagandist claims, many scholars have gone to the other extreme, portraying modern national identities as social and ideological constructs created out of whole cloth by self-serving elites, by impersonal material forces, or by some combination of the two.[3] Among the shortcomings of this interpretive school is that it can become so preoccupied with the manipulative role of social and political elites that – like some of those elites themselves – it loses sight of the role of the popular masses in shaping national identities. One of the most underexamined issues in the existing scholarship is the question of what determines the receptivity or resistance of popular culture to the nationalist ideas disseminated by elites and how the sensibilities and attitudes of the targeted audience shape those ideas.[4]

This problem is, in turn, related to the issue of how to date nationalism's origins. Do modern nationalist movements build on preexisting forms of social and historical identity, or do they fashion ostensibly ancient identities out of thin air? In many cases, historians have clearly established that nationalist claims of ancient roots are quite devoid of foundation. Slovak nationalists' assertions of an unbreakable chain of cultural continuity between their modern community and the ninth-century CE Great Moravian Empire, or Spanish-speaking Mexican nationalists' cooptation of the legacy of the Mayas and Aztecs, serve as ready-made strawmen that scholars of nationalism can knock down to their hearts' content.[5] The most cursory investigation can readily establish that many of the long-since departed states or societies which contemporary nationalists have latched onto in their quest for historical legitimacy actually have little or nothing in common culturally, demographically, or linguistically with their would-be historical descendants. Making such spurious claims to an unbroken chain of historical continuity where no demonstrable connection exists is referred to as a form of "primordialism" – one of the most common features of nationalism and one of the most easily ridiculed.[6]

There are two pitfalls in the debunking of primordialism. One is the failure to acknowledge that some contemporary national cultures may have longer histories of continuous development than others. Exposing the spuriousness of some historical claims does not *ipso facto* reduce all such claims to nonsense, yet many scholars seem to make just that assumption. To be sure, the assertion that the antiquity of a society's origins lends added legitimacy to its latter-day political or territorial claims is based on subjective, ideological, and psychological perceptions, and cannot be rationally proved or disproved. But in questioning this principle, critics of nationalism have jumped to the unwarranted conclusion that no given social identity can possibly be much older than another and, indeed, that national identity did not exist anywhere on the face of the planet prior to 1789, or some other arbitrarily chosen date marking the birth of the modern era. This is a defensive overreaction to nationalism's politicization of history, and it warrants reexamination. I would contend that – to cite a few examples – Armenian, Chinese, or Jewish claims to a chain of cultural transmission linking their modern societies to an ancient past have greater credibility than analogous Slovak or Mexican claims. This does not make Jewish nationalism more real or legitimate than Slovak nationalism (although a credible link to an ancient past may well enhance the mass resonance of a nationalist movement[7]). Nor does this mean that any formulation of national identity, whether associated with an ancient tradition or not, is somehow immune to the constant flux and change of history. What this does suggest is that rumors of nationalism's recent birth as a general phenomenon have been greatly exaggerated.[8]

It is quite true that most modern national identities either took form quite recently or are different in significant respects from their premodern antecedents. It is also true that during the early Middle Ages and beyond, European states were far too weakly constituted to form viable frameworks for the crystallization of national identities.[9] But it is a logical fallacy to deduce from this that national identity could not have existed in any form or at any time prior to the onset of modernity. The fact that most contemporary nations arose in modern times leaves open the possibility that other nations could have existed in pre-modern eras – nations that subsequently disappeared, merged into other collectivities, or evolved into novel cultural, political, and institutional forms. The fact that medieval Europe lacked nation-states by virtue of lacking well-defined states does not preclude the possibility that more firmly established ancient and/or non-European states might have generated, or arisen from, nationalist sentiments. It is certainly *conceivable* that nationalism is in fact an exclusively modern phenomenon, but this should not be an *unquestioned assumption*; it is an assertion that demands proof and that has not, in fact, been convincingly demonstrated.

My own working hypothesis is that the idea of nationhood as well as the phenomenon of national consciousness and its expression in nationalism are not exclusively modern, but have appeared in various forms, among diverse societies, throughout much of the history of literate civilization. I am not alone in trying to push back the chronological boundaries of nationhood. Anthony Smith has argued that the success of modern nationalisms in garnering public support has rested on their selective utilization and adaptation of pre-modern images, myths, and symbols of ethnic community. He has gone so far as to express openness to the idea of nations existing in antiquity. Adrian Hastings contended that literate culture, not the printing press (as Benedict Anderson would have it), is the essential precondition and foundation for the creation of national communities, and went on to explore the phenomenon of national identity in the European Middle Ages and Early Modern period.[10]

In this chapter, I wish to carry Adrian Hastings' thesis to what I see as its logical conclusion. Hastings highlights the centrality of the Hebrew

Bible in shaping European conceptions of nationhood, and he concedes that ancient Israelite or Jewish identity may well have been national in character. But he does not explore this proposition in depth, given that the focus of his work is on medieval and early modern European identities, of which he regards English identity as the earliest example. In these pages, I will argue – as Steven Grosby has done[11] – that ancient Jews developed a recognizably national form of identity and, indeed, that they were not the only ancient society to do so.

I would also like to push Anthony Smith's path-breaking argument a little further, and suggest that his careful distinction between pre-modern ethnic and national identity and modern nationalism may be a bit too careful. Smith holds that national*ism* is a strictly modern phenomenon even though nations may, arguably, have existed in antiquity. Certainly, if by nationalism we mean a political ideology that is viewed as globally applicable, and in the name of whose universal principles individual nations strive for self-determination, then nationalism is strictly modern. But this seems like an overly narrow definition of nationalism – one that assumes and imposes an overly constraining framework of understanding even on modern nationalist movements. After all, even in the modern period, there is no one definitive doctrinal tract to which all nationalists subscribe – no published corpus that has played a role comparable to that of Karl Marx's writings in the development of socialism. Both Benedict Anderson and Anthony Smith have argued convincingly that nationalism should be seen more as an anthropological or cultural phenomenon than as a formal political ideology.[12] Its fundamental characteristic is a preoccupation with the freedom, political-territorial sovereignty, and dignity (sometimes also aggrandizement) of one's own nation as cardinal objectives towards which collective and individual effort are to be directed. I contend that wherever one finds a nation one is likely to find nationalism in this sense of the term. After all, the nation itself is the product of subjective consciousness; it is a human collectivity that regards its common identity as a basis for preserving or claiming some form of political-territorial self-determination, or any population in its aspect as a group on behalf of which such claims are made.[13] The active and self-conscious assertion of such claims constitutes the essence of nationalism.

Therefore, rather than rejecting the idea of ancient nationalism outright, it strikes me as more straightforward and productive to draw distinctions and comparisons between pre-modern nationalism and modern nationalism. Disenchanted readers may well object that all of this is nothing but a meaningless semantic game. But the point is that there is no reason to begin an examination of modern nationalism's pre-modern analogues or origins by conceding in advance that nationalism *per se* is an exclusively or inherently modern phenomenon. To do so is to cede the rhetorical and analytical ground prematurely to scholarship's modernist[14] mainstream.

That said, let me clarify that this is not designed as an exercise in reductionism. It is not my intention to eliminate all distinctions between modern and pre-modern forms of identity, but to refine them. Modern nationalisms do have significant distinguishing features. Chief among them is their attunement to the ideal of political self-determination as an abstract and universally applicable model – as reflected in the fact that every modern nationalist movement *calls itself* a nationalist movement, in effect legitimizing its particular cause by subsuming it under a generic category. On the other hand, when we speak of a nationalist we refer to someone who has taken up the cause of his or her own nation, not that of nations in general. (Thus, while it is true that the nineteenth-century Italian nationalists Mazzini and Garibaldi took up the causes of oppressed peoples other than their own, it is *in their capacity as fighters for their own nation's unity and independence* that we refer to them as nationalists.) This aspect of nationalism is not exclusively modern.

It is my contention that this sort of analytical and comparative discussion can, in fact, best be undertaken through the use of a terminology that allows for the existence of pre-modern and modern nationalisms, just as scholars discuss, compare, and contrast pre-modern and modern forms of agriculture, commerce, art, literature, religion, social class, family life, democracy, warfare, the state, etc. There are many fundamental differences between sacrificing children on the altar of Moloch and pulling into a contemporary drive-in church for a spiritual quickie, yet both rituals are recognizably religious in nature and one can usefully compare and contrast them within that *common framework* without suggesting that they amount to the *same thing*. Conversely, to insist that nationalism is exclusively bound up with modernity is to fall into a pattern of circular logic and tautological argument that is analytically self-limiting if not self-defeating, as I will argue at greater length below.[15]

* * *

What makes the phenomenon of nationalism particularly baffling is that it lies at the intersection of the anthropological and the ideological,[16] the socio-biological and the socially constructed, the emotional and the intellectual. Some of nationalism's psychological building blocks and fundamental behavioral qualities, such as collective territoriality, solidarity based on kinship (real or imagined), and hostility towards outsiders, can be found among humans at every stage of historical development as well as among many non-humans such as wolves and chimpanzees. When we observe a flock of geese in a pond advancing aggressively, necks extended, against the retreating members of another flock until they have driven them over an imaginary line in the water, we instantly and intuitively recognize and understand the general nature of their activity (even if their apparent moderation in stopping short at the line may strike us as alien).[17]

Does this mean that if it walks like a goose and honks like a goose, it's a nationalist? Not quite. (If it goosesteps, it undoubtedly is, but that's another story.) Nationalism can be seen as the cultural and ideological expression of some of the analogous impulses and social-behavior patterns in humans,[18] but in its capacity as a cultural system it also actively shapes those patterns and links them to moral frameworks, political institutions, and social and economic interests. Most fundamentally, nationalism extends and transposes the idea and/or sensibility of kinship to a broader community that cannot possibly verify the integrity of its genealogical connections and, as Benedict Anderson has pointed out, that is too large for each of its members to know all the other members personally. The nationalist conception of kinship can be literal, positing a mythical, common biological ancestor for all members of the nation, or it can be figurative, as in the American notion of the Founding Fathers as common ideological ancestors of an immigrant society.[19] In either case, nationalist kinship serves to bind together people who do not know one another personally in a sense of community that provides the motive and framework for the exercise of political authority over a demarcated territory. Nationalism synthesizes the idea of group solidarity and territoriality with the principle of governmental authority and political sovereignty. It links the intrinsically human connection between collective and individual identity to the conditions and demands of state formation and institutionalized political power. Given humans' versatility and resourcefulness in the manipulation of symbols and the construction of myths, nationalism can be associated with an endless variety of ethical codes, religious beliefs, ideological agendas, and political and territorial frameworks.

A prerequisite for the formation and survival of any national community is the availability of impersonal mechanisms for the broad dissemination – both across the living community and between its generations – of standardized myths, traditions, memories, values, and laws.[20] The primary channels of communication need not be directly accessible to every member of the community; it is enough to have a geographically dispersed elite that is directly connected to the information flow. Personal contact and oral communication between communal leaders and common folk can suffice as a transmission device of last resort at the local level. It is the networking of cultural, social, and political elites that is the *sine qua non* of any nationalist enterprise. On the other hand, the more widely accessible the impersonal medium of communication is, the more likely nationalist consciousness is to become the preeminent and most pervasive source of social and political cohesion.

word as medium

In the beginning was the Logos. The written word was the original medium for the impersonal broadcasting of standardized information. (Of course, it has also been a medium for the expression and communication of non-standardized information, but that does not concern us here.) It was intimately tied to the construction of political communities in the ancient Fertile Crescent, Egypt, and Greece, as well as in China, and it made the formation of national identities possible, though not necessary. The Phoenicians' development of the alphabet out of earlier ideographic systems, and the rapid spread of this extremely simple, yet highly versatile, form of writing among adjacent, Western Semitic societies (all of which spoke very similar languages), made the written word more easily and readily accessible to a broader cross-section of the population than ever before. Even if the literate remained a small minority of the overall population, the growth of literacy among social elites is likely to have had a ripple effect, by way of oral transmission of written information, on broader segments of society. It is probably no coincidence that one of the most fully articulated national identities in the ancient world developed in the western, alphabetic zone of the Fertile Crescent, among the Israelites.[21]

THE ANCIENT JEWS

The history of Jewish identity raises serious questions about the validity of narrowly modernist understandings of nationalism. To be sure, Zionism clearly conforms to the pattern of nineteenth- and twentieth-century movements that utilized modern techniques of mass mobilization and modern conceptions of popular sovereignty in their struggle to nationalize collective identities. There certainly was an element of contrivance, and even artifice, in Zionism's selective adaptation of traditional religious images, symbols, and practices in its creation of a secular, nationalist iconography.[22]

But recognition that Zionism exaggerated its links to the past in order to legitimize its political modernization project need not lead us to dismiss all claims regarding the antiquity of Jewish national identity as spurious. Certainly ethnicity – in the sense of collective identity based on the notion of common ancestry – is the fundamental basis for the Hebrew Bible's classificatory schema for humanity. The seemingly endless series of "begats" that fills so many pages of Genesis, and that has brought tears to the eyes of so many Sunday School students, serves to lay out a genealogical basis for the division of humanity into multiple peoples, while at the same time underlining the common ancestry that all humans share. Genesis 10, in particular, traces the lineage of various peoples back to the three sons of Noah, concluding each genealogy with a sentence along the lines of: "These are the children of Shem, [according] to their clans, their tongues, their lands, their peoples [*goyeihem*]."[23] Kinship, language, and territory are thus explicitly and formulaically identified as the interconnected elements that make up the fundamental and universal rubric of collective identity – of peoplehood and nationhood. I would venture to say that *goyeihem* is in fact best translated – as indeed it commonly is by biblical scholars indifferent to the dictates of nationalism theorists – as "their nations."[24] In Genesis 11, the Tower of Babel story likewise associates ethnic divisions with linguistic ones, suggesting the irreversibility of humanity's ethno-cultural divisions even as it ruefully acknowledges that such differences are a cardinal source of human misunderstanding and conflict. (See Chapter 4.)

This understanding of the "fatal diversity" of human languages and identities – to paraphrase Benedict Anderson[25] – serves as the framework for the biblical conceptualization of the Israelites' particular territorial and political sovereignty. In the biblical view of things, it is the combination of the Israelites' common descent from Abraham and their common commitment to his and Moses' covenants with God – a linkage of ethnic and civic elements, to use modern terminology – that forms the basis of their right to political sovereignty over the bounded territory ("from Dan to Beersheba") of the Promised Land.[26] The legitimacy of monarchic government for the Israelites hinges on a king's sharing his subjects' ethnic identity and on his upholding the Covenantal law of the land:

When you come to the land which the Lord your God gives you, and you possess it and dwell in it, and then say, "I will set a king over me, like all the nations that are round about me"; you may indeed set as king over you him whom the Lord

your God will choose. *One from among your brethren you shall set as king over you;*
you may not put a foreigner over you, who is not your brother ... And when he sits
on the throne of his kingdom, he shall write for himself in a book a copy of this
law ... and it shall be with him, and he shall read in it all the days of his life,
that he may learn to fear the Lord his God, by keeping all the words of this law
and these statutes ... *that his heart may not be lifted up above his brethren* ...[27]

In the biblical formulation, a myth of common origins, an elaborately
defined sense of territoriality, a conception of political legitimacy closely
tied to the principle of equality of all members of the community
(monarch included) before the Law, and the overarching framework of
Covenantal law, form mutually defining and supporting elements of an
institutional and ideological nexus that bears all the marks of politicized,
national-territorial identity – that is to say, nationalism.[28]

A variety of objections can be raised to this interpretation. For
instance, modern nationalism is intimately linked to the idea of popular
sovereignty,[29] whereas the Bible's fundamental conception of political
authority is theocratic. Indeed, most of the means and forms of mass
mobilization associated with contemporary nationalism were non-existent
in ancient times – mass media, universal education, political parties, etc.
The initial articulation and acceptance of the biblical complex of religious, communal, and political ideals was doubtless limited to the
restricted spheres of priestly elites or eccentric prophetic circles. Without
the framework of popular sovereignty linked to mass culture, how can
ancient Jewish notions of identity be deemed nationalist in character?

Such objections can be challenged, in turn. Judaism's theocratic
principle legitimized possession of the Land of Israel by the Children of
Israel – not by their kings. To be sure, ultimate authority over the land
and its people was exercised by God, whose sovereignty was mediated by
the Covenant. But in its capacity as an egalitarian social contract (in the
sense that it created an egalitarian framework for relations among the
human parties to it), the Covenant conferred the functional equivalent of
popular sovereignty on the Israelites.[30] Enlightenment era social-contract
theory, which lies at the basis of modern, secular conceptions of popular
sovereignty and national self-determination, is largely an intellectual
offshoot of biblical Covenant theology.[31] For that matter, few modern
nationalisms are as secular as many theorists tend to assume.[32] Popular
sovereignty continues to be widely understood as conferred by divine will
rather than, or along with, natural law, be it in Serbian eschatological
nationalism or American conceptions of Manifest Destiny.[33]

If one defines nationalism as the propagation of a homogeneous, politicized identity to a territorially bounded community *by means of psychologically and technologically advanced instruments of indoctrination and communication*, then, of course, nationalism must be a strictly modern phenomenon. But there is a tautological element to this reasoning.[34] In Benedict Anderson's formulation, the emergence of print capitalism was a necessary, though not sufficient, condition for the genesis of nationalism. According to this criterion, nationalism cannot possibly have informed the composition of the *Hebrew* Bible; rather its origins can be traced to the production and marketing of the *Gutenberg* Bible. But this approach is, once again, premised on an overly sharp distinction between religious and nationalist sensibilities. If the Jewish religious tradition *is* recognized as containing a nationalist element, then could it not be argued that its scripture and liturgy may have served as media for the propagation and shaping of national identity among the masses? Hearing the Torah read in public every Sabbath and market day from early Second Temple times on must have created (and still does) a sense of simultaneity of experience that was more, not less, powerful than the daily ritual of reading the newspaper that Anderson refers to as the hallmark of modern imagined communities.[35]

I do not mean to reduce the rich body of biblical literature to nothing more than a series of sanctified propaganda pamphlets. My point is not that the Torah is a book about nationalism. It is rather that the Jewish scriptures and liturgy both presuppose and reinforce a strong sense of national particularism that is inextricably intertwined with universalistic themes of ethics and theology. This very tension between particularistic and universalistic ideals is characteristic of some of the most influential modern nationalist ideologies, including American and French-republican nationalisms. (See Chapter 4.)

To be sure, legitimate questions have been raised about what, if anything, the biblical religio-political vision of what an Israelite or Jewish state *ought to look like* had to do with *historical realities* in the original kingdoms of Israel and Judah (tenth–sixth centuries BCE).[36] Archaeological research has provided ample evidence of the actual existence of these kingdoms and of many of the specific monarchs named in the biblical accounts.[37] But it has also demonstrated how widespread pagan cults were throughout these lands during this period. Indeed, the biblical accounts themselves emphasize the ubiquity of idolatry and the perennial inclination to "stray from the path" of purist monotheism on the part of common folk and rulers alike. Moreover, both internal textual evidence from the Bible and unearthed cultic objects from the first half of the first millennium BCE point to a gradual evolution of first monolatry,[38] then full-fledged monotheism, out of earlier religious forms that high-lighted the role of Yahweh amid a broader pantheon.[39] The dating of the Hebrew scriptures is itself a hotly disputed subject, with estimates for the composition of the Book of Deuteronomy, to take one example, ranging from the seventh to the fourth centuries BCE.[40] In other words, a defining text of Judaism may not have been fixed in its final form until after the destruction of the monarchy whose legitimacy is supposed to have rested on that very text.

But as far as the broad thrust of this chapter's argument about the antiquity of nationalism is concerned, it really makes little difference whether monotheistic, Covenantal Judaism crystallized before or after the destruction of the First Temple in 586 BCE. Even if the fundamental texts of the Hebrew Bible did not take their definitive forms until well into the second half of the first millennium BCE, that would still place them firmly in the period of classical antiquity. At the time of their compo-sition, whether before or after the fall of the Davidic monarchy, the Jewish scriptures may well have represented the outlook of an alienated minority of priests and prophets rather than the cultural mainstream of the society they lived in. Yet the fact that an ancient intellectual elite – however marginalized – incorporated such distinctively nationalist ele-ments into its religious perspective would suffice in and of itself to burst the modernist paradigm of nationalism. Indeed, if the original purveyors of the biblical conception of Jewish identity were a narrow elite or even a marginalized coterie, the same can be said of many of the intelligentsias and/or social elites that spearheaded nationalist movements in East Central Europe, the Middle East, and elsewhere over the course of the last century or two.[41]

Moreover, by the late first millennium BCE, the biblical texts had incontrovertibly become the universally accepted basis for Jewish religious belief and communal identity. By this time, when widely held Messianic beliefs were so powerfully political in their implications and repercus-sions, and when Roman rule over Palestine was repeatedly challenged by violent uprisings aimed at the restoration of Jewish territorial sovereignty, it seems clear that Jewish nationhood and nationalism constituted pow-erful social and cultural realities. The sectarian and political disputes that divided the Jewish community in Hasmonean and Roman times (i.e. from the second century BCE on) were based on rival *interpretations* of the commonly accepted, scripturally prescribed relationship among common

Figure 1 This Israeli 10 agorot coin from the mid-1970s bears an image of a palm tree deliberatively evocative of coins issued in the second century CE by the Jewish rebel leader Bar Kokhba. Photograph by David Hagen. All copyrights of this image are the sole property of the Bank of Israel, by whose permission it appears in this publication.

ancestry, Covenantal authority, territorial sovereignty, political legitimacy, and religious belief.[42]

Even some of the symbols and images employed by ancient Jewish nationalists can strike a familiar chord among a modern audience. Some of the coins minted by the modern state of Israel bear motifs borrowed from ancient Judean coins. For instance, the small-denomination 10 Agorot coin (minted in 1975–76) illustrated in Figure 1 bears the image of a seven-branched palm tree, first used on coins dating from the revolt led by Shim'on Ben Kosiba (known by tradition as Bar Kokhba) in 132–5 CE. (See Figure 2.) This was the last major Jewish rebellion against Roman rule in Palestine, coming six decades after the destruction of the Second Temple. The image on the modern Israeli coin is a stereotypically

Figure 2 The Bar Kokhba rebellion coin from the 130s CE which served as the inspiration for the modern Israeli coin in Figure 1. The name "Shim'on" (after Shim'on Bar Kokhba) is inscribed on this coin in a palaeo-Hebrew script that is evocative of a yet earlier period in Jewish history. Courtesy of Sandy Brenner, www.JerusalemCoins.com.

twentieth-century evocation (or "appropriation") of the ancient past in the construction of a modern national identity. Yet a glance at ancient Jewish coins struck during periods of autonomy, independence, or rebellion between the Hasmonean period and the Bar Kokhba revolt (that is, between the second century BCE and the second century CE) suggest that this very technique may represent a reinvention of the wheel, so to speak. The mottoes on these ancient coins, such as the word "Shim'on" (for Shim'on Ben Kosiba) on the coins that served as the inspiration for the modern Israeli coin, or various propagandist slogans of the Bar Kokhba coinage, such as "For the Freedom of Jerusalem," "For the Freedom of Israel," and "Year Two of the Freedom of Israel," were anachronistically inscribed in palaeo-Hebrew – the script of the First Temple period which had long since been supplanted in common usage by an utterly different style derived from Aramaic lettering. Although Phoenician and other Middle Eastern coins were also commonly inscribed in archaic scripts, this stylistic choice could be read as part of a conscious attempt to lend an aura of Davidic-kingdom-era, national authenticity to latter-day Jewish regimes and rebel governments.[43] The nationalist propensity for primordialism is itself an ancient phenomenon!

Ah, but what about the idiosyncratically modern relationship between nation and historical consciousness, some will object. Drawing an analogy, as I have done above, between Judaism's weekly Torah reading and Benedict Anderson's daily newspaper reading calls to mind one of the fundamental differences between pre-modern and modern conceptions of time and history that Anderson and others have emphasized. Torah reading proceeds in a circle, resuming at Genesis, chapter 1 immediately following the conclusion of the last chapter of Deuteronomy, without fail every year. Today's newspaper headlines, by contrast, change from day to day and year to year without ever repeating themselves. The pre-moderns, it is commonly argued, had a cyclical view of time or held to a belief in mystical or theological connections between temporally detached events (such as the destruction of the First and Second Temples on the same day of the year, or – in Christian theology – the crucifixion of Jesus and its prefiguration in the near-sacrifice of Isaac). The moderns, by contrast, are said to have a linear conception of history as a chain of causes and effects continuing endlessly through time – a sense of flux and transience that is compensated for by the belief in the immortality of the nation.[44]

This is a significant and in many ways useful contradistinction.[45] Yet, once again, I contend that it should not be accepted without serious reservations. It is precisely in the Judeo-Christian tradition that the linear conception of history has deep roots. (I would argue that elements of the classical Greco-Roman historiographical tradition are influential here as well.[46]) One of the Hebrew Bible's central themes is the Israelites' movement together through time toward a common destiny, and the fluctuation of their fortunes in accordance with their observance or defiance of their Covenant with God.[47] This theological historicism coexists with ahistorical elements; they are not mutually exclusive.[48] By the same token, modern nationalism is not informed by a purely historicist mentality. Mystical prefigurations and the cyclical reliving of past events are indispensable components of nationalist mythology and ritual. The historicism of nationalism often gives way to imagery suggestive of a sudden collapsing of events hundreds of years apart into a single, transcendent moment that unifies the nation's countless generations across time. Annually recurring independence-day celebrations are an occasion for the reliving – or at least recounting – of a nation's primordial act of self-determination. In many European countries, the anniversary of the

armistice ending the First World War is used to commemorate the
nation's fallen in all wars, somewhat as the Jewish religious fast day of
Tish'ah be-Av marks the destruction of, not just one, but both, temples.
Israel's close juxtaposition of Holocaust Remembrance Day with Independence Day and the Memorial Day for Israel's fallen soldiers is
designed to reinforce certain ideological and quasi-theological beliefs
about the connection between suffering and redemption and the contrast
between victimization in the Diaspora and self-determination in the
ancestral homeland. It does not reflect a strictly historicist approach to
Zionist history.[49] Nor is this phenomenon a peculiarity of the Jewish
case; evidence of it can be found in virtually any nationalist tradition, as
I will try to demonstrate in Chapter 2.

THE ANCIENT GREEKS

The Jewish example is a particularly compelling case of ancient nationalism, both because of its contemporary reconceptualization as political
Zionism and because of its formative impact – via the medium of the
Hebrew Bible – on early modern and modern European constructions of
nationhood. (See Chapter 4.) But it is not the only case of ancient
nationalism. The ancient Greeks provide another striking example of
national identity as a vital political, cultural, and ideological force in the
ancient world. As in the case of the ancient Hebrews, this is a particularly
salient example because of its formative influence on modern Western
(and, hence, global) political institutions and historical consciousness.

It is commonly assumed that, because Greeks' political loyalties in the
classical period were centered on the city-state (*polis*), the notion of
national identity can have little or no relevance for understanding their
societies and institutions.[50] Ironically, this assumption is itself a product
of the very essentialist mentality that contemporary scholars are so vigi-
lant in warning against. At the same time, it in fact ignores some striking
cultural and political manifestations of a budding pan-Hellenic national
consciousness in the late classical era.

To elaborate on the former point first, by what immutable law was it
determined that the geographic and demographic scope of national
identity must be congruent with an objectively determined set of linguistic or cultural boundaries? It is one of the mantras of contemporary
scholarship that the criteria and boundaries of national identity are
subjectively, contentiously, and often quite arbitrarily, determined. Yet
when it comes to the ancient world, Athenians, Spartans, and Thebans

are held to have had no meaningful national identities merely because their primary political loyalties were focused on their individual city-states rather than on Greece as a whole. This is a striking example of anachronistic thinking, informed by the familiar examples of nineteenth-century Italian and German national unification – and, of course, of modern Greek nationalism. In the modern German and Italian contexts, local or regional identity (Bavarian, Lombard, etc.) was regarded as a potential obstacle to the larger purpose of forging a trans-regional national identity. Although, as we shall see further on, pan-Hellenic sentiment did come to play an important role in ancient Greek identity, it is a teleological distortion to project the nineteenth-century national-unification model onto, say, fifth-century BCE Athens and conclude that Athenian identity was nothing but a hindrance to the development of a Greek national identity or that in the absence of a unified Greece there was no framework for nationalism in the Hellenic world. Yet that seems to be the subtext of the widespread assertion or implication that the *polis* was, by definition, too small a unit to qualify as the legitimate object of nationalist sentiment.[51]

True, many *poleis* were so small that a majority of their inhabitants at any one time were likely to know one another personally, and it seems reasonable to agree with Benedict Anderson that imagining oneself to be part of a nation involves a level of abstraction beyond that needed to bind together a community of personal acquaintances. Granted the importance of that *quantitative*, demographic watershed, there remains at least one *polis* – Athens – whose population clearly *was* too large for personal ties to serve as its primary source of affective cohesion. What filled the gap was a *quality* of public sentiment that provides a remarkably vivid example of national identity as an active political force in the ancient world.

Athens was by far the largest of the *poleis* in population and consisted of more than a geographical point on the map, including as it did the city itself, the Piraeus port, and a relatively extensive rural hinterland in Attica. The political history of sixth- and fifth-century BCE Athens was dominated by a process of development and transformation that bears striking resemblance to what is referred to in the contemporary world as the construction of national identity and a state- and elite-led process of national integration. Cleisthenes' constitutional reforms of 508 BCE combined the democratization of political institutions with the intro-duction of new socio-political structures that served to marginalize the political influence of old, territorially circumscribed, clan-based group-ings by creating alongside them new "tribes," each of which comprised members from urban, seaside, and rural districts, respectively. These new "tribal" divisions served as the basis for the distribution of seats on the Council, the allocation of various public offices, and the structuring of communal institutions. In other words, traditional kinship structures were marginalized and/or replaced by public associations that employed the imagery and rituals of kinship to link individuals and their families both psychologically and functionally to Athenian civil society as a whole.[52]

Athens' small size relative to most modern nation-states was significant precisely in so far as it facilitated this process of national integration. In the modern era, mass media, speedy transportation systems, standardized educational curricula, and other instruments not available in the ancient world are employed to promote and maintain a sense of national community among the population of a large territory. In ancient Athens, the territorially circumscribed nature of the state facilitated the creation of a direct democracy that drew on the compulsory participation of all male citizens. This created what was arguably a more powerful sense of involvement in the national enterprise than the typical experience of citizenship in a twenty-first-century CE nation-state. At the same time, this *polis* was big enough (in the late fourth century BCE, Athens comprised some 30,000 adult male citizens and a total population – including slaves and resident aliens – of at least 300,000[53]) to preclude the realistic possibility of each member of the community personally knowing every other member of the community. As Edward E. Cohen also points out, it therefore meets the criteria of an *imagined* national community according to Benedict Anderson's widely accepted definition of the term.[54]

It is true that Athenians continued to think of themselves as a community of interpersonal acquaintance long after the *polis'* size had grown so enormous. This has led scholars to categorize Athens as too intimate a polity to qualify as a nation. I would argue that the fifth- and fourth-century BCE Athenians' projection of this anachronistic image of mutual familiarity onto their outsized *polis* is precisely what distinguishes their identity as national in character. After all, being imagined as bound by deeply personal ties even though they are not is precisely what makes imagined communities imagined.

For a visceral sense of how highly developed this feeling of national community had become by the fifth century BCE, we need only look to Thucydides' rendition of Pericles' funeral oration of 431/430 BCE. This well-known text presents an eloquent and finely nuanced articulation of what it means to be an Athenian and what distinguishes the collective character of Athens from that of the other Greek city-states. Athens' democratic system of government is explicitly highlighted as both the embodiment and guarantor of the *polis'* uniquely well-balanced combination of individualism and civic-mindedness, personal freedom and readiness for self-sacrifice. Seeking to lend meaning to the losses suffered during the first year of the Peloponnesian War, Pericles portrays the willingness of Athens' men to face death in combat as the purest and most selfless form of public service, which more than compensates for whatever faults they may have had in their personal lives:

To me it seems that the consummation which has overtaken these men shows us the meaning of manliness in its first revelation and in its final proof. Some of them, no doubt, had their faults; but what we ought to remember first is their gallant conduct against the enemy in defence of their native land. They have blotted out evil with good, and done more service to the commonwealth than they ever did harm in their private lives ...

So and such they were, these men – worthy of their city. We who remain behind may hope to be spared their fate, but must resolve to keep the same daring spirit against the foe ... I could tell you a long story ... about what is to be gained by beating the enemy back. What I would prefer is that you should fix your eyes every day on the greatness of Athens as she really is, and should fall in love with her ... Make up your minds that happiness depends on being free, and freedom depends on being courageous ... [55]

[Many of the quintessential elements of nationalism as we know it – even a specifically liberal-democratic type of nationalism – are strikingly apparent in this speech:[56] love of country as the ultimate good and death for one's homeland as the ultimate sacrifice that wipes out all stains; the seamless connection between collective identity and personal identity within a framework that still leaves scope for a large measure of individualism and mutual tolerance;[57] the idea that popular sovereignty is the foundation of the state's political legitimacy and the mechanism whereby individual members of the populace – rich and poor alike – identify themselves with the social and political collective; the idea that one's own society has a distinctive character that manifests itself in both private and public spheres and that shapes not just political action but also the educational system, cultural production, public entertainment, private forms of leisure, and patterns of consumption.[58] The words attributed to Pericles seem designed to create an image of Athens as a culturally distinctive collectivity that constitutes the mirror of each individual Athenian's soul. In other words, the Athenian state is not simply constituted by the political participation of its citizens, as in the alleged classical model of the republic; it derives its legitimacy from its ability to express, represent, and sustain the cultural identity of its people.[59]

The implicit or explicit exclusion of various social groups from full participation in the idealized Athenian way of life need not be viewed as incompatible with the idea of nationhood. The cult of masculinity and ethos of warrior machismo implicit in Pericles' address – and the associated marginalization of women[60] – is a stereotypical feature of many nineteenth- and twentieth-century nationalisms. The vast numbers of slaves who played such significant roles in the Athenian economy were certainly not considered worthy of any mention at all in a discussion of Athenian identity, and the relationship of non-citizen residents to the imagined community was often ambiguous.[61] But, as in the marginalization of women, this sort of mentality is a common feature – practically a distinctive characteristic – of modern nationalisms. One need only think of the double standard of American democratic nationalism in the age of plantation slavery or of recent German policies toward second-generation resident aliens of Turkish origin[62] to realize how restrictive the criteria of belonging can be in unquestionably national frameworks of identity.

An ostensibly more difficult problem with labeling as nationalist the bonds of loyalty in ancient Greek city-states is the fact that, by the fifth century BCE, Athenians, Spartans, Thebans, and other Greek-speakers all seem to have regarded their individual *poleis* as part of a greater Hellenic whole.[63] By that period, it was common to refer to Greeks as members of one *ethnos* (usually translated as "nation"); in the fourth century, the term *genos* – a community bound by notional ties of birth, as manifested in shared language and culture – was also used to describe the Hellenes.[64] This appears to give just cause to those sceptics who argue that the borders of the Greek city-states did not correspond to the territorial distribution of a self-identifying ethno-cultural community and that therefore national identity cannot be regarded as an operative factor in the political culture of ancient Greece.[65] But this is to apply an overly rigid standard according to which many latter-day societies could be disqualified from recognition as nations. Are countries in the English-speaking world (e.g. the United Kingdom, USA, Canada, Australia, New Zealand) to be excluded from the category of nationhood because their overarching sense of linguistic, cultural, and liberal-democratic ideological affinity is not reflected in a firmly instituted political federation? Is Germany not a nation-state because it does not include Austria or German-speaking Switzerland? Has nationalism not operated as a powerful force in the Arab world merely because a unified pan-Arab nation-state does not exist? The complexity of the relationship between cultural and political identities in ancient Greece is all too familiar from the point of view of the modern observer. The salient characteristic of political culture in classical Athens was that it linked the legitimacy of the state to the exercise of popular sovereignty and the consequent ability of state institutions to express the will and embody the identity of the social collective. The fact that being affiliated with a greater Hellenic culture was a significant element of this identity did not make it any less national in character.

Indeed, it can be argued that Hellenism itself operated as a pan-national framework of identity, one that was linked to ideas of sovereignty in a negative way: while advocacy of pan-Hellenic political unification may never have been fully articulated, the notion that non-Hellenic states must be prevented from exercising suzerainty over Hellenes appears to have acquired the status of a cliché in the political rhetoric of fifth-century BCE Greece.[66] This pan-national frame of reference shaped and lent focus to the identity of a nation-*polis* such as Athens. The collective resistance of some of the Greek city-states to the Persian invasion of the 490s BCE forms the central, heroic narrative of Herodotus' *Histories* (composed in the early second half of the fifth century BCE), and was to remain a standard historical-ideological reference point for Athenian politicians, orators, and demagogues for many generations. Though not Athenian by birth himself, Herodotus appears to have been addressing a largely Athenian or pro-Athenian reading public that took for granted the distinction between "good" city-states that had participated in the war against the Persians and "bad" city-states that had collaborated with the enemy or refused to join in the fight. Aegina's (the island state just off the coast of Athens) initial acceptance of tributary status under Persia is recorded as having elicited an Athenian accusation that the Aeginetans (their old enemies) were "traitors to Greece."[67] Later, according to Herodotus, in appealing to Sparta for assistance, the Athenians once again invoked the idea of a collective Hellenic heritage and of mutual obligation among Greek *poleis* by suggesting that the subjugation of Athens would constitute a loss for Greece as a whole: "Men of Sparta ... the Athenians ask you to help them, and not to stand by while the most ancient city of Greece is crushed and subdued by a foreign invader [literally: barbarian men]; for even now Eretria has been enslaved, and Greece is the weaker by the loss of one fine city."[68] Subsequently, after rejecting a Persian offer of a separate peace, the Athenians assured the Spartans of their own continued loyalty to the anti-Persian coalition by referring to their common "Greekness" (*to Hellenikon*), as manifested in their common blood, language, religious rituals and way of life.[69]

Whether Athens' leaders actually made such remarks or not at the time of the Persian Wars cannot be known, but from the point of view of this argument, it does not matter. Herodotus, in thus writing of these events a few decades after their occurrence, was preaching to the converted, telling an Athenian audience what it liked to hear about its leading role in the pan-Hellenic struggle and about the close relationship between the flourishing of Athens and the fortune of Greece.[70] Athenians had come to see their cultural ties to the rest of Greece and their historic role in the liberation of Greece as defining elements of their own collective identity. The fact that the Athenians' claim to historic leadership in the pan-Hellenic struggle of the 490s BCE was often used hypocritically and cynically in their own pursuit of imperial dominion over their fellow Greeks does not lessen the significance of the connection between Athenian identity and its pan-Hellenic frame of reference. On the contrary, it represents an all too familiar use (or abuse) of nationalist and pan-nationalist ideology to legitimize hegemonic aspirations.[71] Otto von Bismarck's employment of German nationalism and foreign wars to establish Prussian hegemony over the smaller German states in the 1860s and 1870s comes to mind as a modern analogy.

This pattern is a trademark feature of some of the most famous discourses written by Isocrates (436–338 BCE), the prominent publicist of the post-Periclean era, when a declining Athens was struggling to reassert its power and dominance in the Greek world. Isocrates invoked pan-Hellenic myth, history, and culture – the Trojan War, the early fifth-century Persian War, and the Panathenaic festival – in calling for a new, common front among the Greek states against a once-more intrusive and threatening Persian Empire.[72] Athens, of course, would be the natural leader of such a pan-Hellenic effort.[73] The Athenians and their Spartan partners, after all, had led the Greeks to victory in the Persian Wars in a spirit of patriotic selflessness, "regarding their own cities as their respective abodes [*aste*], while considering Hellas to be their common fatherland [*patris*]."[74] As they had done a century earlier, so too, in the present circumstances (*circa* 380 BCE), Athens and Sparta had to end their internecine warfare and join forces in leading a collective anti-Persian military campaign on behalf of the collective freedom, dignity, and material well-being of Greece.[75]

Similar ideals of pan-Hellenic solidarity were to be invoked in 344 BCE by Demosthenes in his call for Athenian resistance to Philip of Macedon's hegemonic aspirations. It was precisely the Athenians' single-minded devotion to Greek freedoms, Demosthenes argued, that made them the greatest obstacle to Philip's aggrandizement and hence the prime targets of his machinations.[76] For his part, Philip was to try and turn the pan-Hellenic ideal to his own advantage, planning a grand military expedition against the Persian Empire as – among other things – a way of consolidating and legitimizing his own dominion over the Greek *poleis*.

The very fluidity and elasticity of these ancient Greek conceptions of national identity renders them startlingly familiar to the modern sensibility. In the name of the ideal of political freedom for all Greeks, Athens could be defended or attacked, war could be advocated or averted, alliances could be justified or derided. By the same token, it seems as though no significant policy issue could be discussed *without* reference to the historical legacies and political meanings of Athenian and Greek identities, and to the relationship between nation-*polis* and Hellas. In other words, national identity – however widely or narrowly construed – was not just one of many different social and cultural frames of reference; it seems to have been regarded as the *fundamental* source of common purpose and political legitimacy, at least among the Athenian political elites, but presumably also among the broader audiences of male citizens (and permanent residents[77]) whom many of these orators, publicists, and historians were addressing.

Even some of the cultural idiosyncrasies most closely associated with modern nationalist and pan-nationalist ventures manifested themselves within this ancient context. Aristotle's insistence on the need to standardize and formalize the Greek language, to the exclusion of dialectal variation (which he derides as conducive to barbarism), seems like a page torn out of the book of nineteenth-century Central and Eastern European cultural nationalisms.[78] The general fifth-century BCE shift in emphasis from ethnic/genealogical markers associated with regional Ionian, Dorian, Akhaian, and Aiolian identities to more sweepingly inclusive, cultural definitions of common Hellenicity (as Jonathan Hall has put it[79]) seems strikingly similar to modern, often vain, efforts to find common cultural and political ground among ethno-national groups with similar languages or historical experiences (from Czechs and Slovaks to Czechoslovaks, from Croats, Serbs and Slovenes to Yugoslavs). The "appropriation" of history and mythology by a "hegemonic discourse" of nationalism is familiar to us from contemporary examples, such as the Serbian nationalist commemoration of the epic Battle of Kosovo of 1389 and the use of the Kosovo myth to justify certain cultural and political agendas.[80] The pan-Hellenic political slant Isocrates gives to the epic story of the Trojan War fits right into this pattern, as does the general regard the ancient Greeks had for Homer's work as a pan-Hellenic cultural legacy.[81] Isocrates and Demosthenes both refer to the city-state, in the context of a citizen's loyalty and obligation toward it, by the very modern-sounding term "fatherland" (*patris*), and Isocrates, as shown above, extends the concept to Greece as a whole.[82]

My point is that these ancient Greek conceptions and visions of collective identity do more than meet many of the technical, social-scientific criteria for qualifying as expressions of nationalism. They constitute a quintessentially nationalist brew of ethnic, cultural, historical, and political issues, symbols, and references. They have the sound and feel of nationalism. They *smell* like nationalism. Perhaps scholars should stop and have a sniff before dismissing the idea of ancient nationalism as nothing more than the product of an overheated, anachronistic imagination.

CONCLUSION

My purpose here has not been to engage in a comprehensive analysis of identity formation in the ancient world, but simply to suggest how readily the conceptual and terminological apparatus of contemporary nationalism studies could be applied to ancient societies. Other examples from the ancient world may well abound, and the growing importance of the idea of nationhood in late medieval and early modern European worldviews has been increasingly documented.[83] At the same time, I should emphasize that I am not defining nationalism so broadly as to encompass all societies in all periods of history (at which point the term would become useless as a category of analysis). In fact, most societies and polities in the pre-modern world probably fell into categories that cannot be considered national in character: ethnic groups ruled by divine-right monarchies that did not hold up the common ethno-cultural identity of their subjects as a central source of state legitimacy; multi-ethnic empires, such as those of the Persians, Macedonians, and Romans; various forms of stateless societies; collectivities small enough to fall below the Andersonian threshold of imagined community; nomadic groups that may have had a strong sense of common ethnic identity but that lacked the attachment to a bounded territory that is a hallmark of national identity, etc. But even if the ancient Jews and ancient Athenians were to present the only convincing examples of nations and nationalism in the ancient world, they would remain significant because: (a) they fly in the face of the dominant theoretical school of thought that regards nationalism as the exclusive outgrowth of the material and cultural conditions of modernity; (b) these two particular instances of ancient nationalism have served as powerfully influential models in the development of modern European conceptions of nationhood. Indeed, many of the fundamental tensions latent within ancient Jewish and Greek conceptions of nationhood were to manifest themselves within nineteenth- and twentieth-century constructions of national identity, as we shall see.]

Is this to say that, in the field of nationalism, there is nothing new under the sun? The modern era has indeed brought about many significant changes and innovations in the dynamics and character of nationalist politics. The printing press, the spread of literacy, the development of mass-conscription armies, universal enrollment school systems, and (apart from some notable exceptions such as the United States) standardized mechanisms for the institution of universal suffrage, along with a thousand-and-one other modern instruments of communication and integration, have facilitated the dissemination of nationalist ideals and sentiments on a territorial and demographic scale and with a speed and intensity unimaginable in earlier historical epochs. They have contributed to the conceptualization of nationhood as a generally applicable principle of political-cultural organization, one whose global attraction has been enhanced by its close association with the modern power and prestige of the Euro-Atlantic countries.

These and other factors – including the English, American, and French Revolutions, European overseas imperialism, the collapse of multinational empires at the end of the First World War, post-1945 decolonization, and the collapse of the Eastern Bloc and Soviet Union during 1989–91 – have catalyzed the world-wide diffusion of the idea of *popular sovereignty*, and hence *popular identity*, as the legitimizing basis of state authority. Nationalism was, so to speak, an option in the pre-modern world. In the modern era, it has become, for a time, a quasi-universal, globally dominant framework for the exercise of political sovereignty.[84] Nationalism's modularity – the perception of it as a pre-fabricated ideological structure that can be set up as a framework for institutional and cultural development in any society – is a distinctly modern phenomenon.[85]

Paradoxes of
nationalism

It is precisely from its peculiar status as a globally recognized basis for
political legitimacy that many of modern nationalism's fundamental
contradictions and paradoxes arise. As a system that draws on ancient –
dare I say primordial? – notions about the relationship among kinship,
identity, authority, and territoriality, nationalism seems incongruously
juxtaposed with the impersonal principles and bureaucratized institutions
of the modern Weberian state. Yet – as Anthony Smith has argued – by
compensating for and modifying the antiseptic qualities of a Weberian
meritocracy, it lends legitimacy to the rationalized, centralized modern
polity.[86] Often closely associated with the push for collective empowerment through economic and technological progress, nationalism simultaneously offers people the illusion of standing still in time and being one
with their ancestors regardless of the material changes overtaking them.
Yet, hegemonic though it is as a political paradigm, the nation-state
(whose creation or defense is the object of every nationalist movement) is
actually very poorly suited to the ethnographic conditions and political
cultures of many contemporary societies. It is the nation-state's very
universality in the modern era that has given rise to many of the brutal
conflicts associated with it, for in more cases than not the concept of the
nation-state forms a very poor fit with the ethno-culturally heterogeneous
societies whose leaders so fervently embrace it.

Regardless of whether it "works" or "doesn't work," the political
development of modern nationalism is driven by conflicts and compromises over the dilemmas that are intrinsic to it. One of the most fundamental tensions in the nationalist sensibility is that between the
embrace of historical progress and nostalgia for the past, the sense of
moving ever forward in time and the desire to stop the clock. In this, as in
so many other respects, modern nationalism represents the meeting
ground – and even battle-ground – for modern and pre-modern sensibilities, rather than a manifestation of modernity pure and simple.

END NOTES

1 An early version of this chapter's material on ancient Jewish nationalism
   appeared in Aviel Roshwald, "Jewish Identity and the Paradox of
   Nationalism," in Michael Berkowitz, ed., *Nationalism, Zionism and Ethnic
   Mobilization of the Jews in 1900 and Beyond* (Leiden: E. J. Brill, 2004), 11–24.
   My thanks go to Brill Academic Publishers for their permission to use this
   material here.
2 See Eric Hobsbawm and Terence Ranger, eds., *The Invention of Tradition*
   (Cambridge: Cambridge University Press, 1983).

3 Elie Kedourie stated flat out that "Nationalism is a doctrine invented in Europe at the beginning of the nineteenth century." Elie Kedourie, *Nationalism*, 3rd edn (London: Hutchinson, 1966), 9. Kedourie looked at the phenomenon as a modern evil created by misguided intellectuals. For works that explore nationalism as an aspect or function of socio-economic, cultural, and/or political modernity, see Karl Deutsch, *Nationalism and Social Communication: An Inquiry into the Foundations of Nationality* (Cambridge, Mass.: MIT Press, 1966); Ernest Gellner, *Nations and Nationalism* (Ithaca: Cornell University Press, 1983); Eric Hobsbawm, *Nations and Nationalism since 1780: Programme, Myth, Reality* (Cambridge: Cambridge University Press, 1990); Hobsbawm and Ranger, *Invention of Tradition*; John Breuilly, *Nationalism and the State*, 2nd edn (Chicago: University of Chicago Press, 1994); Benedict Anderson, *Imagined Communities: Reflections on the Origin and Spread of Nationalism*, 2nd edn (London: Verso, 1991).

4 Partha Chatterjee seeks to chart a post-modernist theoretical course towards the bridging of this gap in *The Nation and its Fragments: Colonial and Postcolonial Histories* (Princeton: Princeton University Press, 1993). A much more concrete approach can be found in James Gelvin's case study, which highlights the vexed relationship between popular and elite conceptions of political and national identity in post-World War I Syria. James Gelvin, *Divided Loyalties: Nationalism and Mass Politics in Syria at the Close of Empire* (Berkeley: University of California Press, 1998).

5 For a sympathetic account of modern Slovak nationalists' identification with ninth-century Great Moravia, see Stanislav J. Kirschbaum, *A History of Slovakia: The Struggle for Survival* (New York: St. Martin's Press, 1995). See also Peter Toma and Dusan Kovac, *Slovakia: From Samo to Dzurinda* (Stanford: Stanford University Press, 2001), ch. 1. For use of the Mexican example as strawman, see Anderson, *Imagined Communities*, 154.

6 Anthony Smith draws a useful distinction between *primordialism* – the assertion that modern nationalism draws on emotional or even socio-biological impulses that are inherent in human nature – and *perennialism* – the claim that ethnicity is a continuously recurring phenomenon in history and that many modern nations can trace their origins to pre-modern ethnic groupings. In practice, there is often considerable overlap between these two approaches. For purposes of simplicity, in this chapter I am lumping the salient features of perennialism and primordialism together under the common heading of primordialism. Anthony D. Smith, *Nationalism and Modernism: A Critical Survey of Recent Theories of Nations and Nationalism* (London: Routledge, 1998), 21–24, ch. 7, and 223–224.

7 C. A. Bayly makes this point in *The Birth of the Modern World, 1780–1914: Global Connections and Comparisons* (Oxford: Blackwell, 2004), 219.

8 For a witty and engaging exchange of views about the significance of modern nations' pre-modern ethno-cultural roots, see Anthony D. Smith, "Nations and their Past" and Ernest Gellner, "Do Nations Have Navels?" in Smith and Gellner, "The Nation: Real or Imagined?: The Warwick Debates on

Nationalism," *Nations and Nationalism*, vol. 2, no. 3 (1996), 357–370. Alexander H. Joffe discusses the evolution of Gellner's views on nationalism in "Israel in the Eyes of Historians: Some Jewish Historians of Nationalism on Zionism and Israel" (unpublished draft manuscript).

9 Hagen Schulze, *States, Nations and Nationalism: From the Middle Ages to the Present*, trans. William E. Yuill (Oxford: Blackwell, 1996), 6–12. On the fluidity of ethnic and political frameworks of identity in medieval Europe, see Patrick J. Geary, *The Myth of Nations: The Medieval Origins of Europe* (Princeton: Princeton University Press, 2002).

10 Anthony D. Smith, *The Ethnic Origins of Nations* (Oxford: Blackwell, 1986); Anthony D. Smith, "Dating the Nation," in Daniele Conversi, ed., *Ethnonationalism in the Contemporary World: Walker Connor and the Study of Nationalism* (London: Routledge, 2002); Anthony D. Smith, *The Antiquity of Nations* (Cambridge: Polity Press, 2004); Adrian Hastings, *The Construction of Nationhood: Ethnicity, Religion and Nationalism* (Cambridge: Cambridge University Press, 1997); Anderson, *Imagined Communities*, ch. 3. John A. Armstrong has written about *Nations Before Nationalism* (Chapel Hill: University of North Carolina Press, 1982), but he uses the term nation as equivalent to ethnicity, and contends that the link between ethnicity and state legitimacy – i.e. nationalism – is a predominantly modern phenomenon. Again, my point is that, while the perception of this link as universal, as well as the actual global spread of nationalism as the predominant legitimizing basis for state sovereignty, are modern phenomena, there were clear and historically influential examples of nationalism in the ancient world. Ernest Gellner, the brilliant and witty arch-modernist of nationalism studies, actually conceded that the pre-modern ("agrarian") world contained isolated examples of entities resembling nation-states, but he did not explore the theoretical complications that such a concession creates for his materialist theory of nationalism. Ernest Gellner, *Nations and Nationalism* (Ithaca: Cornell University Press, 1983), 138.

11 See the collection of Grosby's articles in Steven Grosby, *Biblical Ideas of Nationality: Ancient and Modern* (Winona Lake, Ind.: Eisenbrauns, 2002). One of the founding fathers of twentieth-century nationalism studies, Hans Kohn, took the idea of ancient Jewish and Greek nationalisms as fairly self-evident. See Hans Kohn, *The Idea of Nationalism: A Study in its Origins and Background* (1944; New York: Macmillan, 1948), ch. 2. At the same time, he wrote that "nationalism as we understand it is not older than the second half of the eighteenth century." Ibid., p. 3.

12 Anderson, *Imagined Communities*, 5; Anthony D. Smith, *Chosen Peoples* (Oxford: Oxford University Press, 2003), 18.

13 I am paraphrasing the definition I employed in Aviel Roshwald, *Ethnic Nationalism and the Fall of Empires: Central Europe, Russia and the Middle East, 1914–1923* (London: Routledge, 2001), 6. See also the Introduction to the present book.

14 I will use the term "modernists" as Anthony Smith and others do, to denote those who espouse the view that nationalism is exclusively rooted in the experience of modernity.

15 In a similar spirit, Tom Garvin makes a brief but bold attack on the modernist school in *Mythical Thinking in Political Life: Reflections on Nationalism and Social Science* (Dublin: Maunsel & Co., 2001), 42–55. See also the nuanced critique of Gellner's and Anderson's claims about the exclusively modern features of nationalist consciousness in Prasenjit Duara, *Rescuing History from the Nation: Questioning Narratives of Modern China* (Chicago: University of Chicago Press, 1995), ch. 2.

16 See Anderson, *Imagined Communities*, 5.

17 Paul R. Ehrlich, *Human Natures: Genes, Cultures, and the Human Prospect* (Washington, DC and Covelo, Calif.: Island Press/Shearwater Books, 2000), 177–178 and 207. My claims about geese are based on personal observation and are unscientific in nature. But for scientific discussion of group territoriality among a number of other bird species, see William Etkin, "Co-operation and Competition in Social Behavior," in William Etkin, ed., *Social Behavior and Organization among Vertebrates* (Chicago: University of Chicago Press, 1964), 25; Robert Carrick, "Ecological Significance of Territory in the Australian Magpie, *Gymnorhina tibicen*," 743 and J. H. Crook, "The Adaptive Significance of Avian Social Organizations," 206–207 in Allen W. Stokes, ed., *Territory*, Benchmark Papers in Animal Behavior, vol. 11 (Stroudsburg, Penn.: Dowden, Hutchinson & Ross, 1974). On group territoriality and violence among chimpanzees, with some comparative discussion of territoriality among other animals, see Jane Goodall, *The Chimpanzees of Gombe* (Cambridge, Mass.: Harvard University Press, 1986), ch. 17. On the role of kinship ties in fostering cooperative and territorial behavior among certain species of fish, see George W. Barlow, *The Cichlid Fishes: Nature's Grand Experiment in Evolution* (New York: Perseus, 2000), 210–214; J. W. Ward and Paul J. B. Hart, "The Effects of Kin and Familiarity on Interactions between Fish," *Fish and Fisheries*, vol. 4, no. 4 (December 2003), 348.

18 For a succinct, socio-biological interpretation of ethno-nationalism, see Pierre L. van den Berghe, "Race and Ethnicity: A Sociobiological Perspective," *Ethnic and Racial Studies*, vol. 1, no. 4 (October 1978), 401–411.

19 See Eric P. Kaufmann, *The Rise and Fall of Anglo-America* (Cambridge, Mass.: Harvard University Press, 2004), 278 (drawing on the terminological distinctions of Anthony D. Smith). See also Chapter 5 of the present book.

20 On the relationship between national identity and social communication, discussed from a modernist perspective, see Karl W. Deutsch, *Nationalism and Social Communication: An Inquiry into the Foundations of Nationality*, 2nd edn (Cambridge, Mass.: MIT Press, 1966).

21 On evidence for the spread of popular literacy in seventh-century BCE Judah, see William M. Schniedewind's compelling argument in *How the Bible Became a Book* (Cambridge: Cambridge University Press, 2004), ch. 6.

22 See Chapter 2.

23 Genesis 10:31. My translation. See Genesis 10:5 and 10:20 for nearly identical versions of this formulation.

24 My thanks to Steven Grosby for drawing my attention to this verse and its significance. See also Steven Grosby, "The Biblical 'Nation' as a Problem for Philosophy," *Hebraic Political Studies*, vol. 1, no. 1 (Fall 2005), 7–23, esp. p. 7, note 1.

25 Anderson, *Imagined Communities*, 46.

26 It is true that various biblical as well as Talmudic texts prescribe and describe the precise boundaries of the Promised Land in diverse ways. See Jean-Christophe Attias and Esther Benbassa, *Israel, the Impossible Land*, trans. Susan Emanuel (Stanford: Stanford University Press, 2003), 24–26, 39–40, 52–56. But, as with modern disputes about the location of legitimate national borders, the effort invested in such debates reflects the common assumption that the nation's territory should in fact be bounded according to a fixed and unchanging blueprint.

27 Deuteronomy 17:14–20, Herbert G. May and Bruce M. Metzger, eds., *The New Oxford Annotated Bible with the Apocrypha: Revised Standard Version* (New York: Oxford University Press, 1977). Emphases are mine.

28 On the Covenant as authoritative throughout the territory of Israel, see Steven Grosby, "Kinship, Territory and the Nation in the Historiography of Ancient Israel," *Zeitschrift für die alttestamentliche Wissenschaft*, vol. 105, no. 1 (1993), 1–18.

29 See Walker Connor, "Nationalism and Political Illegitimacy," in Conversi, ed., *Ethnonationalism*.

30 See Smith, *Chosen Peoples*, 34–35; David Novak, *The Election of Israel: The Idea of the Chosen People* (Cambridge: Cambridge University Press, 1995), 31–42; and Chapter 4 of the present book.

31 See Michael Walzer, *Exodus and Revolution* (New York: Basic Books, 1985), 83.

32 This point is forcefully made in Smith, *Chosen Peoples*, chs. 1–2 and *passim*. See also Chapter 4 of the present book.

33 See Tim Judah, *The Serbs: History, Myth and the Destruction of Yugoslavia* (New Haven: Yale University Press, 1997); Conor Cruise O'Brien, *Godland: Reflections on Religion and Nationalism* (Cambridge, Mass.: Harvard University Press, 1988); Steven Grosby, "The Nation of the United States and the Vision of Ancient Israel," in R. Michener, ed., *Nationality, Patriotism, and Nationalism* (St. Paul: Paragon, 1993).

34 For a more cautious argument along similar lines about the tautological nature of modernist definitions of the nation, see Smith, *Antiquity of Nations*, ch. 5. Smith builds his argument by decoupling "nation" from "nationalism" – a concession I see no need to make. Oliver Zimmer calls into question the assumption that only the apparatus of the modern state is capable of lending institutional form to nationalism. Oliver Zimmer, *Nationalism in Europe, 1890–1940* (Basingstoke: Palgrave Macmillan, 2003), 24.

35 Anderson, *Imagined Communities*, chs. 2–3.

36 See, for instance, Israel Finkelstein and Neil Asher Silberman, *The Bible Unearthed: Archaeology's New Vision of Ancient Israel and the Origins of its Sacred Texts* (New York: Free Press, 2001).

37 For an argument that the First Temple monarchy arose in the context of a broader emergence of "ethnicizing states" in parts of the early first-millennium BCE western Fertile Crescent, see Alexander H. Joffe, "The Rise of Secondary States in the Iron Age Levant," *Journal of the Economic and Social History of the Orient*, vol. 45, no. 4 (December 2002), 425–467.

38 Monolatry is the exclusive worship of one god, without denying the existence of other gods.

39 One of the Hebrew Bible's words for God, *elohim*, is actually the plural form of the generic term for a god–*eloah*. This suggests a deliberate, monotheizing attempt to subsume multiple divinities under the identity of a single god. Amidst the myriad pagan cultic objects unearthed from ancient Israelite sites, one of the most startling is an eighth-century BCE graffito depicting "Yahweh of Samaria" alongside his apparent consort, Astarte (Asherah)! Edward F. Campbell Jr., "A Land Divided: Judah and Israel from the Death of Solomon to the Fall of Samaria," in Michael Coogan, ed., *The Oxford History of the Biblical World* (New York: Oxford University Press, 1998), 309.

40 A strong case for the crystallization of a body of sacred Jewish literature at the earlier end of this spectrum is made in Schniedewind, *How the Bible Became a Book*, 5–7. On the discovery of seventh-century BCE silver-scroll amulets bearing Hebrew inscriptions virtually identical with the priestly blessing in Numbers 6:24–26, see also Gabriel Barkay, "Excavations at Ketef Hinnom in Jerusalem," in Hillel Geva, ed., *Ancient Jerusalem Revealed* (Jerusalem: Israel Exploration Society, 2000).

41 Alexander Joffe similarly points out that the "imagined" quality of ancient nationhood does not detract from its significance or its legitimacy as a category of analysis, if contemporary conceptions about the constructed nature of social identity are to be applied consistently. (Joffe, "The Rise of Secondary States.")

42 See Doron Mendels, *The Rise and Fall of Jewish Nationalism* (New York: Doubleday, 1992), chs. 7–12. On the adaptive redefinitions of Jewish identity in response to the encounter with Hellenistic culture, see Erich S. Gruen, *Heritage and Hellenism: The Reinvention of Jewish Tradition* (Berkeley and Los Angeles: University of California Press, 1998); Erich S. Gruen, *Diaspora: Jews amidst Greeks and Romans* (Cambridge, Mass.: Harvard University Press, 2002); John M. G. Barclay, *Jews in the Mediterranean Diaspora: From Alexander to Trajan* (323 BCE–117 CE (Berkeley: University of California Press, 1996), esp. ch. 14. Barclay argues that, even as Hellenistic influence contributed to a broader, cultural conception of Jewishness – especially in Diaspora communities – an ethnically defined sense of nationhood remained the core element of Jewish identity: "Almost all the literature from the [Hellenistic/Roman era] Diaspora indicates the significance of the 'nation' as the bearer of the Jewish tradition" (405). On the continued importance of the

emotional attachment to the Judean homeland among diaspora communities, see pp. 421–423. For a more problematizing approach to this theme, see Attias and Benbassa, *Israel*, ch. 2.

43 A strong case for this interpretation is made in Leo Mildenberg, *The Coinage of the Bar Kokhba War* (Aarau: Verlag Sauerländer, 1984), 69–72 and Seth Schwartz, "Language, Power and Identity in Ancient Palestine," *Past and Present*, no. 148 (August 1995), 3–47, esp. 27. Schwartz argues that in the course of the Second Temple period, Hebrew "became not the national language of the Jews, but the language whose representation symbolized Jewish nationhood." Ibid., 25. See also A. Reifenberg, *Israel's History in Coins: From the Maccabees to the Roman Conquest* (London: East and West Library, 1953), 9. On use of the Temple's image as a symbol of Jewish freedom in the Bar Kokhba rebellion, see Martin Jessop Price and Bluma L. Trell, *Coins and their Cities: Architecture on the Ancient Coins of Greece, Rome, and Palestine* (London: Vecchi and Sons, and Detroit: Wayne State University Press, 1977), 177–179. Steven Grosby points out that the Bar Kokhba coins' reference to Israel rather than Judah is itself a revival of a term associated with David and Solomon's united kingdom that fell apart in the tenth century BCE. Steven Grosby, "The Chosen People of Ancient Israel and the Occident," *Nations and Nationalism*, vol. 5, no. 3 (1999), 357–380. Conversely the coins' reference to Year Two of Israel's liberation suggests a linear conception of history existing in tandem with a transcendent perspective – a feature that is stereotypical of modern nationalisms (see Chapter 2 of this book). For possible connections between coinage inscription styles and nationalist themes in Phoenician city-states of the fourth century BCE, see John Wilson Betlyon, *The Coinage and Mints of Phoenicia: The Pre-Alexandrine Period* (Chico, Calif.: Scholars Press, 1980; Harvard Semitic Monographs No. 26), esp. 55–56.

44 Anderson, *Imagined Communities*, 22–36. See also Mircea Eliade, *The Myth of the Eternal Return. Or, Cosmos and History* (Princeton: Princeton University Press, 1954), discussed in Chapter 2 of this book.

45 For a brilliant application of this approach to the history of Jewish historical sensibility, see Yosef Hayim Yerushalmi, *Zakhor: Jewish History and Jewish Memory* (Seattle: University of Washington, Press, 1982).

46 Cyclical conceptions of history were certainly common in the classical tradition. But the most highly regarded ancient historian of all, Thucydides, introduced his history of the Peloponnesian War – which he presented as the greatest war ever yet fought – by tracing the progressive development of Greek society from early, primitive conditions to what might be termed the "modernity" of the Periclean era. Thucydides, *History of the Peloponnesian War* 1:1–23, trans. Rex Warner (Harmondsworth: Penguin, 1972), 35–49.

47 Michael Walzer vigorously makes the case for reading the biblical story of the Exodus as progressive history in *Exodus and Revolution*, 12–17 and *passim*.

48 In the medieval Augustinian tradition, Christian theologians held to a sharp contradistinction between the timeless eternity of the divine and the transience of time as known by mortal humans. But in the scholastic theology

of the late Middle Ages, this view was challenged and modified by a neo-Aristotelian conception of time itself as continuously and endlessly flowing into an unbounded future. The progress of history, in this framework of understanding, could be associated with immortality rather than death, meaning rather than insignificance. This approach coexisted, somewhat uneasily, with the idea of a God existing outside of time and with Christian eschatological dogma. Ernst H. Kantorowicz, *The King's Two Bodies: A Study in Mediaeval Political Theology* (Princeton: Princeton University Press, 1957), 274–284.

49 For a finely nuanced analysis of the adaptive integration of the Jewish religious cycle into Israel's framework of nationalist commemoration, see Yael Zerubavel, *Recovered Roots: Collective Memory and the Making of Israeli National Tradition* (Chicago: University of Chicago Press, 1995), ch. 7 and 216–221.

50 See, for example, M. I. Finley, *The Use and Abuse of History* (1971; 1975; London: Penguin, 1990), ch. 7; Gellner, *Nations and Nationalism*, 14; Hobsbawm, *Nations and Nationalism*, 64. Anthony D. Smith explores the influence on modern nationalism of classical Greek and Roman conceptions of loyalty to the political community and readiness to sacrifice oneself for the social collective, but he does so in the context of a concession that these classical models were developed "in epochs that knew nothing of nationalism and its theories of a world of authentic self-realizing nations." Smith, *Chosen Peoples*, 219.

51 M. I. Finley critiques the anachronistic notion that the Greeks ought to have striven after political unification on the nineteenth-century German model yet, in so doing, he does not seriously explore the possibility that Athenian identity, for example, could be deemed national in its own right. He points out that political factions embroiled in conflict within Greek city-states readily turned to outside support against their internal enemies, suggesting that this indicates a mentality incompatible with nationalism. Finley, *Use and Abuse of History*, ch. 7. Yet how many modern nation-states have seen rival groupings seek support from foreigners! Were Francisco Franco's forces in the Spanish Civil War (1936–39) not Spanish nationalists, merely because they sought support from Nazi Germany and Fascist Italy? (Franco and his followers were not very nice, but I have yet to hear of anyone questioning their nationalist credentials.) H. E. Stier (cited and critiqued in Walbank, "Problem of Greek Nationality," 4–11) did in fact make a case for the *polis* as nation, but only by starkly contrasting it with a pan-Hellenic cultural consciousness that he insisted was strictly non-national in character. I contend that city-state and pan-Hellenic identities both contained strikingly nationalist elements that shaped and reinforced one another. Walbank somewhat murkily argues that viewing Greek history through a nationalist prism is anachronistic, but can be analytically useful as long as one distinguishes one's own perspective from that of one's historical subjects. Frank W. Walbank, "The Problem of Greek Nationality," in Frank W. Walbank, *Selected Papers: Studies in Greek and*

Roman History and Historiography (Cambridge: Cambridge University Press, 1985), 1–19. Most recently, Edward E. Cohen has made a strong case for the nationhood of ancient Athens in *The Athenian Nation* (Princeton: Princeton University Press, 2000). Cohen concedes that, by Aristotle's definition of the term, a *polis* was a self-governing community small enough for all inhabitants to know one another personally. But he goes on to point out that, precisely because of that, over-sized Athens fell into the Aristotelian category of *ethnos* – best translated, in this context, as "nation." Ibid., ch. 1. Despite his own, hedging, openness to the idea of ancient nationhood, Anthony Smith remains dissatisfied with Cohen's argument – albeit by contrasting ancient Athens with an "ideal-type" definition of nationhood that is tautologically modern, as Smith himself goes on to point out! Smith, *Antiquity of Nations*, 131–132.

52 N. G. L. Hammond, *A History of Greece to 322 B.C.*, 3rd edn (Oxford: Clarendon Press, 1986), 185–191.

53 Cohen, *Athenian Nation*, 17.

54 "[A Nation] is an imagined political community – and imagined as both inherently limited and sovereign. It is *imagined* because the members of even the smallest nation will never know most of their fellow-members, meet them, or even hear of them, yet in the minds of each lives the image of their communion." Anderson, *Imagined Communities*, 6. Since I first drafted this chapter, I have come across the work of Edward E. Cohen, who makes the identical point about Athens as imagined community. Cohen, *Athenian Nation*, 12. Indeed, Cohen contends that the Athenian nation should be thought of as including the hundreds of thousands of non-citizen, permanent residents (of various legal statuses) who played a very active role in diverse spheres of Athenian public life and who were recognized in sundry ways as forming an integral part of the community. Ibid., chs. 1 and 4.

55 Thucydides 2.42–43, Penguin edn, 148–150.

56 Since first drafting this passage I have come across a similar argument in Cohen, *Athenian Nation*, 96–98, esp. 98.

57 "Just as our political life is free and open, so is our day-to-day life in our relations with each other. We do not get into a state with our next-door neighbour if he enjoys himself in his own way, nor do we give him ... black looks ... We are free and tolerant in our private lives; but in public affairs we keep to the law..." Thucydides 2.37, Penguin edn, 145.

58 "When our work is over, we are in a position to enjoy all kinds of recreation for our spirits. There are various kinds of contests and sacrifices regularly throughout the year; in our own homes we find a beauty and a good taste which delight us every day and which drive away our cares. Then the greatness of our city brings it about that all the good things from all over the world flow in to us, so that to us it seems just as natural to enjoy foreign goods as our own local products." Thucydides 2:38, Penguin edn, 146.
      "....There is a difference, too, in our educational systems. The Spartans, from their earliest boyhood, are submitted to the most laborious training in courage; we pass our lives without all these restrictions, and yet are just as

ready to face the same dangers as they are . . . " Thucydides 2.38–39, Penguin edn, 146.

59 Colin Poole has formulated the traditional distinction between *polis* or classical republic and modern nation very neatly: "The key difference between the republican and the national conceptions of citizenship lies in the relationship of the individual to the political realm. For the republican, the relationship is ideally one of *agency*: citizens *form* the State through their political activity. For the nationalist, the relationship is one of *mimesis*: citizens *recognise* themselves in the State. National subjects find their identity affirmed in the political realm, and for this reason make themselves available to its demands." Colin Poole, *Nation and Identity* (London: Routledge, 1999), 107. Bernard Yack makes a similar argument in "The Myth of the Civic Nation," in Ronald Beiner, ed., *Theorizing Nationalism* (Albany: State University of New York Press, 1999), 111–114. I am arguing that, upon close examination, Pericles' funeral oration blurs the distinction between these two typological categories. Poole himself suggests that "it is possible to wonder whether some form of cultural identity was not presupposed in . . . classical models of citizenship." (Ibid., 107.) He goes on to suggest that, conversely, the classical ideal of citizen participation forms an important aspect of modern, liberal-democratic nation-states. (Ibid., 107–112.)

60 Pericles addresses the women of Athens only once, towards the end of his speech, tersely informing war widows that "the greatest glory of a woman is to be least talked about by men, whether they are praising you or criticizing you." Thucydides 2.46, Penguin edn, 151. This conception of women's role in the social order fits perfectly into the eighteenth-century European (male) worldview. Linda Colley cites a line from a popular 1796 British publication, Thomas Gisborne's *Enquiry into the Duties of the Female Sex*, admonishing women to observe Pericles' strictures. Linda Colley, *Britons: Forging the Nation 1707–1837* (New Haven: Yale University Press, 1992), 254.

61 Again, Edward E. Cohen argues strongly that non-citizens of a variety of statuses were integral parts of the Athenian imagined community. Cohen, *Athenian Nation*, ch. 4.

62 See Rogers Brubaker, *Citizenship and Nationhood in France and Germany* (Cambridge, Mass.: Harvard University Press, 1992), ch. 4.

63 See Thucydides 1.3 for a typically sophisticated discussion of the development of collective consciousness among the Hellenes. Jonathan Hall argues that early ethno-genealogical definitions of Hellenicity gave way to cultural definitions in the fifth century BCE. Jonathan M. Hall, *Hellenicity: Between Ethnicity and Culture* (Chicago: University of Chicago Press, 2002), chs. 5–6.

64 John E. Coleman, "Ancient Greek Ethnocentrism," in J. Coleman and C. Walz, *Greeks and Barbarians; Essays on the Interactions between Greeks and Non-Greeks in Antiquity and the Consequences for Eurocentrism*, Occasional Publications of the Department of Near Eastern Studies and Jewish Studies, Cornell University, no. 4 (Bethesda, Md.: Capital Decisions Limited, 1997), 175–220.

65 M. I. Finley critiques the anachronistic assumption that the Greeks ought to have striven after political unity in *Use and Abuse of History*, ch. 7.

66 Martin Sherwin and Yossi Shain have pointed out that opposition to external imposition of sovereignty can be seen as a characteristic attribute of modern nationalism. Martin Sherwin and Yossi Shain, "A Nation is a Nation, is a nation, is a nation, is a ... A Critique of the Semantic and Methodological Rigor in the Study of Nationalism," unpublished manuscript.

67 Herodotus, *The Histories* 6.49, trans. Aubrey de Sélincourt (Harmondsworth: Penguin, 1972), p. 404. On the role of the Persian Wars in solidifying the Greek distinction between Hellenes and barbarians, see Smith, *Antiquity of Nations*, 163–164.

68 Herodotus 6.106, Penguin edn, 425.

69 Herodotus 8.144, Penguin edn, 575. See Suzanne Saïd's analysis of this passage in "The Discourse of Identity in Greek Rhetoric from Isocrates to Aristides," in Irad Malkin, ed., *Ancient Perceptions of Greek Ethnicity* (Washington, D.C.: Center for Hellenic Studies/Trustees for Harvard University, 2001); Walbank, "Problem of Greek Nationality," 13.

70 On the other hand, in stressing a cultural rather than genealogical definition of what it meant to be Greek, Herodotus may have been trying to puncture certain myths about Athenian ethnic purity. Rosalind Thomas, "Ethnicity, Genealogy, and Hellenism in Herodotus," in Malkin, ed., *Ancient Perceptions*.

71 For a famously cynical dismissal of Athens' official justification for its imperialism, see the words Thucydides places in the mouths of the Athenian representatives in the Melian Dialogue (Thucydides 5.89, Penguin edn, p. 401).

72 See Yun Lee Too, *The Rhetoric of Identity in Isocrates: Text, Power, Pedagogy* (Cambridge: Cambridge University Press, 1995), ch. 4.

73 Indeed, Jonathan Hall argues that the predominant conception of Hellenic identity by the late fifth, early fourth centuries BCE had become "Athenoconcentric," that is, one in which Athenian culture was the standard by which Greekness was to be defined, with non-Athenians being categorized in concentric circles according to their cultural proximity to or distance from the Athenian center of gravity. Hall, *Hellenicity*, 205–220. Suzanne Saïd likewise argues that fourth-century BCE pan-Hellenism was largely a rhetorical and ideological framework for the articulation of Athenian claims, interests, and identity. Saïd, "Discourse of Identity," 286.

74 Isocrates, *Panegyricus* 81, in *Isocrates with an English Translation*, trans. George Norlin, 3 vols. (London: Heinemann, and New York: Putnam, 1928–45), vol. 1, pp. 168 and 169 (Greek original and English translation, respectively). My modification of Norlin's translation.

75 Ibid., *passim*.

76 See Demosthenes, *Second Philippic* 6–12, in *Demosthenes, with an English Translation*, vol. 1, trans. J. H. Vince (Cambridge, Mass: Harvard University Press, 1935), 126–131.

77 Edward E. Cohen notes that Demosthenes' own citizenship status was publicly called into question. Cohen, *Athenian Nation*, 76–77.

78 On Aristotle, see Too, *Rhetoric*, 139–140. For a depiction of the role nineteenth-century intellectual elites played in the creation of standardized national languages in countries such as Slovakia and Finland, see Miroslav Hroch, *Social Preconditions of National Revival in Europe: A Comparative Analysis of the Social Composition of Patriotic Groups among the Smaller European Nations* (New York: Cambridge University Press, 1985). Ernest Gellner points to linguistic standardization as one of the quintessentially modern characteristics of nationalism in *Nations and Nationalism*. See also Stephen Barbour and Cathie Carmichael, eds., *Language and Nationalism in Europe* (Oxford: Oxford University Press, 2001).

79 Hall, *Hellenicity*. Jonathan Hall notes that the term Hellenicity was first coined by E. Hall in *Inventing the Barbarian: Greek Self-Definition through Tragedy* (Oxford: Oxford University Press, 1989).

80 See Tim Judah, *The Serbs: History, Myth and the Destruction of Yugoslavia* (New Haven: Yale University Press, 1997).

81 Isocrates insists that the abduction of Helen was only the pretext for Agamemnon's organization of the Greek expedition against Troy, whose true objective was to secure the safety and honor of *Hellas* (Greece) in the face of barbarian threats. Isocrates, *Panathenaicus* 80 in *Isocrates*, vol. II, pp. 421–422. See also Too, *Rhetoric*, 132–139.

82 Isocrates, *Panegyricus*, 25 and 81, Heinemann ed., vol. I, pp. 132–133 and 168–169; Demosthenes, *On the Navy Boards*, 32 in *Demosthenes*, vol. I, pp. 400–401. Yun Lee Too (ch. 4) contends that Isocrates' pan-Hellenism is little more than a device he uses to elevate the role of Athens, whose culture and institutions, in turn, define for him what it means to be Greek. This may well be so. But, again, the use of a pan-nationalist legitimizing framework for the definition and promotion of a more particularistic variant of national identity is quite typical of recent nationalisms. The relationship between pan-Slavism and Russian nationalism or between pan-Turkism and Turkish nationalism in the late nineteenth and early twentieth centuries are noteworthy examples, as is the complex and self-contradictory phenomenon of pan-Arabism and Arab state nationalisms to this day.

83 Smith, *Antiquity of Nations*; Hastings, *Construction of Nationhood*; Colette Beaune, *The Birth of an Ideology: Myths and Symbols of Nation in Late Medieval France* (Berkeley: University of California Press, 1991); David Collins, S.J., "Latin Lives of the Saints in Germany, 1470–1520: Humanists, History, and Sainthood" (Ph.D. diss., Northwestern University, 2004), ch. 3.

84 This statement may need qualification in light of the contemporary rise of Islamic fundamentalist movements that challenge the legitimacy of national – as opposed to religious – identity as a foundation of statehood, as well as in view of the European integration movement. See the Conclusion to this book.

85 On the notion of modularity, see Tom Nairn, *The Break-Up of Britain: Crisis and Neo-Nationalism* (London: Verso, 1981).

86 Anthony D. Smith, *Nationalism in the Twentieth Century* (New York: New York University Press, 1979), ch. 7. On nationalism as a backlash against the bureaucratic state, see also Isaiah Berlin, "The Bent Twig: On the Rise of Nationalism," in Berlin, *The Crooked Timber of Humanity: Chapters in the History of Ideas*, ed. Henry Hardy (New York: Random House, 1990).

CHAPTER 2

The nation in history and the curved arrow of time

Is it not strange ... that society causes the mind to transfigure the past to the point of yearning for it?[1]

(Maurice Halbwachs)

When, on 11 September 2001, hijackers flew four commercial airliners to their destruction in a murderous attack on American power and population centers, two historical perspectives were immediately adopted by commentators, political leaders, and the mass media alike. One perspective was the Pearl Harbor analogy. Doubtless leaping spontaneously to the minds of thousands of observers across the country, the image of Pearl Harbor was publicly invoked by political leaders within hours of the attacks. In subsequent days, press coverage and opinion polls repeatedly referred back to the 1941 precedent, explored how close an analogy to the 9/11 attacks it actually represented, and compared the qualities of the "generation of 1941" to those of contemporary Americans. On the six-month anniversary of the attacks, the US Postal Service issued a commemorative "Heroes of 2001" stamp in honor of New York City firefighters, featuring Thomas E. Franklin's photograph of three firefighters raising the American flag over the ruins of the World Trade Center in a pose strongly reminiscent of Joe Rosenthal's iconic photo (and the monument it inspired)[2] of Marines planting the Stars and Stripes on Iwo Jima in February 1945.[3] (See Figures 3 and 4.) The nearly six decades separating World War II era marines from twenty-first-century firefighters evaporates in the framework of the postage stamp, which suggests that the same

---

I take the phrase "arrow of time" from Stephen Hawking, *A Brief History of Time: From the Big Bang to Black Holes* (New York: Bantam, 1988), ch. 9. See also Eviatar Zerubavel's richly insightful discussion of the role played by linear, circular, and other arrows of time in the structuring of collective memory, in *Time Maps: Collective Memory and the Social Shape of the Past* (Chicago: Chicago University Press, 2003), ch. 1.

Figure 3 The United States Marine Memorial in Rosslyn, Virginia. Photograph by author.

Figure 4 "Heroes USA" first-class postage stamp, issued by the United States Postal Service in 2002, after the photograph by Thomas E. Franklin. Courtesy of the United States Postal Service. Stamp Designs © 2002 United States Postal Service. Displayed with permission. All Rights Reserved. Written authorization from the Postal Service is required to use, reproduce, post, transmit, distribute, or publicly display these images. Also courtesy of the North Jersey Media Group. Photograph © 2001 *The Record* (Bergen County, New Jersey), Thomas E. Franklin, Staff Photographer. Also courtesy of The Bravest Fund.

spirit of defiance and triumph in the face of brutal and deceitful aggression animates the men of both generations. On a similar note, in public events marking the first anniversary of the September 11 attacks, politicians' speeches were laced with references to previous, iconic moments in American history. Indeed, a number of prominent public speakers, such as the governors of New York and New Jersey, largely confined their remarks to recitations of the Declaration of Independence and Lincoln's Gettysburg Address.[4] Timeless images from the nation's distant past were cobbled together to form an improvised framework of meaning for the shocking events of the previous year.

The other historical perspective dominating much of the discussion in the immediate aftermath of the national disaster was the idea that "everything had changed"[5] and that nothing in American life would ever be the same, but that the country would eventually emerge the stronger for it.[6]

Two distinct, at once contradictory and complementary, modes of telling historical time are encapsulated in these reactions. One mode is to search for archetypal experiences as points of reference in confronting the shock of historical change. This approach deals with the trauma of unending movement away from a familiar past and into an uncertain future by curving the arrow of time[7] into a cyclical pattern – or by collapsing two temporally distant events into a single, meta-historical experience. The other approach embraces the idea of linear historical development by associating it with Progress – even if it takes the form of "one step backward, two steps forward."

There is nothing new about the idea of cyclical and linear views of history. But most contemporary theories of nationalism suggest a radical dichotomy between the two sensibilities. Most notably, Benedict Anderson's now classic study draws a sharp distinction between the ahistorical conception of time said to have informed the pre-modern, universalistic, religious mental universe, and the linear historicism of the modern, secular, particularistic religion that is nationalism.[8] The sociologist of memory, Eviatar Zerubavel, has called into question such radical contradistinctions between the pre-modern and modern structuring of temporal sensibility.[9] In this chapter, I contend that there is in fact a constant tug-of-war – as well as mutual influence – between linear and non-linear conceptions of national history, and that this shapes much of the cultural production and political content of nationalism.

* * *

One of the most succinct and clearly articulated expositions of the cyclical/cosmic sense of time as a characteristic of ancient, agricultural societies is Mircea Eliade's *Myth of the Eternal Return*.[10] In this book, the Romanian-born scholar of comparative religion pointed out that the religious observances of agricultural civilizations were closely tied to cycles of sowing and harvest, and to the ever-repeating rotation of seasons that determined the schedule of planting and reaping. Time, for these peoples, did not progress in a straight line, but went round in circles. Their religious festivals commemorated, not events on a historical timeline, but the archetypal deeds of gods – immortal beings whose acts of procreation and outbursts of destructive rage in the course of the original process of Creation manifested themselves in the eternal sequence of spring, summer, fall, and winter. Symbolic representations and reenactments of such primordial events in human religious observances were deemed critical to the smooth operation of the life-sustaining cycle and, in reenacting the roles of the divinities, humans could, as it were, take part in the original events of Creation, entering the cosmic, meta-historical dimension occupied by the gods themselves. Day-to-day existence, and the ups and downs of human history, constituted "profane time," which had no significance in and of itself, according to Eliade. People could sustain themselves through profane time and find meaning in their existence only by participating in the cyclical, cosmogonic rituals.

In setting forth this picture, Eliade was drawing a sharp distinction between the ancient circle of time, and the subsequent development of a this-worldly, linear conception of chronology and history. The latter perspective, he argued, was introduced by Judaism and developed by Christianity, both of which shared a conception of human historical fate as shaped by God in accordance with the vice or virtue of his human subjects. The daily existence of men and women, which had hitherto fallen into the category of profane time, thus acquired a sacred quality. The idea of progressive change over time – unilinear history – as the central human experience had been launched.[11] This perspective is said to have come most fully into its own in modern times.

Yet, as Eliade himself was quick to point out, these two paradigmatic conceptions are not mutually exclusive in practice. Judaism and Christianity both incorporate cyclical patterns of religious observance and meta-historical conceptions of sacral meaning, as delineated in Chapter 1 of this book. This coexistence of linear and cyclical/meta-historical senses of time continues to characterize the modern sensibility. In Eliade's account, this is partly a function of the intellectual and experiential gap between elites (those who are capable of having a marked impact on history) and masses (who, as relatively passive objects of history, seek

solace in archaic, ahistorical sensibilities). But he readily conceded that
secular intellectual elites themselves – deprived of the Judeo-Christian
promise of salvation at the end of the historical road – seek escape from
the terrifying, unilinear descent into oblivion by constructing neo-
cyclical theories of history such as Hegelianism and Marxism. (As a
professor at the University of Chicago after the Second World War,
Eliade chose to concede rather less about his own pre-war enthusiasm for
the Romanian Iron Guard's fascist and anti-Semitic cult of national
regeneration.[12])

Eliade's nuanced understanding of the coexistence and dynamic
interaction of so-called archaic and modern conceptions of time within
the framework of contemporary civilization is sadly absent from much of
the theoretical literature on nationalism. Benedict Anderson's influential
work in particular claims that the development of nationalism was
directly linked to the replacement of religious notions of cyclical and
meta-historical time by the modern, secular conception of simultaneous
human movement forwards through what he, quoting Walter Benjamin,
refers to as "homogeneous, empty time."[13] Not only does this view, as
argued in Chapter 1, misrepresent the complex and ambiguous features of
pre-modern notions of history, it also presents a one-sided picture of the
modern mental calendar. It cries out for revision in light of many of the
historical case studies of nationalism that have appeared in recent years as
well as of sociological studies such as Eviatar Zerubavel's on the structures
of collective memory.[14]

The fundamental premise of the prevalent, Andersonian model, namely
that the modern age is defined by secularization and that nationalism arose
to fill the void left by religion, is itself simplistic and misleading, as
Anthony Smith and others have persuasively argued and as many case
studies have demonstrated.[15] Linda Colley's acclaimed work *Britons*, for
instance, identifies an embattled Protestant identity as the vital element
that gave rise to and shaped British nationalism, and imbued it with its
most enduring qualities.[16] Both the medium and the message of British
nationalism were steeped in religious meaning, according to Colley. The
King James Bible and John Foxe's *Book of Martyrs* were two widely disseminated texts from the sixteenth century on that contributed decisively –
along with sermons, pamphlets, and the like – to a sense of common
British cultural and religious identity bound up with a common history of
victimhood at the hands of Catholic monarchs and with a common destiny as God's new chosen people. Even as narrowly Protestant conceptions
of British identity declined in the wake of Catholic emancipation in 1829,

the idea of Britain as a Christian nation continued to imbue imperialist projects and collective self-imagery with missionary overtones well into the early twentieth century.[17] Moreover, the transposition of Anglo-Puritan values to the Promised Land of New England played a critical role in the crystallization of American political culture and identity.[18] Religious gestures, symbols, and rhetoric continue to pervade political life and public ceremonial in the United States, as the American government's Annual National Prayer Breakfast suggests.[19] Given that British and American national identities are often cited as historically path-breaking, globally influential examples of modern, secular, national identity, the presence within them of such powerful strains of religiosity is particularly striking.[20]

This is not to say that national identity can simply be reduced to a subset of religion. Clearly, secular forms of national identity are not only possible, but have been extremely powerful and influential. Moreover, even when nationalist ideals are expressed in religious idioms, they remain primarily concerned with the temporal rather than the spiritual dimension of human experience, or at least with collective salvation on earth rather than in heaven.[21] The point is not that nationalism is a form of religion, but that nationalism coexists with religion, often overlaps extensively with it, and is almost always colored by the legacy and/or persistent influence of religious sensibilities and worldviews – as Anthony Smith has vividly demonstrated.[22] Even militantly anti-religious manifestations of national identity, as in the case of the radical revolutionary tradition in France or Labor Zionism in Israel, have adapted certain aspects of religious symbolism and thinking and deployed them in the service of their secular-nationalist agendas.

Upon close examination, it appears that the very aspect of nationalist thought commonly considered most distinctively modern – its conception of time and history – is among the most clearly marked by religious influence and pre-modern precedents. Modern nationalism's embrace of the unidirectional, linear sense of history is itself derived from the Judeo-Christian historicization of the path to salvation. But a great deal of nationalist rhetoric, imagery, and mythology also reflects a persistent urge to transcend historical time, much as Judaism and Christianity have held on to elements of the Myth of the Eternal Return in their religious calendars and theological doctrines.[23] Indeed, one of the keys to a nationalist movement's or regime's public acceptance lies in its ability to bridge the gap and overcome the tensions and contradictions between these two dimensions of temporal imagination.

TRANSCENDING HISTORY: THE FRENCH AND CZECH CASES

Manipulating history in wartime France

In the opening passage of his three-volume memoir of the Second World War, Charles de Gaulle draws a curious distinction between "la France" and "les Français." "All my life," he says, "I have pictured for myself a certain idea of France."[24] He goes on to liken his image of his country to the princess in a fairy tale or to a painting of the Madonna and to suggest that it has been created for great things. To the extent that it falls short of greatness, the blame lies not with "the spirit [*génie*] of the fatherland," but with "the shortcomings of the French." Only by being inspired to follow noble visions and carry out grand projects can the French people be led to live up to the glory of the country they inhabit, the nation they compose.[25]

This approach represents more than a trite literary device. It encapsulates the manner in which de Gaulle the politician and statesman sought to frame the entire French experience of World War II. He saw it as one of his central tasks as a leader to persuade his compatriots that the meaning of their crushing and humiliating 1940 defeat at the hands of the Germans could be understood only in the larger framework of French history. But this was History with a capital H, a History that transcended the quotidian experience and that allowed the most terrible setbacks to be interpreted as opportunities to establish existential contact with the eternal. More specifically, it allowed him to represent himself and the small band of followers who initially aligned themselves with his London-based Free French movement as the embodiments of French national identity, of *la France*. The fact that they at first constituted a tiny and obscure minority of exiles, flouting the authority of a French government that had concluded an armistice with the Germans, was irrelevant. Picking Joan of Arc's symbol, the Cross of Lorraine, as their emblem, the Free French (and the resistance movement within France that came to affiliate itself with the Free French) presented themselves as the embodiment of Joan's spirit of defiance in the face of all odds, of her religious faith in the ultimate victory of the nation. It was only half in jest that exasperated British and American officials remarked that de Gaulle saw himself personally as a latter-day Joan of Arc.[26]

This is not to suggest that de Gaulle's endeavor was primarily mystical or religious in nature. The overwhelming bulk of his efforts were focused on the political and military here and now, on the daily struggle to keep his movement alive in the face of German occupation, French apathy,

British ambivalence, and American hostility. In his propaganda too, he laid primary emphasis on the ups and downs of the war and on the long-term material advantages that would, he was convinced, allow the Allied coalition to prevail.[27] The Free French movement was very much connected to history with a small H, and had, perforce, to be obsessed with steering its way through the daily uncertainties and unpredictable contingencies of the wartime experience. But precisely because the outcome of the conflict seemed so unpredictable and because the events of spring 1940 had left the French feeling so hopeless and despairing, it seemed vital to connect the this-worldly struggle of the war to a transcendent vision of France the eternal. The Free French movement's claim to legitimacy depended on its professed unique ability to mediate between the devastating historical experience of the 1940s and the meta-historical ideal of a glorious and sovereign France. On the face of it, those two images could not have been more at odds with one another. Yet by upholding the cause of national liberation in the face of defeat, Free France could bridge the gap between these images and redefine the Fall of France as the opportunity for its resurrection. In the aftermath of liberation, as propaganda efforts came to focus on the restoration of a sense of unity that would transcend the bitter and violent divisions of wartime, the identification of the Free French movement with Joan of Arc was more strongly emphasized than it had been in the midst of the conflict itself. As founder (1958) and first president (1959–69) of the Fifth Republic, de Gaulle himself struck poses and invoked symbols that identified him with past leaders and regimes stretching from the medieval era to the twentieth century – all rolled into one personage claiming to embody the changeless substance of the French national soul.[28]

For its part, the right-wing, authoritarian Vichy regime that had negotiated the armistice with Germany also invoked seemingly timeless French social and political values in its struggle to portray itself as the guardian of the nation's soul. In Philippe Burrin's words, "everything in the Pétainist vision expresses a formidable aspiration to exit time."[29] Yet for all its reactionary qualities, Burrin argues, this was a regime that presented itself as the epitome of political modernity. The Vichy regime declared itself to be undertaking a National Revolution that would lead France towards the future by breaking definitively with the Third Republic's legacy of parliamentary factionalism, industrial unrest, and military defeat. The ostensibly non-ideological "Labor, Family, Fatherland" replaced the original French Revolution's "Liberty, Equality, Fraternity" as the state slogan, calling to mind a way of life that transcended all of France's historical epochs, defunct regimes, and factional struggles. This transformed France – a France brought into touch with its trans-historical essence – was to have an honorable role to play in the New Europe that Nazi Germany was supposed to be creating.

Guiding France through this attempted rupture with the immediate past of the interwar period as well as the entire heritage of the Revolution of 1789 was the hero of World War I's Battle of Verdun, Marshal Philippe Pétain. The language and imagery of Pétainist propaganda had a decidedly religious and meta-historical aura to it. In his radio address of 17 June 1940, Pétain employed the phrase that was to become the hallmark of his regime: "I make France the gift of my person in order to ease her misfortune." (In subsequent proclamations, he was to employ the royal "we.") Eighty-four years old and ready to enjoy the rewards of a lifetime of public service, the marshal had selflessly chosen to give up the comforts of retirement for his country's sake. The image invoked, absurd as it might be, was that of Jesus sacrificing himself for the salvation of humanity.[30]

In its propaganda, the Vichy regime combined brash visions of a new, vigorous, youthful France with the quasi-deified image of the aged patriarch watching protectively over his people. Widely disseminated placards portrayed a white-haired Pétain casting his benevolently unfocused gaze towards a distant horizon while a virile young generation reverently beheld his visage or marched confidently ahead in lockstep.[31] One poster called on French children to pray to the Virgin Mary and the patron saints of France to intercede with God on behalf of the continued "vigor and health of our glorious and venerable Marshal Pétain."[32] The very paradox of an octogenerian leading the National Revolution epitomized one of Vichy's central messages: this was a revolution that would take France into the future by reconnecting it with its timeless, glorious, pre-modern past, liberating it from its sense of linear continuity with the turbulent historical experience of the previous 150-odd years.[33]

The cult of Joan of Arc was ideally suited to promoting this idea. Contesting the Free French movement's appropriation of the Cross of Lorraine as its emblem, the Vichy regime elevated Joan of Arc to Madonna-like status in its nationalist iconography. While the Free French played on her resistance to a foreign occupier as an inspiration to the anti-German struggle, Vichy emphasized the English identity of the fifteenth-century occupiers, a message better suited to the collaborationist regime's effective alignment with Nazi Germany. As the caption on one Vichy propaganda poster put it, "So that France may live, one must drive the English out of Europe as Joan of Arc did."[34] The annual festival of Joan of Arc, already embraced by the Third Republic during the interwar period, was the occasion of heightened attention under Vichy. Official ceremonies in her honor were held across the country, with public dignitaries, schoolchildren, and members of government-sponsored associations such as the official veterans' organization in attendance. A plethora of officially produced and disseminated pamphlets and posters about Joan blanketed the country, cinemas played newsreel footage of the ceremonies, and an oratorio in her honor was broadcast over the radio. In a 1941 Pétainist biography of the saint, the fifteenth-century adolescent and the twentieth-century octogenarian were identified as two sides of the same miraculous coin of redemption that heaven had bestowed on France in its need.[35]

The nation's progress through the seamlessly unilinear flow of ordinary time could have meaning and direction only if it was illuminated by associations with superhuman figures and archetypal events from the distant past. An essential element in the battle for public acceptance and political legitimacy, both the Free French and Vichy were convinced, lay in their ability to present themselves as the essential links between the meta-historical and the historical. In their rivalry over the legacy of Joan, which Robert Gildea has highlighted, Vichy and the Free French were each laying claim to a transcendent symbol of spiritual triumph and national redemption.[36] Whoever seized the halo of this sainted figure could light the nation's way through the darkness of the war years and beyond. In the country whose great revolution of 1789 is widely regarded as a critical watershed in the development of modern nationalism, a religious icon from the late Middle Ages continued – well into the twentieth century – to play a powerful symbolic role in shaping collective identity and in defining (or, rather, deliberately obfuscating) the nation's relationship with historical time.[37]

The Czech national revival

In adopting and propagating this perspective, the competing wartime French national movements were far from unique. Nearly every modern nationalist ideology, movement, and regime has sought to establish connections between chronologically far-flung events by creating mythical structures designed to bridge yawning gaps in time. The nationalist "invention of tradition"[38] can serve to weave the dramatic epiphanies of destiny that punctuate the nation's passage through time into an unchanging fabric of meaning that transcends the endless chain of banal causes and unanticipated effects that marks the ordinary progress of history.

Derek Sayer's masterful history of Czech national identity provides a vivid illustration of this phenomenon. Significantly, Sayer calls into question the exclusive modernity of nationalism, making a strong case for the emergence of a powerful sense of Czech national identity during the religious wars of the fifteenth–seventeenth centuries.[39] But he also contends that the Habsburg/Catholic defeat of Czech Protestant resistance at the Battle of the White Mountain in 1620 inaugurated the successful repression and eradication of Czech national culture and identity. By the late 1700s, the surviving social elites of the provinces of Bohemia and Moravia (the Czech heartland) had been successfully co-opted into the Habsburg Empire's administrative, political, and clerical establishments and had been thoroughly assimilated into German language and Austro-German culture. Czech high culture was dead and the Czech language was largely reduced to an array of peasant dialects. When Vienna's late eighteenth- and nineteenth-century attempts to consolidate centralized state power provoked the reassertion of historic regional rights and cultural distinctiveness, German-speaking Bohemian aristocrats and intellectuals found themselves hard pressed to define just what it was that made them Czech. The nineteenth-century Czech national "awakening" really constituted "the (re)invention of the 'imagined political community' of the modern nation."[40] The critical element in this enterprise was the establishment of a sense of connection with the Czech nation in its previous, early modern, incarnation. To be effective, this tie to the distant past had to span across the historical chasm of the preceding two centuries' national oblivion.

The nationalist use of history therefore had to be radically ahistorical in method – ahistorical not just in the sense that it interpreted past events in light of a contemporary political agenda, but in the deeper sense that it circumvented the strictly continuous sequence of historical time. Thus, in Alfons Mucha's early-twentieth-century artistic masterpiece, *Slovanska epopej* (Slav Epic), dramatic episodes from the history of the Slavic peoples generally, and the Czechs in particular, are presented in a series of gigantic paintings that tell the story of the nation's inexorable rise to spiritual greatness in the face of material adversity. A fanciful image of the Slavs in their original homeland is followed by a depiction of the creation of a Slavonic-language Christian liturgy, and, several panels later, by scenes from the fifteenth-century Hussite religious reformation and the wars that ensued. The series ends with "The Apotheosis of the History of the Slavs," in which a Christ-like image hovers over a festive parade of people in peasant attire celebrating their commitment to humanity. In Derek Sayer's words:

Mucha transposes his historical subject matter into another dimension, a timeless realm of essential truths that stands above the ephemera of mere events ... [He] wrenches historical events out of their diverse contexts and reinscribes them in a new space, which is that of the epic of his title ... They are not historical illustrations but the exact opposite: history serves in them as itself the illustration of the national and Slavonic Idea that animates them.[41]

Of course, there was a fixed sequence to the events depicted in these panels, but it was a sequence that connected far-flung historical dots into a line of continuity that lay outside the realm of ordinary time.

Mucha's approach, Sayer argues, was typical of the nationalist perspective. It followed the pattern of the linguists who standardized the Czech language and revived it as a literary medium, the historians who narrated the story of the Czech nation, and the ethnographers who gathered folktales, collected songs, and preserved peasant costumes. All were engaged in attempts to create and affirm a national experience capable of lending meaning and purpose to history by virtue of standing outside of time. Even the Communist regime of the Cold War years resorted to presenting itself as a remanifestation of the Hussite movement in what Sayer terms "this fairy tale of the eternal return of the ever-same ... "[42] And, of course, the Czech approach was not unusual, but was paralleled by sundry other ethnic-revival and nationalist movements across not just East Central Europe, but much of the world.[43]

As the rival claims of Vichy and the Free French to the legacy of Joan of Arc and the example of the Czechoslovak Communist Party presenting itself as a Hussite revival remind us, the nationalist myth of eternal return can transcend the most radical political differences. By the same token, it often forms the symbolic centerpiece of factional and ideological struggles, a Holy Grail that confers legitimacy on its possessor and whose control is the object of endless competition. Rival groupings can differ about what the Holy Grail is – that is, which episodes and figures from the past are to be regarded as embodying timeless elements of the national character. But they all seem to agree on the need for such a Grail. Thus, the liberal-democratic founding father of Czechoslovakia, Tomáš Masaryk, gained early notoriety in the Czech cultural and political arena by denouncing as nineteenth-century forgeries a group of supposedly medieval manuscripts touted by right-wing nationalists as proof of the antiquity and unchanging spirit of Czech nationhood. But Masaryk himself invoked the memory of the fifteenth-century Czech religious reformer and martyr, Jan Hus, as a point of departure and source of inspiration for his own conception of the Czech national spirit as a long-suppressed synthesis of religious faith with political rationalism and progressive, humanist values. In rejecting the forged manuscripts and upholding the legacy of Hus, Masaryk was asserting the superiority of a modern, scientific approach to national history over the blatant fabrications of unscrupulous chauvinists. Jan Hus had really existed in the fifteenth century, while the allegedly ancient manuscripts had not. But in a broader sense, Masaryk was resorting to myth-making of his own, for to suggest that Hus embodied the Czech national character or that the creation of a modern liberal democracy would constitute a manifestation of the spirit of Hussite religious reform was to make unfalsifiable, and hence unverifiable, claims. Masaryk too was invoking a timeless image as a way of orienting the nation in its march through time and as a means of legitimizing his particular ideological agenda for the nation's historical development.[44]

THE NEW YORKER'S MAP OF HISTORY

If nationalists raise selected events and personalities out of the historical continuum and into the realm of the meta-temporal, they also make a point of marginalizing entire stretches of history that do not fit their ideological mold. As Ernest Renan famously put it in his 1882 Sorbonne lecture on nationalism: "Forgetting, I would even go so far as to say historical error, is a crucial factor in the creation of a nation, which is why progress in historical studies often constitutes a danger for [the principle of] nationality."[45] Nationalist amnesia can take a variety of forms. Renan's example of an event consigned to oblivion by common national agreement was the St. Bartholemew's Day massacre of 1572, in which thousands of French Protestants were slaughtered in cold blood by their Catholic compatriots. As Benedict Anderson has pointed out, his use of this example was paradoxical, for in mentioning this "forgotten" event, Renan felt no need to clarify what it was: he clearly assumed that everyone in his audience was perfectly familiar with it. His point was not that the massacre had literally been forgotten, but rather that a semi-conscious decision had been made not to commemorate it, not to integrate it into the mythology of the nation. The consensus among French Catholics and Protestants, clericalists and secularists, not to mark St. Bartholemew's

Day in their calendars, the general agreement to interpret the event as a tragic exception that proved the rule of French unity, itself constituted a powerful affirmation and manifestation of that unity.[46]

Some sixty years after Renan delivered his lecture, the French were engaged in a variation on this exercise. De Gaulle's triumph over Pétain in the context of the Allied victory in World War II led to a deliberate and systematic rewriting of history under de Gaulle's Fifth Republic (1958–). As Henry Rousso has shown, the mythmaking apparatus of the state was thrown full force behind an attempt to present the history of the Resistance and the Free French movement as the main story of France during the war.[47] The Vichy regime was portrayed as little more than a grab-bag of traitors and collaborators who had wandered down a historical blind alley and whose nefarious deeds served as a dark backdrop against which the wartime heroism of the French people could shine all the brighter. For several decades, virtually no scholarship was devoted to the history of Vichy, the regime's extensive collaboration in the deportation of Jews to Nazi concentration camps was largely unacknowledged, and the wide base of popular support it originally enjoyed was actively denied. The civil-war-like conditions that marked the liberation of France in 1944 were virtually unmentionable. It was left to American scholars in the 1970s to pioneer serious research into the history of Vichy France and to present it as a regime whose ideologies, institutions, and personalities had been at least as deeply rooted in French history and society as de Gaulle's Free French movement.[48]

Of course, Americans themselves have been no less guilty of such tricks of the nationalist trade. For many years following Reconstruction, the importance of slavery as a social and economic institution, and its centrality to Southern identity as well as to the origins of the Civil War, was underplayed in American school textbooks in both North and South. Here again was a case of an embarrassing episode in history that everyone knew about vaguely, but that much of white America agreed was best left in the margins of the national epic.[49] As late as 1961, the federal government's Civil War Centennial Commission strove to make commemoration of the conflict a focus for national unity by jointly honoring the memory of General Grant and General Lee and by highlighting the common spirit of heroism and self-sacrifice in which soldiers on both sides of the fray had gone off into battle.[50]

Such forms of institutionalized amnesia do not really represent a departure from the linear conception of history as a continuous unfolding of interconnected events. De Gaulle was not trying to ignore the years

1940–44; he was laying claim to them. Pre-1960s American textbooks were not trying to make the Civil War disappear; they were redefining or evading what that conflict had been about. But another form of nationalist forgetting does subvert the linearity that is supposed to be the hallmark of the modern historical sensibility. This variation on the theme might be termed the New Yorker's Map of History. A widely disseminated and copied poster image of Saul Steinberg's 29 March 1976 *New Yorker* cover, "View of the World from 9th Avenue," caricatures the stereotypical image New Yorkers supposedly have of the United States by presenting a distorted map of the country, in which the New York City skyline takes up the entire foreground and Los Angeles looms up alarmingly close from the back, with the entire breadth of the landscape between the two coasts reduced to a handful of Lilliputian landmarks. In what Eviatar Zerubavel has referred to as their "social punctuation of the past," some nationalist roadmaps of history bear at least a superficial resemblance to this perspective.[51] In cases where national independence is a recent phenomenon, coming on the heels of a protracted period of foreign subjugation, much is made of the intimate connection between the present period of self-determination and an ancient era (real, mythical, or a little of both) of dignity and freedom. The vast stretches of time in between are summed up in a handful of images, relegated to complete obscurity, or consigned to a separate cartographic dimension that remains unconnected to the main roadmap of nationalist history.

In her study of the interplay of history, memory, and myth in the evolution of Israeli national consciousness, Yael Zerubavel refers to this phenomenon as enclosing historical epochs in parentheses.[52] We have already seen elements of this approach in the Czech national myth's marginalization of Bohemia's and Moravia's seventeenth- and eighteenth-century history. In the Zionist case, the period to be bracketed was the nearly two millennia of dispossession and exile that had marked Jewish history between the Roman destruction of Jewish society in Palestine in the first and second centuries of the Common Era and the inception of the modern Zionist movement in the late nineteenth and early twentieth centuries.

The early generations of Zionists were not just trying to save the Jews of Europe from material deprivation and political, religious, and physical persecution. They were also intent upon recasting the Jewish national character in the mold of the heroes of old. Secular Zionists of every political stripe agreed that centuries of living as a dispersed and despised minority had turned a once proud nation into a physically enfeebled and spiritually cowed people. Indeed, many Zionists consciously or unconsciously accepted certain anti-Semitic stereotypes about the Jews as an uncouth, unattractive, and economically parasitical people, while attributing these alleged characteristics to the intensity and duration of their persecution rather than to any innate qualities.[53] The central task of the national revival was to restore this downtrodden people's physical and spiritual dignity and vitality by reestablishing their autonomous existence in their ancestral homeland.

This enterprise necessarily involved more than a concerted organizational, political, and economic effort. It was a multifaceted cultural and psychological undertaking as well. The revival of Hebrew as a spoken language was the most uniquely successful aspect of this project.[54] It encapsulated the effort to turn back the hands of time and establish a direct sense of affinity – an ability to communicate, as it were – with the Hebrew-speaking Jews of the Davidic kingdom (1000–586 BCE)[55] and with the national-historical texts of the Hebrew Bible. As Yael Zerubavel has shown, Zionist literature, school textbooks, and even reconfigured religious holidays (notably Lag Ba-Omer) sought to highlight heroic episodes from Jewish antiquity such as Bar Kokhba's failed second-century CE anti-Roman rebellion as inspirations for the (hopefully more successful) twentieth-century pioneers of Jewish liberation.[56] Modern heroes of the Zionist movement were presented as cast in the mold of their ancient predecessors. Widely disseminated photographs of the father of Zionism, Theodor Herzl, portrayed him in the guise of a visionary prophet, while the fallen defender of a Jewish settlement in northern Galilee, Yosef Trumpeldor, was mourned and commemorated as a Jewish fighter who had incarnated the qualities of a Bar Kokhba.[57]

It should be emphasized that the primary proponents of this perspective were not religious in the conventional sense of the term; they were forward-looking modernizers and firm believers in doctrines of historical progress as holding the key to Jewish national regeneration. Zionist institutions and the Israeli political establishment were dominated by socialist- and other secular-nationalist movements and parties that rejected the God-fearing ways of traditional Judaism as marked by a fatalism and obscurantism bred of powerlessness and exile.[58] But the modernizing sensibility was not seen as precluding a tie to the distant past. On the contrary, it was this drive to renew the link with antiquity that legitimized the programs of mainstream Zionism and that struck a resonant chord among wide sectors of Jewish society in Eastern Europe and elsewhere. The religious and liturgical tradition itself had always

*more
complicated
than this*

presented the Return to Zion as the defining feature of collective salvation
for the Jews. Zionists affirmed the worthiness of this goal, but rejected
what they saw as passive waiting for a divinely anointed Messiah who
would lead the Israelites back to the Promised Land in favor of an activist
approach that stressed self-reliance, organization, and bold cultural,
political, and economic initiatives as the way to fulfill this dream. In
charting their course towards a reconnection with the ancient experience
of collective existence on the native soil, secular Zionists were laying out a
program for shedding the stultifying influence of the immediate past.

Hence, as Yael Zerubavel argues, linear and circular conceptions of
time came to coexist in the Israeli national tradition, not just in the sense
that the national holiday calendar – like its religious counterpart – went
round in circles, but in the sense that history itself was not portrayed as
proceeding in a straight line. The twentieth-century history of the Yishuv
(Zionist settlement in Palestine) and the State of Israel was taught and
commemorated in standard, linear fashion, as a steady sequence of
political and cultural initiatives, immigration waves, and diplomatic and
military battles for survival, with each new endeavor building on the
foundations of earlier sacrifices and achievements. The history of Ancient
Israel and Judah was portrayed as running along a similarly straight
timeline. Educational curricula, dramatic archaeological digs, and military-political triumphs (notably, the reunification of Jerusalem in the
1967 Six Day War) combined to create a tangible sense of intimate
connection between new Israel and ancient Israel. But the nearly two
millennia stretching between these two timelines did not fit this pattern,
for the entire point of Zionism and the State of Israel was to undertake a
radical break with the exilic experience of passivity and humiliation.
Hence, school textbooks, fiction, poetry, and political rhetoric alike
underplayed the history of the Jewish diaspora. The Zionist version of
Jewish history converted the unhappy diaspora experience into a sort of
chronological detour that eventually led back to a point close to where the
original, linear story had left off, with the people once again established as
a thriving, self-sufficient community on its native soil.[59]

While the Israeli case furnishes a particularly striking example of this
nationalist foreshortening of historical time, it is – as Eviatar Zerubavel has
pointed out – hardly exceptional.[60] The Czech national renewal described
above similarly sought to marginalize the centuries separating the Battle of
the White Mountain from the nineteenth-century "reawakening." We
have seen how the Vichy regime endeavored to establish a sense of connection to France's pre-1789 history. Modern Greek nationalism focused

on classical antiquity and Periclean Athens as the most vital points of reference for the recreation of a vibrant Hellenic culture. Nineteenth-century Greek linguistic standardizers even sought to institute a modified form of classical Greek as the accepted form of written communication, in defiance of the spoken language's nearly two-and-a-half millennia of evolution since the days of Thucydides. Centuries of foreign rule were to be consigned to relative oblivion, apart from furnishing negative lessons about the importance of political sovereignty to national dignity.[61] Irish nationalists have had similarly ambivalent approaches to the centuries of English rule over their island, highlighting key incidents of resistance and oppression while at the same time struggling to create a direct sense of connection to a romanticized medieval past. In the words of Douglas Hyde, "what we must endeavour to never forget is this, that the Ireland of today is the descendant of the Ireland of the seventh century, then the school of Europe and the torch of learning."[62] In Ireland – as in Israel and to a lesser extent Greece – the establishment of mandatory instruction in a standardized and modernized version of the people's original tongue[63] – has been the most prominent and substantive aspect of the effort to skip back over time.[64] By the same token, the failure to reestablish Gaelic as a widely spoken language and the brilliant impact generations of Irish writers have had upon English literature highlight just how difficult it is to change the legacy of political history and the course of cultural evolution.[65]

CONCRETIZING THE TRANSCENDENT

Monuments

Nations are possessed with an insane ambition to perpetuate the memory of themselves by the amount of hammered stone they leave. What if equal pains were taken to smooth and polish their manners?[66] (Thoreau)

Linguistic revival is but one of many ways in which nationalist movements attempt to defy the relentless passage of years. Various other stereotypical aspects of nationalism serve to concretize the sense of a transcendent national experience that bridges awkward historical chasms and lends purpose and meaning to the forward progress of the nation through time. As the Zerubavels have pointed out, independence day and other national holidays cycle around every year, bringing each generation in touch both with the primordial act of national creation/liberation, and with all the previous generations that have celebrated that event.[67]

Monuments to fallen soldiers and national heroes serve a comparable function. The Tomb of the Unknown Soldier has, since the aftermath of the First World War, become a widespread nationalist tradition whose power lies not only in the anonymity of the individual remains lying within it, but also in the non-specificity of the time it refers to.[68] It is not only the Unknown Soldier who stays nameless; the war in which the Unknown Soldier gave up his life has essentially become any war and every war. Even if, in some cases, information is actually provided about the specific battlefield from which the remains within originated, this is marginal to the symbolic import of the monument. The central message is that the Tomb represents the unnamed heroes of all the wars ever fought on behalf of the nation. Eternal flames that burn in honor of the dead remain, like the essence of the nation's soul, constant and unchanging through the years. And like independence day celebrations, memorial days are annually recurring occasions for nations to renew spiritual and emotional contact with their fallen heroes of all times. Conflicts fought in vastly different periods and for fundamentally different reasons are all conflated into a single, institutionalized commemoration that contains strikingly ahistorical elements in its approach to the nation's past.

Of course, the great bulk of monuments, including war memorials, contain strong elements of historical specificity as well.[69] It was largely a twentieth-century innovation to list the names of the war dead on memorials, the ubiquitous French town and village monuments to the local fallen of the First World War being a notable example.[70] Such memorials are erected in honor of particular men, from particular places, who fell at a particular time and in a particular war. The Vietnam War Memorial in Washington, D.C. is one of the most prominent national examples of this approach.[71] Yet even in the case of some such monuments, the sense of historical specificity becomes blurred over time. Many local World War I monuments in France as well as in the United States have additional plaques added to them in honor of the dead of subsequent twentieth-century conflicts. One monument serves to commemorate all, and the names of those who died in the Second World War and various colonial conflicts blend fairly seamlessly into the lists of those fallen before them.

More significantly, ahistorical monuments and historically specific ceremonies and memorials not only coexist but also complement each other's symbolic functions. Late nineteenth-century Germania monuments, built to celebrate Bismarck's successful wars of German national unification, sought to symbolically supersede regionalist sentiments and tensions associated with Bismarck's policies by linking the commemoration of recent victories with a personified image of national unity free of any particular dynastic or recent historical association. The very name Germania harked back to the nation's primeval common ancestors as described by the Roman historian Tacitus.[72] In France, the 1929 death of World War I commander Marshal Foch was the occasion of a solemn military parade accompanying Foch's body to the Hôtel des Invalides, where the hero of the nation's most recent war was laid to rest in the building that housed Napoleon's remains and which was decorated with seventeenth-century images of the nations defeated by Louis XIV, during whose reign the Invalides had been constructed. As Jean Tulard puts it, in this ceremony, "the infantry men joined . . . the regiments of Louis XIV and the soldiers of the [Napoleonic] Grande Armée."[73] The country's most recent bloodletting was given a higher meaning by blurring the temporal chasm that separated it from earlier episodes of glorious self-sacrifice.

The cumulative impact of the war memorials in the United States capital is not dissimilar. The Tomb of the Unknown Soldier in Arlington National Cemetery in Virginia lies just across the Potomac River from the National Mall in Washington, D.C. – site of the major national war memorials (Vietnam, Korea, and World War II[74]). Visitors making their way along the tourist pilgrimage route in and around the American capital are more likely to be impressed by the overarching theme of continuity among the variously designed monuments than they are to be jarred by inconsistencies of style and message (perhaps with the exception of the starkly mournful and non-triumphalist Vietnam War Memorial). Like so many other aspects of what Anthony Smith has called the national myth-symbol complex,[75] the National Mall's ensemble of memorials serves to connect discrete historical episodes and human tragedies into a larger, more meaningful whole that transcends any particular historical period. The memorials to specific wars mark the nation's advance from challenge to challenge and triumph to triumph in the course of historical time, while the Tomb of the Unknown Soldier links all these periods and experiences into an overarching sense of devotion, honor, and sacrifice that knows no limitation of time or space.[76]

The conjoining of historical specificity with symbolic transcendence of time was strikingly apparent in the design and presentation of the United States World War II Memorial, opened in May 2004. The occasion was marked by a special advertising supplement in the *Washington Post*

Magazine, which quoted from the memorial's main inscription to explain the symbolic significance of the monument's spatial arrangement at the midpoint between the Washington Monument and Lincoln Memorial: "Here in the presence of Washington and Lincoln ... we honor those Twentieth Century Americans who took up the struggle during the Second World War and made the sacrifices to perpetuate the gift our forefathers entrusted to us: A nation conceived in liberty and justice." Having established the memorial's link to the nation's immortal leaders and timeless values, the essay went on without so much as a figurative bat-of-an-eyelid to assert that "America was transformed between 1941 and 1945 ... [The memorial's words and bas-reliefs] show, in effect, where the country was at the start of the war; what individuals did during it ... and why, in the aftermath, America was changed forever."[77] For the nationalist sensibility, there is no contradiction in portraying a cataclysmic event at one and the same time as a radical rupture with, and a vital link to, the nation's past.

Land

The land that holds the nation's fallen war heroes alongside all the other dead of generations past, is itself one of the most important and compelling objects of nationalist devotion and worship.[78] Nationalist poems and hymns, such as "America the Beautiful," sing the praises of the country's physical endowments. The *Wandervogel,* Germany's late nineteenth- and early twentieth-century scouting organization, emphasized exploration of the land as the path to spiritual renewal and patriotic inspiration.[79] Instilling "knowledge of the land [of Israel]" was the central mission of Zionist scouting movements.[80] Carving the nation's symbols upon the land further reinforces the association between nation and territory, as at Mt. Rushmore in South Dakota, where the landscape has been shaped into the explicit form of a national monument. As Benedict Anderson has pointed out, even the contours of the nation's borders as depicted on a two-dimensional map can become a powerful nationalist logo.[81]

From what stems this fascination with geography? To be sure, the possession of territory is an indispensable prerequisite for the exercise of political sovereignty, so nationalism without a territorial dimension would not be nationalism at all. (Even diasporic nationalism, as in the Jewish and Armenian cases, is associated with nostalgia for a homeland and yearning for territorial sovereignty.) But, as Anthony Smith has also argued, the

patriotic cult of the land has to do with more than the practical requirements of statehood.[82] As the repository of the dead, the land constitutes a
direct, concrete link to the nation's past – an immutable past that serves
forever as a source of inspiration and reassurance to the nation's living.[83]
Archaeologists can lend substance and scientific legitimacy to nationalists'
romantic fascination with the land, by digging into the earth to unveil the
material remains of the nation's past alongside the bones of its ancestors.[84]
The excavation of the ancient Jewish, anti-Roman rebel outpost on
Masada, and its conversion into a tourist-pilgrimage site, is the most
famous example of this sort of nationalist-archaeological synthesis. The
choice of Masada as the site for the swearing in of recruits to the Israeli
army's armored units serves momentarily to erase two millennia of elapsed
time, as Israel's contemporary defenders unite in spirit with their ancient
predecessors.[85]

Moreover, the natural landscape is a national monument in its own
right, organically linked to the historical monuments built upon it.[86]
(Significantly, in the United States, the National Park Service is jointly
the custodian of both the national parks and a wide array of federally
owned historic sites, monuments and national cemeteries.[87]) The landscape is worshipped as a national possession, symbol, even an embodiment of the national spirit, which is seen as unchanging and unaffected
by the ephemeral events of human history. The same mountains, streams,
forests, that earlier generations gazed upon are still there to be admired by
those of later times. As Eviatar Zerubavel puts it, "constancy of place is a
formidable basis for establishing a strong sense of sameness."[88] The more
urbanization, industrialization, and environmental degradation take
place, the more nationalist imagery of the land seems to focus on images
of pristine countryside unsullied by human intervention. Even the most
militant opponents of the environmentalist movement eagerly wrap
themselves in the mantle of the nation's landscape when appealing for
public support, as in George W. Bush's much trumpeted and never-
to-be-fulfilled 2000 campaign promise to devote himself to a restoration
of the United States' neglected national parks, or in his use two years later
of Mt. Rushmore as the spectacular backdrop for an announcement that
his response to the national rash of forest fires would be to lift various
curbs on logging by the timber industry.[89]

Feeling rooted in the natural or pastoral landscape allows the nation to
overcome the perceived chasm between civilization and nature and to escape
the uncertainties of historical time by finding refuge in the seeming
immobility of geological time.[90] Nineteenth- and twentieth-century

German *völkisch* nationalists became intoxicated by their own myths about the forest as the primeval haunt of an undefiled German national spirit, recalling the forbidding, swamp-ridden woods from which Arminius' fearsome warriors had emerged to slaughter the Roman legions in the year 9 CE.[91] Nineteenth-century British and American landscape painting was torn between the embrace of the railroad and other symbols of industrial development as harbingers of progress, and attachment to images of unsullied countryside and untouched nature as parts of a timeless heritage whose image provided a sense of continuity and changelessness amidst the dislocating pressures of modernization. The image of the West as a wasteland awaiting development by America's pioneers encapsulated the sense of a nation marching forward through history, while linking that image of linear progress through time and space to the timeless, archetypal theme of a chosen people setting forth to inherit a promised land. Across the Atlantic, early nineteenth-century English landscape and pastoral paintings won renewed appreciation from the late Victorian and Edwardian eras onward, when insecurities over mounting threats to Britain's industrial and imperial primacy strengthened the cult of the pastoral as haven for an immutably pristine sense of Englishness.[92] Thomas Lekan has documented how German nature-conservation efforts in the Rhineland from the late nineteenth century onwards were infused with a similar concern to link regional and national identity to the enduring beauty of the native landscape in a period of rapid socio-economic and environmental transformations.[93] And during World War I, in George Mosse's words, images of unsullied national landscapes "served to direct attention away from the impersonality of the war of modern technology and the trenches toward preindustrial ideals of individualism, chivalry, and the conquest of space and time."[94] The more nations are transformed by urbanization and industrial modes of production, the more attractive apparently unchanging images of nature – and pastoral or agricultural forms of human interaction with nature – have become as symbols of those nations' inner essences.

Peasantry

Indeed, in many European countries, the nationalist fascination with nature, landscape, and native soil contributed to the nineteenth- and twentieth-century idealization of the peasant – the tiller of the soil. To be sure, the cult of the peasant was never a nationalist monopoly, having been a central aspect of nineteenth- and early twentieth-century Russian populism and twentieth-century Chinese Communism, among other movements. Nationalist interest in the peasantry was certainly influenced by left-wing populist ideologies as well as by the obvious political importance of winning peasant support in countries where a large chunk if not a majority of the population remained rural well into the twentieth century. But nationalist romanticization of peasant culture, traditions, and folkways clearly exceeded – and often seemed irrelevant to – the requirements of mass mobilization in the countryside. Indeed, in modern nationalist iconography, the peasant typically played a role more in keeping with the fantasies of urban intellectuals than with the economic needs or political interests of the rural population itself. Moreover, instances abound of the peasantry being glorified as repository or embodiment of nationalist values long after the lives of actual peasants have been radically transformed by the inroads of capitalism, urbanization, and industrialization.

It was as people of the soil – the nation's soil – that the peasantry-in-the-abstract was worshipped by many modern nationalist movements.[95] Working the land for their living, the peasants were seen as more intimately and organically connected to it than those city dwellers who merely resided upon the national territory. As largely illiterate people, heavily dependent on oral transmission of cultural knowledge, peasants were seen as maintaining age-old traditions relatively uninfluenced by the modern spread of ideas through the printed word. Indeed, the national language itself had often been kept alive, albeit in the form of sundry dialects, by the peasantry in countries where members of social and intellectual elites had been assimilated into alien cultures. (We have seen this in the Czech case, discussed earlier in this chapter.) Nineteenth- and twentieth-century ethnographers, many of them pursuing a nationalist agenda, strove to record rural folk traditions before the steady inroad of modernization led to their disappearance.

In both these capacities – as people "rooted" in the native soil and as bearers of ostensibly ancient traditions – peasants embodied qualities of timelessness and authenticity that were highly prized by nationalist ideologues. As supposed repositories of the most organically continuous, distinctive, and unadulterated aspects of national culture and character, the peasants were to be studied and their lifestyles recorded for all time. Their stories were to be adapted into published folktales (like those of the Brothers Grimm) and epic poems (such as the Finnish Kalevala[96]), their superstitions described, their music recorded or reworked into orchestral format (as in the compositions of the Czech Antonín Dvořák or the

Hungarian Béla Bartók).[97] Peasant costumes were to be trotted out on national festivals and featured in museums and fairs, as in the case of the embroidered peasant women's clothing that remains a fixture of pro-Palestinian cultural exhibits. Where a peasant ethnic base was not to be found at all, it had to be created. The socialist Zionist pioneers saw the virtual absence of a Jewish peasantry in Eastern Europe as one of the marks of the artificiality of Jewish existence in the Diaspora; the movement to establish collective farms (*kibbutzim*) in Palestine was designed to normalize the nation's socio-economic existence while simultaneously reconnecting it organically and spiritually to the Land of Israel.[98]

kibbutzim

To return briefly to our French case study, the image of the peasant-soldier as the embodiment of simple, manly connection and devotion to the fatherland has long been a feature of nationalist literature and propaganda in France, particularly on the right wing of the political spectrum. This trend reached its apogee under the virulently anti-socialist Vichy regime, which placed the peasantry on a pedestal and portrayed it as the guardian of the most genuinely French traditions. Precisely because it had often played such a faceless, reactive, and oppositional role in the revolutionary upheavals of French history since 1789, the peasantry could be represented as embodying values that transcended the country's chaotic and unstable succession of regimes. Indeed, for much of this period, the peasants had been bastions of conservative monarchism and traditional Catholicism in the face of the radical politics of Parisian intellectuals and working-class activists. Only under the Third Republic (1871–1940) had the rural masses been more or less integrated into officially propagated French culture and convinced to accept a moderate republican form of government.[99] Marshal Pétain seems to have aspired to reverse this process by portraying old-fashioned peasant values as the epitome of real Frenchness and supplanting what he saw as the corrupt influence of urban civilization with the earthy, story-book simplicity of rural culture. "La terre, elle ne ment pas" ["the land, it does not lie"] – was one of his most renowned, if vacuous, phrases, suggesting that France's answer to its degrading 1940 defeat lay not in the modernist ideologies of the urban intelligentsia but in an introspective return to ahistorical, peasant values.[100] In remarks made to American journalists in October 1940, Pétain claimed that "the France of tomorrow will be at one and the same time very new and very ancient. She will become once again that which she should never have ceased to be – an essentially agricultural nation. Like the giant in the fable, she will rediscover all her forces by regaining contact with the earth."[101]

This romanticized, ahistorical conception of the peasant as embodiment of the nation's soul was not the exclusive province of the French far right, any more than the cult of Joan of Arc was. The idealization of the peasant – and of the peasant-soldier – had been a recurring theme in the history of French political culture, and had been one of the distinguishing characteristics of the French Third Republic's nationalist dramaturgy, as Gérard de Puymège has argued. Indeed, the interment of the Unknown Soldier at the Arc de Triomphe on 11 November 1920 was accompanied by a parade that prominently featured symbols of rural, agricultural France as a salute to the nameless peasant warriors who had died in the defense of the very soil that they had tilled and that their surviving comrades had gone back to tilling.[102] Throughout much of the twentieth century, France's republican governments looked upon the peasantry as a demographic recruitment pool for a stable, hard-working bourgeoisie and as a reservoir of stable French national values. The phrase "la France profonde" was commonly used to denote the rural sector that constituted the semi-mystical well-spring of national identity. In contemporary France, the virtual disappearance of the traditional peasant way of life in the face of modernization and globalization is seen as posing a fundamental challenge to the essence of the nation's identity.[103]

Cults of the peasantry often embodied the paradoxical nature of nationalism. In idealized and homogenized form, with many regional variations and unpleasant realities ironed out of the official folkloric tapestry, peasant culture was propagated as a national inheritance to be shared in and cultivated by members of all social classes and educational strata, serving to bring those social elements most affected by international currents of modernization back in touch with their own nation's traditions. Intellectual elites' championing of the peasantry as embodiment of the national soul also often served as an ideological weapon in the economic and political marginalization and persecution of urban-based ethnic minorities, such as the Jews in Eastern Europe[104] or the Greeks and Armenians in Anatolia.[105] But by the same token, it was the self-proclaimed and self-appointed task of countless nationalist intellectuals and political leaders to bring the peasantry into the modern age. In Central and Eastern Europe, as well as in many parts of the Middle East, South and East Asia, Africa, and Latin America, modern nationalism presented itself as a movement of liberation, not only from the political and military grip of outsiders, but from the legacy of traditional lifestyles and mentalities thought to have weakened the nation and made it economically and politically vulnerable to external control and exploitation.

Romanticized for its attachment to timeless traditions, the peasantry was just as readily derided for living outside of history. Backward rural folk were to be cajoled, maneuvered, or forced into the mainstream of historical progress if the nation as a whole was to achieve genuine self-determination and gain its rightful place in the international system. Educating the peasants, integrating them into a national market economy, socializing them into a homogeneous national culture through military conscription, suppressing their challenges to economic and political power structures – these have been standard objectives of modern nation-states. It was precisely because the stereotypical nationalist agenda sought to transform peasant society beyond recognition that the task of creating an official version of traditional peasant culture and preserving it for all generations to come was so important. Even as rural folkways gave way before the bulldozer of modernization, the official cult of the peasant would ensure that the nation's march into modernity would be guided by values, images, and symbols that were held to be timeless in nature and that could serve to inform and protect the nation's sense of self in the face of the ceaseless assault of historical change.[106] Yet such carefully cultivated preoccupations with the symbolic value of the traditional farming lifestyle have inevitably led to very self-conscious crises of national identity as the last vestiges of "authentic" village life disappear. Contemporary France is, once again, a notable case in point.[107]

So deeply ingrained and widespread is the notion that the peasantry is the repository or well-spring of authentic national identity, untouched by the forces of historical change, that it has even colored the analysis of some of the most rigorously modernist and materialist scholars of nationalism. Mirsoslav Hroch, who is famed for his application of a nuanced Marxist paradigm to the analysis of nationalism's development among the small nationalities of Europe, seems to take it for granted that peasant customs are the most genuine manifestations of national tradition. In the midst of his coldly materialist dissection of the conditions contributing to nationalism's emergence as a mass movement, he startlingly refers to the peasants as "the natural repositories of the nation's linguistic and cultural tradition . . ." and contends that "the role of the peasantry as the objective substratum of national existence was irreplaceable."[108] In his acclaimed deconstruction of nationalist and post-nationalist forms of historical memory – upon which this chapter has drawn heavily – Pierre Nora suggests that the pre-national peasant communities of the past had no need of designated memorials to historical events because they came into intimate contact with the past through the rhythm and rituals of their daily lives. In other words, the simple villagers of pre-modern France are alleged to have had an authentic, organic link to the past which their alienated modern descendants have been obliged to replace with artificial forms of commemoration. Nora's critical analysis of history and memory itself thus seems to incorporate elements of nostalgia for a historical Never-Never Land when time was not unilinear and when past and present were merged in a mystical union.[109] Similarly, the budding historiographical genre known as subaltern studies seeks to rediscover the indigenous sources of national identity in formerly colonized countries by retroactively "giving voice" to the rural underclasses that were ignored and marginalized by both imperial administrators and their own Westernized countrymen.[110] Each of these influential approaches to the study of national identity and memory seems to unwittingly participate in the romantic cult of the peasant and the search for a timeless past that are themselves hallmarks of modern nationalist sensibility. Post-modern scholarship itself sometimes bears witness to the continued appeal of the Myth of Eternal Return.

CONCLUSION: NATIONALIST ZEN AND THE ART OF WHITEWATER RAFTING

The single most distinctive characteristic of the modern sensibility is its self-conscious focus on its own modernity. What the substance of modernity (let alone post-modernity!) is, no one can agree on, but we are all convinced that there is something qualitatively distinctive about the contemporary era, which marks the period as fundamentally different from all that has come before. In many respects – the development of technological and scientific knowledge, the industrial revolutions, population growth and urbanization, the crystallization of the centralized, bureaucratic state, the advance of global communications and transportation systems, etc. – the nature of the difference is manifestly apparent. But when it comes to assessing the impact of these multiple forms of modernization on human identities, we enter much murkier waters. How fundamentally have the natures of our individual and collective identities been transformed by all these material and organizational changes to our physical and social environments?

The modern intersection of centralized state power with the idea of popular sovereignty and the global diversity of cultural identities has certainly contributed to the universal replication of the nation-state as a framework for the establishment of government authority on a foundation of collective identity. The nation-state is also widely hailed as the vehicle that conveys the nation along the unilinear process of historical evolution toward modernity itself. But, at one and the same time, one of the central attributes of nationalism is its attachment to the past and its dogged resistance to assimilation into a global culture of modernity. National identity, and the institutions a nation-state establishes to define, preserve, and cultivate that identity, are media for the reconciliation of past and future. As such, nationalism has a profoundly ambiguous approach to history.[111] The relentlessly unidirectional historical rapids that the nation seeks to navigate are best mastered, it seems, by looking on the River of Time as a unified whole that – like the Mighty Mississippi or the Blue Danube – retains an immutable aspect amidst the ephemeral currents that run through it.

The conception of the nation as an immortal collective entity that provides comfort and a sense of meaning for the mortal, modern secular soul, is fully acknowledged in much of the modernist school's writing on nationalism. But this view is based on an insistent claim that the modern, nationalist conception of time is exclusively unidirectional. Within this bleak modern context of a temporal journey with no return, so the argument goes, the idea that the nation will go on forever provides a this-worldly solace of a kind that cosmological religion can no longer offer.[112] But what I have been suggesting is that the modern nation seeks to resist the flow of time in more profound ways – in ways that would commonly be considered as characteristically pre-modern. The nation is not just eternal – it is timeless. It is the timelessness of the nation that lends structure and meaning to the flux and change of historical time. This atemporal quality is embodied by certain archetypal figures (e.g. Joan of Arc) and events (e.g. the Bar Kokhba revolt) with which the nation regularly needs to reconnect. The annual, calendrical cycle of national holidays – sometimes fused with religious commemorations, as in the Israeli version of Lag Ba-Omer or in the church services associated with memorial days – is, as the Zerubavels have argued, one of many ways in which this radically non-linear conception of national history is super-imposed upon the forward march of events.[113]

These are not just obscure analytical categories designed to keep academics (un)gainfully employed – although they do serve that purpose admirably. It is true that, during ordinary times (if there is such a thing), the general public may appear unaffected by such arcane phenomena as the tension between linear and non-linear understandings of national history. But at times of national crisis, when the path to the future suddenly seems obscured, the nature of the timeless nation's relationship to historical time (past, present, and future) can suddenly become an explosively divisive question. The success of competing claims to legitimate political leadership can then hinge in part on each party's ability to convince the popular audience that it in fact holds the key to reconciling the experience of the current, unstable moment in time with the nation's unchanging past and transcendent destiny. The Vichy–Free French competition over Joan of Arc's legacy is a striking example of how ideological opponents have striven to gain tactical advantage and attract maximal popular support by claiming for themselves – and denying their rivals – the unique ability to interpret the immutable events of the past and to use them as guideposts in leading the nation through the minefield of the present and into the promised land of the future.[114]

* * *

As many of the examples cited in this chapter may have already suggested, the most compelling historical experiences that nations repeatedly reenact, relive, and commemorate are not necessarily great triumphs and victories. More often than not, it is the great national defeats and martyrdoms that provide grist for the mill of national consciousness. Indeed, the memory of *violation* serves as a mechanism for lending focus to the collective will, the *volition*, of the nation, as Chapter 3 argues.

END NOTES

1 Maurice Halbwachs, *The Social Frameworks of Memory* (French original first published in 1925), in Lewis A. Coser, trans. and ed., Maurice Halbwachs, *On Collective Memory* (Chicago: University of Chicago Press, 1992), 51.

2 The monument popularly known as the Iwo Jima Memorial is officially designated as the United States Marine Memorial. It commemorates fallen Marines from all the nation's wars. Here is yet another example of a single moment in history – the raising of the flag at Iwo Jima – being depicted as the encapsulation of a trans-historical, national experience.

3 United States Postal Service, *Philatelic News* public information release, Stamp Release #02–017, 11 March 2002: http://www.usps.com/news/2002/philatelic/sr02_017.htm. Franklin's photo first appeared on 2 September 2001 in *The Record* (New Jersey), the newspaper for which he worked as a staff photographer, and was also featured on the front cover of the *Newsweek* issue dated 11 September 2001. See http://www.september11news.com/FDNYFireman.htm. The analogy with the Iwo Jima image is pointed out explicitly on the website of the non-profit fundraising organization ("The Bravest Fund") devoted to the emergency-worker victims of the September 11 attacks, founded by the three firemen featured in the Franklin photograph: http://www.bravestfund.com.

4 On speeches planned for the first September 11 anniversary, see Andrei Cherny, "Sept. 11, 2002: A Time to Speak Up," *The Washington Post*, 31 August 2002, op. ed. page.

5 A "Google" search of the Internet conducted on 27 May 2003 unearthed approximately 670 websites containing the phrase "everything has changed" with reference to the events of 11 September 2001. For further reflections on the ambiguous conceptions of time encapsulated in the rhetoric about September 11, see Amy Kaplan, "Homeland Insecurities: Reflections on Language and Space," *Radical History Review*, no. 85 (Winter 2003), 82–93, esp. p. 83 (my thanks to Pradeep Ramamurthy for this reference); E. Zerubavel, *Time Maps*, 48 and 89.

6 See, for instance, the comments by New York Mayor Giuliani on the morrow of the attack. CNN.com, 12 September 2003: http://www.cnn.com/2001/US/09/11/new.york.scene/.

7 Again, the phrase "arrow of time" is the title of chapter 9 of Hawking, *A Brief History of Time*.

8 Benedict Anderson, *Imagined Communities*, 2nd edn (London: Verso, 1991). See also the distinction between national elites' linear sense of time and popular-traditional, inchoate forms of memory in John R. Gillis, "Introduction" (esp. p. 6) in John R. Gillis, ed., *Commemorations: The Politics of National Identity* (Princeton: Princeton University Press, 1994). For a nuanced critique of Benedict Anderson's approach to religion and nationalism, see Anthony D. Smith, *Chosen Peoples* (Oxford: Oxford University Press, 2003), 20–21.

9 E. Zerubavel, *Time Maps*, chs. 1–2, esp. pp. 23–25 and 46–48.

10 Mircea Eliade, *The Myth of the Eternal Return: Or, Cosmos and History* (Princeton: Princeton University Press, 1954).

11 See also Donald Harman Akenson, *God's Peoples: Covenant and Land in South Africa, Israel and Ulster* (Ithaca: Cornell University Press, 1992), 28–31. For a different perspective, see Maurice Halbwachs, who argued that Judaism and Christianity sanctify original, narrowly demarcated periods of paradigmatic history (e.g. the period from the Exodus to the end of the Davidic monarchy or the life of Jesus) that remain isolated and separate from the subsequent flow of time. Halbwachs, *Social Frameworks*, ch. 6.

12 Matei Calinescu, "The 1927 Generation in Romania: Friendships and Ideological Choices (Mihail Sebastian, Mircea Eliade, Nae Ionescu, Eugène Ionesco, E. M. Cioran)," *East European Politics and Societies*, vol. 15, no. 3 (2002), 649–677; Irina Livezeanu, *Cultural Politics in Greater Romania: Regionalism, Nation Building, and Ethnic Struggle, 1918–1930* (Ithaca: Cornell University Press, 1995), 310.

13 Anderson, *Imagined Communities*, 24 and 33.

14 See E. Zerubavel, *Time Maps*, 23–25, 46–48 and *passim*.

15 A. Smith, *Chosen Peoples*. On changing understandings of the relationship between philosophical rationalism and religious sentiment during the Enlightenment and in modernity generally, see the review essay by Jonathan

Sheehan, "Enlightenment, Religion, and the Enigma of Secularization," *American Historical Review*, vol. 108, no. 4 (October 2003), 1061–1080; Steven B. Smith, *Spinoza, Liberalism, and the Question of Jewish Identity* (New Haven: Yale University Press, 1997), 1–7 and *passim*. See also Carl L. Becker, *The Heavenly City of the Eighteenth-Century Philosophers* (New Haven: Yale University Press, 1932).

16 Linda Colley, *Britons: Forging the Nation, 1707–1837* (New Haven: Yale University Press, 1992), ch. 1. On religion and the earlier development of English nationalism, see Adrian Hastings, *The Construction of Nationhood: Ethnicity, Religion and Nationalism* (Cambridge: Cambridge University Press, 1997), ch. 2.

17 On the nineteenth- and early twentieth-century persistence of these influences, see Hugh McLeod, "Protestantism and British National Identity, 1815–1945," in Peter van der Veer and Hartmut Lehmann, eds., *Nation and Religion: Perspectives on Europe and Asia* (Princeton: Princeton University Press, 1999).

18 Bernard Bailyn, *The Ideological Origins of the American Revolution* (Cambridge, Mass.: Harvard University Press, 1967), 32–33; Robert N. Bellah, *The Broken Covenant: American Civil Religion in Time of Trial* (New York: The Seabury Press, 1975), ch. 1.

19 Conor Cruise O'Brien, *Godland: Reflections on Religion and Nationalism* (Cambridge, Mass.: Harvard University Press, 1988), ch. 4. See also Robert N. Bellah, "Religion and the Legitimation of the American Republic," in Robert N. Bellah and Phillip E. Hammond, *Varieties of Civil Religion* (San Francisco: Harper & Row, 1980); Robert N. Bellah, *Beyond Belief: Essays on Religion in a Post-Traditional World* (New York: Harper & Row, 1970), ch. 9.

20 On Britain and/or the United States as prototypes or globally influential models of the modern nation-state, see Liah Greenfeld, *Nationalism: Five Roads to Modernity* (Cambridge, Mass.: Harvard University Press, 1992), chs. 1 and 5; Tom Nairn, *The Break-Up of Britain: Crisis and Neo-Nationalism* (London: Verso, 1981). On British and American ideas of chosenness, see Clifford Longley, *Chosen People: The Big Idea that Shapes England and America* (London: Hodder & Stoughton, 2002) as well as my own discussion in Chapter 4 of the present book.

21 See Talal Asad, "Religion, Nation-State, Secularism," in van der Veer and Lehmann, *Nation and Religion*. On the relationship between transcendent religious belief and this-worldly nationalism, see also Steven Grosby, "Nationality and Religion," in Montserrat Guibernau and John Hutchinson, eds., *Understanding Nationalism* (Oxford: Blackwell, 2001).

22 A. Smith, *Chosen Peoples*, chs. 1–2 and *passim*.

23 On Judaism's mix of linear and cyclical elements, see Yosef Hayim Yerushalmi, *Zakhor: Jewish History and Jewish Memory* (Seattle: University of Washington Press, 1982), 41–42.

24 "Toute ma vie, je me suis fait une certaine idée de la France." Charles de Gaulle, *Mémoires de guerre*, vol. 1: *L'Appel, 1940–1942* (Paris: Plon, 1954), 1. All translations from the French are my own, unless otherwise indicated.

25 Ibid.
26 Robert Gildea, *The Past in French History* (New Haven: Yale University Press, 1994), 162–164; H. R. Kedward, *Resistance in Vichy France: A Study of Ideas and Motivation in the Southern Zone 1940–1942* (Oxford: Oxford University Press, 1978), 122 and 133; Alexander Werth, *De Gaulle: A Political Biography* (1966; Harmondsworth: Penguin, 1967), 101 and 160.
27 See, for instance, the text of de Gaulle's BBC radio broadcast of 18 June 1940 in de Gaulle, *Mémoires de guerre*, vol. 1, 267–268.
28 For more detailed analyses of these themes, see Pierre Nora, "Gaullistes et Communistes," in Pierre Nora, ed., *Les Lieux de mémoire*, vol. III: *Les France*, part 1: *Conflits et partages* (Paris: Gallimard, 1992); Michel Winock, "Jeanne d'Arc," in ibid., part 3: *De l'archive à l'emblème* (Paris: Gallimard, 1992), 722; Stanley Hoffmann and Inge Hoffmann, "The Will to Grandeur: de Gaulle as Political Artist," *Daedalus*, vol. 97, no. 3 (Summer 1968), 829–887.
29 Philippe Burrin, "Vichy," in Nora, ed., *Les Lieux*, vol. III: *Les France*, part 1: *Conflits*, 336.
30 Dominique Rossignol, *Histoire de la propagande en France de 1940 a 1944: L'utopie Pétain* (Paris: Presses Universitaires de France, 1991), 77–81 (the Pétain quotation is on p. 78); Gildea, *Past in French History*, 25.
31 See the reproductions in Rossignol, *Histoire de la propagande*, following page 166.
32 Poster reproduced in Rossignol, *Histoire de la propagande*, 109.
33 See Herman Lebovics, "Creating the Authentic France: Struggles over French Identity in the First Half of the Twentieth Century," in John R. Gillis, ed., *Commemorations: The Politics of National Identity* (Princeton: Princeton University Press, 1994), 247–248.
34 "Pour que la France vive, il faut comme Jeanne d'Arc bouter les Anglais hors d'Europe." Quoted in Roger Caratini, *Jeanne d'Arc: De Domrémy à Orléans et du bûcher à la légende* (Paris: l'Archipel, 1999), 362.
35 Gildea, *Past in French History*, 154–165, esp. 162–164; Rossignol, *Histoire de la propagande*, 84–87; Philippe Pétain, speech delivered in his name on 10 May 1942, in Philippe Pétain, *Actes et écrits*, ed. Jacques Isorni (Paris: Flammarion, 1974), 230–232; René Rémond, "La fille aînée de l'Église," in Nora, ed., *Les Lieux*, vol. III: *Les France*, part 3: *De l'archive*, 578; Nadia Margolis, "The 'Joan Phenomenon' and the French Right," in Bonnie Wheeler and Charles T. Wood, eds., *Fresh Verdicts on Joan of Arc* (New York: Garland, 1996), 275; Winock, "Jeanne d'Arc," 722.
36 Gildea, *Past in French History*, 162–164. On the slippery slope that could lead from invocation of Joan of Arc as anti-British symbol to drawing inspiration from her spirit of resistance to foreign occupation, see Kedward, *Resistance in Vichy France*, 205–206.
37 Clearly the right-wing tradition in France was more closely bound to such ahistorical conceptions of nationhood than was the republican tradition. As David A. Bell has put it, "The republicans, unlike their opponents on the right, distinguished between the past as heritage and the past as

blueprint ..." David A. Bell, *The Cult of the Nation in France: Inventing Nationalism, 1680–1800* (Cambridge, Mass.: Harvard University Press, 2001), 204. Likewise, in the case of Poland, Brian Porter suggests that an ahistorical conception of the nation as a timeless social organism was the distinctive intellectual premise that served as the point of departure for the early-twentieth-century Polish National Democrats' elaboration of their proto-fascist ideology. Brian Porter, *When Nationalism Began to Hate: Imgaining Modern Politics in Nineteenth-Century Poland* (New York: Oxford University Press, 2000), 204 and *passim*.

38 Eric Hobsbawm and Terence Ranger, eds., *The Invention of Tradition* (Cambridge: Cambridge University Press, 1983).

39 Derek Sayer, *The Coasts of Bohemia: A Czech History* (Princeton: Princeton University Press, 1998). For striking examples of the powerful grip ethno-national conceptions exercised on the minds of the fifteenth-century Hussites defending Czech lands against German-dominated Catholic armies, see Howard Kaminsky, *A History of the Hussite Revolution* (Berkeley: University of California Press, 1967), 297–298, 369. My thanks to Brian Hodson for drawing my attention to this source.

40 Sayer, *Coasts of Bohemia*, 13.

41 Ibid., 151 and 153.

42 Ibid., 284.

43 For other East Central European examples, see Maria Bucur and Nancy M. Wingfield, eds., *Staging the Past: The Politics of Commemoration in Habsburg Central Europe, 1848 to the Present* (West Lafayette, Ind.: Purdue University Press, 2001).

44 Sayer, *Coasts of Bohemia*, 144–147, 155–157; Karel Čapek, *Talks with T. G. Masaryk*, trans. Dora Round, ed. Michael Henry Heim (North Haven, Conn.: Catbird Press, 1995), 120 and 133, 141–144 and translator's gloss on 251; H. Gordon Skilling, *T. G. Masaryk: Against the Current, 1882–1914* (University Park, Penn.: Pennsylvania State University Press, 1994), 6–7, 35–37, 101–103, and ch. 3; Robert Pynsent, *Questions of Identity: Czech and Slovak Ideas of Nationality and Personality* (Budapest: Central European University Press, 1994), 180–182; Roman Szporluk, *The Political Thought of Thomas G. Masaryk* (Boulder: East European Monographs, 1981), chapter 4.

45 Ernest Renan, "What Is a Nation?," trans. Martin Thom, in Geoff Eley and Ronald Grigor Suny, eds., *Becoming National: A Reader* (New York: Oxford University Press, 1996), 45.

46 See Benedict Anderson's discussion of this in *Imagined Communities*, 199–201.

47 Henry Rousso, *The Vichy Syndrome: History and Memory in France since 1944*, trans. Arthur Goldhammer (Cambridge, Mass.: Harvard University Press: 1991).

48 The path-breaking book was Robert O. Paxton, *Vichy France: Old Guard and New Order, 1940–1944* (New York: Knopf, 1972). See also Michael R. Marrus and Robert O. Paxton, *Vichy France and the Jews* (New York: Basic Books,

1981). In the wake of the publication in 1973 of a French edition of Paxton's book, the French historiographical floodgates were unleashed on Vichy. Rousso, *Vichy Syndrome*, 251–271.

49 See Kirk Savage, "The Politics of Memory: Black Emancipation and the Civil War Monument," in Gillis, ed., *Commemorations*; Anderson, *Imagined Communities*, 201.

50 John Bodnar, *Remaking America: Public Memory, Commemoration, and Patriotism in the Twentieth Century* (Princeton: Princeton University Press, 1992), 206–216. Bodnar notes that, given the growing centrality of the civil rights movement to American politics at the time, themes of slavery and emancipation did gain a place in the Civil War centennial events.

51 E. Zerubavel, *Time Maps*, 83. E. Zerubavel invokes another of Steinberg's cartoon themes to illustrate the converse phenomenon – namely, how collective memory can create huge, artificial gulfs between chronologically proximate events. Ibid., 87.

52 Yael Zerubavel, *Recovered Roots: Collective Memory and the Making of Israeli National Tradition* (Chicago: University of Chicago Press, 1995). Eviatar Zerubavel discusses this sort of phenomenon as "the social construction of historical discontinuity." E. Zerubavel, *Time Maps*, 95; see also his discussion on pp. 25–34. See also Ella Belfer, *Zehut kefulah: Al ha-metach bein artsiut le-ruchaniut ba-olam ha-yehudi* [A Split Identity: The Conflict between the Sacred and the Secular in the Jewish World] (Ramat-Gan, Israel: Bar-Ilan University Press, 2004), 171–172.

53 Theodor Herzl, the father of modern Zionism, was notably influenced by anti-Semitic stereotypes in his perception of European Jewry. Steven Beller, *Theodor Herzl* (New York: Grove Weidenfeld, 1991); Jacques Kornberg, *Theodor Herzl: From Assimilation to Zionism* (Bloomington and Indianapolis: Indiana University Press, 1993).

54 The Hebrew revival is uniquely successful in having reestablished the language as the first tongue of the great majority of Israel's native-born Jewish population, in contrast to, say, Irish Gaelic, which is learned – with varying degrees of success – as a second language by most of the Irish Republic's citizens. John McWhorter, *The Power of Babel: A Natural History of Language* (2001; New York: HarperCollins, 2003), 277–279.

55 During the Second Temple period (late sixth-century BCE – 70 CE), Aramaic gradually supplanted Hebrew as the dominant spoken language among the Jewish community in Palestine. Seth Schwartz, "Language, Power and Identity in Ancient Palestine," *Past and Present*, No. 148 (August 1995), 3–47.

56 Of course, there already were, ready-to-hand, a number of traditional religious holidays – most notably Hanukah – that commemorated ancient episodes of national heroism. See Jean-Christophe Attias and Esther Benbassa, *Israel, the Impossible Land*, trans. Susan Emanuel (Stanford: Stanford University Press, 2003), 193–194.

57 On Herzl as prophet, see Michael Berkowitz, *Zionist Culture and West European Jewry before the First World War* (Cambridge: Cambridge

University Press, 1993), 136–137. On the Zionist reinterpretation of the Lag Ba-Omer festival as a commemoration of Bar Kokhba's rebellion and on the cult of Trumpeldor, see Y. Zerubavel, *Recovered Roots*, 55–56, 96–102 and *passim*.

58 There was, to be sure, a religious-Zionist movement that challenged important aspects of this perspective, while incorporating and/or adapting important features of it. Religious Zionism's influence in Israel has grown since the 1967 Six Day War. But secular nationalism continues to predominate in Israeli Jewish society and political establishment alike.

59 Y. Zerubavel, *Recovered Roots*.

60 E. Zerubavel, *Time Maps*, ch. 4.

61 The Greek Orthodox Church took issue with this perspective. An influential current in Greek nationalism also looked to the Byzantine Empire as a precedent and frame of reference in defining the new state's territorial aspirations. This Great Idea, as it was called, served as a framework for reconciling secular and religious conceptions of the Greek national idea; it also led Greece into a disastrous foreign policy in the aftermath of the First World War. Paschalis M. Kitromilides, "'Imagined Communities' and the Origins of the National Question in the Balkans," *European History Quarterly*, vol. 19, no. 2 (April 1989), 149–192; Eleni Bastéa, *The Creation of Modern Athens: Planning the Myth* (Cambridge: Cambridge University Press, 2000), 22–23, 118–119, 146–147; A. Smith, *Chosen Peoples*, 199–205.

62 Douglas Hyde, *The Necessity for De-Anglicising Ireland* (lecture first delivered in 1892), limited edition (Leiden: Academic Press, 1994). Hyde himself had been born into a Presbyterian, Anglo-Irish family! (Ibid., Introduction by Joep Leerssen.)

63 This was the culmination of a linguistic revival movement spearheaded by Douglas Hyde.

64 On the conception of the nation's language as a vital aspect of its ethno-cultural and historical "authenticity," see Joshua A. Fishman, *Language and Nationalism: Two Integrative Essays* (Rowley, Mass.: Newbury House Publishers, 1972), 44–52.

65 R. V. Comerford, "Nation, Nationalism, and the Irish Language," in Thomas E. Hachey and Lawrence J. McCaffrey, eds., *Perspectives on Irish Nationalism* (Lexington: University Press of Kentucky, 1989).

66 Henry David Thoreau, *Walden: or, Life in the Woods* (1854; New York: Random House, 1991), 48.

67 E. Zerubavel, *Time Maps*, 46–48; Y. Zerubavel, *Recovered Roots*, 138–144. Linda Colley writes that, for eighteenth- and nineteenth-century British national consciousness, "time past was a soap opera written by God, a succession of warning disasters and providential escapes which they acted out afresh every year as a way of reminding themselves who they were." Colley, *Britons*, 19.

68 On the origins and development of the Unknown Soldier tradition, see George Mosse, *Fallen Soldiers: Reshaping the Memory of the World Wars* (New York: Oxford University Press, 1990), 94–98.

69 The seminal discussion of "sites of memory" and modern historical imagination is Pierre Nora, "Entre mémoire et histoire: La problématique des lieux," in Nora, ed., *Les Lieux de mémoire*, vol. 1: *La République* (Paris: Gallimard, 1984).

70 Thomas W. Laqueur, "Memory and Naming in the Great War" and Daniel J. Sherman, "Art, Commerce, and the Production of Memory in France after World War I," in Gillis, ed., *Commemorations*; A. Smith, *Chosen Peoples*, 238–250. On the function of World War I memorials as loci of mourning rather than symbols of nationhood, see Jay Winter, *Sites of Memory, Sites of Mourning: The Great War in European Cultural History* (Cambridge: Cambridge University Press, 1995), ch. 4.

71 John Bodnar writes of the Vietnam memorial: "It could be viewed by people as an embodiment of the ideas of patriotism and nationalism and as an expression of comradeship with and sorrow for the dead. But unmistakably the latter theme predominated over the former, a point which troubled opponents of the original design." Bodnar, *Remaking America*, 9.

72 Reinhard Alings, *Monument und Nation: Das Bild vom Nationalstaat im Medium Denkmal – zum Verhältnis von Nation und Staat im deutschen Kaiserreich, 1871–1918* (Berlin: Walter de Gruyter, 1996), 444–447 and 506–510.

73 Jean Tulard, "Le Retour des cendres," in Pierre Nora, ed., *Les Lieux de mémoire*, vol. II: *La Nation*, part 3 (Paris: Gallimard, 1986), 109.

74 It is curious that the sequence of these memorials' construction was the inverse of the chronological order of the historical conflicts they commemorate. I have no idea what, if anything, that signifies.

75 Anthony D. Smith, *The Ethnic Origins of Nations* (Oxford: Blackwell, 1986), 15–16, 57–68.

76 For a different perspective, see Gillis, "Introduction," in Gillis, ed., *Commemorations*. For more on the glorification of death in combat as a nationalist *Leitmotiv*, see Philippe Contamine, "Mourir pour la patrie: Xe–XXe siècle," in Nora, ed., *Les Lieux*, vol. II: *La Nation*, part 3.

77 Susan Richmond, "The National WWII Memorial ... A Lasting Tribute to a Generation" (advertising supplement produced by *The Washington Post*'s Advertising Department in collaboration with the American Battle Monuments Commission), *The Washington Post Magazine*, 23 May 2004, pp. 21–55. For critiques of the World War II Memorial's over-reliance on inscriptions and unimaginative design, see Blake Gopnik, "Many Words, Little Eloquence," *The Washington Post*, 23 May 2004, pp. N1 and N6; and Paul Goldberger, "Down at the Mall: The New World War II Memorial Doesn't Rise to the Occasion," *The New Yorker*, 31 May 2004, 82–84.

78 Many of the British, American, and other soldiers who died overseas in the twentieth century's world wars were actually buried overseas in nationally segregated cemeteries near the battlefields where they fell. But these cemeteries themselves became symbolic extensions of their native soil.

79 Walter Laqueur, *Young Germany: A History of the German Youth Movement* (New York, Basic Books, 1962); Mosse, *Fallen Soldiers*, 108. On museums'

use of habitat dioramas to encapsulate the distinctive fauna and flora of the native land and add yet another dimension to the sense of national territoriality and to the link between nature and nation, see Karen Wonders, "Habitat Dioramas and the Issue of Nativeness," unpublished paper.

80 See Meron Benvenisti, *Conflicts and Contradictions* (New York: Villard Books, 1986), ch. 2.

81 Anderson, *Imagined Communities*, 175. On the seamless continuity between monumental architecture and landscape in the nationalist imagination, see Anthony D. Smith, "The Origins of Nations," *Ethnic and Racial Studies*, vol. 12, no. 3 (July 1989), 340–367.

82 See A. Smith, *Chosen Peoples*, pp. 36–37 and ch. 6.

83 Again, for a parallel line of argument, see ibid., ch. 9.

84 Neil Silberman writes that "the standard archaeological narrative requires that a certain ancient trait be identified, celebrated as noble and timeless, and linked to the present across a long period of ignorance or neglect." Neil Asher Silberman, "Promised Lands and Chosen Peoples: The Politics and Poetics of Archaeological Narrative," in Philip L. Kohl and Clare Fawcett, eds., *Nationalism, Politics, and the Practice of Archaeology* (Cambridge: Cambridge University Press, 1995), 256. Of nineteenth- and early twentieth-century Irish archaeology, Elizabeth Crooke writes that, "raising the status of the ancient past was a method of shortening the distance between the present and the 'ancient nation' . . ." Elizabeth Crooke, *Politics, Archaeology and the Creation of a National Museum in Ireland: An Expression of National Life* (Dublin: Irish Academic Press, 2000), 151.

85 Y. Zerubavel, *Recovered Roots*, chs. 5, 8, and 11; Nachman Ben-Yehuda, *The Masada Myth: Collective Memory and Mythmaking in Israel* (Madison: University of Wisconsin Press, 1995). On the controversy surrounding the role of Masada's defenders in the broader context of Judaean society during the Great Revolt against Rome, as well as the questions raised regarding the alleged mass suicide on Masada on the eve of its capture by Roman forces in 73 CE, see also Neil Asher Silberman, *Between Past and Present: Archaeology, Ideology, and Nationalism in the Modern Middle East* (New York: Henry Holt, 1989), chapter 5. See also the discussion in Chapter 3 of the present book.

86 Anthony Smith also makes this point in *Chosen Peoples*, 136.

87 See Bodnar, *Remaking America*, ch. 7.

88 E. Zerubavel, *Time Maps*, 41.

89 See the CBS News report at http://www.cbsnews.com/stories/2002/08/22/politics/main519472.shtml. The text of Bush's 15 August 2002 speech is available at the White House website: http://www.whitehouse.gov/news/releases/2002/08/20020815.html. In January 2003, the National Parks Conservation Association responded to a series of Bush administration deregulation proposals by calling on the White House to "halt its attacks on national parks." *The Washington Post*, 15 January 2003, p. A17.

90 For a somewhat contrasting interpretation, see A. Smith, *Chosen Peoples*, 37 and 134–137. Smith argues that the point of nationalist landscape worship is to link national history to the organic evolution of nature.

91 Simon Schama, *Landscape and Memory* (New York: Knopf, 1995), ch. 2.

92 Ibid., 444–446; Stephen Daniels, *Fields of Vision: Landscape Imagery and National Identity in England and the United States* (Princeton: Princeton University Press, 1993), chs. 6–7; Stephen Daniels, "The Political Iconography of Woodland in Later Georgian England," in Denis Cosgrove and Stephen Daniels, eds., *The Iconography of Landscape: Essays on the Symbolic Representation, Design and Use of Past Environments* (Cambridge: Cambridge University Press, 1988), 73; W. J. T. Mitchell, "Holy Landscape: Israel, Palestine, and the American Wilderness," in W. J. T. Mitchell, ed., *Landscape and Power*, 2nd edn (Chicago: University of Chicago Press, 2002); Longley, *Chosen People*, 233–234. See also the discussion of this theme in A. Smith, *Chosen Peoples*, 36–37 and 137–141. On the symbolic relationship between wilderness and spiritual awakening in the American Puritan tradition, see Bellah, *Broken Covenant*, 8–12.

93 Thomas M. Lekan, *Imagining the Nation in Nature: Landscape Preservation and German Identity, 1885–1945* (Cambridge, Mass.: Harvard University Press, 2004), Introduction, ch. 1, and *passim*.

94 Mosse, *Fallen Soldiers*, 107. One suspects that these images were more effective on the home front than among the soldiers who actually had to fight and die on the industrialized battlefield. Even Ernst Jünger, the World War I veteran who articulated the right-wing myth of the front generation in post-war Germany, emphasized the incongruity between the battered landscape of the Western Front and the timeless qualities of heroism supposed to have characterized the behavior of the frontline fighters. Ernst Jünger, *Storm of Steel* (1920; New York: Howard Fertig, 1996).

95 For a similar treatment of the national cult of the peasantry, see A. Smith, *Chosen Peoples*, 35–37.

96 Ibid., 192–194.

97 For a discussion of how Bartók sought to reconcile his conception of Hungarian folk music as the expression of a distinctive national essence with his recognition of the mutual influence among East Central European ethno-musical traditions, see Katie Trumpener, "Béla Bartók and the Rise of Comparative Ethnomusicology: Nationalism, Race Purity, and the Legacy of the Austro-Hungarian Empire," in Ronald Radano and Philip V. Bohlman, eds., *Music and the Racial Imagination* (Chicago: University of Chicago Press, 2000). On European nineteenth- and twentieth-century folk-song scholarship as an ahistorical enterprise that selectively mapped musical traditions in order to legitimize ethnically exclusive territorial claims and that made timeless national monuments out of the inherently temporal experience of song and dance performance, see Philip V. Bohlman, "The Remembrance of Things Past: Music, Race, and the End of History in Modern Europe," in ibid.

98 Belfer, *Zehut*, 26–27; Attias and Benbassa, *Israel*, 157–167; A. Smith, *Chosen Peoples*, 90–91; Steven G. Marks, *How Russia Shaped the Modern World: From Art to Anti-Semitism, Ballet to Bolshevism* (Princeton: Princeton University Press, 2003), 55.

99 Eugen Weber, *Peasants into Frenchmen: The Modernization of Rural France, 1870–1914* (Stanford: Stanford University Press, 1976).

100 Gérard de Puymège, "Le Soldat Chauvin," in Nora, ed., *Les Lieux*, vol. II: *La Nation*, part 3, 71; Burrin, "Vichy," 334–335.

101 Comments at a reception for American correspondents, 22 October 1940, in Pétain, *Actes et écrits*, 545. In a speech given two years later, Pétain called on the peasantry to view itself as the vanguard of French national renascence. Pétain, address delivered to the Peasant Corporation of the département of Corrèze, 8 July 1942, in Philippe Pétain, *Discours aux Français, 17 juin 1940 – 20 août 1944*, ed. Jean-Claude Barbas (Paris: Albin Michel, 1989), 264. The importance de Gaulle and his successors in the French Fifth Republic have placed on protecting French farmers through European agricultural subsidies suggests that the French nationalist mystique of the peasant is not a monopoly of the far right.

102 Puymège, "Le Soldat Chauvin," 69–71.

103 Stanley Hoffmann, "Paradoxes of the French Political Community," in Stanley Hoffmann *et al.*, *In Search of France: The Economy, Society, and Political System in the Twentieth Century* (1963; New York: Harper & Row, 1965), 3–7, 15; Richard Kuisel, "The France We Have Lost," in Gregory Flynn, ed., *Remaking the Hexagon: The New France in the New Europe* (Boulder: Westview Press, 1995), 33–34.

104 See, for example, Livezeanu, *Cultural Politics in Greater Romania*, 11–13, 190–192.

105 The cult of the Turkish peasant was conducted in tandem with the persecution and displacement of Greek and Armenian urban/mercantile minorities in Anatolia under the nationalist Young Turk regime during the First World War. See Ahmed Emin Yalman, *Turkey in the World War* (New Haven: Yale University Press, 1930), 182–186 and chs. 9, 10–13; Feroz Ahmad, *The Making of Modern Turkey* (London: Routledge, 1993), 40–46; Erik Zürcher, *The Unionist Factor. The Role of the Committee of Union and Progress in the Turkish National Movement, 1905–1926* (Leiden: E. J. Brill, 1984), 76–77; Erik Zürcher, *Turkey: A Modern History* (London: I. B. Tauris, 1993), 129–131, 134–135.

106 To be sure, peasants are more than objects acted upon by socio-political establishments. Peasant communities and movements have often articulated their own conceptions of national identity that have been greeted with varying degrees of openness or hostility by nationalist elites. See Keely Stauter-Halsted, "Rural Myth and the Modern Nation: Peasant Commemorations of Polish National Holidays, 1879–1910," in Bucur and Wingfield, *Staging the Past*; Florencia E. Mallon, *Peasant and Nation: The Making of Postcolonial Mexico and Peru* (Berkeley: University of California

Press, 1995); Peter Sahlins, *Boundaries: The Making of France and Spain in the Pyrenees* (Berkeley: University of California Press, 1989), Conclusion. The classic case study of the modernization and nationalization of peasant life is Eugen Weber's *Peasants into Frenchmen*, which also emphasizes the importance of the interplay between peasant interests and state pressures in the late nineteenth- and early twentieth-century national-cultural integration of rural France.

107 Kuisel, "The France We Have Lost."

108 Miroslav Hroch, *Social Preconditions of National Revival in Europe: A Comparative Analysis of the Social Composition of Patriotic Groups among the Smaller European Nations*, trans. Ben Fowkes (1985; New York: Columbia University Press, 2000), 180.

109 In discussing the industrial era's romantic fascination with the rural culture of the past, Nora himself rather nostalgically refers to peasant society as a "collectivité-mémoire par excellence." Nora, "Entre mémoire et histoire," xvii. David A. Bell has noted that, "despite Nora's presentation of ... [his edited series] as a dispassionate analysis of the workings of national memory, much of it adopted a frankly elegiac, rueful tone ... " Bell, *Cult of the Nation*, 211. See also Hue-Tam Ho Tai, "Remembered Realms: Pierre Nora and French National Memory," *American Historical Review*, vol. 106, no. 3 (June 2001), 906–922.

110 Thus, Partha Chatterjee explicitly distances himself from nationalist romanticization of the peasantry, but then goes on to claim that developing a workable approach to the research and writing of an "Indian history of peasant struggle" will lead to "a fundamental restructuring of the edifice of European social philosophy as it exists today." In other words, the consciousness and social structure of India's rural underclasses represent such a profoundly alien alternative to Western rationalist structures that their very study will lead to the overthrow of Western cultural hegemony that India's nationalist elites were never able to achieve. Partha Chatterjee, *The Nation and its Fragments: Colonial and Postcolonial Histories* (Princeton: Princeton University Press, 1993), ch. 8. Quotation from p. 169.

111 Cf. the discussion in Prasenjit Duara, *Rescuing History from the Nation: Questioning Narratives of Modern China* (Chicago: University of Chicago Press, 1995), 27–33.

112 Anderson, *Imagined Communities*, 22–36.

113 E. Zerubavel, *Time Maps*, 46–48, 101–102, ch. 4. Anthony Smith articulates a similar idea when he writes that "myth-memories of golden ages" can serve "to posit an identity beneath the flux of historical change. Beneath the many developments, and different periods, of the history of the community, there remains an eternal core, as it were, which provides the ground on and over which history 'writes.' " A. Smith, *Chosen Peoples*, 213. See also Mordecai Roshwald, *The Transient and the Absolute: An Interpretation of the Human Condition and of Human Endeavor* (Westport, Conn: Greenwood Press, 1999), ch. 8. In another variation on this theme, Brian Vick argues

that early nineteenth-century German nationalist intellectuals combined cyclical and linear conceptions of history: "Time's arrow consequently resembled more the graph of an ever-looping, upward-tending cycloid than that of a straight line." Brian E. Vick, *Defining Germany: The 1848 Frankfurt Parliamentarians and National Identity* (Cambridge, Mass.: Harvard University Press, 2002), 63.

114 In a similar vein, on the use of epic myths as guides to the nation's destiny, Anthony Smith writes: "The myth-memories of ... earlier ages give to the present a new direction and significance, as the members [of the nation] interpret it in the light of the virtues of past epochs. In consequence, golden ages have come to provide 'maps' for the road to national destiny and 'moralities' for the tasks required to travel along that auspicious path ..." A. Smith, *Chosen Peoples*, 216–217. See also Anthony D. Smith, *The Antiquity of Nations* (Cambridge: Polity Press, 2004), ch. 8. My emphasis here is on the intense *competition* among rival political groups for *exclusive possession* of the Holy Grail of epic memory.

CHAPTER 3

Violation and volition

The ideal of self-determination – the free exercise of collective volition – is so central to any nationalist ideology as to appear virtually synonymous with it.[1] In many cases, what lends focus and meaning to the idea of self-determination is an archetypal image of violation – something Vamik Volkan has referred to as a "chosen trauma."[2] The memory of what others have done to the nation helps define the meaning and value of liberty and to highlight the necessity of shaking off foreign yokes or of fighting to maintain independence and security.[3] The biblical account of the Israelites' progress into freedom takes as its point of departure their enslavement in Egypt. The story of the American Revolution begins with the British crown's flagrant trespassing on the traditional rights of the colonists. Their supposed defeat at the Battle of Kosovo in 1389 sets the scene for the Serbs' epic tale of historical suffering and eventual political-territorial resurrection. In a similar vein, nineteenth-century Polish romantics depicted their occupied and partitioned country as the "Christ of nations," its very physical dismemberment freeing it of worldly concerns and allowing it to develop a spiritual ideal of freedom that would lead not only to its own liberation but to the redemption of humanity.[4]

[handwritten margin note: Israel's fate = fate of humanity]

But, of course, the moral and political implications of a people's historical victimization are rarely obvious or straightforward. Nor is a nation's fixation on its experience of humiliation a static phenomenon. It varies in intensity and significance over time, manifesting itself along a spectrum of possibilities ranging from outbursts of xenophobic violence to banal commercial slogans, as in the 1931 Chinese tooth-powder advertisement that urged consumers to brush their teeth with the locally manufactured product as a way of reminding themselves of the need to cleanse the nation of its humiliation at the hands of foreign powers.[5] The interplay of contemporary power-political relations and threat perceptions with collective memories of martyrdom and violation molds and/or constrains the exercise of national volition in diverse ways and to varying degrees. It often colors disputes about fundamental policy choices. For *treatment of minorities* example, the issue of what ethical constraints should bind the nation in its relations with internal minorities or neighboring peoples is often framed by conflicting understandings of the nation's own legacy of violation. The biblical commandment, "you shall not wrong a stranger or oppress him, for you were strangers in the land of Egypt" (Exodus, 22:21), represents one end of the spectrum of ethical possibilities. The most extreme alternative is the unconditional assertion of the primacy of one's own nation's rights over those of others, as a form of compensation for the past violations suffered by one's people. Heated disputes can also arise between rival ethno-national claimants to the priceless legacy of violation. Conversely, some myths of violation can develop into more flexible frameworks of collective identity capable of accommodating more than one *examples?* ethno-national group within their fold.

The case studies that inform this chapter's exploration of this theme range from the relatively mild Alamo controversy to the periodically explosive conflict over Muslim and Jewish holy sites in Jerusalem. It is precisely because the geopolitical, religious, and ethnographic settings of these disputes are so diverse that the points of similarity among them are so striking. By the same token, the differences among them are also profound and speak to the importance of institutional settings, historical contexts, power relationships, and cultural matrices in shaping how the violation-volition dynamic plays out.

SHRINES OF MARTYRDOM

The Alamo

At the entrance to the Alamo in downtown San Antonio, Texas, posted notices enjoin gentlemen to remove their hats and urge visitors to maintain a respectful silence (a rule observed largely in the breach). (See Figure 5.) For the site is more than a museum or even a monument. Owned by the state of Texas, the Alamo is maintained and administered by the Daughters of the Republic of Texas (DRT) – a private foundation entrusted with this responsibility by the Texas state legislature. For the DRT, the site is a shrine dedicated to the memory of the men who were massacred on 6 March 1836 on Mexican General Santa Anna's orders, after refusing his demand that they surrender the Alamo without a fight. The Alamo is to be preserved for all time as a reminder of the mixed emotions of horror and pride associated with that formative event in the

Figure 5 The Alamo, San Antonio, Texas, *circa* 1909. This famous façade of the Alamo Church is not original to the building, but was constructed by the US Army in 1850 as part of a renovation project. Black-and-white negative of half of a stereograph image. Stereograph by Stereo-Travel Co., 1909. Photographer unknown. Courtesy of the Library of Congress, Prints and Photographs Division.

development of Texan identity. In thus fastening upon a memory of violation as the focal point for collective self-definition, the custodians of the site are playing out a variation on a dialectical theme that shapes many a case of national consciousness.

In associating Texan political identity with nationalism, I do not mean to impute secessionist designs to the citizens of the Lone Star State. In the contemporary context, being a proud Texan is not in conflict with being a patriotic American. On the contrary, it is partly defined in terms of unwavering devotion to the United States. But its fiercely guarded sense of cultural and historical distinctiveness and its zealous attachment to all the trappings of state sovereignty within the larger Union,[6] justify treating Texan identity as an example of sub-nationalism – a sense of collective identity and special destiny linked to political control of a bounded territory, nesting within a broader sense of loyalty to a larger political-territorial entity.[7]

That Texans exhibit such a marked sense of sub-national identity is a legacy of their state's peculiar early history. Of the fifty American states, Texas is the only one that can boast of a prior – if brief (1836–45) – history as a sovereign republic,[8] and one that fought its own successful war of independence at that.

The history of English-speakers' settlement in Texas began on the fabled note of a bankrupt Connecticut-born businessman by the auspicious name of Moses Austin initiating negotiations in 1820 with the Spanish provincial governor in San Antonio. He talked the governor into accepting a proposal for the establishment of a colony of American settlers in the sparsely populated province of Tejas (as Texas was called in Spanish). The validity of the original March 1821 agreement was soon cast into doubt by Mexico's independence from Spain in September of that year, and Moses did not live to see his people settle in the promised land. But when his son Stephen took up the question with the new Mexican government, permission to settle was granted in 1823 on condition that all the newcomers accept Mexican citizenship and the Catholic faith. Despite the 1824 administrative merger of Tejas with the neighboring, predominantly Hispanic province of Coahuila, the influx of both legal and illegal Anglo-American immigrants was so great that by 1835 they outnumbered Spanish-speakers in the province of Coahuila y Tejas by a ratio of about four to one (30,000 to 7,800).[9]

The framework of understanding between the parties to the original settlement agreement (and similar agreements subsequently negotiated with other American colonists) was steadily eroded under the impact of mutual suspicions. The rapid growth of the Anglo-American population, whose loyalty to the Mexican state and sincere adherence to the Catholic religion were highly questionable, led to concern among Mexico's political authorities over their ability to maintain long-term control over

Tejas. Friction mounted over the institution of slavery, formally banned under Mexican law yet allowed to persist among the Anglo-Americans, many of whom had brought slaves with them to their new homes in Tejas. An 1830 ban on further immigration from across the Mexican–American frontier succeeded in antagonizing the English-speakers of Tejas, but failed to be effectively enforced.

Tensions came to a head amidst Mexico's internal struggle between defenders of the country's original, federal constitution and the military-dominated, centralist forces under General Santa Anna, who seized power and assumed the presidency of Mexico in 1834 (following a brief earlier stint as president in 1833). Santa Anna's order for the expulsion of illegal settlers and the disarming of legal residents threatened the survival of the Anglo-American community in Tejas. But the Anglo-Americans were able to find common cause with a significant component of the local Hispanic elite, a number of whom joined ranks with Stephen Austin and his followers in defending the federal constitution and the institutions of provincial autonomy against Santa Anna's repressive centralizing program.

A series of confrontations between military garrisons and local residents rapidly escalated into armed conflict, as Texians and Tejanos (Anglo-American and Hispanic inhabitants of Texas, respectively) took up arms against the national authorities in late 1835. The insurgents, joined by volunteers (many of them European-born) from across the border in the United States, succeeded early on in seizing San Antonio and fortifying the town's abandoned barracks and former mission known as the Alamo before reinforcements were able to reach the local Mexican army contingent. Ignoring orders from the cautious rebel commander, Sam Houston, to beat a tactical retreat,[10] the defenders of the Alamo decided to attempt to hold their position against the Mexican troops advancing northwards under General Santa Anna's personal command. The result was the notorious battle of 6 March 1836, which ended with the slaughter of all the armed defenders, including a handful who were taken prisoner but then summarily put to death on Santa Anna's personal orders.[11] The corpses of the dead were then put to the torch.

News of the Alamo's fate spread quickly, reported by Tejanos who had been present in San Antonio around the time of the battle and by the widow of one of the Alamo's defenders, whose life, along with that of her daughter and of Alamo commander William Travis' slave, had been spared and who was allowed to leave after the conclusion of the battle. Details about the circumstances of the various defenders' deaths and even about the number of men who had participated in the suicidal endeavor remained sketchy and contradictory. In the meantime, on 3 March 1836, the rebel convention at Washington-on-the-Brazos had declared the independence of Texas. Following the massacre of another group of captured rebels at Goliad and a controversial retreat by the prudent Sam Houston's forces, on 21 April 1836 Santa Anna's pursuing contingent was literally caught napping by its intended prey at the San Jacinto river. Bellowing "Remember the Alamo!" as they took advantage of their enemies' siesta, Houston's soldiers took few prisoners on the battlefield in the course of the one-sided slaughter that ensued. Santa Anna himself was spared when captured on the morrow of his defeat and then released after agreeing to recognize the independence of Texas and to order the with-drawal of all remaining Mexican forces from the territory of the new republic.

The successful rebellion against Santa Anna's Mexico had not been an exclusively Anglo-Texan affair. Prominent Tejanos such as Juan Seguín and José Antonio Navarro[12] had been involved in both the military and political aspects of the fight for Texas independence, and the role of members of the Spanish-speaking landowning elite in supporting the rebellion was initially recognized through the award of high offices to a number of Tejanos. The republic's first vice-president was the Yucatán-born signer of the Texas Declaration of Independence, Lorenzo De Zavala.[13] But the overall impact of the war was to heighten the hostility of Texas' Anglo majority towards everything associated with Mexican cul-ture and language. Within a few years, Spanish-speaking Texans had been driven out of positions of political prominence. De Zavala felt excluded from any substantive decision-making role and left office within months of assuming it, dying shortly thereafter. Seguín was forced into exile in Mexico for a number of years. The admission of Texas into the United States as the 28th state in December 1845, followed by the US Army's 1846–48 conquest of the rest of the present-day American Southwest from Mexico, assured Texas' future as an Anglo-American-dominated society. For many decades to follow, a very thin Tejano upper-class stratum was tolerated on the margins of Texas' socio-political establishment while the great mass of Tejano and Mexican immigrant peasants, cattlemen, and laborers were economically marginalized, racially stigmatized, and routinely brutalized in the Texas Rangers' (the state milita) counter-insurgency campaigns.[14]

* * *

The struggle for independence from Mexico forms the central myth[15] of Texan identity, and the Alamo takes center stage in this story. (Of course, the legend of the Alamo has also become part and parcel of American national folklore.) The Daughters of the Republic of Texas, an organization whose membership is limited to those women who can document their genealogical ties to the generation that lived in Texas during its decade of independence, sees itself as custodian, not just of the physical site of the Alamo, but of the history and identity of Texas as represented by the shrine.[16] A series of panels set up on the Alamo's grounds, entitled "The Wall of History," lays out a timeline of the critical events in this official version of Texas' birth and rise to greatness. Itself a relatively recent innovation designed to quell critics of the DRT's custodianship by giving due recognition to the roles of non-Anglo peoples in the history of Texas and the Alamo, the Wall of History emphasizes the Mexican government's attempts to arrogate centralizing powers not granted it by the Mexican constitution and its restriction on further migration into the territory by American settlers as the fundamental causes of the 1836 rebellion. Nowhere is any mention made of the institution of slavery and its role as a point of friction between slave-owning Texians and the Mexican government. Even though Mexico City's attempt to crack down on slavery could easily be dismissed as a cynical maneuver designed to limit the influx of independent-minded Anglo-Americans, the very mention of this issue would embarrass the DRT's effort to portray the conflict as a clear-cut struggle between light and darkness, freedom-loving Texans and Santa Anna's forces of oppression.

But why make the site of a resounding military defeat the focal point of Texan identity? Precisely because the disaster at the Alamo can be used to lend meaning to the subsequent military and political victory. The idea of self-determination has little substance or appeal unless it is understood as a prize to be won through struggle; it is hard to define its focus unless it is directed against a clearly identified foe. The more difficult the struggle and the more wicked and dangerous the foe, the greater the sense of pride and purpose associated with the sustained assertion of collective will. Indeed, a common yardstick for the measurement of a nation's strength and tenacity is the degree to which its individual members are willing to risk all and even sacrifice themselves on its behalf.

The events of March 1836, as commemorated by traditional Texas patriots, encapsulate this theme. Santa Anna's brutality vividly highlights the nobility of the Alamo's defenders. The latter's decision to disregard Sam Houston's orders and stay at the Alamo, followed by their defiant cannon shot in response to Santa Anna's warning to surrender or die, established the selfless devotion of the Alamo's defenders to the cause of a free Texas. Without their subsequent massacre, the defenders' determination to fight at any cost would not have been so clearly and dramatically demonstrated. Conversely, had it not been for their refusal to surrender, there might not have been a massacre, and the arbitrary and unjust nature of Mexican rule would not have been so dramatically exposed. As it is, the Mexican slaughter of the defenders and the subsequent burning of their bodies stand as primordial acts of violation that lend context and meaning to the epic story of Texas' creation. According to the traditional version of events, the defenders of the Alamo exercised their free will in its ultimate form by choosing death over dishonor.[17] In so doing, they inspired others to continue the struggle until its victorious conclusion secured the ability of Texans to exercise their free will in the framework of an independent republic, and, later, as a self-governing state within the American Union. On a more pragmatic plane, the resistance at the Alamo is depicted as not having been undertaken in vain, but rather as having both bought time for, and inspired a zeal for vengeance among, Sam Houston's men, who gave Santa Anna's forces their just deserts at the Battle of San Jacinto while Houston nobly spared the Mexican general's life. At all levels – the spiritual, psychological, and tactical – the themes of violation and volition are intimately intertwined.

This message is driven home hard, with obvious religious overtones, at the Alamo shrine. The central building is, appropriately enough, the former chapel from the days when the site was a Spanish Catholic mission. Side rooms along the nave display the equivalent of saints' relics: the walking cane of the last courier to ride out from the besieged Alamo, guns and knives of the martyred defenders, a log from the chimney corner of Alamo defender Davy Crockett's home in Tennessee. At the front and center of the building, instead of a church altar, plaques bear the names of the Alamo's sacrificial victims, with one marker dedicated to the unknown fighters who died there. Outside the Alamo compound, on the city-owned Alamo square, a cenotaph erected on the centenary of the 1836 battle bears an image of the bodies of the martyrs being burned, with a figure representing the "Spirit of Sacrifice" rising above them.[18] The inscription underneath reads: "From the fire that burned their bodies, rose the eternal spirit of sublime heroic sacrifice which gave birth to an empire state."

The familiar Christian themes of martyrdom as the greatest expression of faith and suffering as the path to salvation could not be laid on any thicker. The image of the Alamo is also informed by classical motifs of self-sacrificing patriotism. Indeed, within weeks of the Alamo's fall, analogies were being drawn between the heroism of the fallen Texans and the Spartan fighters who chose to die defending Greece against the king of Persia's Asiatic hordes at the mountain pass of Thermopylae in 480 BCE.[19]

As with centers of religious devotion, the Alamo's symbolic power is maintained – as Holly Beachley Brear has documented – through institutionalized rituals that take place there on an annual basis and whose organizers' access to the Alamo is carefully controlled by the custodians of the shrine. Only two honorific societies other than the DRT itself – the Order of the Alamo and the Texas Cavaliers (both, roughly speaking, male counterparts of the DRT) – are regularly allowed to conduct ceremonies in the Alamo shrine. Other associations must seek special permission from the DRT for holding activities on the premises, and permission is frequently denied. By the same token, a systematic effort is made to publicly propagate the carefully guarded official meaning of the shrine through mechanisms such as tourism, the quasi-pilgrimages of school field trips to the Alamo, and the annual San Antonio fiesta held shortly after the Texas Cavaliers' secret induction ceremony at the shrine and presided over by a Fiesta "King" chosen from among the Cavaliers' ranks.[20]

The official cult of the Alamo imparts a sense of emotional power and transcendent meaning to Texan identity and Texan self-determination. The community of sacrifice and the community of self-determination are one and the same, if the former is defined very broadly as including not just the Alamo defenders themselves, but all those on whose behalf they gave their lives and all those who have inherited the prize of Texas freedom along with the sense of obligation to those who died for that prize.

This form of collective myth has considerable inclusive power. In some ways, the Alamo myth draws broad boundaries for Texan identity, boundaries wide enough to encompass all residents of the state who make the conscious choice to "remember the Alamo." Indeed, the volunteer fighters at the Alamo themselves hailed from various states of the American Union, many of them were European-born immigrants, and a few were Hispanic Texans – Tejanos.

Yet the very distinction the historical narrative makes between Texians and Tejanos points to the tension between Texan identity as a culturally pluralistic framework and Texas patriotism as a more narrowly bounded ethno-cultural phenomenon. Texians became Texans after independence, but the metamorphosis of Tejanos remains laced with ambiguities. The core of the Alamo myth, after all, revolves around the confrontation between virtuous Anglophones and evil Mexicans. Cultivated as a symbol of unity and continuity, the Alamo has therefore also had an alienating and divisive impact on Texan society. As we shall see further on, responses to this have varied, ranging from attempts to highlight the role of Tejanos in the original struggle against Santa Anna to outright rejection of the Alamo as a legitimate symbol of the Lone Star State's identity.

The Temple Mount/al-Haram al-Sharif

Whereas the Alamo is a modern shrine that evokes associations with ancient Greco-Roman and Christian conceptions of death with honor and transcendence through martyrdom, elsewhere in the world, ancient religious shrines themselves constitute loci of powerful nationalist sentiments. Nowhere is this more notoriously or dramatically evident than at the Temple Mount in Jerusalem.

The site of a pagan temple in the second millennium BCE, the Temple Mount served as the location for the Jews' First Temple, constructed, according to biblical sources, by King Solomon in the tenth century BCE. From its inception, it served the dual function of center for religious worship as well as symbol of centralized state authority. Its destruction by the Babylonians in 586 BCE coincided with the defeat and dismantling of the Kingdom of Judah and the exile of tens of thousands from among the country's social elites. Return from exile under the more benevolently disposed Persian Empire towards the end of the sixth century BCE led to the construction of the Second Temple over its predecessor's ruins. Renovated and expanded on a magnificent scale by the Romans' puppet king, Herod, in the late first century BCE, the Second Temple was ultimately destroyed by the Romans as they crushed the Jewish revolt (the Great Revolt) of 66–70 CE. Further conflicts between Jews and Roman imperial overlords in the following century contributed to the steady dispersal of most of Palestine's Jewish community into the diaspora.

The memory of the Temple and the mourning over its repeated destructions have exercised a powerful grip on Jewish national consciousness ever since. As early as the Bar Kochba revolt of 132–135 CE, the image of the temple was invoked on rebel coinage as a symbol of national regeneration.[21] By the same token, the religious fast day of Tish'ah be-Av was instituted as an occasion to mourn the destruction of the First and Second Temples and the exile from the Promised Land associated with those destructions. The perceived relationship between the fate of the Temple and the destiny of the Jews was complex and filled with ambiguities. On the one hand, the equation of the Temple's destruction with national suffering and exile was very clear. Yet the precedent of the sixth century BCE suggested that destruction was to be followed by redemption, exile by return. If the suffering of the Jews was the result of their transgressions against the Covenant, their repentance and reinvigorated commitment to the Covenant would bring about God's forgiveness and their collective salvation and return to a sovereign existence in the Promised Land.

Beyond that, the Second Temple's destruction had itself been associated not only with profound despair but also with a successful reorientation of Jewish religious practice and communal identity. While the Romans were besieging a Jerusalem that had fallen under the control of Jewish Zealots, the rabbinical scholar Jochanan Ben Zakkai was smuggled out of the city and – whether with the Romans' express permission or on his own initiative – went on to establish a new center of rabbinical authority in the coastal town of Yavneh.[22] The final fall of Jerusalem brought about the virtual obsolescence of the priestly caste that had administered the Temple and the end of the daily animal sacrifices that had marked worship there. This left rabbinical Judaism, with its emphasis on biblical exegesis, legal and ethical analysis, and religious devotion through righteous living and prayer, as the main current of Judaism. The regeneration of the Jews need not await the reconstruction of the Temple; it had already begun at the academy of Yavneh. With Torah and synagogue as the central loci of communal life, Jewish identity could be preserved and transported to any part of the globe, even as the memory of the Temple and its destruction preserved the element of topographic particularity in Jewish identity.[23]

From 70 CE on, then, the memory of the Temple's destruction was closely associated with the Jewish conception of self-determination in a variety of ways. The Temple's fate and the bitter experience of exile were interpreted as divine punishments for violations of the Covenant, just as the prophets had argued at the time of the First Temple's demise.[24] The theological connection between the fall of the First and Second Temples, allegedly on the same date, lent these tragedies a transcendent quality that removed them from the ephemeral, unilinear flow of seemingly meaningless events. More specifically, the earlier sequence of the First Temple's destruction followed by the building of the Second, of Babylonian Exile followed by redemptive Return, held forth the promise of a similar reversal of fortune in the Jews' future. Indeed, the idea that Jewish suffering represented punishment for deviations from the Law allowed them to view their very hardship as evidence of the Covenant's validity. For true believers, there was a foolproof, if circular, logic to this theological system: the people's collective suffering was proof of the Covenant's existence; this, in turn, held forth the reassurance that mending their ways and adhering strictly to the commandments of the Torah as interpreted by the Talmudic sages would lead the Jews to redemption. In this manner, the people were obliged to take an active hand in the determination of their own fate.

Conversely, the horrific persecutions endured from Roman times onwards could themselves serve as evidence of the Jews' fortitude and faith in the face of overwhelming material odds.[25] The martyrdom stories traditionally recounted on Yom Kippur (The Day of Atonement) recall the fate of rabbinic sages whose dying words were expressions of faith spoken as they underwent the gruesome tortures of sadistic Romans. In the absence of viable political or military instruments of self-determination, it was the Jews' tenacious adherence to their tradition, at the price of vicious persecution, that constituted the central expression of their volition, of their will to survive and ultimately regain a sovereign existence on their own land. The more pain they endured, the more tests of faith they passed, the more credit they accrued in the Covenantal accounting ledger. The massacres of entire Jewish communities in the Rhineland during the Crusades and in Polish-ruled Ukraine during Bohdan Khmelnitsky's seventeenth-century rebellion were understood as collective martyrdoms – deaths willingly endured for the sanctification of the Lord's name. Such latter-day horrors were commemorated and mourned in a manner that assimilated them, theologically, liturgically, and calendrically, with one another, just as the destructions of the two Temples were seen as manifestations of the same principle whose traditional occurrence on the same date was more significant than their separation in time by over half a millennium. On the one hand, this provided some sort of framework of understanding by identifying traumatic events with archetypal experiences of catastrophe that had already been woven into the fabric of collective identity and historical memory. On the other hand, the more this primordial suffering was reenacted, the more the Jews could expect their quota of pain to have been fulfilled and Redemption to be at hand. Enduring so much grief as the price of faith allowed the Covenantal tables to be turned on God; leading Jewish rabbinical and spiritual figures periodically called on God to put an end to the disproportionate suffering of his people and lead them to their just reward.[26]

The consciousness of violation has been no less central to the ideology and identity of secular Zionists than it has been to the Orthodox outlook, but whereas the suffering of violation was itself a primary medium for self-determination in the religious tradition, it was viewed as a spur to more direct, political and military, forms of self-determination in modern Zionism. Rather than waiting for God to send the Messiah to lead the Jews back to the Promised Land, it was up to the Jews to take matters into their own hands, to recognize that the only escape from the perennial phenomenon of anti-Semitism was to take an active hand in redeeming themselves. While the city of Jerusalem certainly retained potent symbolic force for secular Zionists, the Temple Mount itself and the site of Jewish worship at the Herodian retaining wall on the western side of the Temple Mount (the Western Wall, also known as the Wailing Wall) were not as central to early twentieth-century Zionist consciousness as they are today. In their search for a suitably ancient symbol that would better represent their own activist conception of national self-determination and that would distance their movement from what they derided as the passive fatalism of traditional Judaism, many Zionist writers, historians, and archeologists were to find Masada a far more appealing candidate. This isolated outpost, the site of a fortified Herodian palace atop a forbidding mountain crag in the Judean desert, had been seized and held by a group of armed fighters and their families during the Great Revolt, and had not fallen to the Romans until 73 CE, three years after the fall of Jerusalem. The ancient Jewish historian Josephus Flavius (the main source of information about the siege and fall of Masada) described the fortress' defenders as members of a radical Jewish fringe group of terrorists and assassins (the *Sicarii*) whose ruthless behavior towards their fellow Jews had led to their expulsion from rebel-held Jerusalem. But, as Nachman Ben-Yehuda has documented, this information was glossed over in the Zionist myth of Masada, which focused on the idea that the defenders of this outpost had exercised the ultimate act of self-determination by taking their own lives and those of their wives and children rather than enduring humiliation, rape, torture, murder and/or enslavement at the hands of the Romans.[27] Choosing their manner of death, they came to be widely regarded as a source of inspiration by a movement determined that modern Jews should choose their own manner of living. The arduous hike to the top of Masada took on the role of a secular pilgrimage for Zionist youth movements determined to establish a tangible link to the ancient Jewish community in Palestine while circumventing the symbolic framework of traditional Diaspora Judaism.[28] The slogan "Masada shall not fall again" became a powerful invocation of collective will to survive as a sovereign nation – a Zionist "remember the Alamo" – in the newly created state of Israel, where recruits to the military's armored units are still sworn in at evocative ceremonies held atop the ancient desert fortress. For some veterans of the pre-independence Zionist youth movements and armed formations, Masada remained a more potent symbol of Jewish resolve than the Western Wall of the Temple Mount even after the dramatic capture of East Jerusalem in the 1967 Six Day War.[29]

Nonetheless, the dynamic of Muslim–Jewish relations within British-ruled Palestine set in motion a process that – alongside the growing Zionist fascination with Masada – progressively accentuated the significance of the Temple Mount and its environs to the national-religious consciousness of Zionists and Palestinian nationalists alike.[30] (See Figure 6.)

The platform once occupied by the Temple is also sacred to Muslims as al-Haram al-Sharif (the Noble Sanctuary). Islamic tradition identifies it as the spot from which the Prophet Muhammad ascended directly to heaven following his miraculous passage by night from Mecca to Jerusalem. The Haram is home to the al-Aqsa Mosque and the Shrine of Omar (also known as the Dome of the Rock), first constructed following the Islamic conquest of Jerusalem from the Byzantine Empire in the seventh century CE. Dominating the city's skyline, these sites mark Jerusalem as the third holiest city (after Mecca and Medina) in the Islamic hierarchy of topographic sanctity.[31] One of the early major outbreaks of ethnic violence between the two communities arose from a 1929 clash over the rights of Jews praying at the Western Wall – a site that was at that time controlled by an Islamic trust (*waqf*) and that was hemmed in by an Arab residential neighborhood that practically abutted onto the Wall, leaving it accessible only by a narrow blind alley. Jewish worshippers' attempts to set up benches and male/female partitions in the alley were resisted by the Muslim authorities as illicit acts of appropriation. Muslim authorities had long tolerated informal Jewish prayer at the Western Wall, as distinct from an institutionalized Jewish presence there. If the Jews succeeded in establishing what amounted to a house of prayer at this site, what would stop them from ultimately challenging Muslim control over the Islamic shrines that dominated Jerusalem from atop the Temple Mount? As far as the Muslim authorities were concerned, the institutionalization of Jewish collective worship at the Wall was a threat that had to be nipped in the bud. The founding father of Palestinian nationalism, the Grand Mufti (Islamic juridical authority) of Jerusalem, Haj Amin al-Husseini, forcefully reaffirmed Muslim claims dating to the

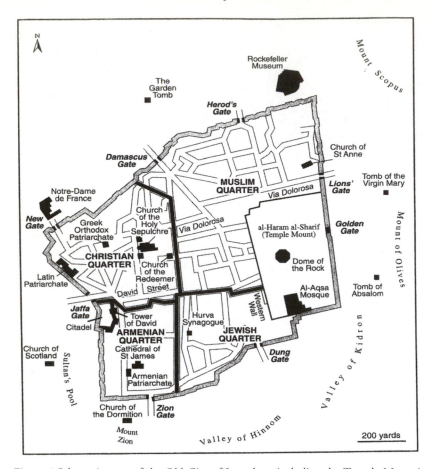

Figure 6 Schematic map of the Old City of Jerusalem, including the Temple Mount/
al-Haram al-Sharif. Reproduced from "Map 12: Jerusalem: the old city" in Bernard
Wasserstein, *Divided Jerusalem: The Struggle for the Holy City* (New Haven: Yale
University Press, 2001), p. 321.

previous century to the effect that the Western Wall was itself holy
to Islam in its capacity as the legendary *Buraq* – the site where the
Prophet Muhammad had tethered his winged horse al-Buraq before
ascending the Temple Mount and rising to heaven.[32] In a transparently
provocative move, the Muslim authorities opened up the blind alley
beside the Wall into a thoroughfare for passers-by and their beasts of
burden – a deliberately humiliating way to remind Jews praying at their

holy site of their proper place in the Islamic scheme of things.[33] In August, members of Betar, the youth movement of the right-wing, secular Zionist Revisionist movement (to which the contemporary Likud bloc is ideological heir), responded by arming themselves with batons and marching to the Western Wall, where they held a vocal demonstration.[34] The Mufti then lit the tinder box, spreading rumors of an imminent Jewish assault on Muslim holy places and mobilizing mass violence against Jewish communities throughout Palestine over the course of a week.[35]

In their attempt to contain the problem, the British essentially upheld the *status quo ante* at the Wall (albeit with greater leeway for some forms of organized Jewish worship at the Wall than the Mufti and his Supreme Muslim Executive were prepared to accept).[36] But this obviously did nothing to dissipate the mutual resentments and suspicions associated with the dispute. On the contrary, in its capacity as a symbol of double violation (as a remnant of the destroyed Temple and as a site of latter-day humiliation of, and violence against, Jews), the Wall had acquired new value as a nationalist symbol in the eyes of secular Zionists.[37] Furthermore, the massacre of over sixty defenseless Jewish residents of Hebron in the course of the riots marked the events of 1929 as a turning point for the Yishuv (the Jewish community in Palestine). The violence instigated by the Mufti was seen by many as identical in nature to the anti-Semitic pogroms that had made helpless victims of Eastern European Jews for generations. Even as it sought to hold militarist imagery at arm's length, the mainstream of the Labor Zionist movement that dominated the Yishuv henceforth associated the ideal of Jewish national self-determination more intimately than before with the theme of armed self-defense in the face of aggression and individual willingness to sacrifice all on behalf of the community.[38]

For Palestinian Arabs too this was a turning point. The Mufti's charges of a Zionist plot against Jerusalem's Muslim shrines became established as a standard motif in Palestinian nationalist lore from 1929 on.[39] Moreover, the episode marked a watershed, not only in the nationalist mobilization of Palestinian Arabs, but also in the generation of active interest in Palestinian affairs by the broader Muslim world.[40] The connection between contemporaneous experiences of national triumph, frustration, or defeat and the historical-religious symbolism of the Temple Mount/ Haram was further intensified in the context of the Arab–Israeli wars of 1948–49 and 1967 and of the post-1967 Palestinian–Israeli conflict, as we shall see in this chapter's final segment.

Who was the victim and who the oppressor? What is the authentic version of the original tale of violation, and who is the rightful heir to the legacy of that experience? Such questions form critical points of friction between rival nationalisms and rival versions of national identity. Disputes over the identities of martyrs and the circumstances and meanings of their sacrifices lend emotional focus and power to clashes and disputes within and among ethno-national groups. So it is in the case of the Alamo.

Disputing the meaning of the Alamo

For decades after the 1836 battle, the Alamo's physical remnants were largely neglected. By the turn of the century, the site's chapel was owned by the State of Texas, but remained in disrepair. The adjacent barracks (a former convent from the Alamo's days as a Spanish mission), where much of the battle had centered, had been converted into an unsightly commercial building by its owner, a wholesale company. The initiative to restore and preserve the Alamo began soon after 1900, in response to the wholesaler's intention of selling its portion of the site to a hotel. Two figures in the Austin chapter of the recently formed Daughters of the Republic of Texas (DRT) played important roles in this effort: Clara Driscoll, from a family of wealthy Anglo-Texan landowners and railroad developers, and Adina De Zavala, granddaughter of the first vice-president of the Republic of Texas, Lorenzo De Zavala. Driscoll had the financial wherewithal to purchase the building, while De Zavala played a crucial role in initiating the preservation effort and in both sparking Driscoll's original interest in it and winning the public's support for the undertaking. The State of Texas was quickly shamed into reimbursing Driscoll by purchasing the structure from her, immediately handing custody of the entire Alamo site to the DRT. But the DRT soon found itself divided into rival factions, as the two women clashed over the extent and nature of the preservation effort to be undertaken at the newly secured site. The Driscoll faction's intention of razing the old barracks at the Alamo and preserving only the chapel itself incurred the wrath of Adina De Zavala, who was committed to preservation not only of the sites of the Alamo heroes' last stand, but also of structures that had been important parts of the complex during Spanish colonial times and which, she claimed, had in any case been the major scene of fighting during the

1836 battle. Driscoll's faction withdrew from De Zavala's chapter of the DRT to form its own chapter, and a dispute ensued over which group had legal custody of the Alamo.[41]

What followed in 1908 was what historians have dubbed a "second battle of the Alamo,"[42] in which Adina De Zavala barricaded herself inside the barracks to prevent the Driscoll faction from leasing the building to another commercial firm pending a final determination of the custody issue. Her fear was that the lessor would further disfigure or demolish the structure. In what served as a momentarily successful publicity stunt, De Zavala refused to leave the premises for three days, until she obtained assurances from the governor of Texas that the state would take control of the barracks pending final adjudication of the custody dispute, leaving the existing building intact. Within a few years, however, the Driscoll chapter had succeeded in garnering enough support within the DRT to purge De Zavala's chapter from the organization, thus gaining legal control over the Alamo site and shutting De Zavala out of any further involvement with administration of the shrine. A temporary suspension of the DRT's custodianship in 1912 raised hopes of an architectural victory for De Zavala, who had the sympathetic ear of Texas' governor. But with Driscoll threatening to mobilize the public against him during the upcoming election campaign, the governor discreetly went out of state while his lieutenant-governor had the Alamo barracks shorn not only of the wholesaler's additions but of their entire second story, leaving the chapel as the dominant structure at the Alamo, more or less in accordance with Driscoll's vision. De Zavala spent the rest of her life as a sort of DRT version of Leon Trotsky,[43] exiled from the organization she had helped place on the political map, but continuing to denounce the Driscoll landscaping vision as a betrayal of the restorationist revolution De Zavala had initiated. For decade after decade, she devoted herself to speaking and writing about her understanding of the Alamo's historical meaning and to organizing and lobbying on behalf of a full restoration of the old convent/barracks structure that, to her mind, represented "the main building of the Alamo Mission."[44]

What was the significance of this feud, so full of sound and fury, among historical preservationists? At one level, it clearly had to do with personal ambition and clashing egos. Having taken the lead in the struggle to restore the Alamo, it must have been hard for Adina De Zavala, granddaughter of Texas' first vice-president, to find herself dependent upon the generosity of the wealthy Clara Driscoll, without whose purchasing power the cause may well have proved doomed from the outset. By the same token, Driscoll clearly felt that her initial purchase of the old barracks building gave her the moral right to dispose of the structure as she saw fit in the course of carrying out her aesthetic vision for the Alamo, which was inspired by European models of landscaped plazas or gardens dominated by solitary, monumental structures. This plan clashed with De Zavala's more conservative preservationist effort, which laid greater stress on the importance of historical accuracy in depicting the layout of the Alamo at the time of the 1836 battle. Two powerful personalities became fixated on these design differences as stakes in their broader struggle to gain credit for saving the Alamo and to secure control over the "master symbol" of Texan identity, to borrow Richard Flores' expression. Whoever controlled the Alamo, it seemed, gained custody of the soul of Texas.[45]

But, as Flores has documented, the clash was not devoid of ethno-political connotations in its own time – connotations that have grown more explicit in recent years, as the Second Battle of the Alamo has itself become the object of heated interpretive disputes.[46] Although her parentage was half Irish, De Zavala identified most strongly with her Yucatán-born grandfather, who had numbered among the founding fathers of Texas. For her part, Driscoll clearly saw herself as a member of the Anglo-Texan establishment (despite herself being wholly of Irish background). By her own account, in her struggle to preserve the former convent-turned-barracks, De Zavala was not only striving to convey a sense of the authentic layout of the site *circa* 1836, but to remind visitors of the Alamo's original history as a Spanish mission. Driscoll and the DRT presented the state's history as shaped by a struggle between predominantly Anglo-American lovers of political freedom and economic progress and an essentially backward and oppressive Mexican social and political culture whose lasting contribution to Texan civilization was little more than a lingering air of exotic charm associated with things Spanish. For her part, De Zavala called for a more nuanced and inclusive conception of Texan history and identity and sought to promote a shift in mentality that would allow Texans of Hispanic heritage to be considered no less Texan and American than those of German or other European origin.[47]

In her own day, the favorable attention De Zavala received in the American press emphasized her descent from "the best Spanish blood"[48] – an exotic and noble lineage in the racist perspective of the day, as distinguished from the despised alternative of being viewed as Mexican. As Richard Flores notes, even while she argued for the acceptance of

Mexican-Americans as Americans pure and simple, De Zavala did not describe herself as a member of the oppressed community.[49] But she remains a potent symbol of resistance to the received, Anglo-Texan version of the state's history and vision of its identity. Many Tejanos see in her struggle a symbol and expression of their own contribution to the defense of the Alamo. Her dramatic role in the preservation of the monument has been hailed by Tejanos as an early effort to place Texans of Hispanic background on an equal footing with Anglos in the legacy of heroism and sacrifice that constitutes the core element of the Texan myth. After all, by holding out in the former barracks for three days until her demands for the building's preservation were temporarily met, De Zavala created a theatrical second siege, taking center stage in the defense of the state's heritage and identity. By the same token, Driscoll's eventual victory encapsulates the use of the Alamo as an instrument of repression. As such, the Second Battle of the Alamo has come to be seen by many Tejanos as a symbol of their historic marginalization in an Anglo-Texan dominated society. Just as the role of Tejanos in the struggle against Santa Anna was followed within a decade by their removal from positions of power and prominence, so too a Tejana's critical role in the preservation of the Alamo was followed by her exclusion from the running of the shrine and, for many years, the virtual suppression of her memory in the official version of history-according-to-the-DRT.

The rise to social, economic, and political prominence of a new generation of Latino Texans in the last few decades, along with the wider impact of the civil rights movement and the greater scope allowed for expressions of non-Anglo ethnic identity within American society since the 1960s, have combined to bring ever greater pressures to bear on the institutional guardians of Texan identity.[50] They have responded by modifying their presentations of the Alamo's history in an effort to preserve the overarching structure of its significance as symbol of selfless heroism in the face of tyranny and brutality. In its museum exhibits and school curricula, the state of Texas has endeavored to distance itself from the traditional DRT approach in the hopes of constructing a more pluralistic framework of Texan civic identity. A critical component of this effort has been the integration of Tejano characters into the primordial myth of violation. At the Bob Bullock Texas State History Museum in Austin, a short film on Texan history highlights the role of Juan Seguín in the founding of the republic, in an effort to portray the struggle of 1836 as a fight between Texans of every ethnic heritage on the one hand and an oppressive Mexican state on the other.[51] And the DRT itself, seeking to fend off calls for the removal of the Alamo from its custody, has responded to its critics by hiring a university-trained scholar as its official historian and curator and by moving in the direction of a more inclusive history of the Alamo.[52] Space is dedicated in the Alamo chapel to the memory of Gregorio Esparza, a Tejano who fought and died there alongside the other victims of Santa Anna's ferocity and whose role was brought to light by Adina De Zavala's "discovery" and interview of his surviving son in 1901.[53] The Wall of History recently set up on the Alamo grounds (see above) ignores the role of slavery in the build-up to the Texas War of Independence, but does frame the story of the 1836 siege in the broader context of the site's history, beginning its timeline with the founding of the Spanish mission and highlighting the role of Tejanos in the defense of the Alamo. The long-dead Juan Seguín is recruited yet again to the defense of Texas' founding myth, his 1837 eulogy over the Alamo's fallen defenders being featured prominently on the Wall. The DRT, an organization that did not amend its bylaws to allow for African-American membership until 1986,[54] advertises its new-found multi-cultural sensitivity by "respectfully" dedicating the Wall of History to

the native peoples who built Mission San Antonio de Valero [the original name of the Alamo] and to the successive custodians of the site: Franciscan friars, Spanish and Mexican soldiers, Texians and Tejanos, members of the United States and Confederate armies, government officials, entrepreneurs, historians, and dedicated preservationists. Each has contributed to a history that will ensure that the Alamo will endure as a patriotic symbol for all times.[55]

(Could this be interpreted to mean that all are welcome to dip into the Alamo's bottomless pool of social and cultural capital as long as they don't question its patriotic meaning?) Finally, the display even takes the huge step of acknowledging Adina De Zavala's role in the site's pre-servation, although without mentioning her staging of the Second Siege or her eventual purging from the DRT – or even making it clear that the dispute over preservation plans pitted her directly against Clara Driscoll. Her posthumous rehabilitation is capped by the placement of her photograph alongside that of Clara Driscoll, each of them identified simply as "DRT member."[56]

But concessions of this nature are not sufficient to create a sudden consensus over the meaning of the Alamo. Dissatisfied by what they see as the condescension and tokenism of such gestures, some Tejanos and those sympathetic to their perspective have reacted by seeking to debunk the myth of the Alamo altogether. Unable to gain a convincingly equal standing in the official myth of violation, they call into question its historical legitimacy.[57] They have been aided in this by the critical work of historians and anthropologists who continue to expose how the symbolic power of the shrine has been manipulated over the years to the advantage of social and ethno-racial elites and who call into question the accuracy of some of the factual claims on which the official Alamo myth still rests. For many critics, the cultural hegemony of this myth – its recent incorporation of "inclusive" sub-narratives notwithstanding – remains a relic and reminder of the often brutal history of political and economic dispossession of Tejanos (apart from a small, upper-class elite) from the second half of the nineteenth century onwards.[58] In the eyes of some Latino commentators, Adina De Zavala and her latter-day apologists have got it all wrong, perpetuating what Rolando Romero has termed a Tejano "me-too" version of the Alamo's history, knocking on the gates of the Alamo legend in a humiliatingly vain attempt to gain full admittance into an Anglo-constructed edifice rather than tearing the whole mythical structure down.[59]

Revisionist attacks on their sacrosanct shrine have, in turn, antagonized traditional Texan patriots, stoking the flames of the low-grade culture war over the Alamo. Of course, these tensions have a broader resonance throughout the United States, for both the Alamo myth and the Latino sense of historical dispossession are part of the fabric of American national culture. Disputes have continued to rage over issues ranging from the legitimacy of the DRT's continued administration of the site to the specific circumstances of its defenders' deaths. Controversies over seemingly trivial historical minutiae take on Olympian proportions in light of the enormous symbolic burden resting on the relatively small set of available historical data.

A quintessential example of this is the Davy Crockett controversy. A legendary frontiersman from Tennessee, whose progressive political agenda had won him few friends and many enemies during his three terms in the US Congress, Crockett had resolved to begin his life anew in Texas following his failure to win reelection in 1834. Commanding an independent contingent of volunteer fighters at the Alamo, his choice to stand by the decision of the commander, William Travis, to stay and fight rather than abandon the position, earned him a hallowed place in the Alamo's official hagiography. A fierce storm of protests therefore arose when, in the 1970s, historians began calling into question the accepted story about the manner of his death. In the received version, Crockett was shot to death alongside his comrades during close-quarter fighting in the final stage of the Mexican army's assault. However, according to a number of sources, including the diary of Mexican army captain José Enrique de la Peña, Crockett was one of a handful of men taken prisoner and brought before Santa Anna after the end of the fighting. Furious that his troops had not followed his order to kill all defenders of the Alamo on the spot, Santa Anna had these survivors summarily executed. In their comparative analysis of the documentary evidence, most historians now find the latter account more credible than the traditional story of Crockett dying in combat, rifle in hand.[60]

One might well wonder what difference this apparently minor historical emendation could possibly make to the image of Crockett or the legend of the Alamo. After all, the "revisionist" account still has him killed on Santa Anna's orders following his valiant attempt to fend off the Mexican army's attack. Indeed, this version highlights even more starkly than the traditional story how cold-bloodedly ruthless Santa Anna was, for it shows him holding fast to his decision to take no prisoners even after the heat of battle had dissipated and in the face of a plea for clemency on the part of the Mexican general who brought the captives before him. Moreover, de la Peña highlights the dignified demeanor of Crockett and his half-dozen or so fellow captives in the face of a virtual lynch mob of Santa Anna's subordinate officers, who used their swords to put them to a gruesome and less-than-immediate death: "Though tortured before they were killed, these unfortunates died without complaining and without humiliating themselves before their torturers."[61] What more could one ask for in the way of a picture-perfect martyrdom?

But this is not good enough for True Believers, who have been raised on the image of Crockett dying in combat and who are disturbed in the very core of their beliefs by the notion that such a hero could possibly have allowed himself to be taken prisoner. Historians who have vouched for the authenticity of the de la Peña diary have been the targets of hate mail from outraged devotees of the Crockett myth. At least one such letter writer identified so completely with his hero that he seemed to take the revision of the accepted legend as an assault on his own manhood: "[B]efore I would have allowed a pompous, filthy-mouthed dog-of-a-man such as 'General' Santa Ana [*sic*] to capture me I'd shoot myself two to three times, vitally."[62] For rigid traditionalists, the primordial act of violation has to adhere to a very specific script and cannot be tampered with in any way if the foundations of Texan identity and dignity are to remain inviolate.[63]

For their part, as Holly Beachley Brear has argued, by the very act of attacking the Alamo myth, many of its critics continue to refocus attention on it and thus, in a way, to keep it alive.[64] Indeed, for the most vehement opponents of the official legend, the Alamo remains a potent symbol, but one which must be turned around and used to remind Latino Texans and other ethnic and racial minorities of the historic violations of their rights and of the continued ambiguities surrounding the place of minority cultures in the Texan and American frameworks of identity.[65] Thus, in his history of the Chicanos, Rodolfo Acuña includes a chapter whose very title – "Remember the Alamo: The Colonization of Texas" – urges readers thus to invert the meaning of the famous battle cry of Sam Houston's vengeful army.[66] Even as Acuña indicts the official memory as an instrument of exploitation, he cannot resist a triumphalist dig, suggesting that the cult of the Alamo's martyrs originated as little more than a form of psychological compensation on the part of "white Texans" who were "never able to live down the fact that the Mexicans had won the battle . . ."[67]

Ultimately, whether by seeking to gain entrée for Tejanos into the official framework of the Alamo story, as Adina De Zavala did, or by calling into question the very legitimacy of the Alamo myth as a whole, critics of the traditional legend have continued to share with its most die-hard defenders the common assumption that staking a convincing claim to the Alamo's legacy of violation (either by gaining recognition for one's group's role in defending the Alamo or by exposing how the story of the Alamo has been used to oppress one's group) is critical to the effective and legitimate exercise of collective volition in the context of Texan society. Such themes are replicated around the world, in many different geopolitical contexts. The certification of an ethnic group's victimhood is commonly seen as the key to establishing the legitimacy – in its own eyes and those of others – of its claims to a share of power, to self-rule, or to outright secession. Denying rival claims of violation generally goes hand-in-glove with the assertion of one's own group's victimization. Such disputes often take much bloodier form than the relatively civil and restrained debates over the meaning of the Alamo.

Ireland's sacred parades

For the parties to the Northern Irish conflict, it is the perennial flare-up of tensions over the Orangemen's marching season that brings each side's sense of historic and potential victimization into powerful symbolic focus.[68] The annual series of marches by the Unionists' Orange Order climaxes around the anniversary of William of Orange's 12 July 1690 triumph over the forces of England and Scotland's recently usurped

Catholic monarch, King James II, at the Battle of the Boyne. For many in England and Scotland, the battle marked the final postscript to the Glorious Revolution that consolidated the victory of constitutional monarchy and Protestantism over the threat of Stuart tyranny and French-backed Catholicism. But in the context of the Irish soil on which the fighting took place, it confirmed the subordination of the island's Catholic majority to a socially and politically dominant Protestant minority backed by the power of the Anglo-Scottish (soon to be British) crown. Among the Protestants themselves, Anglicans (members of the official Church of Ireland – sister institution to the officially established Church of England) dominated a status hierarchy and juridical regime that left Presbyterians and other dissenting sects bereft of many privileges until legal reforms in the early nineteenth century and the official disestablishment of the Church of Ireland in 1869.[69]

The Orange Order (also known as the Loyal Orange Institution) was not founded until just over a century after the Battle of the Boyne. The year was 1795 and the recent overthrow of the monarchy in revolutionary France, with which Britain was at war, was giving hitherto subordinate groups in Ireland dangerous new ideas about political equality and national freedom. At that point, Ireland's Anglicans were feeling most immediately threatened by the United Irishmen, an organization founded by members of the Scottish Presbyterian settler community in the northern province of Ulster. The United Irishmen were agitating for a self-governing Irish republic, an idea that touched a highly resonant chord among the impoverished and long-oppressed Catholic peasantry. Catholic restiveness led to a number of highly publicized, horrifically brutal attacks against Protestants in heavily mixed regions of rural Ulster, such as County Armagh. The ensuing outburst of localized sectarian violence made a mockery of the United Irishmen's aspirations to a republican nationalism transcending religious divisions. Following their successful repulse of a Catholic peasant militia's assault on a Protestant community near the town of Portadown in County Armagh, a group of armed Protestants resolved to follow up on their local triumph by forming a loyalist organization loosely modeled on the Freemasons and named after William of Orange. The Orange Order was dedicated to the stalwart defense of Ireland's political and religious status quo against what it saw as the existential threat posed by Catholic fanaticism and republican sedition. Enjoying the support of elements of the Anglican gentry and of government authorities, the Orangemen unleashed a campaign of terror against political dissidents of all denominations.

Following the British authorities' brutal suppression of the United Irishmen's 1798 uprising, the Orange Order continued to thrive and expand as a network of fraternal lodges devoted to the memory of William of Orange's military triumph over his Papist foes and to the defense of Ireland's Union with Britain. The fixation on the events of 1690 served not only to celebrate the victory of Protestantism but also to remind fellow Protestants of just how tenuous their position in Ireland really was. Shamelessly provocative triumphalism and a profound sense of vulnerability have long been two sides of the same coin in the militantly self-assertive political tradition of Unionism. The political and religious status quo could not be taken for granted; it had been won through battle, and it must be defended with militant zeal, else the victory on the Boyne might be snatched away just as quickly as it had been won. Despite Parliament's intermittent nineteenth-century attempts to ban or restrain the Order and its provocative marches, the Orangemen succeeded in establishing themselves as a fixture of Protestant socio-political life in Ulster and as a bastion of determined opposition to proposed changes in Ireland's political status quo. Indeed, it was the coalescence of northern Ireland's denominationally diverse Protestant community around the values and mentality of the Orange Order that helped block the all-Ireland Home Rule proposals of the late nineteenth and early twentieth centuries and that ultimately led to the 1922 partition of Ireland and the grant of parliamentary self-government to the Protestant-majority and Protestant-dominated north within the framework of a continued union with Britain.[70] (Northern Ireland is composed of the bulk of the old province of Ulster. Three of Ulster's nine counties form part of the Irish Republic.) Throughout the following half century, until Britain's suspension of Northern Ireland's Parliament and imposition of direct rule at the height of the sectarian Troubles in 1972, the Orange Order and the Ulster Unionist Party (UUP) that was its creation dominated the patronage systems and defined and defended the symbolic frames of reference that undergirded Protestant political hegemony in Northern Ireland.

In the early twenty-first-century context of a still-partitioned Ireland whose future is under negotiation, the theme of defining self-determination as a defense against the threat of existential violation remains very much alive on both sides of the communal divide. Northern Ireland remains split between a beleaguered Protestant majority that looks to continued union with Britain as the bulwark of its position and a large Catholic minority whose political and economic marginalization under the post-1922 political dispensation was all the more galling in light of the attainment of independence by the rest of the island.[71] The Orange Order has lost much of the political power it wielded prior to 1972, but it remains an influential mobilizer of Protestant political opinion and a highly visible framework of Protestant associational life. The initial acceptance by mainstream Protestant political leaders (many of whom were themselves members of the Orange Order) and voting public alike of the 1998 Good Friday Agreement, with its provisions for a power-sharing deal between Catholics and Protestants in Ulster and for the creation of an intergovernmental ministerial council between Northern Ireland and the Republic of Ireland,[72] only served to provoke certain diehard stalwarts within the Orange Order – along with members of more radical Unionist associations – into acts of militant defiance. In their eyes, the very future of the Unionist political order that constituted the political and institutional embodiment of their identity now hinged on their ability to maintain (or recreate) a broad coalition of Protestant denominations and interests bound together by the shared memory of past victories-snatched-from-the-mouth-of-defeat and a common commitment to keep the Union Jack flying over Ulster.[73] The more mainstream Protestant public opinion became alienated from their views, the more the radicals among the Protestant orders fell back on their old parading tradition to draw a clear line in the sand.

It is the annual marching season that Orangemen live for. Culminating in commemorations of Anglo-Irish Protestantism's triumph over its religious and national enemies at the Battle of the Boyne, the marching season serves as an opportunity to reassert Protestants' determination to hold on to Northern Ireland's union with Britain in the face of Catholic hopes for the eventual unification of Northern Ireland with the Catholic-dominated Irish Republic. It is at one and the same time a reminder of British Protestantism's ultimate triumph in the wake of a century and a half of intermittent persecution and military aggression by Catholic rulers and Catholic states (first Spain, then France) in post-Reformation Europe, and of Unionist determination to hold fast in the face of the never-ending threat of engulfment by Irish nationalism. For Catholics, this series of parades – often accompanied by provocatively noisy "blood and thunder bands"[74] – constitute an intolerable provocation, particularly when their traditional routes take them directly through Catholic-populated towns and neighborhoods.

The most violent flashpoint associated with the Orange marches in recent years has been the town of Portadown's annual Drumcree parade.[75] Portadown's Orange Lodge No. 1 is the historic mother of all Orange lodges, and the Anglican (Church of Ireland) parish church of Drumcree, which lies roughly a mile outside of town, is located near the site of the 1795 skirmish that led to the founding of the Orange Order. Ever since 1807, with intermittent interruptions during nineteenth-century bans on the Orange Order and its activities, the anniversary of the Battle of the Boyne has been marked on the Sunday before 12 July (as well as on the 12th itself) by a solemn march from the lodge's hall in the city center to the Drumcree church, where prayers of thanks are given for William of Orange's historic triumph. The lodge members then march back into town by another route, to form a full circuit.

When the tradition first began, Portadown was, naturally, less developed than it is today and the march's path simply followed main thoroughfares leading out of and into town. With Portadown's growth over the years, much of the traditional setting of the march has been transformed from rural landscape to urban neighborhoods – neighborhoods with a largely Catholic population. Altered demographic and political contexts have changed the meanings of the march for onlookers and participants alike.[76] In the framework of the post-1969 Troubles, Catholic neighborhoods along the parade path have resented what they see as provocative intrusions into their residential areas by a group of unreconstructed representatives of the old Protestant ascendancy in Northern Ireland. Unionist militiamen's participation in many Orange marches added to the aura of aggression that came to be associated with the annual marching season. Catholics' bitterness was all the greater for the fact that their attempts to conduct marches of their own in counterpoint to the Protestant parades were seriously restricted by the Royal Ulster Constabulary (RUC – Northern Ireland's Protestant-dominated police force). Portadown's St. Patrick's Day March (17 March) was repeatedly restricted to a straight, back-and-forth path designed to prevent it from encroaching on Protestant neighborhoods where it might provoke unrest.

There was a dual double-standard at play here that was doubly insulting to Catholic pride. Most obviously, Protestant opposition stood in the way of Catholic marches encroaching on Unionist neighborhoods while the Orangemen were still being allowed to violate Catholic space. More subtly and interestingly, a great deal of importance was attached (by both sides) to the symbolic significance of completing a full circuit on their marches. Catholics found it egregiously humiliating that they were restricted to a back-and-forth pattern, returning to their march's starting point by exactly the same route they had taken away from it. Portadown's

Orange Lodge No. 1, for its part, was allowed to proceed along a roughly elliptical route. St. Patrick's Day celebrants were reduced to a frustrating, unidimensional pacing to and fro within the narrow confines of their neighborhood, whereas Protestant marchers were free to demarcate a territorial zone in the full two-dimensional sense of the term, infringing on Catholic residential areas along the way. The discrepancy between the shapes of the parade routes could be seen as symbolizing the gap between the Catholics' historic status in Northern Ireland as a tolerated (or not so tolerated) minority and Protestant Unionists' claim to territorial-political dominion.

For their part, of course, the Orangemen vehemently and violently resisted periodic attempts by the RUC and British authorities to modify their route, seeing in it an outrageous assault on a tradition that was central to their identity and an insult to the memory of the martyrs who had fallen in defense of British Ulster and Protestant pride through the ages. That Catholic neighborhoods turned to the Provisional IRA for assistance in organizing violent resistance to the marches only confirmed the Orangemen in their belief that the protests over the Drumcree tradition were nothing more than propagandist devices and intimidation tactics cynically employed by their mortal enemies with a view to the ultimate annihilation of Protestant Ulster's collective traditions and identity. Adding to the mystique of martyrdom associated with the marches was the memory of the Battle of the Somme – Britain's catastrophic World War I offensive on the Western Front in the course of which a large cohort of Irish Protestant volunteers died precisely in the month of July. Ever since 1916, the climax of the marching season had commemorated not just the triumph on the Boyne but also the sacrifice on the Somme. British authorities' meddling in the matter of the march route was tantamount to violating the sanctified memory of the loyal Irish Protestants who had laid their lives down for King and Country. Most fundamentally, Protestants feared that giving an inch over the sacred route of their march would mark the start of a descent down the slippery slope of losing Northern Ireland altogether. In a sense, their annual completion of the full circle to Drumcree and back signified not just their continued, implicit claim to control of Portadown, but their larger commitment to maintaining a protective perimeter against internal and external threats to the status of Northern Ireland as a whole.[77] As a Northern Irish member of the British Parliament put it in 1985, the marchers "are not motivated out of a desire to break the law, but a sense of historic necessity to express . . . their legitimate pride in possession of their lands. They know instinctively that they only survive by their solidarity and determination."[78]

Drumcree and the marching season as a whole have been seen by Northern Ireland's Catholics as an outrageous flaunting of the Unionist Protestants' continued grip on power in Northern Ireland, undertaken in celebration of a military victory that allowed Britain to consolidate its arbitrary colonial rule over a persecuted Irish Catholic people. It is a bitter reminder to Catholic Irish nationalists of the historic condition of violation that served as the impetus to the bloody, early twentieth-century struggle for Irish independence, and of the failure of that struggle to achieve the liberation of the island's six northern provinces from British rule.[79] By the same token, the Provisional Irish Republican Army's (IRA) legacy of bombing outrages and murders combined with its longtime refusal to undertake a fully verifiable disarmament feeds directly into the Protestants' age-old fear of making themselves vulnerable to a bloodthirsty rule of Catholic terror. It lends a sense of timeliness and legitimacy to the Orange Order's insistence on continuing to take its provocative marches through the heart of Catholic neighborhoods. After all, the Orangemen can argue, in the face of the legacy and possible renewal of nationalist terror, is it not better to take the battle to the enemy's camp than to make oneself vulnerable through a compromise on traditional marching routes that could be taken as an indication of a broader willingness to abandon traditional frameworks and symbols of Unionist identity?

As in the case of the Arab–Israeli conflict discussed below, the marching season's association with legacies of violation and aspirations to self-determination – and its symbolic significance for each side's sense of relative status and dignity[80] – is so great for both parties to the dispute that it appears to stand in the way of any pragmatic compromise. Periodic efforts by the British authorities to modify the route of the marches so as to circumvent Catholic neighborhoods is taken as the thin end of the wedge by die-hard Unionists, who feel they have their backs to the wall as it is and are convinced that any symbolic concession will only encourage the British government to finally abandon its supporters in Ulster to their enemies. Orange Lodge No. 1 did agree to some modifications of its tradition in the mid-1980s, most notably agreeing to alter the outward-bound segment of the route to Drumcree so as to circumvent a Catholic neighborhood.[81] But vicious confrontations erupted over police attempts to change the second part of the loop, which took the Orangemen by Catholic homes along the Garvaghy Road. In a 1995 standoff, the RUC backed down from its efforts to block the Orangemen from marching down the Garvaghy Road, ultimately agreeing to let the march proceed along its traditional route provided it was unaccompanied by the often provocative musical bands.[82] The local member of the British Parliament, David Trimble, made a name for himself by marching at the head of the parade on this occasion, with the radical Protestant firebrand Ian Paisley at his side. (Paisley was not even an Orangeman, belonging instead to a more notorious Protestant order known as The Apprentice Boys.) Trimble's role in this short-lived triumph propelled him into the leadership of the mainstream Ulster Unionist Party (UUP) a few months later. But in the following year, a renewed standoff at Drumcree led to widespread sectarian rioting and violence across the province. In the aftermath of this disaster, the Parades Commission (created in 1997–98 as a non-governmental, quasi-judicial arbiter of marching disputes[83]) and the RUC have become much more resolute in blocking the Garvaghy Road to Orange marches pending a negotiated settlement of the dispute.[84] This stance has served as grist to the mill of radical Unionists convinced that Britain is stabbing Ulster's Protestants in the backs and that defiance in the face of compromise (be it imposed or negotiated) is an existential necessity.[85]

Yet it must also be emphasized that political attitudes and perceptions are far from monolithic within the two Northern Irish communities. Within the Orange Order, as Dominic Bryan has shown, the possibility of overarching political compromise has opened up profound fissures.[86] The old, middle-class, socially and politically respectable leadership of the Orange Order has increasingly shied away from open confrontation with the police force, preferring to negotiate compromises over parade routes rather than face the RUC across barricades. Disaffected working-class members of the Order, along with blood-and-thunder bands and members of more radical fraternal associations, have responded with accusations of cowardice and spinelessness, challenging the legitimacy of the Orangemen's established leadership. This internal splintering has contributed to the overall weakening of the Orange Order's status as a mainstream Protestant institution.[87]

For all the back-to-the-wall intransigence associated with symbolic flashpoints such as Drumcree, then, the political implications of such violation-volition traditions are not set in stone. The importance and meaning of these traditions can be subject to intense debate and multiple interpretations within the communities that identify with them. Hardliners on both sides of Northern Ireland's sectarian divide still hold fast to a conception of collective identity that is so inseparable from the memories, myths, and symbols of past victimhood and/or threatened violation, that the very success of a political compromise would call into question their sense of who they are. Yet, as of 2005, the Good Friday Agreement has yet to fall entirely to pieces and many Catholic nationalists and Protestant Unionists alike remain willing to contemplate a power-sharing arrangement that would serve to prevent a return to the violence of the Troubles. Indeed, one of the watershed events leading to the conclusion of the Good Friday Agreement was the horrific bombing at Omagh in 1998, carried out by a breakaway faction of the IRA. Claiming twenty-nine civilian victims on both sides of the sectarian divide, this atrocity had the opposite of its intended polarizing effect, as public opinion in both communities shifted dramatically in favor of a compromise solution to the three-decade-long reign of violence in Northern Ireland. A sudden sense of shared victimhood aroused a will on both sides to try and redefine the political implications of such violations. The changed atmosphere in the wake of Omagh allowed Unionist leader David Trimble and Gerry Adams, the head of Sinn Féin (the political wing of the IRA), to meet in public for the first time.[88]

It is true that the process of implementing the Good Friday Agreement subsequently stalled, in part over the IRA's long unwillingness to undergo a complete and verifiable disarmament. Moreover, the November 2003 triumph in Northern Ireland's Legislative Assembly elections of Ian Paisley's radically anti-Catholic Democratic Unionist Party (DUP) and Sinn Féin over more moderate parties within the two respective communities seemed to herald a new polarization of sectarian relations. Yet even Paisley's DUP has been willing to engage in limited cooperation with Sinn Féin on local councils, and has – at least nominally – focused its political efforts on trying to alter the Good Friday Agreement's framework for power-sharing and political devolution in Northern Ireland rather than on doing away with it altogether.[89] For his part, following a series of violent outrages by the IRA that provoked strong condemnations from the Irish Republic's government as well as from prominent supporters of the Irish nationalist cause in the American political establishment, Sinn Féin leader Gerry Adams felt constrained in April 2005 to call publicly on the IRA to disarm.[90] This was followed three months later by the IRA's public commitment to disarming ("decommissioning"), a process that was certified as completed by the Independent International Commission on Decommissioning on 26 September 2005.[91] On the other hand, the 2005 marching season was marred by violent rioting and gunfire directed against police forces by Protestant paramilitaries in Belfast, in protest over the rerouting of an Orange parade in that city.[92]

In brief, peaceful and violent scenarios for Northern Ireland's future both remain open. Among Northern Ireland's Catholics and Protestants, the blood of martyrs past continues to color many people's visions of the political present and future. But for every person who remains convinced that the sacrifices of the past can only be redeemed by the attainment of an exclusionary form of sectarian self-determination, there is at least one other who is eager to prevent any more martyrs from being created – even at the price of calling into question the uncompromising conceptions of collective will in whose name so many victims have been claimed in years gone by.

What I am suggesting is that memories of oppression and martyrdom need not be one-sided in their political implications. They may shape the contours of national debates, but they should not be seen as predetermining their outcomes. The choices that are made in the name of national self-determination can change the understanding of past violations and imminent threats, no less than violation shapes volition. By the same token, the range of realistic choices does vary tremendously depending on the geopolitical and historical context, as I will argue in the next section.

THE INTERPRETIVE VISE OF WARFARE

As Anthony Smith reminds us, traditions of martyrdom – like all nationalist myths and memories – can be interpreted and employed in many different ways.[93] Up to this point, our comparative perspective has focused on some of the striking similarities across the globe in the ways religious notions of martyrdom have been transposed to, or fused with, nationalist myths of violation to produce powerful frameworks for the creation and/or preservation of identities and the justification of struggles for self-determination. Yet the volition-violation relationship has been far from static; in each case, varied understandings of it have been articulated within each ethno-national community. By the same token, some historical and geopolitical contexts create much greater latitude for interpretive flexibility and freedom of choice than others. Every ethnic and national community is free to make choices; some communities have more freedom of choice than others.

In the cases of the Alamo controversy and the Temple Mount/ al-Haram al-Sharif conflict, the parallels in the religio-nationalist imagery and symbolism surrounding the two shrines are quite remarkable. Yet, as a flashpoint in a broader political conflict over territorial sovereignty and collective survival, East Jerusalem is at the center of a series of concentric circles of violence, bloodshed, and warfare, as we shall see below. For its part, the main activity the Alamo draws is tourism. Few visitors to this prime attraction in the sleepy town of San Antonio are even aware that a controversy exists over the meaning and history of the shrine. A cultural war may be raging over symbolic possession of the Alamo, but its protagonists are a relatively small group of intellectuals, civic associations, and fraternal orders. It is being waged in the context of a society that has, in recent decades, largely been spared the more violent manifestations of ethnic conflict.

The key contextual difference here is that there currently is no territorial dimension to the ethno-cultural conflict whose symbolic centerpiece is the Alamo. The debates that rage over who was the victim and who the oppressor, who the tyrant and who the martyr, are no longer linked to a broader questioning of the borders or political status of Texas. Mexico has long since abandoned the pursuit of any claims to its former possessions north of the Rio Grande, and most Chicanos and Tejanos no longer harbor serious aspirations to territorial secession from Texas or the United States.[94] The Alamo controversy gains its edge from the defensiveness of old-fashioned Texan patriots who feel threatened by attempts to deconstruct the myths on which they base their identity, and by the bitterness and resentment many Latinos feel over past and present patterns of ethno-racial discrimination against them in Texan society and over the continued disparity between the economic and educational opportunities available to Anglo-Texans and Hispanic Texans. More fundamentally, perhaps, the controversy is fueled by each side's concern with protecting its sense of dignity and gaining recognition and acceptance of its identity within the Texan and American civic arenas.[95] But all this takes place largely within a commonly accepted political-territorial framework of Texanness (or should I say Tejanidad?). The ultimate question remains how one defines being Texan – where the *ethno-cultural* boundaries of Texas should lie and how much tinkering with the symbols of Texan identity is acceptable in the interests of inclusiveness, rather than whether the state of Texas should exist or where its *territorial* boundaries should be drawn. The clash of symbolic meanings in Jerusalem encapsulates a struggle over more fundamental issues of physical survival and political sovereignty. But even here, as I will argue towards the end of this section, some latitude may remain for the reframing of the violation-volition nexus.

Before exploring the extent of such flexibility, let us look more closely at the constraints that warfare and extreme violence undeniably impose on nationalist interpretations of suffering.

* * *

At the risk of stating the obvious, it must be emphasized that the perceived *threat or experience* of violation is at least as potent a force as its *memory* in shaping the conception of national will and the exercise of political power.[96] In practice, it is very difficult to distinguish the one from the other. Indeed, perceived threats to collective dignity and national well-being often include both challenges to official myths of violation and overt acts of violation, oppression, or exploitation. The cult of past martyrdoms and the awareness of contemporary dangers to national honor, sovereignty, and/or security are commonly intertwined in a dynamic, ever-changing relationship.

In brief, the role of historical myths and symbols of identity in shaping the dynamics of ethno-national politics cannot be understood outside the geopolitical context in which they operate. Nationalist cults of martyrdom and collective memories of victimization have a far more dramatic impact on mass behavior and governmental decision-making during periods of turmoil than in days of peace, in the absence of a commonly accepted rule of law (be it national or international) than in the framework of a shared conception of political legitimacy. During periods of social and political stability, the imagery of violation may have relatively little impact on the exercise of collective volition. Most Texans nowadays are far likelier to be moved to fervent emotion by a victory of the San Antonio Spurs in the National Basketball Association (NBA) championships than by the ins and outs of the Alamo controversy.[97] But when the preexisting social, political, or international order falls apart, the violation-volition nexus comes to the foreground of people's consciousness, is actively exploited by parties to ethnic or nationalist conflict, and plays an important role in polarizing differences between rival ethno-national groups and deepening the sense of enmity between them.

War produces the fullest manifestation of this phenomenon. In the context of armed conflict, the distinction between national/religious symbols of martyrdom and the individual experience of peril and suffering is readily obscured, and governments actively play on this blurring of boundaries in their effort to engage and maintain mass commitment to the national war effort. The threat of sexual violation often plays a prominent role – whether implicit or explicit – in such propaganda campaigns. The nation is typically depicted as a woman, chaste yet vulnerable, threatened by an enemy intent upon ravaging her. The image of the virginal Joan of Arc, particularly as it developed in the nineteenth and twentieth centuries, contained potent elements of, and variations on, this theme.[98] In the words of the nineteenth-century French romantic nationalist historian, Michelet: "Let us always remember, Frenchmen, that among us *la patrie* was born from the heart of a woman, from her tenderness, from her tears, from the blood she shed for us."[99] Yet even as Joan embodied the pure, Madonna-like essence of French national purity that had to be defended against the brutality of the country's enemies, the battlefield heroism of this adolescent woman and her eventual martyrdom made her an inspiring model for France's uniformed men in time of war. If a young maiden was willing and able to don men's clothes, take sword in hand, and sacrifice herself for her country, surely the nation's men would not shirk their duty in its time of need.[100]

Joan of Arc's combined qualities of nationalist machismo and female sexual purity make her a somewhat unusual figure. Nationalist iconography more commonly segregates these images along lines of gender. One of the propagandist themes employed by Southern apologists during and after the American Civil War portrayed the Confederate struggle as one waged on behalf of the honor and safety of Southern women, who had to be defended against the depredations of unchained slaves and marauding Yankees alike.[101] Some of the leaders of the Texas war of independence had warned of similar threats posed by Tejanos.[102] In First World War propaganda posters of Allied and Associated and Central Power countries alike, women were commonly portrayed as tender mothers and wives patiently awaiting the return of their sons and husbands gone off to war, as caretakers for the wounded (see Figure 7), or as vulnerable creatures threatened with rape by the bestial enemy. Allied outrage over the German "rape of Belgium" conflated the image of individual sexual violation with the treatment of a country as a whole. (See Figure 8.) The willingness of French soldiers to endure the horrors of life and death in the trenches was strengthened by their sense that they were fighting to protect the purity and innocence of their wives and families behind the lines from the pollution and devastation of war.[103] Conversely, the fear that their wives and girlfriends were taking advantage of their absence to betray them served to undermine the morale of troops at the front.[104] Likewise, Iraqi armed resistance to US military occupation from 2003 on was bolstered from the start by rumors about American soldiers' use of night-vision goggles to visually undress Iraqi women, and subsequently reinforced by the graphically documented sexual humiliation of Iraqi men at Abu Ghraib

Figure 7 "The Greatest Mother in the World." First World War American Red Cross poster (*circa* 1917). Artist: Alonzo Earl Foringer (born 1878). Courtesy of the Library of Congress, Prints and Photographs Division.

prison. Nothing lends such visceral force to males' sense of national violation and the will to resist it as does the notion of their mothers, sisters, wives, and daughters being threatened by the enemy, the fear that their social and cultural control over women may be threatened by a licentious,

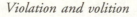

Figure 8 "Remember Belgium." American First World War bond-issue poster advertising the Fourth Liberty Loan. Artist: Ellsworth Young. First published in New York: United States Printing and Lithograph Co., *circa* 1918. Courtesy of the Library of Congress, Prints and Photographs Division.

invading culture, and the image of their own emasculation at the hands of occupiers.[105] Sadly, in many cases, invading armies and militias do in fact engage in systematic campaigns of rape and murder designed to terrorize and dehumanize their victims.[106]

When war subsides, such images and experiences move to the background, but the sense of threat and fear of violation can rapidly resurface when societies are suddenly forced to cope with the collapse of overarching geopolitical, institutional, and ideological frameworks of stability – as in East Central Europe following the demise of Communism.[107] The power of myths and images of violation to shape the nationalist imagination waxes and wanes in response to broader changes in historical circumstances. Once again, though, this is not to say that these myths do not themselves contribute to the shaping of those circumstances. A long-cultivated sense of collective victimization can contribute to conflict between ethnic groups and nations. The outbreak of conflict, in turn, creates conditions in which the bitter determination to overcome one's history of violation becomes much more widely and deeply rooted, shaping public consciousness and mass behavior much more powerfully than during peacetime.

The Yugoslav wars

The late twentieth-century Yugoslav wars illustrate the complexity and ambiguity of this political dynamic. The sudden disintegration of long-standing domestic and international frames of political reference at the end of the Cold War instilled new vigor in preexisting Serb and Croat perceptions of vulnerability and historical memories of violation. The resulting explosion of ruthless ethnic warfare created the impression, fostered by some of the journalistic and mass-media coverage of events, that these Balkan peoples had always been at each other's throats, and that the obsessive nursing of collective grievances was a peculiarly entrenched characteristic among these ethnic groups.[108] In response to such wide-spread stereotyping, some analysts went to the other extreme, arguing that the divisive form of ethnic nationalism that brought the Yugoslav state to an end was the product of the calculated machinations and manipulations of self-serving leaders such as Serbia's Slobodan Milošević and Croatia's Franjo Tudjman. The impression that these communal resentments and hatreds had always lain just beneath the surface of a nominally harmonious Yugoslav civil society was, according to this view, simply a testimony to the Machiavellian sophistication of unscrupulous politicians and propagandists skilled at the implanting of false memories, rather than a reflection of authentic historical experience.[109]

Each of these views seems one-sided and overly simplistic. There certainly was a significant sector of pre-1991 Yugoslav society that identified itself with Yugoslavia as a whole, that took seriously the official Communist slogan of "brotherhood and unity" among the country's constituent ethnicities, and that regarded historic traditions of ethno-national martyrdom and victimhood as relics of the past. "Mixed" marriages among Serbs, Croats, and Muslims had been common in the country's urban centers, and some 5.4 percent of the country's citizens had chosen to designate their ethnicity as Yugoslav rather than Serb, Croat, etc. in the 1981 census.[110] For many members of the country's younger generations, who had no personal memory of the bitter conflicts of the World War II years and who mingled freely with one another across ethnic lines in the context of both work and leisure, the rapid collapse of Yugoslavia and the sudden imposition of unidimensional categories of ethnic identity capable of determining issues of life and death were devastating blows that hit them out of the blue.[111] Slobodan Milošević's cold-blooded manipulation of ethnic tensions between Albanians and Serbs in Kosovo and his use of this issue to propel himself to power in Serbia amidst the collapse of Communism has been extensively documented.[112]

On the other hand, Milošević, Croatia's President Tudjman, and their ilk, had plenty of ready-to-hand material to work with. The genocidal policies of Croatia's fascist Ustaša government towards that country's Serb minority during the Second World War was a matter of historical record, was commemorated at the museum on the site of the infamous Jasenovac concentration camp, and remained a living memory for survivors of the World War II generation. As Croatia moved towards independence in 1990–91, its new government's open nostalgia for the Ustaša era played directly into the worst fears of the country's Serb minority. Croatia's Serbs were readily convinced that history had come full circle and that the intervening decades of relative interethnic peace had been nothing but an ephemeral illusion.[113] Croats, for their part, could look back on a long history of suppression of their national aspirations within the framework of a Yugoslav state whose first, post-World War I incarnation had really functioned quite transparently as a framework for an expanded Serbian monarchy.[114]

Indeed, ethnic tensions had remained part of the fabric of Yugoslav politics throughout the period of Communist rule that followed the

Second World War.[115] Under the regime of the anti-Nazi partisan leader and Communist strongman Marshal Tito (who was of mixed Croat and Slovene parentage), Yugoslavia's adaptation of the Soviet ethno-federal model provided each major nationality with the symbolic apparatus of self-determination – a juridically autonomous territorial republic – nested within the framework of a unified, Communist-run, Yugoslav state.[116] This approach – combined with the strong arm of Tito's police-state dictatorship – may have helped assuage some non-Serbs' lingering grievances over the Serb-dominated nature of the interwar Yugoslav state and their fear of continued domination by the most populous of Yugoslavia's nationalities. But it left many Serbs, who felt that they were the historic founders of Yugoslavia who had suffered the most in the struggles to create and defend the state, feeling cheated of their national birthright. Their diminished influence in Titoist Yugoslavia also struck many Serbs as out of keeping with their numbers: in 1981, Serbs comprised over 8 million out of 22 million Yugoslavs, with the next largest nationality, Croats, coming to just under 4.5 million.[117]

Many non-Serbs, in turn, felt threatened by such demographic disparities and remained deeply suspicious that the Yugoslav Communist ideal of a cultural and political "drawing together" (*zbližavanje*) of the South Slav nationalities would, if successful, amount to little more than a cover for Serb cultural and political imperialism. Internal debates within Communist Yugoslavia's political and ideological establishments never succeeded in definitively resolving whether the term "Yugoslav" represented a new, unificatory ethno-national identity into which all the country's constituent ethnicities would eventually merge, or whether it denoted no more than a supra-ethnic, political identity that would always function at a separate plane from the discrete ethno-cultural components of the federation.[118] More generally, Communist ethno-federalism (be it in the Soviet Union, China, or Yugoslavia) never succeeded in resolving the dilemma of how to satisfy people's need for symbolic representation of their ethnic identity without creating the expectation of more substantive, political self-determination.[119]

Conversely, to the extent that real autonomy did come to be exercised by Yugoslavia's constituent republics in the latter decades of Communist rule, it was the source of friction between ethnic majorities and minorities within each republic and between individual ethnic groups and the federal government. The cultural revival spearheaded by Croat intellectuals and students – with the support of a faction within the Croatian Communist Party – during the late 1960s and early 1970s was defined from the start as a defensive response to what was depicted as years of economic exploitation and cultural repression at the hands of the Serbs. The movement soon adopted an intolerant stance towards ethnic Serbs residing in Croatia and began to articulate demands for the transfer of Croat-inhabited sections of the Bosnian republic to Croatia. The rapid escalation of nationalist tensions provoked a political crackdown and purge by Belgrade at the end of 1971, followed three years later by the promulgation of a new constitution intended to assuage nationalist resentments by granting greater self-government to the federal republics (Serbia, Croatia, Slovenia, Montenegro, Bosnia, and Macedonia) as well as to the two autonomous provinces nesting within the Serbian republic – Vojvodina and Kosovo. The latter reform only contributed to tensions in Kosovo, which in the 1980s became the scene of low-level violence and persistent friction between an Albanian majority emboldened by its growing control of the province's public institutions and a Serb population that felt both physically and culturally threatened by its minority status within the region. The devolution of power to Vojvodina and Kosovo also diluted Serbia's influence in the collective, inter-republican presidency that assumed control of Yugoslavia after the 1980 death of Communist Yugoslavia's authoritarian founding father, Marshal Tito.[120]

It was against this background that, a few years after Tito's death, influential members of the Serb intelligentsia began to articulate a stridently revanchist form of ethnic nationalism. Playing on the perception of Serb victimization in Kosovo, these figures undertook a broader attempt to assert the Serbs' control over Kosovo and their pride of place among the peoples of Yugoslavia as a whole.

Kosovo was a particularly powerful focal point for this movement because of its historic role as the site of a 1389 battle pitting a Serb-led coalition against an Ottoman army. Although that day's fighting ended in a stalemate, the execution of Serbian Prince Lazar following his capture and the subsequent subjugation of Serbia by the Ottoman Empire led to the battle's commemoration in epic poetry and Serbian Orthodox Church tradition as a glorious defeat in which the Serbian leader – later sainted by the Church – was martyred for his people. (The Ottoman sultan, Murad I, was also assassinated by a Serbian fighter who managed to gain access to his tent.) The Serbs' suffering on the Field of Crows (Kosovo Polje) and under subsequent Ottoman rule was compared to the pain of Jesus on the Cross and the travails of the Jews in Babylonian exile. The Serb sacrifice, some claimed, had saved the rest of European Christendom from subjugation by the Turks. And, some day, the Serbian people would secure their own earthly salvation by virtue of their many centuries of suffering, rising up to regain the freedom their ancestors had died defending.[121]

It was precisely in Kosovo that the Serbs' contemporary sense of disempowerment in the context of an increasingly decentralized Yugoslav federation was most acutely felt. In the years following ethnic Albanian nationalist demonstrations in 1981, many among the Serb minority in Kosovo had faced harassment by members of the province's fast-growing ethnic Albanian majority and many more had become increasingly alarmed by rumors of an orchestrated campaign of rape and terror being directed against them. High Albanian birth rates combined with a steady flow of Serb emigration from Kosovo left Serbs as less than 10 percent of the total population by 1990 (down from 23.6 percent in 1961 and 13.2 percent in 1981) in a region that they regarded as theirs by historic right. Under these circumstances, Serbs felt mortally threatened by growing ethnic Albanian demands for full republican status for Kosovo in the Yugoslav federation, alongside Serbia and the other republics rather than as a province within the Serbian republic.[122]

Here was a neatly arranged package of historical memories, martyrdom myths, and immediate fears ready for exploitation by nationalist intellectuals who had long chafed at the bit while political leaders and official media had intoned saccharine slogans about Communist internationalism and the fraternal bonds uniting the peoples of Yugoslavia. In September 1986, the Serbian Academy of Arts and Sciences drafted a clarion call to action in the form of a memorandum – leaked prematurely to the press – which depicted the situation of the Serb people and Serbian republic in the gravest possible terms.[123] Referring to Communist internationalism and the existing constitutional setup of Yugoslavia as failed systems that had served to cloak the progressive marginalization of Serbia, the memorandum characterized the plight of Kosovo's Serbs as a "physical, political, legal and cultural genocide."[124] Events in Kosovo, it claimed, were emblematic of the broader patterns of political, economic, and cultural discrimination that were tearing away at the fabric of Serbian national life in Yugoslavia. If current trends were not rapidly reversed, warned the Academy, Serbs would not only be ethnically cleansed from their historic heartland of Kosovo, but would face the loss of their cultural heritage and the marginalization of their national identity at the hands of the other national republics of Yugoslavia. The reassertion of Serbian control over Kosovo and Vojvodina in the framework of a fundamental, constitutional restructuring of the Yugoslav federation was a matter of the highest priority if the Serb people – whose sacrifices on behalf of Yugoslavia outweighed those of any of its other constituent nations – were to survive as a member of "the family of cultured and civilized nations of the world."[125]

Sounded as it was on the eve of the collapse of East European Communism, the brazen new tone of Serbian nationalism did not fall on deaf ears among Serbia's political leadership. While the mainstream of the Serbian state and party leadership had mixed feelings about such divisive sentiments, the maverick new head of the Serbian Communist Party, Slobodan Milošević, appears to have seen in the agitation over Kosovo an opportunity to associate himself with and exploit a popular cause that, in its breadth of appeal and in the intensity of emotion it evoked, far surpassed any ideal hitherto articulated by the Communist Party. Appearing before a crowd of agitated Serbs in Kosovo in April 1987, Milošević responded to their claims of abuse at the hands of the ethnic Albanian police by declaring "No one should dare to beat you." Broadcast on Serbian state television, the statement marked the formal conversion of the republic's Communist Party boss to the cause of Serbian nationalism.[126]

While Milošević and his cronies subsequently succeeded in using the Kosovo issue to gain complete control over the Serbian government and Communist Party (soon to be renamed the Socialist Party), the aggressive style and substance of his policies destroyed the fragile structures of collective federal government and inter-republican balance of power that held post-Tito Yugoslavia together. Croatian voters responded by unseating the Communists in the republic's first multi-party elections in May 1990. The newly elected nationalist government headed by the former Communist partisan and latter-day Holocaust denier Franjo Tudjman immediately drafted a new constitution, which defined the republic as homeland of the Croatians, omitting all mention of Croatia's sizable (12 percent of Croatia's population in 1981[127]) and territorially concentrated Serb minority. (Previously, Croatia had been defined as "the national state of the Croatian nation *and the state of the Serbian nation in Croatia.*"[128]) As mentioned above, Tudjman's regime also openly flirted with the moral and symbolic rehabilitation of the only recent historical example of a sovereign Croatian state – the genodical Ustaša regime of World War II.[129]

The ethnic-Serb militias that were rapidly organized in response (first in Croatia and soon thereafter in contested Bosnia and Herzegovina) were no less eager to identify themselves in name and appearance with the

Second World War-era Serb monarchist Četnik forces – notorious for their atrocities against Croat and Muslim civilians. As in civil war reenactments in the United States, the donning of outdated uniforms, waving of long-discarded banners, and reversion to period-piece hair and beard styles[130] seemed to reverse the passage of years and gave participants the feeling of reliving the passionate struggles of their forefathers. But in the Yugoslav case, the guns were loaded with live ammunition and the romantic yearning to recapture a bygone generation's sense of manly honor was quickly supplemented and supplanted by a thirst to avenge one's fallen in the all too real ethnic wars that followed. With one Yugoslav republic after another declaring full independence over the course of 1991–92, ethnic identity, which had been nested within a broader framework of trans-ethnic political institutions, was left by default as the exclusive basis of cultural and political identities alike across the lands of the collapsed federation.[131]

Indeed, the escalation of warfare involving both armies and irregular forces, first between Serbs and Croats in Croatia, then between Serbs and Muslims (and, periodically, between Croats and Muslims) in Bosnia, and finally, in the late 1990s, between Serbs and Albanians in Kosovo, set in motion a vicious circle of atrocious violations that propelled a downward spiral into the most intolerant and exterminationist conceptions of self-determination. Although Tudjman's unapologetically chauvinistic Croatian nationalist regime contributed heavily to the escalation of hostilities, Serb nationalist militias, backed by Serb elements of the former Yugoslav National Army (JNA), committed the most egregious and systematically organized atrocities in these conflicts.[132] The psychological dynamic of Milošević's official cult of national victimhood was self-sustaining. The more the international press implicated Serb forces in "ethnic cleansing" operations and orchestrated massacres, the easier it was for Milošević's propaganda machine to convince its audience that Serbs were the maligned victims of a defamation campaign launched by their enemies and detractors. The nation would be doomed to the worst of fates unless it fought savagely for its very survival. Contemporaneous adversaries were identified with the nation's historic foes, lending the struggle an elemental, timeless quality that seemed to free its Serb protagonists from responsibility for their own actions while imputing existential blame to the undifferentiated members of rival nationalities simply by virtue of the community they were identified with. Bosnian Muslims were commonly referred to as Turks, as though these Serbo-Croatian-speaking former Yugoslavs were the living representatives of the Ottoman

Turks whose imperial rule had oppressed Serbs from the fifteenth to the nineteenth centuries.[133] The equation of contemporary Croats with the World War II-era Ustaša did not require much of a stretch, given the new Croatian state's attempts to minimize the nature and extent of the crimes committed by its World War II-era predecessor against the country's Serbs, Jews, and Gypsies. Germany's December 1991 initiative extending diplomatic recognition to the newly independent Slovenian and Croatian republics (which placed pressure on other European states to follow suit) was portrayed as evidence that Germans were reprising their familiar role as enemies sworn to the eradication of Serbian independence (as manifested in the heavy-handed Austrian occupation of Serbia during World War I and the vicious Nazi occupation of the Second World War).[134] The span of years dividing the present generation from German invasion and Turkish massacres disappeared in the blink of an eye, as Serbia's newly transformed geopolitical and ideological environment enabled its leaders to infuse the traditional iconography of national martyrdom and suffering with renewed meaning.

In these circumstances, their sense of ethno-national violation was the lens through which many Serbs *came to view* both their current political circumstances and their historical past, to the ever greater exclusion of other emotional and psychological prisms. This does not mean that they had seen things so unidimensionally all along, nor does it mean that Milošević called this mentality into being out of thin air. In the midst of a general crisis that had thrown the established framework of the Communist Party-imposed inter-ethnic compromise and coexistence into serious question, political leaders and intellectual elites had turned to, and played on, selected aspects of historical memory to produce a situation in which pre-war memories that diverged from the theme of endemic violation seemed like little more than counterfactual delusions, superficial products of empty Communist propaganda about brotherhood and unity, rather than aspects of a complex and contradictory historical reality.[135] What took place here – as among the Croats – was a radical narrowing of perspectives to a tightly focused obsession with one strand of the variegated fabric of the pre-Milošević Yugoslav experience. In the hell that engulfed much of former Yugoslavia during the 1990s, the cult of victimhood became a self-perpetuating phenomenon that reduced the ideal of self-determination to little more than an overriding compulsion to lash out at enemies, real and imagined, and to terrorize, murder, or expel aliens from within the nation-state. Only when every one of Milošević's ill-conceived campaigns to extend Serbia's borders to embrace all Serbs had ended in either stalemate (in Bosnia) or mass expulsions of ethnic Serbs from neighboring regions (Croatia's Krajina and parts of Kosovo) did his political star begin to wane.

And yet, inexorable and irreversible as such precipitous descents into mayhem can sometimes appear, peoples do (sometimes) find ways out of self-limiting fixations on their own past suffering and present vulnerability, even when persistent warfare has appeared to eliminate any alternative perspective. Precisely when the cult of victimhood becomes most obviously self-defeating, some voices may be raised that suggest more constructive ways of applying the lessons of violations past and present. Such a scenario can even (possibly) be imagined in the case of that seemingly most intractable of ethno-national clashes, the Israeli–Palestinian conflict.

Jerusalem revisited: constraints and possibilities

Real-time threats of violation merge with traditional cults of martyrdom and suffering in shaping national identities and the exercise of national will in the Middle East as elsewhere. The tension surrounding the ultimate disposition of the Temple Mount is the example *par excellence* of how memories of violation and present fears of annihilation or subjugation can reinforce one another. As we have already seen, in the first half of the twentieth century, the Jewish and Muslim holy places in Jerusalem became much more than objects of religious devotion and reminders of ancient historical experiences. They evolved into potent symbols in an ongoing, life-and-death struggle over political sovereignty, territorial control, and national self-determination. These roles have become further accentuated in the context of the post-1948 Arab–Israeli conflict.

When East Jerusalem fell to Transjordan's Arab Legion during the Israeli War of Independence (1948–49), the residents of the Jewish Quarter were expelled. In violation of Article VIII of the April 1949 Israeli–Jordanian armistice agreement, Jews were denied access to the Western Wall throughout the nineteen years of Jordanian rule.[136] (Transjordan was renamed Jordan in December 1948, following the kingdom's occupation of the West Bank and East Jerusalem.) In Israeli eyes, divided Jerusalem, the western half of which functioned as the country's capital (largely unrecognized by the international community), encapsulated the half-full/half-empty quality of the cup of national redemption for a people that relished its newly won independence but remained acutely aware of the existential vulnerability of its political and military position. The Old City and the Western Wall that lay so tantalizingly unattainable just beyond the armistice line in Jerusalem became objects of nostalgic yearning among Israeli Jews of most ideological persuasions, religious and secular alike. The sentiment was most viscerally captured by the late Naomi Shemer's "Jerusalem of Gold," a gripping song of romantic, quasi-religious longing (composed, it so happened, on the eve of the 1967 Six Day War), which quickly acquired the status of an unofficial national anthem.[137]

After East Jerusalem came under Israeli control in the course of the 1967 conflict, with Israel proclaiming its full sovereignty over the unified city (including a large swath of West Bank land extending well beyond the old municipal boundaries) soon after the war's end, the symbolic and ideological dynamics of Zionist self-determination shifted once again. The religious stream of Zionism, which had been a relatively marginal current of the movement, gained new-found zeal and recruited more followers in the aftermath of the seemingly miraculous military victory and the fall of Judaism's holiest places under the Jewish state's control. The religious-Zionist Gush Emunim movement spearheaded the campaign to settle Jews in the West Bank (with extensive backing from the ruling Labor Party), while the Jewish Quarter of East Jerusalem, which had been subjected to ethnic cleansing by Jordan's army in 1948, was rebuilt and settled by secular and religious Jews alike. While Gush Emunim claimed the mantle of the early socialist-Zionist pioneers, secular Israeli Jews of every political stripe found themselves profoundly moved by the capture of the Temple Mount and the resumption of Jewish worship at the Western Wall. Israel's Labor Zionist-led government cleared Arab houses away from the Western Wall, opening up the narrow alley beside it into a capacious public plaza. A steady flow of archaeological digs in the Jewish Quarter and at the foot of the Temple Mount unearthed startling remnants of the city's ancient Jewish past, ranging from a stretch of fortification hastily improvised at the end of the eighth century BCE in anticipation of an Assyrian siege, to the late Second-Temple-era basement and *mikvah* (ritual immersion pool) of a high-ranking *kohen*'s (priest's) house, the soot from the conflagration of 70 CE still clearly visible along the walls. Integrated almost seamlessly into the reconstructed Jewish Quarter, these archaeological landmarks created a sense of intimate contact between the Israeli Jews of today and their besieged and martyred ancestors of yesteryear.[138]

For all the sense of national triumph and fulfillment following the reunification of Jerusalem, the situation at the Temple Mount itself still

arouses mixed feelings among Israeli Jews. Their 1967 victory notwithstanding, the topographical configuration of the Temple Mount serves as
a continued reminder of their primordial sense of violation. The Muslim
shrines still sit astride the paved platform that is the summit of the
Temple Mount while Jews pray at the Western Wall below, their physical
subordination to the Islamic holy places belying their political-military
control of the city. Immediately after the conclusion of fighting in 1967,
Israeli Defense Minister Moshe Dayan recognized the continued jurisdiction of the Islamic *waqf* (religious trust) authorities over the summit
of the Temple Mount and the religious sites atop it, and assigned day-
to-day security responsibility for the area to the *waqf*'s uniformed
guards.[139] From the start, then, the sense of a triumphant reversal of
national fortunes associated with the reunification of Jerusalem was
tempered by the recognition that certain critical elements of the symbolic
status quo ante were to be indefinitely maintained. Jews were once more
free to worship at the Western Wall, but the Western Wall itself was a
bare remnant of a once glorious Temple, a painful reminder of the
Temple's destruction that remained physically overshadowed by the gold-
plated dome of the Shrine of Omar resting resplendently atop the Temple
Mount/Haram – where Israeli authorities prohibited Jewish worship.
Occasional incidents of stones being cast down on Jews at the Western
Wall plaza by rioting Palestinians on the Temple Mount above serve to
rub in this disjuncture between the distributions of political and symbolic
power in Jerusalem.[140]

For traditional, Orthodox Jews, there is no practical conflict between
Muslim control of the Temple Mount and Jewish religious practice and
communal identity. Religious law forbids Jews from ascending to the site
of the demolished Temple pending the arrival of the Messiah, for fear
that they might inadvertently wander onto the uncertain location of the
Temple's Holy of Holies, the innermost sanctuary and site of the Divine
Presence, access to which had been permitted to the high priest only, once
a year, at the climactic moment of the Day of Atonement. For their part,
until access to tourists was cut off by Israeli authorities in September 2000
following the ourbreak of the al-Aqsa Intifada, secular Jews had no
compunction about visiting the Temple Mount as curious onlookers,
removing their shoes in accordance with Islamic practice before entering
the Shrine of Omar and lining up to gaze at the piece of exposed bedrock
at the center of the Shrine, traditional location of Abraham's aborted
sacrifice of Isaac and of the Prophet Muhammad's ascent to heaven, and
possible site of the Holy of Holies in the Second Temple.

And yet, and yet – secular Israelis were fascinated by the ongoing archaeological excavations that exposed a section of the Herodian southern retaining wall around the corner from the Western Wall, that opened up long-hidden stretches of the Western Wall itself, and that revealed the survival of ancient tunnels extending beneath the Temple Mount – secret passageways apparently used by priests to make a clean exit from the area of the Temple in the event of ritual contamination.[141] If the surface of the Temple Mount was bound to remain the privileged domain of Muslims, the area around and beneath the Muslim shrines was beginning to present a more ambiguous aspect.

For a small handful of Orthodox Jews, the longstanding theological stalemate over the Temple Mount was itself open to question. The traditional ban on Jewish access to the Temple Mount for fear of trespassing upon the Holy of Holies could be seen as a symbolic expression of the broader passivity of exilic Jewry, its contentment to await the coming of the Messiah rather than actively reassert its political-territorial self-determination. Religious Zionists had broken with this tradition of physical and political passivity and accepted the secular Zionist premise that the initiative for the ingathering of the Jews must come from the Jews themselves. If for most Israeli Jews, the unification of Jerusalem was the ultimate vindication of this approach, for a few religious Zionists it represented the prelude to an even more dramatic, eschatological finale. Given the latest archaeological knowledge, the most up-to-date surveying techniques, and careful interpretations of Talmudic descriptions of the Temple, some asserted, the location of the Holy of Holies could be determined accurately enough to allow Orthodox Jews to limit the forbidden zone to a designated sector atop the Temple Mount rather than extending it to the Temple Mount in its entirety. This would allow religious Jews to join their secular counterparts on the Temple Mount, where they could conduct collective prayers with dignity on the actual site of the Temple rather than limiting themselves to the retaining wall beneath. For a small but highly vocal group of fundamentalists, who formed an organization calling itself the Temple Mount Faithful, the logical next step was obvious – accurate pinpointing of the Holy of Holies and construction of a Third Temple in place of the Muslim holy places. Here was the ultimate synthesis of traditional-messianic and modern-activist notions of self-determination; the sense of violation that had shaped Jewish consciousness since 70 CE was to be ended by an assertion of collective will undertaken in defiance of the demographic, cultural, and political realities of the Middle East, an expression of faith through direct action rather than prayer, a hastening of the Messiah's arrival by *initiating* the rebuilding of the Temple that traditional rabbinic Judaism had looked forward to as the *result* of the Messiah's coming.[142]

* * *

The adherents of the most radical forms of such neo-messianic zealotry remain a tiny minority within the religious-nationalist wing of Zionism. But the uncovering by Israeli authorities of plots by extremists to blow up the Muslim shrines atop the Haram, along with the broader Israeli fascination with archaeological tunneling around the Temple Mount, sufficed to convince broad sectors of the Palestinian Arab public as well as the wider Arab and Muslim worlds that the Israeli government was planning or conniving at the destruction of the Muslim holy places. More fundamentally, for Palestinians and the broader Arab and Muslim worlds, Israel's assertion of sovereignty over East Jerusalem flies in the face of the centuries-old Islamic supremacy in the city, as symbolized by the gold-capped Shrine of Omar's domination of the Old City's skyline. One of the prime motivations for building the Shrine of Omar and al-Aqsa mosque atop the Temple Mount in the first place had been to lend concrete form to Islam's claim to be the true successor to Judaism and Christianity.[143] (As mentioned above, the Temple Mount also came to be identified as the spot from which the Prophet Muhammad had departed the earth by ascending directly to heaven.) In the post-1967 arrangement, the Arab *waqf* police's continued responsibility for security on al-Haram al-Sharif is not enough to assuage the feeling that Israel's overarching control over the city is a violation of Islam's position as the rightful heir to the traditions of Judaism and Christianity and as the supreme faith throughout the Middle East. This broadly defined sense of Islam's historical/theological pride of place among the religions of the book lends a religious tincture to the most secular Palestinian and pan-Arab nationalist movements. (Even many Christian Arabs regard Islam as the creation of the Arab people, the defining framework of Arab civilization, and hence as a national heritage for the Arab people as a whole.[144]) Scorned for their rejection of Muhammad's prophecy and historically tolerated (along with Christian minorities) in the Islamic world as a juridically subordinate People of the Book, the Jews are seen as defying divine will and History's judgment by asserting their political-territorial sovereignty over Islam's third holiest city. For a historically powerless and religiously despised people, whose Middle Eastern minority communities had for centuries lived on Muslim sufferance, to emerge suddenly as a military and political power capable of imposing its control over Arab-claimed lands, Arab populations, and Muslim holy sites constitutes a particularly galling violation of national pride and religious and political dignity.

Palestinian feelings of humiliation and outrage over Israeli control of East Jerusalem and al-Haram al-Sharif are a distillation of the broader sense of violation that is central to Palestinian national consciousness. The historical Big Bang in Palestinian nationalist cosmology is the Nakbah – the Calamity of 1947–49, when Palestinian Arab armed opposition to the United Nations' plan for partitioning Palestine between Jews and Arabs backfired, resulting in the new State of Israel's military defeat of the Palestinians and the neighboring Arab states who invaded Palestine in 1948, and the consequent flight – either in anticipation of Israeli occupation or as a result of expulsion by advancing Israeli forces – of hundreds of thousands of Palestinians.[145] Almost as though they were taking a page from the book of Jewish collective consciousness, Palestinians seized upon their own defeat and exile as defining events in their nation's history. Keeping alive the memory of the Nakbah was crucial to maintaining a commitment to reversing the defeat and bringing exiles home from the diaspora. The sense of collective trauma and the corresponding determination to survive as a nation was sharpened by its carefully cultivated association with the sense of personal loss on the part of Palestinian families that yearned for their native towns and villages, their homes and lands. The rusting keys and tattered title deeds to long-lost houses are passed down from generation to generation among some Palestinian refugee families as a way of maintaining a physical link with their ancestral homes, of keeping alive the memory of where they come from, and of expressing the expectation of imminent return.[146]

From early on, Palestinians saw themselves as the victims not only of victorious Israelis but also of the Arab states that proved such inhospitable and exploitive hosts to Palestinian refugees. In Ghassan Kanafani's classic 1962 novella, *Men in the Sun*, three Palestinian refugees desperate to support their families with remittances die in the desert inside the overheated tank of a water truck in the course of a botched attempt to have themselves smuggled into Kuwait. The deep sense of humiliation at the hands of Jews and fellow Arabs alike is conveyed most powerfully through the character of the smuggler, himself a Palestinian who literally lost his manhood in an explosion while fighting the Jews in the 1947–49 war. The death of his human cargo takes place while he is delayed at a Kuwaiti checkpoint by officials who toy with his papers while crudely teasing him about his supposed – physically impossible – patronage of a prostitute across the border in Iraq. By the time he emerges from this experience of sexual humiliation, all he can do for the desperate men who had remained concealed in the water tank is dump their bodies on a rubbish heap in the hope that they will be discovered there in time for a proper burial. There is no attempt at subtlety here; the reader is to be left in no doubt that this is a people that has been robbed of every last shred of dignity by Jews and Arabs alike.[147]

The events of June 1967 added new dimensions to the Palestinian violation-volition nexus. The success of Israel's preemptive strike against its hostile neighbors' massing armies represented a further humiliation that fed the fires of frustrated Arab nationalism.[148] The Israeli military occupation of the remaining territories (the West Bank and Gaza Strip) of pre-1948 Palestine brought hundreds of thousands of Palestinians under Israeli control, without extending to them the benefits of Israeli citizenship conferred upon the rump Palestinian Arab population living within the Jewish state's pre-1967 boundaries. The construction of Jewish settlements in the occupied territories and the diversion of scarce water resources to serve Jewish settlements' agricultural needs presented Palestinians with the prospect of further dispossession and displacement. At the same time, the defeated armies in 1967 were Egyptian, Syrian, and Jordanian – not Palestinian. In other words, the suffering brought on by this new disaster was Palestinian, but the failure was the failure of the Arab states, not the Palestinian nationalist movement. Indeed, guerrilla and terrorist operations against Israel mounted by Yasser Arafat's Fatah organization and other Palestinian armed formations increased in scope and intensity in the aftermath of the Arab armies' defeat. Fatah's decision to stand its ground (with Jordanian army artillery support) at al-Karama, Jordan in 1968 against superior Israeli forces engaged in a cross-border raid took on tremendous symbolic significance as a demonstration of Palestinians' willingness to sacrifice themselves in the struggle against the enemy.[149] The perceived contrast between the Arab armies' rout in 1967 and the Palestinian fighters' martyrdom in 1968 reinforced the sense that the original Nakbah had ultimately arisen from a failure of military strategy and political will on the part of the Arab states rather than from any misjudgments or shortcomings on the part of the Palestinian Arabs themselves.

Thus, in the nationalist myth cultivated by Yasser Arafat's Fatah movement (which became the dominant component of the Palestine Liberation Organization – PLO), the Palestinians' constant suffering was portrayed in defiant terms as a function of their position at the frontline of the Arab world's confrontation with the Zionist enemy, a badge of honor that put to shame the neighboring regimes that had, time and again, failed in their promise to liberate Palestine from the Jews. The more military defeats and national disasters Palestinians underwent, the more spiritual and political victories their leaders could claim. As Rashid Khalidi has suggested, this outlook conferred tremendous resilience upon the Palestinian nationalist movement, while also shielding its leaders from a sense of accountability for their often calamitous miscalculations and misjudgments.[150]

Framed within this historical and psychological context, al-Haram al-Sharif has been an explosive point of focus for the concentric circles of Palestinian nationalism, pan-Arab nationalism, and Islamic fundamentalism. The symbolic significance Jerusalem holds for the Jews combined with Israel's control over the Muslim shrines in the city has undoubtedly elevated its importance for the Arab world generally and Palestinians specifically. Medina may officially be the second holiest city in Islam (after Mecca), but its location in Saudi Arabia means its status can be taken for granted, whereas Jerusalem – technically the third holiest city – has become the source of intense frustration and the object of profound yearning. The influx of worshippers from the West Bank and Gaza on Friday afternoons combined with the provocative posturings of the Temple Mount Faithful organization have, on occasion, made al-Haram al-Sharif the flashpoint for violent Palestinian demonstrations in the course of which rocks have been hurled at Israeli police stationed just outside the compound and onto the Western Wall plaza below.[151] Heavy-handed responses by Israeli security forces have on occasion served to further inflame passions. In the course of an October 1990 riot atop the Haram, sparked by the Temple Mount Faithful's attempts to initiate Jewish prayers within the compound, Israeli forces shot seventeen Palestinians dead. The resultant aura of martyrdom (following the 1990 incident, Palestinian survivors dipped their hands in the blood of the dead and wounded and left their imprints on the walls of buildings on the Haram) adds to the Haram's luster in the eyes of Muslims and Palestinian nationalists, as do intermittent Israeli security-related restrictions on access to East Jerusalem by Palestinians from outside the city.[152]

This Molotov cocktail of emotions can be ignited by the slightest suspicion of infringement on the already unstable status quo. Israel's 1996 opening of an entrance in the Muslim Quarter to an ancient tunnel – the remains of a Hasmonean-era aqueduct linked to recently exposed northern sections of the Western Wall[153] – immediately set off Palestinian fears that Israeli archaeological excavations in the vicinity of the Temple

Mount were aimed at literally undermining the foundations of the Muslim shrines and inducing their physical collapse. The ensuing riots spread throughout the occupied territories and culminated in deadly exchanges of fire between Israeli troops and Palestinian Authority forces. In September 2000, then Israeli opposition leader Ariel Sharon's visit to the Temple Mount in the company of his retinue of bodyguards sparked riots that escalated into the blood-soaked Second Palestinian Intifadah (Uprising), known among Palestinians as the al-Aqsa Intifadah (after the mosque on al-Haram al-Sharif). The name of the *intifadah* suggested a fusion of religious and nationalist motifs, the Palestinian leadership portraying the struggle as a fight to uphold and defend the role of the Palestinian nation as a defender of some of Islam's holiest shrines against the threat of violation at the hands of the Jews. The *waqf* authorities, for their part, have in recent years engaged in excavation activities beneath the al-Aqsa Mosque that are ostensibly designed to create additional space for worshippers underground, but that also serve to provoke Israeli outrage by asserting Muslim control over the subterranean portion of the Haram, where ruins of the ancient Jewish temple presumably lie.[154] As Menachem Klein has argued, the focus on the Haram/Temple Mount issue at the Camp David talks and in the *intifadah* that followed, and the Palestinian leadership's flagrant denial of a Jewish connection to the site, has further elevated the national significance of symbolic sovereignty over the Temple Mount for a broad range of secular Israelis who might have given little heed to the matter a few years earlier.[155]

* * *

All this is not intended to suggest that the struggle over Jerusalem and the Temple Mount/al-Haram al-Sharif is at the root of the broader Arab–Israeli conflict. On the contrary, one of the central points of this section is to underline the importance of evolving political contexts in shaping the meaning of such symbols of suffering and redemption. What this discussion does suggest is that the clash over the holy sites in Jerusalem epitomizes some of the critical psychological elements of the broader confrontation between these rival nationalisms. Meron Benvenisti has used the term "double-minority syndrome" to describe a vital aspect of this conflict.[156] As in the case of Protestants and Catholics in Northern Ireland, he argues, Israeli Jews and Palestinian Arabs each feel that they are the vulnerable minorities with their backs to the wall. Protestants may constitute a slight majority of the population in Northern Ireland, but they would become an instant minority in the unified Ireland that Catholics dream of, while Northern Irish Catholics, for their part, feel they have long been mistreated by a Protestant-dominated United Kingdom. Likewise, Israeli Jews feel like a threatened and vulnerable minority among the tens of millions of hostile Arabs in the Middle East as a whole, while Palestinians see themselves as the victims of a militarily powerful Israeli foe and as an oppressed minority in a Jewish-dominated Palestine. The intractability of the conflict stems in part from this mutual sense of historical victimization and current vulnerability, which leaves each side feeling that it is not in a position to make any substantive concessions to the other party. The conflict over the final status of East Jerusalem and the Temple Mount/al-Haram al-Sharif encapsulates this broader syndrome, for each side sees this site as representing the memory and/or the threat of national perdition, while simultaneously holding forth the promise of collective redemption. Religious fervor and nationalist emotion, the history of subjugation and the quest for self-determination, the legacy of martyrdom and the prospect of salvation, the keen memory of violation and the stubborn exercise of volition – all these mutually reinforcing elements of nationalism-in-general and Palestinian and Israeli nationalisms in particular are brought into powerful focus for Jews and Arabs alike at the very same location.

Indeed, of all the issues embraced by the tangled web of proposals and counter-proposals, offers and retractions, at the failed Israeli–Palestinian–American Camp David summit of 2000, the one concerning the Temple Mount/al-Haram al-Sharif was the most nettlesome.[157] Various ideas were floated at Camp David concerning the possible division of control over East Jerusalem. The Palestinians appeared willing to consider the recognition of Israeli sovereignty over the Old City's Jewish Quarter and the Western Wall plaza, the rest of the Old City to become part of a Palestinian state with its capital in East Jerusalem. The Israelis offered the Palestinians full sovereignty over Arab neighborhoods on the outer fringes of East Jerusalem, where the Palestinian capital would be established. Arab neighborhoods in the heart of East Jerusalem, including the Old City, would remain under formal Israeli sovereignty while gaining functional autonomy, with the following exception: the Palestinian state would have full control over the *waqf* administration of al-Haram al-Sharif and full sovereignty over a road connecting the new Palestinian capital (on the outskirts of East Jeruslaem) with the Haram, by way of the Muslim Quarter of the Old City. At the same time, Israel would retain formal political sovereignty over the Palestinian-administered Temple Mount/al-Haram al-Sharif and a small area would be set aside atop the Temple Mount for Jewish worship. (This latter point would have represented a change in the *status quo* Moshe Dayan had established in 1967 when he banned any organized Jewish prayer in the Haram.)

Claiming to be shocked by Israel's position regarding the Temple Mount/al-Haram al-Sharif, the Palestinians dismissed these proposals out of hand. Leaders of the Palestinian delegation (including Mahmoud Abbas – Yasser Arafat's successor as president of the Palestinian Authority, as of January 2005) provoked their negotiating partners by casting doubt on the very notion that a Jewish temple had ever stood on the spot that Muslims themselves commonly refer to as *bayt al-maqdis* (a direct Arabic translation of *beit ha-miqdash*, "the house of the sanctuary" – the Hebrew term for the temple).[158] For their part, the Israelis refused to consider a complete abandonment of some kind of vestigial sovereignty claim to the Temple Mount. In an attempt to break the logjam, following the failure of the Camp David talks, President Clinton proposed – among various scenarios – that, while the surface of al-Haram al-Sharif would fall under Palestinian sovereignty, a final agreement could also recognize theoretical Jewish claims to the subterranean portions of the Temple Mount, where archaeological remains of the Second Temple lie buried. In practice, any excavation or tunneling work would require the joint agreement of the Israelis and Palestinians, which would mean an effective freeze on any such activity.[159] The mind-boggling complexity of such an arrangement, along with the ambiguity of its practical ramifications, highlights the difficulty of disentangling the rival claims to this magnetic pole of sacredness. The awkwardness of trying to separate the surface of the Temple Mount from its underside is an apt metaphor for the broader challenges involved in demarcating a definitive boundary between two peoples claiming the same land, of drawing a clear line between present and past, and of establishing a psychological distinction between the memory of dispossession and the fear of destruction.

As the failed Camp David talks of 2000 illustrated, the symbolic power of Jerusalem's holy places is intimately related to a fear of having their collective dignity violated on the part of both parties to the conflict. In the context of a partition of the city that would have signaled Israel's abandonment of its nationalist myth of an eternally unified Jerusalem, Israeli Prime Minister Barak felt he had to save face by retaining a symbolic toehold on the Temple Mount. For the Palestinians, any sharing of authority with the Israelis over the Haram was deemed utterly incompatible with the site's wholeness and purity as a Muslim place of worship and holy site. Moreover, the suggestion of Israeli sovereignty over the ground beneath the Temple Mount fed into the longstanding

Palestinian conviction that the Israelis would like to undermine the Muslim shrines from below.[160] Even a symbolic sharing of control – let alone sovereignty – over any part or aspect of the Haram would likely be seen among Palestinians as a mark of national humiliation and in much of the Muslim world as a selling out of Islamic interests. To realize the dream of Palestinian national self-determination on such a note of violation could have been portrayed by opponents of a peace deal as a fundamental contradiction in terms. With the failure of the Camp David summit, the Palestinian armed revolt and terror campaign that ensued (the al-Aqsa Intifada), and the electoral defeat of the Barak government, the two sides' positions on symbolic and pragmatic issues alike became dramatically polarized.

It is, then, impossible to dismiss the power of Jerusalem's sacred symbols to shape both sides' conceptions of national dignity and fears of national humiliation. Clearly, much more than the clash of material interests is at stake in such conflicts. The Temple Mount/al-Haram al-Sharif issue is unquestionably filled with more than enough explosive potential to blow any reasonable framework of negotiation to kingdom come.[161] Making compromises over this fraught issue might be all the harder in juxtaposition with broader concessions on matters of central significance to Israeli and Palestinian national identities and security interests. Agreeing on how to partition the lands of pre-1948 Palestine, how to balance Israel's concern for security with Palestinian demands for national dignity and territorial contiguity, Israeli insistence on maintaining its internal demographic status quo with Palestinian demands for the return of refugees to their ancestral homes – all this would be hard enough without adding Jerusalem's holy places to the equation. In the event that painful and controversial concessions are made on all these overarching issues, it may prove all the more difficult for either side to give way on its claims over sacred sites. Holding fast to uncompromising positions over Jerusalem's holy places may be political leaders' only way of saving face over the wholesale abandonment of hitherto unbending stances on other issues.

But having acknowledged that, it is important not to fall into the trap of regarding these symbols as though their power to shape politics emanated from an entirely self-contained sphere of sacredness. In Jerusalem, symbolic disputes are seamlessly intertwined with security concerns. The alleviation of the latter may modify many people's conception of the former. The close intermingling of Jewish and Arab neighborhoods in this city raises very pressing and immediate life-and-death concerns for

Israelis, who have repeatedly been targeted by ruthless suicide bombings along the main thoroughfares and shopping districts of the western part of town. The prospect of yielding control over any portion of East Jerusalem to a Palestinian state is highly threatening to Israelis as long as the Palestinian Authority is seen as providing safe shelter for organizations that cast the Palestinian–Israeli struggle as a war to the death between Islam and Judaism and that are officially and openly committed to the destruction of the State of Israel and dedicated to the murder of as many of its citizens as possible.[162] If the Palestinian Authority were to succeed in suppressing the activity of Hamas, Islamic Jihad, and their ilk, the idea of sharing sovereignty over East Jerusalem – and over mandatory Palestine as a whole – would become much less unpalatable for Israelis. Once again, the historical memory of suffering and the imminent threat of bloodshed act synergistically in dissuading Israelis from relinquishing control over any part of East Jerusalem. Diminishing the power of the second element of this equation would undercut the potency of the first. By the same token, the opportunity to rid themselves of Israel's intrusive control over their lives may ultimately motivate Palestinians in East Jerusalem and elsewhere to make painful concessions of their own and to rethink how much they are willing to sacrifice for the sake of gaining exclusive sovereignty over the Haram.

It would, then, be a mistake to view the disruptive power of the Temple Mount controversy and of the two peoples' associated memories and fears of violation as entirely precluding the possibility of reasonable compromise. The glimmer of a possible territorial and political settlement between Israelis and Palestinians may one day help dissipate the heavy fog of martyrdom that hangs low over Jerusalem's stones. The prospect of relieving the ongoing suffering brought on by Israeli military occupation, Palestinian terrorism, and general economic upheaval may counterbalance the memory of past suffering and sacrifice that confers such inestimable value upon uncontested possession of East Jerusalem and the Temple Mount. This was the assumption of the Israeli and Palestinian negotiators of the 1993 Oslo accords, who left the resolution of the Jerusalem question to the final stage of the process of compromise and accommodation that they were attempting to initiate.[163] Indeed, to discuss the dispute over Jerusalem as though the entire city were an undifferentiated mass and the rival claims to it a zero-sum game is misleading. Opinion surveys confirm that most Israeli Jews have little or no interest in the Arab neighborhoods in East Jerusalem outside of the Old City. Likewise, a slim majority of Palestinians evince little interest in pursuing claims to overwhelmingly Jewish West Jerusalem. It is essentially in the Old City, and particularly at the Temple Mount/al-Haram al-Sharif complex, that both sides' most intense sentiments of national and religious attachment to Jerusalem physically intersect.[164]

It is true that past experience offers little reason for optimism: particularly when it comes to symbolic issues, each side's definition of what constitute the non-negotiable elements of self-determination represents a violation of the other side's sense of collective dignity. Yet one can be allowed to hope that, at some point in the future, a de-escalation of polarizing violence will modify the psychological framework that has allowed the violation-volition complex in its most negative form to determine the dynamics of negotiations between the parties to the conflict. Greater freedom from the imminent threat of violence may allow imaginative leaders to act on their recognition that a compromise over the loci of national-religious sanctity may constitute the ultimate act of redemptive sanity.

CONCLUSION

What all of these cases suggest is that the power and meaning of national martyrdom and violation myths grow and decline, shift and change form, in the face of evolving socio-cultural conditions and power relationships.[165] National narratives of suffering and sacrifice do not have the power in and of themselves to send people flying at one another's throats. In the context of institutional and geopolitical arrangements that preclude the serious possibility of changing political boundaries or redistributing national territory, people may lose interest in hallowed tales about the shedding of their forefathers' blood at the hands of their enemies. Indeed, the mere passage of generations and cultivation of a skeptical public attitude towards political and cultural authority can engender cynicism about such foundational myths even in the midst of ongoing conflict. Yael Zerubavel provides a splendid example of this in discussing the evolution of the myth of Yosef Trumpeldor in contemporary Israeli society. A hero of the early Zionist settlement effort in Upper Galilee, Trumpeldor lost his life in defending the small outpost of Tel Hai against Arab attackers in 1920. As he expired in his comrades' arms, he is reputed to have uttered the words, "Never mind – it's worth dying for the country." Generations of Israelis have been raised on this story of noble self-sacrifice, and have gone on school field trips to visit the monument in Trumpeldor's honor at Tel Hai. So obsessively have history textbooks, school teachers, and scout-troop leaders dwelled on the inspiring theme of Trumpeldor's actions and words that many jaded Israelis are convinced that the operatic pathos of his famous last words are a complete fiction – a stereotypical nationalist cliché concocted in a bygone age of romantic naiveté. A widespread joke-turned-popular-belief suggests that Trumpeldor's last words were actually a foul Russian curse phonetically similar to the heroic Hebrew phrase. The irony is that the authenticity of the official story about Trumpeldor's final utterance is actually well attested and not disputed by historians. For once, the hero of the nationalist myth actually played his part to the hilt in real life. But a generation of Israelis tired of hearing about the Zionist pioneers' selfless spirit of sacrifice refuses to believe that anyone felled by a fatal gunshot wound would have either the inclination or the presence of mind to give vent to such a melodramatic outburst.[166]

This Israeli counter-example notwithstanding, it is at times when the sense of real, physical threat to the nation's existence or security is most acute that nationalist myths of violation, martyrdom, and sacrifice are most likely to become the prisms through which the world is seen, the dominant frameworks of political understanding and decision-making. In this role, they can serve to accentuate the sense of existential threat and the tendency to lash out desperately, as current enemies are identified with primordial foes and immediate dangers with age-old patterns of violation. The Yugoslav example is a classic demonstration of the powerfully self-fulfilling quality of such perspectives.

Yet even under the bleakest of circumstances, the element of human choice should not be discounted. Nationalist ideologies do not have the intrinsic power to turn human beings into glassy-eyed zombies willing and eager to butcher one another in the names of their martyred forebears. People choose how to interpret their nation's history of suffering. To take a final example from Zerubavel's Israeli case study, the lessons to be learned from the desperate stands taken against the Jews' ancient Roman oppressors by the followers of Bar Kokhba (see Chapters 1 and 2) and the fighters at Masada have been the subject of public disputes. In the 1980s, critics began to call into question the way such tragic episodes were taught in the country's schools and employed in political discourse. Rather than drawing inspiration from the readiness of their ancient forebears to lay down their lives for a doomed cause, the critics argued, Israelis should draw sobering conclusions from their fatal mistakes. The Jewish revolts against the Romans brought catastrophic destruction and exile upon the Jewish people – consequences that were inevitable and entirely foreseeable, given the enormous disparity in power between Judaean rebels and imperial Rome's legions. The moral of these stories was not that Israel must always fight for its national objectives against all odds, but that it should make careful distinctions between vital interests and unattainable and potentially self-destructive dreams (e.g. between survival as a state and incorporation of the West Bank and Gaza into the territory of the state). The application of critical analysis could convert myths of violation from inspirations for desperate defiance into object lessons in how *not* to act if national survival was the ultimate rationale for the existence of the state.[167]

For their part, Palestinians face a choice between the blood-crazed religious messianism of organizations such as Hamas and the practical possibilities of compromise offered by the late Yasser Arafat's successors in the leadership of the Palestinian Authority. Hamas' founders and leaders have portrayed the struggle over Palestine, not as a conflict between rival nations with overlapping territorial claims, but as the embodiment of a transcendent struggle between Islam and Judaism that can only end with the eradication of all Jews from Palestine and a resultant End of History.[168] For Hamas, the religious overtones of the struggle have become its central theme, its nationalist aspects reduced to the status of superficial epiphenomena. The more suffering and blood-shed is incurred in this apocalyptic war to end all wars, the firmer becomes the assurance of a final reward for the Muslim faithful. Yet as the conflict drags on from year to year with no tangible benefit to be seen, more and more Palestinians may turn away from this eschatological vicious circle and back to a more bounded, pragmatic, nationalist vision that leaves open the door to a compromise that can limit human suffering instead of seeking redemption through it.[169]

The cultural politics of the geopolitically much less constrained Alamo debate demonstrates how – at least under relatively ideal circumstances – national violation myths can be adapted to serve multiple political agendas, including pluralistic visions of national (or, in the case of Texas, sub-national) identity. The most effective strategy adopted by Texas institutions and museums in trying to maintain the function of the Alamo as a focal point for Texan identity has been to co-opt non-Anglos into the story of the Alamo. Highlighting the role of figures such as Gregorio Esparza and Juan Seguín in the original fight for Texan independence and the contribution of Adina De Zavala to the preservation of the Alamo shrine is designed to shift the emphasis of the Alamo myth from the confrontation between Anglos and Mexicans to the ethno-culturally pluralistic legacy of a Texas that was created through the joint efforts of Anglos and Latinos with a shared commitment to political freedom and democratic government. The continued interpretive disputes notwithstanding, such approaches have softened the edges of the debate. And to the extent that the public comes to view some of the new, self-consciously inclusive, approaches to history as themselves predictably didactic and preachy, it may remain disinclined to revert to the equally cliché-ridden scripts of traditional martyrdom myths.

It is, after all, profoundly ironic that myths of national violation are so commonly used to impose deterministic constraints on the exercise of national self-determination. In theory, the independent nation is idealized as a historical free agent, able to choose its destiny without regard for external constraints, in accordance only with its ancestral traditions and internal deliberations. Yet if, in practice, the exercise of national volition continues to revolve obsessively around a sense of victimhood and a commitment to the reversal of violations past, how much freedom of choice is there left for the nation to enjoy? It is by reinterpreting violation myths to open up elastic new possibilities for peacemaking and coalition-building, that a negative conception of national liberty (freedom *from* external oppression) can be expanded into a genuine form of self-determination.[170]

* * *

Myths of violation are closely linked to conceptions of national chosenness, for to be a martyr is to have a special role to play in human salvation. As with the violation-volition nexus, the idea of chosenness helps shape the ideological and psychological frameworks within which national debates unfold, but those debates can lead to a variety of potential conclusions. Some view their chosenness as a license to kill, while others feel that it imposes a special set of obligations towards the rest of humanity – a notion that is itself replete with contradictory implications, as Chapter 4 will show.

END NOTES

1 See, for example, Brian Vick's discussion of nineteenth-century German liberal nationalists' idealization of national unification and independence as a framework for absolute freedom from the influence of external forces. Brian Vick, *Defining Germany: The 1848 Frankfurt Parliamentarians and National Identity* (Cambridge, Mass.: Harvard University Press, 2002), ch. 6.

2 Vamik Volkan, *Bloodlines: From Ethnic Pride to Ethnic Terrorism* (New York: Farrar, Straus and Giroux, 1997), 48–49 and *passim*. Volkan illustrates his

point with a list of examples similar to, though not identical with, those I employ at the end of this paragraph. I came across Volkan's book after having first drafted this section. On the theme of martyrdom and the mythologizing of defeat in nationalist ideology and symbolism, see also Anthony Smith, *Chosen Peoples*, ch. 9; Wolfgang Schivelbusch, *The Culture of Defeat: On National Trauma, Mourning, and Recovery*, trans. Jefferson Chase (New York: Henry Holt, 2001).

3 On the ways in which nationalist mythmaking can transform calamitous military defeats into rallying points for collective self-assertion, see Schivelbusch, *Culture of Defeat*, Introduction and *passim*.

4 Brian Porter, *When Nationalism Began to Hate: Imagining Modern Politics in Nineteenth-Century Poland* (New York: Oxford University Press, 2000), ch. 1.

5 Paul Cohen, *China Unbound: Evolving Perspectives on the Chinese Past* (London: RoutledgeCurzon, 2003), 158. My thanks to Erez Manela for this reference.

6 Article 1, Section 1 of the Texas Constitution emphasizes that: "Texas is a free and independent State, subject only to the Constitution of the United States . . . " The constitution's full text can be downloaded from: http://www.capitol.state.tx.us/txconst/toc.html. T. R. Fehrenbach notes that well into the twentieth century, "Texas history was taught in Texas schools before the study of the United States began." T. R. Fehrenbach, *Lone Star: A History of Texas and the Texans* (1968; New York: Collier, 1980), 712.

7 Michael Keating argues convincingly that national identity need not be viewed as an all-or-nothing proposition. In practice, many people identify with multiple frameworks of national identity, one often embedded within, or overlapping with, another. Michael Keating, *Plurinational Democracy: Stateless Nations in a Post-Sovereignty Era* (Oxford: Oxford University Press, 2001), ch. 1 and *passim*.

8 Hawaii was a kingdom before its annexation by the United States.

9 This background narrative draws on the following sources: Jan Bazant, *A Concise History of Mexico from Hidalgo to Cardenas: 1805–1940* (Cambridge: Cambridge University Press, 1977), ch. 2; Nettie Lee Benson, "Territorial Integrity in Mexican Politics, 1821–1833," in Jaime E. Rodriguez, ed., *The Independence of Mexico and the Creation of the New Nation* (Los Angeles: UCLA Latin American Center Publications and Irvine: Mexico/Chicano Program, 1989); Richard R. Flores, *Remembering the Alamo: Memory, Modernity, and the Master Symbol* (Austin: University of Texas Press, 2002), 22–31; Stephen L. Hardin, *Texian Iliad: A Military History of the Texas Revolution, 1835–1836* (Austin: University of Texas Press, 1994); Andreas V. Reichstein, *Rise of the Lone Star: The Making of Texas*, trans. Jeanne R. Willson (College Station: Texas A&M University Press, 1989); Randy Roberts and James S. Olson, *A Line in the Sand: The Alamo in Blood and Memory* (New York: The Free Press, 2001); Andrés Reséndez, *Changing National Identities at the Frontier: Texas and New Mexico, 1800–1850* (Cambridge: Cambridge University Press, 2005), ch. 5.

10 James L. Haley, *Sam Houston* (Norman: Oklahoma University Press, 2002), 119 and 124.

11 One Louis Rose is said to have escaped the Alamo on the evening before it fell. Walter Lord, "Myths and Realities of the Alamo," *The American West*, vol. 5, no. 3 (May 1968), 18–25.

12 Navarro was actually of Corsican background.

13 See Margaret Swett Henson, *Lorenzo de Zavala: The Pragmatic Idealist* (Fort Worth: Texas Christian University Press, 1996).

14 Rodolfo Acuña, *Occupied America: A History of Chicanos*, 4th edn (New York: Longman, 2000), ch. 3; José E. Limón, *Dancing with the Devil: Society and Cultural Poetics in Mexican–American South Texas* (Madison: University of Wisconsin Press, 1994), 22–26.

15 By myth, in this context, I mean the package of selected historical records, fictions, interpretations, and images that play a role in defining and maintaining collective identity and imparting to those who partake of that identity a sense of a common past, distinctive character, and shared destiny. On myths' central importance to nationhood, see Anthony Smith, *Ethnic Origins of Nations* (Oxford: Blackwell, 1986), 13–16.

16 Holly Beachley Brear, *Inherit the Alamo: Myth and Ritual at an American Shrine* (Austin: University of Texas Press, 1995), ch. 6.

17 As Holly Beachley Brear puts it, according to the traditional myth, "it is the Texans' choice to die rather than the Mexicans' choice to defeat them." Brear, *Inherit the Alamo*, 35.

18 Entry on "Alamo Cenotaph" in *The Handbook of Texas Online* (website maintained by the Texas State Historical Association), http://www.tsha.utexas.edu/handbook/online/articles/view/AA/gga2.html.

19 Roberts and Olson, *Line in the Sand*, 172–173.

20 Brear, *Inherit the Alamo*, chs. 2 and 5.

21 Martin Jessop Price and Bluma L. Trell, *Coins and their Cities: Architecture on the Ancient Coins of Greece, Rome, and Palestine* (London: Vecchi and Sons; Detroit: Wayne State University Press, 1977), 177–179.

22 S. Safrai, "The Era of the Mishnah and Talmud (70–640)," in H. H. Ben-Sasson *et al.*, eds., *A History of the Jewish People* (Cambridge, Mass.: Harvard University Press, 1976), 319–322, 325–330.

23 The shift in importance from Temple to synagogue was, of course, the culmination of a long process of historical development. By the same token, the Temple had already long served as a focal point for Jewish identity in the Diaspora during its existence, as the memory of the Temple was to do following its destruction.

24 Anthony J. Saldarini, "Good from Evil: The Rabbinic Response," in Andrea M. Berlin and J. Andrew Overman, eds., *The First Jewish Revolt: Archaeology, History, and Ideology* (London: Routledge, 2002), 222–223.

25 On this theme, see Neil Asher Silberman, "The First Revolt and its Afterlife," in Berlin and Overman, eds., *First Jewish Revolt*, 238–240.

26 Yosef Hayim Yerushalmi, *Zakhor: Jewish History and Jewish Memory* (Seattle: University of Washington Press, 1982), ch. 2; David G. Roskies, *Against the Apocalypse: Responses to Catastrophe in Modern Jewish Culture* (Cambridge, Mass.: Harvard University Press, 1984), ch. 2; H. H. Ben-Sasson, "The Middle Ages," in Ben-Sasson *et al.*, eds., *History of the Jewish People*, 417–418; David R. Blumenthal, "God at the Center: Selected Meditations on Jewish Spirituality," *Studies in Formative Spirituality*, vol. 19, no. 3 (November 1988), 267–281 (esp. 268 and 270–271).

27 Nachman Ben-Yehuda, *The Masada Myth: Collective Memory and Mythmaking in Israel* (Madison: University of Wisconsin Press, 1995). See also Yael Zerubavel, *Recovered Roots: Collective Memory and the Making of Israeli National Tradition* (Chicago: University of Chicago Press, 1995), chs. 5, 8, and 11.

28 See the preceding chapter for a fuller summary of Yael Zerubavel's concept of Zionism's "placing parentheses" around diasporic history.

29 Ben-Yehuda, *Masada Myth*, 128–129.

30 This narrative draws heavily on the following publications: Bernard Wasserstein, *Divided Jerusalem: The Struggle for the Holy City*, 2nd edn (New Haven: Yale University Press, 2002), ch. 10; Daniel Bertrand Monk, *An Aesthetic Occupation: The Immediacy of Architecture and the Palestine Conflict* (Durham, N.C.: Duke University Press, 2002); Karen Armstrong, *Jerusalem: One City, Three Faiths* (New York: HarperCollins, 1996), 380–382.

31 Armstrong, *Jerusalem*, ch. 12.

32 The association of al-Buraq with the Western Wall appears to be a mid-nineteenth-century innovation associated with Muslim concerns over intensified Jewish interest in the site. The small mosque marking the location of al-Buraq is located on the *inside* of the Wall, within the al-Haram al-Sharif plaza controlled by the Muslim *waqf* authority. Shmuel Berkovitz, *The Temple Mount and the Western Wall in Israeli Law* (Jerusalem: The Jerusalem Institute for Israel Studies and the Teddy Kollek Center for Jerusalem Studies, 2001), 22–23. Rashid Khalidi claims that the tradition antedates the nineteenth century, but – in an endnote – acknowledges some inconsistencies about this in the Islamic sources. Rashid Khalidi, *Palestinian Identity: The Construction of Modern National Consciousness* (New York: Columbia University Press, 1997), 17 and 216, note 25.

33 Y. Porath, *The Emergence of the Palestinian–Arab National Movement, 1918–1929* (London: Frank Cass, 1974), ch. 7.

34 Yaacov Shavit notes that Revisionist leader Vladimir (Ze'ev) Jabotinsky was caught off guard by the Betar demonstration. Yaacov Shavit, *Jabotinsky and the Revisionist Movement, 1925–1948* (London: Frank Cass, 1988), 90.

35 Porath, *Palestinian-Arab Movement, 1918–1929*, ch. 7. For an attempt to exonerate the Mufti of responsibility for inciting violence, see Philip Mattar, *The Mufti of Jerusalem: Al-Hajj Amin al-Husayni and the Palestinian National Movement*, rev. edn (New York: Columbia University Press, 1988), ch. 3, esp. p. 49. For a critique of Mattar's approach, see the discussion in Monk, *Aesthetic Occupation*, 77.

36 Yehoshua Porath, *The Palestinian Arab National Movement: From Riots to Rebellion, 1929–1939* (London: Frank Cass, 1977), 6–8.

37 The head of the Jewish Agency's Political Department, Labor Zionist leader Chaim Arlosoroff, wondered "how did it happen that around us a system of provocations should develop, built up and directed with cunning; that we make out of an issue which has never been the centre of our world [the Wailing Wall] a new idol . . . [?]" Cited in Monk, *Aesthetic Occupation*, 130.

38 Anita Shapira, *Land and Power: The Zionist Resort to Force, 1881–1948*, trans. William Templer (New York: Oxford University Press, 1992), 173–186.

39 Such charges had been raised some years earlier, but the 1929 riots and the airing of the dispute before the subsequent investigatory commission brought them to the foreground of nascent Palestinian Arab consciousness. See Monk, *Aesthetic Occupation, passim*.

40 Avraham Sela, "The 'Wailing Wall' Riots (1929) as a Watershed in the Palestine Conflict," *Muslim World*, vol. 84, no. 1–2 (January–April 1994), 60–94; Porath, *Palestinian-Arab Movement 1918–1929*, ch. 7 and p. 308 and Porath, *Palestinian Arab Movement 1929–1939*, 8–13, 295–296.

41 This discussion draws heavily on the following sources: Flores, *Remembering the Alamo*, ch. 4; Brear, *Inherit the Alamo*, 89–94; Roberts and Olson, *Line in the Sand*, ch. 7.

42 See, for instance, Roberts and Olson, *Line in the Sand*, 209.

43 Thankfully, unlike the ill-fated Bolshevik exile, De Zavala lived into advanced old age and died a natural death.

44 Flores, *Remembering the Alamo*, 70.

45 Ibid., Conclusion.

46 Ibid., ch. 4. See also Roberts and Olson, *Line in the Sand*, ch. 7.

47 Flores, *Remembering the Alamo*, 84–86.

48 Excerpt from 1908 article on De Zavala published in the magazine *Human Life for June*, in Flores, *Remembering the Alamo*, 68.

49 A comparable case is presented by Jovita Gonazalez, the upper-class, university-trained Tejana folklorist of the 1920s and 1930s, whose ambivalent stance towards Mexican–American rural lower classes in general and insurgents/bandits in particular is explored in Limón, *Dancing with the Devil*, ch. 3. (My thanks to John Tutino for this reference.)

50 See Roberts and Olson, *Line in the Sand*, ch. 11.

51 The role of Tejanos in the Texas Revolution is also highlighted in Joseph Tovares' 2004 PBS television documentary, "Remember the Alamo." John Lee Hancock's 2004 feature film, *The Alamo*, also incorporates elements of the new historiography into his retelling of the story. See Randall M. Miller's review of these two films in *American Historical Review*, vol. 110, no. 2 (April 2005), 485–486.

52 For an account of some of the disputes that have raged over the administration of the Alamo and the adjacent municipal square, see Jan Jarboe, "We Will Never Surrender or Retreat," *Texas Monthly*, vol. 22, no. 5

(May 1994), 124–128. See also the exchange between DRT critic Holly Beachley Brear and the Alamo's official historian and curator, Richard Bruce Winders: Holly Beachley Brear, "The Alamo's Selected Past," *Cultural Resource Management*, vol. 22, no. 8 (1999), 9–11; Richard Bruce Winders, "A Response to the Alamo's Selected Past," *Cultural Resource Management*, vol. 23, no. 3 (2000), 31.

53 Timothy M. Matovina, *The Alamo Remembered: Tejano Accounts and Perspectives* (Austin: University of Texas Press, 1995), 62–72. Santa Anna ordered that Esparza's body be turned over to his family for burial rather than burned along with the rest of the Alamo defenders, in honor of his prior service as a soldier in the Mexican army and the fact that his brother had fought on the Mexican side in an earlier battle.

54 Gary Cartwright, "Divine Secrets of the Alamo Sisterhood," *Texas Monthly*, vol. 32, no. 5 (May 2004), 62–68.

55 This quotation is taken from, and these observations are based on, the DRT's glossy fold-out publication that reproduces the contents of the Wall of History display, sold at the gift shop on the Alamo grounds. The quoted text appears at the bottom of the publication's final panel.

56 The DRT's website (http://www.drtl.org/History/Alamo4.asp) also includes information on De Zavala's contributions. Both the website and the Wall of History point to the role of Texas' then lieutenant-governor in the destruction of the second floor of the convent/barracks building without mentioning the part played by Driscoll and her faction of the DRT.

57 Matovina, *Alamo Remembered*, Conclusion.

58 See Limón, *Dancing with the Devil*, 22–26.

59 Rolando J. Romero, "The Alamo, Slavery and the Politics of Memory," http://www.sip.uiuc.edu/rromero/alamo.htm (extended version of author's identically titled chapter in Arturo J. Aldama and Naomi H. Quiñonez, eds., *Decolonial Voices: Chicana and Chicano Cultural Studies in the 21st Century* [Bloomington: Indiana University Press, 2002]).

60 Dan Kilgore, *How Did Davy Die?* (College Station: Texas A&M University Press, 1978), 14–17 and *passim;* José Enrique de la Peña, *With Santa Anna in Texas: A Personal Narrative of the Revolution*, trans. and ed. Carmen Perry (College Station: Texas A&M University Press, 1975), 53–54. James E. Crisp, one of the leading advocates of the de la Peña diary's authenticity and reliability, discusses the ins and outs of the de la Peña and Crockett controversies in his *Sleuthing the Alamo: Davy Crockett's Last Stand and Other Mysteries* (New York: Oxford University Press, 2005), chs. 2–4. See also Roberts and Olson, *Line in the Sand*, ch. 10. On the fascination with Crockett's choice of rifles, see Bill Ball, "The Most Famous Rifle of Texas! Recreating Colonel Crockett's Rifle at the Battle of the Alamo," *Guns Magazine*, January 2004.

61 De la Peña, *With Santa Anna*, 53.

62 Hate mail addressed to historian Dan Kilgore, as quoted in Crisp, *Sleuthing the Alamo*, 105.

63 Crisp, *Sleuthing the Alamo*, ch. 4. I am no expert on the de la Peña diary controversy, although James Crisp's arguments strike me as convincing. Thomas Ricks Lindley questions the authenticity and reliability of the de la Peña diary in *Alamo Traces: New Evidence and New Conclusions* (Lanham: Republic of Texas Press, 2003), 260–274, 346–363. From the point of view of my own discussion here, it does not matter whether or not the de la Peña diary contains genuine eyewitness testimony. What is interesting is the heated nature of the emotions aroused by the controversy.

64 Brear, *Inherit the Alamo*, 122. Brear – herself a critic of the DRT's interpretation of history – has suggested that many of the attacks on the DRT's custodianship of the Alamo are themselves reflections of male antagonism towards female control of a shrine to masculinity. Brear at one point argues that the very concept of historical truth as applied to the Alamo is nothing more than a gendered construction employed to undermine female authority over the shrine to Texas Liberty! Assaulted by fact-wielding chauvinists, the DRT may thus have a new claim to the hallowed nationalist role of victimhood. Holly Beachley Brear, "We Run the Alamo, and You Don't: Alamo Battles of Ethnicity and Gender," in W. Fitzhugh Brundage, ed., *Where these Memories Grow: History, Memory and Southern Identity* (Chapel Hill: University of North Carolina Press, 2000).

65 See, for example, Romero, "The Alamo"; Suzanne Bost, "Women and Chile at the Alamo: Feeding US Colonial Mythology," *Nepantla: Views from South*, vol. 4, no. 3 (2003), 493–522.

66 Acuña, *Occupied America*, ch. 3.

67 Ibid., 367.

68 On the centrality of the sense of victimhood to sectarian identities in Northern Ireland, see Mike Morrissey and Marie Smyth, *Northern Ireland After the Good Friday Agreement: Victims, Grievance and Blame* (London: Pluto Press, 2002).

69 This narrative and analysis draws on the following sources: Marc Mulholland, *The Longest War: Northern Ireland's Troubled History* (Oxford: Oxford University Press, 2002), 98–99 and *passim*; Chris Ryder and Vincent Kearney, *Drumcree: The Orange Order's Last Stand* (London: Methuen, 2002), ch. 1; Dominic Bryan, "Drumcree and 'The Right to March': Orangeism, Ritual and Politics in Northern Ireland," in T. G. Fraser, ed., *The Irish Parading Tradition: Following the Drum* (Basingstoke: Macmillan; New York: St. Martin's Press, 2000); Dominic Bryan, *Orange Parades: The Politics of Ritual, Tradition and Control* (London: Pluto Press, 2000); Ruth Dudley Edwards, *The Faithful Tribe: An Intimate Portrait of the Loyal Institutions* (London: HarperCollins, 1999); Michael Ignatieff, *Blood and Belonging: Journeys into the New Nationalism* (1993; New York: Farrar, Straus & Giroux, 1995), ch. 6.

70 See James Loughlin, "Parades and Politics: Liberal Governments and the Orange Order, 1880–86," in Fraser, ed., *Irish Parading Tradition*.

71 On the ethnicization of Northern Ireland's sectarian division, see Máiréad Nic Craith, *Culture and Identity Politics in Northern Ireland* (Basingstoke: Palgrave Macmillan, 2003), esp. ch. 4.

72 See Thomas Hennessey, *The Northern Ireland Peace Process: Ending the Troubles?* (New York: Palgrave, 2001), part IV.

73 On the traditional function of Orange parades as a unifying force among Ulster's diverse Protestant denominations and political parties, see Neil Jarman, "For God and Ulster: Blood and Thunder Bands and Loyalist Political Culture," in Fraser, ed., *Irish Parading Tradition*, 159–160 and Dominic Bryan, "Drumcree," in ibid., 201 and 203–205.

74 Jarman, "For God and Ulster."

75 This discussion of the Drumcree marches draws extensively upon the following sources: Ryder and Kearney, *Drumcree*, pp. 31–32, chs. 3–4, and *passim*; Morrissey and Smyth, *Northern Ireland After the Good Friday Agreement*, 23 and 50.

76 See Bryan, *Orange Parades, passim* on how evolving historical and socio-political conditions have transformed the meanings and perceptions of the marches. For a more innocuous example of how shifts in historical contexts transform the symbolic meaning and power of traditions, see David Cannadine's discussion of the use of carriages in British royal processions: David Cannadine, "The Context, Performance and Meaning of Ritual: The British Monarchy and the 'Invention of Tradition', *c.* 1820–1977," in Eric Hobsbawm and Terence Ranger, eds., *The Invention of Tradition* (Cambridge: Cambridge University Press, 1983), esp. 142–143 and 156.

77 See Ryder and Kearney, *Drumcree*, 105.

78 Remarks by Harold McCusker as quoted in Bryan, *Orange Parades*, 161–162.

79 Mulholland, *The Longest War*, 98–99, 172.

80 On the central role played by perceptions of lost or threatened status in fuelling ethnic conflicts, see Donald L. Horowitz, *Ethnic Groups in Conflict*, 2nd edn (Berkeley: University of California Press, 2000), ch. 5.

81 Ryder and Kearney, *Drumcree*, ch. 4.

82 Dominic Bryan, T.G. Fraser, and Seamus Dunn, *Political Rituals: Loyalist Parades in Portadown* (Coleraine, Northern Ireland: Centre for the Study of Conflict, University of Ulster, 1995), also available online at http://cain.ulst.ac.uk/csc/reports/rituals.htm, section entitled "Update 1995."

83 See the Parades Commission's website: http://www.paradescommission.org/index.cfm.

84 As of 2005, the Orange Order continued to request permission to conduct its marches along its traditional return route, and the Parades Commission continued to ban it from the Garvaghy Road section of that route. "Determination Made in Relation to the Portadown District LOL [Loyal Orange Lodge] No. 1 Parade Notified to Take Place in Portadown on Sunday, 24 April 2005," Parades Commission document available as download at http://www.paradescommission.org/parades/Parade.cfm?id=10061.

85 Ryder and Kearney, *Drumcree*, chs. 6–7, 11–12.

86 Bryan, *Orange Parades*, 176–181 and *passim*.

87 In March 2005, the Orange Order broke its hundred-year-old official ties to David Trimble's Ulster Unionist Party. The Order's leadership now tends to support Ian Paisley's Democratic Unionist Party, which opposes the Good Friday Agreement. "Orange Order Severs Links to UUP," BBC News (UK edition) website, 12 March 2005, http://news.bbc.co.uk/1/hi/northern_ireland/4342429.stm. On the other hand, Paisley's DUP gained more votes than the UUP in the November 2003 elections to the Northern Ireland Assembly, calling into question the UUP's status as representative of the "mainstream" of Unionist opinion. See below.

88 Hennessey, *Northern Ireland Peace Process*, 197.

89 Nicholas Watt and Angelique Chrisafis, "Adams Urges Bill of Rights to Keep Peace Process Alive," *The Guardian*, 5 February 2004.

90 "A Generous Offer of Murder," *The Economist*, 12 March 2005, 56; Lexington, "The Last-Chance Saloon," *The Economist*, 17 March 2005, 42; Simon Freeman, "Adams Calls on IRA to End Armed Struggle," (London) *Times Online*, 6 April 2005, http://www.timesonline.co.uk/article/0,19809-1557645,00.html.

91 "IRA Says Armed Campaign Is Over," BBC News World Edition, 28 July 2005, http://news.bbc.co.uk/1/hi/northern_ireland/4720863.stm; "IRA 'Has Destroyed All its Arms'," BBC News World Edition, 26 September 2005, http://news.bbc.co.uk/2/hi/uk_news/northern_ireland/4283444.stm.

92 "NI Sees 'Worst Rioting in Years,'" BBC News World Edition, 11 September 2005, http://news.bbc.co.uk/2/hi/uk_news/northern_ireland/4234626.stm.

93 Smith, *Chosen Peoples*, ch. 9 and *passim*.

94 A watershed event in this process was the 1915 uprising by dispossessed and impoverished Tejano farmers with the encouragement of Mexican revolutionaries from across the border. The uprising was brutally crushed by the Texas Rangers and led to an intensification of the racialized segregation of Latinos in Texas. Yet by the same token, in the aftermath of the failed revolt, Tejano elites definitively dissociated themselves from the rhetoric and ideology of secessionism that had animated the rebellion and focused their energies more wholeheartedly on striving for greater substantive and symbolic inclusion of their community in the civic and political life of Texas. Benjamin Heber Johnson, *Revolution in Texas: How a Forgotten Rebellion and its Bloody Suppression Turned Mexicans into Americans* (New Haven: Yale University Press, 2003).

95 See Chapter 5 for a discussion of the relationship between civic and ethnic frameworks of national identity.

96 Donald Horowitz argues that a (usually) irrational fear of collective annihilation lies at the bottom of many ethnic groups' seemingly exaggerated responses to any real or imagined slight at the hands of their rivals. Horowitz, *Ethnic Groups in Conflict*, 175–179.

97 During the Spurs' triumphal parade through "the Alamo City" following their victory in the 2003 NBA championships 300,000 fans lined the streets of San Antonio. Sonja Garza, "Fans Flock to the River Walk," *San Antonio*

Express-News, web-posted 19 June 2003: http://www.mysanantonio.com/
specials/spurschamps/stories/1014060.shtml.

98 As Michel Winock makes clear, different aspects of the Joan of Arc myth
lent themselves to exploitation by rival ideological currents in nineteenth-
and twentieth-century France. Michel Winock, "Jeanne d'Arc," in Pierre
Nora, ed., *Les Lieux de mémoire*, vol. III: *Les France*, part 3: *De l'Archive à
l'emblème* (Paris: Gallimard, 1992).

99 Jules Michelet, as quoted in Winock, "Jeanne d'Arc," 702.

100 See the image of Joan inspiring French troops "on the road to victory" on a
World War I propaganda poster, reproduced in Régine Pernoud and Marie
Véronique Clin, *Joan of Arc: Her Story*, trans. and rev. Jeremy du Quesnay
Adams (New York: St. Martin's Press, 1998), between pp. 164 and 165. See
also Stéphane Audoin-Rouzeau and Annette Becker, *14–18: Understanding
the Great* War, trans. Catherine Temerson (New York: Hill and Wang/
Farrar Straus and Giroux, 2002), 130–131. On an idealized image of Joan
from the sixteenth century, see Claude-Gilbert Dubois, "Rôle historique et
fonction prophétique de Jeanne d'Arc dans *Les merveilleuses Victoires des
femmes* de Guillaume Postel (1553)," in Jean Maurice and Daniel Couty,
eds., *Images de Jeanne d'Arc* (Paris: Presses Universitaires de France, 2000).

101 Cecilia O'Leary, *To Die For: The Paradox of American Patriotism* (Princeton:
Princeton University Press, 1999), 102. On the myth of the Lost Cause, see
also Schivelbusch, *Culture of Defeat*, ch. 1.

102 Roberts and Olson, *Line in the Sand*, 144.

103 To be sure, this cannot be viewed as the main source of military discipline
during the war. British, Dominion, and colonial soldiers fought on during
1914–18 even though they were stationed on foreign soil and the English
Channel or open ocean separated their loved ones back home from the
German foe. On the mechanisms for sustaining British troop morale during
the Great War see J. G. Fuller, *Troop Morale and Popular Culture in the British
and Dominion Armies, 1914–1918* (Oxford: Oxford University Press, 1990).

104 Stéphane Audoin-Rouzeau, *Men at War, 1914–1918: National Sentiment and
Trench Journalism in France during the First World War*, trans. Helen
McPhail (Oxford: Berg, 1992), ch. 5, esp. 128–135; Audoin-Rouzeau and
Becker, *14–18*, 45–54.

105 The more the subordinate/sheltered status of women is seen as a distinctive
attribute and essential quality of a community's religio-national identity, the
more threats to, or encroachments on, that status are viewed as attacks on
the nation's essence. For a singularly paradoxical example of this, see
Douglas Northrop, "Nationalizing Backwardness: Gender, Empire, and
Uzbek Identity," in Ronald Grigor Suny and Terry Martin, eds., *A State of
Nations: Empire and Nation-Making in the Age of Lenin and Stalin* (New
York: Oxford University Press, 2001). Northrop points out that Soviet
ethnographers of the 1920s designated the veiling and seclusion of women in
parts of Muslim Central Asia as important distinguishing characteristics of
the newly formalized Uzbek nationality. Northrop contends that, when a

Soviet cultural-modernization campaign later in the same decade targeted the very social practices that had been highlighted as markers of Uzbek identity, the indigenous backlash was all the more intense because there was no alternative, "authentically Uzbek," socio-cultural framework of national identity available for people turn to.

106 The Bosnian Serb militias' conduct toward Muslim communities during the Bosnian war of 1992–95 is among the most notorious recent examples of this phenomenon. See Eric D. Weitz, *A Century of Genocide: Utopias of Race and Nation* (Princeton: Princeton University Press, 2003), ch. 4. On atrocities against civilians during the First World War, see Audoin-Rouzeau and Becker, *14–18*, ch. 2.

107 See Vladimir Tismaneanu, *Fantasies of Salvation: Democracy, Nationalism, and Myth in Post-Communist Europe* (Princeton: Princeton University Press, 1998).

108 See the discussion in Tom Jackson, "Demonization and Defence of the Serbs: Balkanist Discourses During the Break-Up of Yugoslavia," *Slovo*, vol. 16, no. 2 (Autumn 2004), 107–124. An influential book that many critics perceived as representative of an overly deterministic outlook on the Yugoslav wars is Robert D. Kaplan, *Balkan Ghosts: A Journey through History* (New York: St. Martin's Press, 1993), the first part of which deals with the lands of Yugoslavia from a rather bleak historical perspective. Of course, given the history of the region, it's hard to see how one could treat it from a jolly historical perspective.

109 Bogdan Denitch writes: "Rather than being caused by a popular upsurge of national hate from below, the civil war was the result of policy decisions from the top combined with an all-too-effective use of the mass media, especially television." Bogdan Denitch, *Ethnic Nationalism: The Tragic Death of Yugoslavia* (Minneapolis: University of Minnesota Press, 1994), 62. In their influential study of Yugoslavia's collapse (which also appeared as a six-part documentary film) Laura Silber and Allan Little argue that "Yugoslavia was, in many ways, better placed than any other Communist state to make the transition to multi-party democracy, either as a single state, or as a group of successor states ... This chance was deliberately snuffed out." They do go on to concede that "in retrospect the appearance of a stable and prosperous Yugoslavia may have been deceptive. Ethnic grievances had been suppressed, not dispelled, by the centralized Communist system." In fact, I would argue that this concession goes too far in the opposite direction, making it sound as though ethnic tensions had remained static but suppressed under Communism, rather than developing in dynamic interaction with the Communist regime. Laura Silber and Alan Little, *Yugoslavia: Death of a Nation*, rev. edn (New York: Penguin, 1997), 26. V. P. Gagnon, Jr. argues that ethnic conflicts were engineered by self-interested Serb and Croat elites as a means of *demobilizing* the masses – i.e. diverting them from rallying behind substantive movements for political and economic reform. V. P. Gagnon,

Jr., *The Myth of Ethnic War: Serbia and Croatia in the 1990s* (Ithaca: Cornell University Press, 2004), Conclusion and *passim*. For a brief overview of the debates about the role of historical memory in Yugoslavia, see the opening pages of Peter Fritzsche, "The Case of Modern Memory," *Journal of Modern History*, vol. 73, no. 1 (March 2001), 87–117.

110 "Annex: Demographic Characteristics of Yugoslavia in the Late 1980s," in Thomas S. Szayna, ed., *Identifying Potential Ethnic Conflict: Application of a Process Model* (Santa Monica, Calif.: RAND, 2000).

111 Andrew Baruch Wachtel, *Making a Nation, Breaking a Nation: Literature and Cultural Politics in Yugoslavia* (Stanford: Stanford University Press, 1998), ch. 4; Slavenka Drakulić, *The Balkan Express: Fragments From the Other Side of War* (New York: Norton, 1993), 49–52 and *passim*; Roger Cohen, *Hearts Grown Brutal: Sagas of Sarajevo* (New York: Random House, 1998), 120–121, 156–158, and *passim*.

112 For a detailed and damning dissection of Milošević's role in the Yugoslav catastrophe, see Silber and Little, *Yugoslavia*.

113 Ignatieff, *Blood and Belonging*, ch. 1. On the vandalizing of the Jasenovac museum by Croat militias in 1991 during the Croat–Serb war, see ibid., 31–35.

114 On Serb dominance in interwar Yugoslavia see Ivo Banac, *The National Question in Yugoslavia: Origins, History, Politics* (Ithaca and London: Cornell University Press, 1984), 375–378; Lenard Cohen, "The Social Background and Recruitment of Yugoslav Political Elites, 1918–48," in Allen H. Barton *et al.*, eds., *Opinion-Making Elites in Yugoslavia* (New York: Praeger, 1973), 59–62; Jozo Tomasevich, *Peasants, Politics, and Economic Change in Yugoslavia* (Stanford: Stanford University Press, 1955), 241–260; István Deák, *Beyond Nationalism: A Social and Political History of the Habsburg Officer Corps, 1848–1918* (New York: Oxford University Press, 1990), 209; John Lampe, *Yugoslavia as History: Twice There Was a Country* (Cambridge: Cambridge University Press, 1996), 156–159, 171–173, 189–194, and ch. 7. For an attempt to place the decisions and policies of the interwar Serbian leadership in the best light possible, see Alex N. Dragnich, *The First Yugoslavia: Search for a Viable Political System* (Stanford: Hoover Institution Press, 1983) and Alex N. Dragnich, "The Anatomy of a Myth: Serbian Hegemony," *Slavic Review*, vol. 50, no. 3 (Fall 1991), 659–662.

115 Writing in 1984, Walker Connor observed that: "The most thorough case of permeation of a [Communist] party apparatus by nationalism is that of Yugoslavia." Walker Connor, *The National Question in Marxist-Leninist Theory and Strategy* (Princeton: Princeton University Press, 1984), 555.

116 In Tito's words: "The boundaries of the federated units within the federal state of Yugoslavia do not denote separatism but unity." Quoted in Tim Judah, *The Serbs: History, Myth and the Destruction of Yugoslavia* (New Haven: Yale University Press, 1997), 140. On the evolution of the Yugoslav Communists' approach to the nationalities question, see Connor, *National Question*, ch. 6 and *passim*.

117 Szayna, "Demographic Characteristics."

118 Sabrina P. Ramet, *Nationalism and Federalism in Yugoslavia, 1962–1991*, 2nd edn (Bloomington: Indiana University Press, 1992), ch. 3.

119 Connor, *National Question*, ch. 12.

120 Ramet, *Nationalism and Federalism*, ch. 7 and 187–201; Lampe, *Yugoslavia*, 298–302, 331–333; Silber and Little, *Yugoslavia*, 34.

121 Volkan, *Bloodlines*, 58–64, 66–69; Judah, *The Serbs*, ch. 3 and *passim*.

122 Ramet, *Nationalism and Federalism*, ch. 7 and pp. 187–201; Lampe, *Yugoslavia*, 298–302, 331–333; Miranda Vickers, *Between Serb and Albanian: A History of Kosovo* (New York: Columbia University Press, 1998), chs. 10–11; Judah, *The Serbs*, 149–153; Noel Malcolm, *Kosovo: A Short History* (New York: New York University Press, 1998), ch. 17; Silber and Little, *Yugoslavia*, 34. Throwing Montenegrins – generally regarded as ethnically Serb – into the mix adds a few percentage points to the Serb proportion of Kosovo's population.

123 Extensive, translated excerpts from the "Memorandum of the Serbian Academy of Science and Arts" are printed in Peter F. Sugar, ed., *Eastern European Nationalism in the Twentieth Century* (Washington, D.C.: The American University Press, 1995), 332–346.

124 Ibid., 338.

125 Ibid., 344.

126 Silber and Little, *Yugoslavia*, ch. 2.

127 Ramet, *Nationalism and Federalism*, 206.

128 Marcus Tanner, *Croatia: A Nation Forged in War* (New Haven: Yale University Press, 1997), 230. My emphasis.

129 Sabrina P. Ramet, *Balkan Babel: The Disintegration of Yugoslavia from the Death of Tito to the Fall of Milošević* (Boulder: Westview, 2002), 164–167, 378–380; Tanner, *Croatia*, ch. 15; Alex J. Bellamy, *The Formation of Croatian National Identity: A Centuries-Old Dream?* (Manchester: Manchester University Press, 2003), 69–71.

130 Ramet, *Nationalism and Federalism*, 257.

131 On the tendency of political instability and physical insecurity to reinforce ethnic boundaries irrespective of trans-ethnic cultural commonalities, see Fredrik Barth, "Introduction," in Fredrik Barth, ed., *Ethnic Groups and Boundaries: The Social Organization of Culture Difference* (1969; Prospect Heights, Ill.: Waveland Press, 1998), 36–37.

132 Silber and Little, *Yugoslavia*, chs. 13, 18, pp. 345–350, and *passim*; Weitz, *Century of Genocide*, ch. 4.

133 See report on "Bosnia-Hercegovina: Sarajevo," *Human Rights Watch Reports*, vol. 6, no. 15 (October 1994): http://hrw.org/reports/1994/bosnia3/; Cohen, *Hearts Grown Brutal*, 360.

134 The surprise German move, which scuttled a Franco-German effort to make recognition of former Yugoslav republics contingent on their fulfillment of various political conditions, was regarded with suspicion by many of Germany's European Community partners as well. Daniela Heimerl and Wim van Meurs, "The Balkans between Paris and Berlin," *Southeast*

European and Black Sea Studies, vol. 4, no. 3 (September 2004), 343–360. For an impassioned indictment of the German (and Austrian) initiative, see Denitch, *Ethnic Nationalism*, 51–52.

135 In a fitting irony, the hilltop position from which Serb militias first shelled Bosnia's capital, Sarajevo, was the site of a memorial to the interethnic solidarity of the anti-fascist struggle of the Second World War. Scott A. Bollens, "City and Soul: Sarajevo, Johannesburg, Jerusalem, Nicosia," *CITY: Analysis of Urban Trends, Culture, Theory, Policy, Action*, vol. 5, no. 2 (July 2001), 169–187.

136 On Jerusalem as partitioned city, see Raphael Israeli, *Jerusalem Divided: The Armistice Regime, 1947–1967* (London: Frank Cass, 2002); Meron Benvenisti, *City of Stone: The Hidden History of Jerusalem*, trans. Maxine Kaufman Nunn (Berkeley: University of California Press, 1996), 24–33, 56–64.

137 Benvenisti, *City of Stone*, 31; Oren Yiftachel, "Territory as the Kernel of the Nation: Space, Time and Nationalism in Israel/Palestine," *Geopolitics*, vol. 7, no. 2 (Autumn 2002), 215–248, esp. 234–235.

138 Meir Ben-Dov, *In the Shadow of the Temple: The Discovery of Ancient Jerusalem*, trans. Ina Friedman (New York: Harper & Row, 1985); Hillel Geva, ed., *Jewish Quarter Excavations in the Old City of Jerusalem Conducted by Nahman Avigad, 1969–1982*, vol. 1: *Architecture and Stratigraphy, Areas A, W, and X-2: Final Report* (Jerusalem: Israel Exploration Society/Institute of Archaeology, Hebrew University, 2000), 44–82.

139 Benvenisti, *City of Stone*, 73, 102.

140 Roger Friedland and Richard Hecht, *To Rule Jerusalem* (Cambridge: Cambridge University Press, 1996), 380.

141 Ben-Dov, *Shadow of the Temple*, chs. 4–8, esp. pp. 145–147.

142 Gershom Gorenberg, *The End of Days: Fundamentalism and the Struggle for the Temple Mount* (New York: Oxford University Press, 2000), 132–137 and ch. 7; Ian Lustick, "Israel's Dangerous Fundamentalists," *Foreign Policy*, no. 68 (Fall 1987), 118–139. See also the website of the Temple Mount Faithful at: http://www.templemountfaithful.org/.

143 This is suggested by the deliberate choice of location (in consultation with a Jewish convert to Islam) and by the inscriptions within the Shrine of Omar warning against the error of believing in Jesus' divinity. Wasserstein, *Divided Jerusalem*, 10–11; Armstrong, *Jerusalem*, 239.

144 Albert Hourani, *Arabic Thought in the Liberal Age, 1798–1939* (1962; Cambridge: Cambridge University Press, 1983), 309–311.

145 The definitive account is Benny Morris, *The Birth of the Palestinian Refugee Problem, 1947–1949* (Cambridge: Cambridge University Press, 1987).

146 Cf. the discussion in Khalidi, *Palestinian Identity*, 192–200.

147 "Men in the Sun," in Ghassan Kanafani, *Men in the Sun and Other Palestinian Stories*, trans. Hilary Kilpatrick (Cairo: American University of Cairo Press, 1991). For a nation that has been thus degraded, one may infer, surely any form of violence is justified in response. Kanafani went on to become the spokesman for George Habash's Marxist-Nationalist terrorist

organization, the Popular Front for the Liberation of Palestine (PFLP), before being assassinated in 1972. Dalia Karpel, "With Thanks to Ghassan Kanafani," *Haaretz English Edition*, 15 April 2005: http://www.haaretz.com/hasen/spages/565228.html.

148 The definitive treatment of the Six Day War is Michael B. Oren, *Six Days of War: June 1967 and the Making of the Modern Middle East* (New York: Oxford University Press, 2002).

149 Khalidi, *Palestinian Identity*, 196–197.

150 Ibid., 197–200.

151 See, for example, Wafa Amr, "Israeli Police Storm Holy Site after Jews Stoned," *Irish Examiner*, 30 July 2001.

152 Friedland and Hecht, *To Rule Jerusalem*, 378–384.

153 Dan Bahar, "The Western Wall Tunnels," in Hillel Geva, ed., *Ancient Jerusalem Revealed* (Jerusalem: Israel Exploration Society, 2000).

154 Gorenberg, *End of Days*, 181–186, 196–202; Menachem Klein, *The Jerusalem Problem: The Struggle for Permanent Status*, trans. Haim Watzman (Gainesville: University of Florida Press, 2003), 97–100, 181, 106–109.

155 Klein, *Jerusalem Problem*, 81, 109–110, 161–164.

156 Lecture by Meron Benvenisti, University of Minnesota, *circa* 1976. See also Meron Benvenisti, *Conflicts and Contradictions* (New York: Villard Books, 1986), 123–125. See also Bollens, "City and Soul."

157 This discussion draws on Klein, *Jerusalem Problem*, 71–81 and *passim*. See also Hussein Agha and Robert Malley, "Camp David: The Tragedy of Errors," *New York Review of Books*, vol. 48, no. 13 (9 August 2001).

158 Klein, *Jerusalem Problem*, 76, 81.

159 Ibid., 100–111, 199–203; Wasserstein, *Divided Jerusalem*, 348–349; Rivka Gonen, *Contested Holiness: Jewish, Muslim and Christian Perspectives on the Temple Mount in Jerusalem* (Jersey City: Ktav, 2003), 173; Yossi Beilin, *The Path to Geneva: The Quest for a Permanent Agreement, 1996–2004* (New York: RDV Books/Akashic Books, 2004), 221–222.

160 Klein, *Jerusalem Problem*, 73.

161 I do not mean to suggest that the meanings of these sites are fixed and unchanging. For a critique of what he regards as the pervasive, uncritical treatment of Jewish and Palestinian architectural and archaeological symbols as though they objectively embodied national identities and conflicts, see Daniel Monk's *An Aesthetic Occupation*. I fully agree with Monk that the conflict shapes the meaning of the monuments and artifacts of Jerusalem, no less than those symbols color the conflict. At least I think that is what he is arguing. The stunningly impenetrable nature of his prose makes it hard to be sure. (Ibid., Introduction.)

162 Hecht and Friedland, *To Rule Jerusalem*, ch. 14.

163 For an argument in favor of postponing the negotiation of Jerusalem's final status until all other Israeli–Palestinian issues have been resolved, see Beilin, *Path to Geneva*, 164. For a general critique of the Oslo Accords' gradualist

approach to peacemaking and its vulnerability to sabotage by radical opponents of compromise, see Yossi (Joseph) Alpher, "Oslo's Lessons for Peacemaking," *The Jerusalem Report*, 23 September 2002, 54.

164 Shlomit Levy, "An Analysis of Israeli Jewish Opinion on the Status of Jerusalem," Nader Izzat Sa'id, "An Analysis of Palestinian Opinion on the Status of Jerusalem," and Jerome M. Segal, "Is Jerusalem Negotiable?" in Jerome M. Segal, Shlomit Levy, Nader Izzat Sa'id, and Elihu Katz, eds., *Negotiating Jerusalem* (Albany: State University of New York Press, 2000). To be sure, the issue is somewhat complicated by the presence of some Jewish residential areas in parts of formerly Jordanian-controlled Jerusalem beyond the Old City, such as the French Hill and Gilo neighborhoods.

165 Cf. the discussion in Cohen, *China Unbound*, ch. 6, esp. 169–172.

166 Zerubavel, *Recovered Roots*, chs. 3, 6, 9, esp. pp. 159–160.

167 Ibid., chs. 10–11.

168 Friedland and Hecht, *To Rule Jerusalem*, 372–376.

169 As of December 2004, opinion polls indicated for the first time in years that a slim majority of Palestinians opposed terrorism against Israelis, seeing it as counter-productive to their own national interests. Khaled Abu Toameh, "Poll: Decrease in Palestinian Support of Terror," *The Jerusalem Post*, 8 December 2004.

170 Isaiah Berlin argued that, at the level of the individual, negative liberty (freedom *from* governmental and societal oppression and intrusion) represented a more desirable value than positive liberty (the classical republican ideal of human self-realization through integration and active engagement *in* the collective life of a political community). Berlin saw the latter conception of freedom as potentially totalitarian in its implications. Isaiah Berlin, "Two Concepts of Liberty," in Berlin, *Four Essays on Liberty* (London: Oxford University Press, 1969). What I am suggesting does not contradict that view, given that I am discussing the idea of national rather than individual freedom. I would in fact argue that a disproportionate emphasis on the negative conception of *national* freedom can imperil the negative liberty of the *individual*. That is to say, national fixations on myths and memories of victimization and martyrdom can legitimize regimes that are intolerant of internal dissent and that demand the total mobilization of society in the name of reversing, avenging, and/or preventing the violation of the nation's safety and dignity. This sort of political culture can easily infringe on an individual's right to freedom from excessive social and political control. (Of course, one must keep in mind that many nations do face very real and immediate threats of oppression or annihilation that leave them little immediate choice but to focus obsessively on collective defense.) Berlin himself regarded such forms of nationalism as dangerous, observing that: "To be the object of contempt or patronizing tolerance on the part of proud neighbours is one of the most traumatic experiences that individuals or societies can suffer. The response, as often as not, is pathological exaggeration of one's real or imaginary virtues . . . " Isaiah Berlin, "The Bent

Twig: On the Rise of Nationalism," in Berlin, *The Crooked Timber of Humanity: Chapters in the History of Ideas*, ed. Henry Hardy (New York: Random House, 1990), 246. Liah Greenfeld similarly highlights the role of *ressentiment* (resentment born of envy) in the generation of illiberal conceptions of nationalism. Liah Greenfeld, *Nationalism: Five Roads to Modernity* (Cambridge, Mass.: Harvard University Press, 1992), 15–17 and *passim*. For a thoughtful critique that points to the oversimplifications inherent in Berlin's sharp distinction between negative and positive liberty, see Colin Poole, *Nation and Identity* (London: Routledge, 1999), ch. 3.

CHAPTER 4

Chosenness and mission

"You shall become for me a kingdom of priests and a holy nation," God proclaimed to the Children of Israel.[1] The special relationship with divine holiness monopolized by an elite caste in other ancient societies was to be enjoyed by the Chosen People as a whole (or at least aspired to, given the continued, prominent ritualistic role of the priestly caste in pre-70 CE Judaism).[2] The immediate impression this verse leaves is of a unique privilege conferred upon an unusually lucky people. On second thought, however, one cannot help but wonder: what if some of the Israelites wanted to choose an alternative career path? Having consented to be chosen, can a nation opt out of the arrangement? How much freedom of choice does a chosen people have? And what mission does it think it has been chosen to carry out?

The contradictory implications of chosenness raised fundamental theological and political dilemmas for the ancient Jews. They have assumed global significance in the modern era, with the rise of great powers such as Britain, France, and the United States, each of which has had its national identity and historical trajectory heavily influenced not simply by the ideas of chosenness and mission, but by internal debates about the implications of those ideas.[3]

THE BIBLICAL PARADIGM

Given that it is a collection of writings composed over more than half a millennium, the Hebrew Bible itself presents a varied and evolving set of ideas about chosenness. The notion's first iteration comes in Genesis, in the chapter immediately following the Tower of Babel story.[4] The Tower of Babel itself can be seen as representing a mixed message. The terse biblical narrative begins with a line of background information, explaining that in those days, "all the land was one language and common words..."[5] In and of itself, this primordial monoculturalism does not seem to pose a problem. It is humanity's use of its cooperative potential to attempt the construction of a tower reaching into the heavens that constitutes the fatal expression of *hubris* on its part. Regarding the skyscraper as symptomatic of a united humanity's limitless power and ambition, God launches a preemptive cyber-attack, destroying humans' ability to communicate with one another. The mutually estranged people abandon their common architectural enterprise and disperse across the face of the earth, laying the foundation for the fractured, multinational humanity of history-as-we-know-it.

In its narrative structure, this account bears more than a passing resemblance to the Garden of Eden episode, in which a primordial idyll is disrupted by human presumption. In depicting the multiplicity of human languages and identities as the result of a divine act of sabotage, the Tower of Babel story implicitly idealizes a world without ethno-linguistic boundaries as a paradise lost. By the same token, that loss appears final, that paradise irretrievable. However much we might mourn the disappearance of a universal human society, it is in the experienced reality of cultural pluralism and national particularism that we are all fated to live.[6]

It is against this backdrop that the theme of chosenness first emerges. For to accept the reality of ethno-cultural particularism is not necessarily to embrace moral or religious relativism. Instead, as far as the scriptural agenda is concerned, recognition of the pluralistic reality simply begs the question of which particular way of life most closely approximates the divinely appointed ideal. A convergence of views among the nations may be unattainable until the End of Days, but in the historical interim, an individual nation may strive to rebuild the relationship with God. Indeed, it appears to be just as important for God to establish an intimate relationship with a nation, for it is He who takes the initiative in Genesis 12:1–3:

The Lord said to Abram, "Go forth from your native land and from your father's house to the land that I will show you. And I will make of you a great nation, and I will bless you ... I will bless those who bless you and curse him that curses you; and all the families of the earth shall be blessed by you."[7]

In subsequent passages, the nature of the relationship between God and the descendants of Abram (renamed Abraham) is further elaborated and refined, most importantly in the context of the revelation at Sinai, following the Israelites' liberation from slavery and their exodus from Egypt. Central to this relationship are the intertwined concepts of Chosen

People, Covenant, and Promised Land. God has chosen to offer the Israelites the privilege of binding themselves in a Covenant with Him. Under the terms of this deal, the people accept the authority of God's Law as revealed to Moses, in exchange for which they are to gain possession of the Promised Land. Their continued existence in the Promised Land, enjoying political freedom, security from their enemies, and bountiful harvests, is made conditional on their committed adherence to the Law, across the generations.[8] Rather than concentrating its energies on building towers, the Chosen People is to ascend spiritually through the pursuit of justice: "Justice – pursue justice so that you may live, and you will gain possession of the land that the Lord your God is giving you."[9]

This theological package deal is subject to multiple interpretations. The crudest one comes in the Book of Joshua, where the Israelites' status as the Chosen People is invoked as a justification for the violent dispossession of the indigenous Canaanite inhabitants of the Promised Land. (Archaeological evidence, along with portions of the often self-contradictory biblical texts, suggests that whatever conquest of Canaan by Israelites did actually occur was incremental and piecemeal, accompanied by a good deal of cultural and linguistic assimilation of the newcomers into the local population.)

In other biblical passages, chosenness is depicted as a moral burden. All nations are considered bound by the universal Covenant made between God and Noah after the Flood. This Covenant consists of basic provisions such as a ban on murder. But the Israelites are additionally bound by the far more exacting standards of the Law as revealed at Sinai and are to be held to a higher ethical standard than other peoples. Their adherence to the Covenant of Sinai is to be assessed by such measures as their pursuit of the Golden Rule and their capacity for empathy, love, and tolerance towards minorities: "Do not oppress the stranger, for you know the soul of the stranger, for you were strangers in Egypt."[10] And again: "When a stranger resides with you in your land, you shall not wrong him. The stranger who resides with you shall be to you as one of your citizens; you shall love him as yourself, for you were strangers in the land of Egypt . . ."[11]

In their variation on the theme, prophets such as Isaiah narrow the gap in the circle of particularism and universalism. In their view, the Jews have been chosen to fulfill a mission toward all humanity. Their own adherence to the Law and to the principles of social justice is to serve as an inspiration to all nations of the world. At the End of Days, proclaims Isaiah,

...from Zion shall come forth law,
The word of the Lord from Jerusalem.
Thus He will judge among the nations
And arbitrate for the many peoples,
And they shall beat their swords into plowshares
And their spears into pruning hooks:
Nation shall not take up
Sword against nation;
No more shall they know war.[12]

Waxing similarly exuberant, the prophet Zephaniah foresees a return to the linguistic harmony that preceded the Tower of Babel, with God giving all the nations a mutually intelligible tongue in which to worship him in unison.[13]

The vision of the Hebrew prophets, of course, serves as a doctrinal launching pad for the radical universalism of Pauline Christianity, which dismisses national differences between Jew and Gentile as irrelevant in the context of a common faith in Jesus and a common disregard for the now superseded Law of Moses. In Christian eyes, the Old Covenant with the Chosen People has fulfilled its theological-historical role by paving the way for the New Covenant between God and all humanity. This approach has run into contradictions and moral dilemmas of its own. If a sense of national chosenness can be abused as a license to kill, so too can a commitment to the establishment of universal religious conformity. There is a fine line between dismissing differences among peoples as immaterial in the context of shared values, and actively suppressing human diversity in the name of absolute truths.

In any event, the historical trajectory of Christian universalism led back to a vexed partnership with national particularism and to new variations on the theme of chosenness.[14] Rome's adoption of Christianity as its official religion in the fourth century CE marked the convergence of the universalizing faith with the all-embracing empire. But the fall of the Western empire in the following century put an end to this brief congruence of religious and political-territorial spheres. The bishops of Rome's attempts to translate their spiritual authority over medieval Christendom into concrete power were vigorously resisted by the emperors and kings of Europe's feudal polities, and even the papal claim of primacy within the Church was rejected by the rulers and clergy of the Byzantine Empire. Moreover, European monarchs became adept at using the idea of the universal Christian covenant to their own particular advantage. Some expanded their territorial dominions into non-Christian lands in the course of armed campaigns of proselytism and forced conversion, as in Charlemagne's late-eighth-century conquest of Saxony or the Spanish monarchy's Reconquista in Iberia and its subsequent ravaging of the New World. Some claimed that their polity possessed a special virtue that allowed it uniquely to embody the ideal vision of the universal Christian covenant. Such arguments were made both by the Habsburg rulers of the Holy Roman Empire of the German Nation and by their arch-rivals, the kings of France – "eldest daughter of the Church." Colette Beaune notes that, as early as the late twelfth century, "Robert the Monk wrote of 'the holy race of the Franks whom God has chosen as his people and his heritage.' "[15]

In the Greek Orthodox sphere, the Byzantine tradition of clerical subjection to monarchic authority and the custom of establishing self-governing (autocephalous) churches for regions and states beyond the effective reach of the Orthodox Ecumenical Patriarchate in Constantinople created institutional frameworks particularly conducive to the identification of one's own realm as chosen by God to play a special role in the fulfillment of his will on earth.[16] Russian monarchs from the sixteenth century onwards pressed their clergy to articulate Russia's claim to the status of Christianity's Third Rome (in the wake of the fall of Constantinople – the Second Rome – to the Ottomans in 1453).[17] The Serbian Orthodox Church cultivated the image of Serbia as a nation martyred in the name of Christianity and awaiting collective resurrection.[18] (See Chapter 3.) Anthony Smith notes that, on the periphery of the Roman Empire, Armenia (having established Christianity as its official religion in 301 CE) very early on adopted the idea of being a chosen nation held together by its members' self-sacrificing devotion to the Christian covenant in the face of external aggression by Zoroastrian, and later Muslim, forces. The sense of a special Armenian national covenant was enhanced by the sixth-century split between the Armenian Apostolic Church and the ecumenical mainstream of Christendom.[19]

Since Christianity preserved the Hebrew Bible as an integral part of its scriptures, the original Judaic conception of chosenness was ready to hand as a paradigm for such assertions. But hitching the Jewish notion of particularistic chosenness to the Christian concept of a universal covenant did not always make for a smooth ride. The Jewish approach allowed in principle for a live-and-let-live relationship between the Chosen People and the unchosen others – as long as the former fulfilled the Covenant of Sinai and the latter abided by the Covenant of Noah. In medieval and Renaissance Western and Central Europe, Catholic universalism made it particularly difficult to reconcile a claim to chosenness with an acceptance of multiple political sovereignties, let alone multiple covenants. Major dynasties such as the French Bourbons and the Habsburgs each aspired to some form of universal dominion in the name of their own supposed status as God's anointed rulers. France's "most Christian" monarchs strove for European hegemony and claimed the role of protectors of the holy places in Palestine,[20] while the Habsburgs desperately tried to convince themselves and others that their predominantly German realm really was Holy and Roman and an Empire.[21] When the Protestant Reformation challenged both the temporal authority in Germany of the Holy Roman Empire and the spiritual legitimacy of the Catholic Church, the result was a century and a half of savage conflicts that culminated in the devastating Thirty Years War (1618–48).

The 1648 Peace of Westphalia famously enshrined the plurality of political sovereignties as a formally recognized attribute of the European diplomatic system, with the crucial provision that each local ruler within the Holy Roman Empire was to determine which form of Christianity – Catholic, Lutheran, or Calvinist – would prevail within his or her bounded territory. In effect, the principle held true for Europe as a whole, with the European powers agreeing to disagree about whose particular version of the universal Christian covenant was the chosen version. By the same token, the formal partition of a once exclusively Catholic Western and Central Europe into discrete Catholic, Lutheran, Calvinist, and Anglican domains intensified the identification of polity with covenant, however much any given national church might claim to be part of a universal one in principle.[22] The Protestant emphasis on translation of both the Hebrew Bible and the New Testament into vernacular languages, which converged with the mass-marketing possibilities of the printing press,[23] further enhanced the accessibility and influence of the Israelite model as a source of inspiration for ideas about chosenness. At the same time, the steady centralization of power and incremental homogenization of legal, administrative, and cultural institutions within European states led to an ever-increasing identification between rulers and their realms, between states and their populations. The resultant rise of modern nationalism made the ancient example of Jewish nationhood seem more salient to people's experience than ever before. Moreover, Christian scholarship on the Hebrew scriptures from the late Renaissance through the Reformation and early Enlightenment had led to an intense fascination in some circles with the ideal of a Mosaic-style theocratic republic. The conviction that one's own community was the

New Israel proved particularly influential in John Calvin's sixteenth-century Geneva, in the newly independent Dutch republic of the seventeenth century, in England from the seventeenth century on,[24] and among the Puritan founders of New England.[25]

The modern movement towards the secularization of politics ultimately weakened but did not eliminate the direct influence of biblical models on political institutions and collective identities. As I have argued in previous chapters and as Anthony Smith, Adrian Hastings, and others have contended, the modern break with religious modes of thought was often only skin deep.[26] Well into the eighteenth-century Age of Reason, the Hebrew Bible remained an intimately familiar point of reference (both positive and negative) for political theorists and literate masses alike, continuing to exert profound influence on the development of political cultures. Even in times and places where Scripture no longer served as a direct source of legitimacy for political ideologies, the legacy of its earlier centrality to European thought was clearly discernible. After all, the idea of the social contract that became so fundamental to modern political theory and practice was itself heavily influenced by the biblical idea of the Covenant.[27] The Israelites had collectively agreed to a covenant with God that not only established his sovereignty over them, but also created a legitimizing framework for the development of egalitarian moral, contractual, and political relations *among themselves.*[28] In the case of the modern nation-state as conceived of by Enlightenment philosophers, the polity's legitimacy was supposed to be derived from the social contract that its members had implicitly or explicitly concluded *with one another.*[29] And the familiar Christian claim that one's kingdom had been chosen by God to spread the true word of the Gospel could readily be modified into the conviction that one's nation had been appointed by History to diffuse the light of Reason. Greco-Roman distinctions between civilization and barbarism, republican civic virtue and corrupt tyranny, also contributed heavily to modern conceptions of national mission, and eighteenth-century Enlightenment thinkers (unlike their seventeenth-century predecessors) tended to be more comfortable invoking classical models than biblical precedents. But it is difficult to miss the parallels between the Puritan idea of being God's elect and the American sense of Manifest Destiny, or between the French monarchs' self-description as Most Christian Kings and the French revolutionaries' conviction that their nation had a unique duty to spread liberty to the far corners of Europe.[30]

As with the biblical case, modern conceptions of national chosenness and mission are subject to conflicting interpretations and beset with moral and ideological dilemmas. In cases where the ideas of chosenness and/or global mission serve as constitutive elements of national identity, differences over what it means to be chosen and what the nature of the mission is form ideological fault lines along which rival interests are ranged. How liberating or constraining is the legacy of the primordial covenant from which the nation derives its unique identity? Which vision of social and political justice best embodies the covenant's principles? To the extent that the chosen nation actively spreads its gospel among the nations of the world, how is it to maintain its distinctiveness from them? These are among the most fundamental issues that confront both ideologues and decision-makers and around which competing interests and parties array themselves in chosen and missionary nations.[31]

CHOOSING TO BE CHOSEN:[32] THE AMBIGUITIES OF
COVENANTAL NATIONHOOD

Choosing to be a nation and being chosen as a nation are closely related concepts. The primordial covenant – be it mythical or historical – that first brought the nation into being is the basis for its special relationship with God and/or History. Not every national covenant is necessarily linked to a claim of chosenness, but for most chosen peoples the idea of covenant is a focal point of collective identity. It was an original exercise of will – a common commitment to a certain (potentially universal) vision of the ideal life – that first marked the people as distinct from all others, according to this conception of national identity. The main exception to this pattern is the racist version of chosenness. In the Nazi conception of German identity, for instance, it was the inherent biological nature of Germans that was supposed to form the basis for their superiority to all other peoples. No original act of choice was involved in determining either their status or that of their intended victims (according to the Nazi myth). The exercise of national will was certainly one of Hitler's consuming obsessions, but it was to serve as a means of realizing the Volk's preexisting potential, rather than forming the basis of that potential.

Among those nations that chose to be chosen, how much freedom of choice did their primordial covenants leave for the contracting parties' descendants?[33] For that matter, how much freedom of choice was involved in the primordial covenanting itself? A Talmudic interpretive story goes to the heart of this ambiguity. According to this account, when the Israelites gathered at Mount Sinai to hear the terms of God's Covenant with them, God did not rely exclusively on the attractions of the virtuous life as the people's incentive for accepting the pact; He also suspended the mountain over their heads until they signed on the dotted line. Like Marlon Brando in "The Godfather," he made them an offer they couldn't refuse. Having thus effectively called into question the moral legitimacy of the Covenant of Sinai, the Talmud hastens to salvage its contractual authority by arguing that the Israelites' reaffirmation and renewal of it on subsequent occasions was genuinely voluntary in nature.[34]

Of course, no amount of interpretive ingenuity can once and for all resolve the inherent problem every national/political community confronts in trying to reconcile the principles of consent and constraint. To return to the biblical archetype, it is one of the cardinal principles of the Mosaic Covenant that it be taught and passed on from generation to generation and that straying from its provisions will bring down the wrath of heaven upon the nation. While enjoying the fruits of the Covenant in the Land of Israel, the Jews remained obligated by its terms. Conquered and then exiled from their national territory, Jews believed that it was only through a renewed, collective devotion to the Covenant that their fate could be reversed and their territorial sovereignty under the House of David restored. For that matter, it was their continued observance of the Law that defined them as a nation despite their dispersion. At the same time, while in theory the original terms of the Covenant of Sinai were absolute and immutable, in practice the tradition of rabbinical interpretive debates and authoritative rulings as recorded in the Talmud and continued in subsequent *responsa* literature served to adapt the Law to changing socio-economic and political conditions as well as to evolving ethical norms and legal practices.[35] With the rise of modern Zionism, Jewish communities became divided over whether the people of the Covenant had the right and obligation to seize the initiative in recreating a Jewish state in the Promised Land or whether they were obliged to continue waiting for God to take the initiative in fulfilling his end of the covenantal bargain. Such tensions between the notions of chosenness and freedom of choice, destiny and self-determination, shape the experience of many covenantal nations.

America's constitutional covenant

In no contemporary instance is the idea of covenant more central to national identity than it is in the United States of America. By a broad consensus, the events of the American Revolution and its aftermath are regarded as acts of creation that first gave rise to a nation whose very existence was destined to transform the world. Divine Providence is widely regarded as having furnished the necessary preconditions – a resource-rich Promised Land awaiting settlement by Puritan colonists – for these events.[36] As John Adams put it on the eve of the War of Independence: "I always considered the settlement of America with reverence and wonder, as the opening of a grand scene and design in Providence for the illumination of the ignorant, and the emancipation of the slavish part of mankind all over the earth."[37] In their collective choice of a new political covenant, the revolutionaries of Adams' generation are popularly seen as having brought this potential to its first fruition, giving birth to a new chosen nation.

The two defining moments in what might be termed America's Covenanting Era are its start and end points: the Declaration of Independence (1776) and the drafting and ratification of the Constitution (1787–90).[38] And herein lies an element of profound ambiguity. The Declaration of Independence justifies its specific claims by appealing to universal values: the natural right to "life, liberty and the pursuit of happiness" and the general principle that "when a long train of abuses and usurpations, pursuing invariably the same Object evinces a design to reduce ... [a people] under absolute Despotism, it is their right, it is their duty, to throw off such Government..."[39] This is as much an apologia for revolution in general as it is a justification of this specific revolution. As such, it casts doubt on the permanence of the new polity that it calls into being, for it implies that as soon as its government falls into corruption or disrepair, it in turn can legitimately be overthrown.[40] Presumably, it is for each generation to judge whether or not the national covenant still serves the cause of justice. As the French theorist of nationalism Ernest Renan was to put it just over a century later, "a nation's existence is ... a daily plebiscite."[41] Indeed, under the loose Articles of Confederation that held the former colonies more or less together, popularly elected state legislatures effectively reigned supreme in an America whose national government consisted of so many gossamer threads blowing in the political wind.[42]

By contrast, the constitution drawn up in 1787 and ratified over the following three years was designed to provide enough flexibility to accommodate changing conditions, needs, and pressures within a strong and permanent framework of national government. In Isaac Kramnick's words, what framers of the constitution such as James Madison "wanted ... was nothing less than a complete reversal of 1776."[43] To be sure, among the mechanisms Article V of the constitution provided for the document's emendation was that, at the request of two-thirds of the state legislatures, a national convention could be called that would be empowered to propose amendments to the Constitution (subject to the approval of three-fourths of the states). Seemingly true to the spirit of the Declaration of Independence, this provision suggested the possibility of what would amount to future constitutional conventions that could effectively (though not technically) wipe the national-covenantal slate clean. But this prospect has always seemed so daunting, the threat this would pose to the very essence of national identity so fundamental, that no serious attempt has ever been made to undertake this radical procedure. (Amendments to the Constitution have been proposed and ratified singly, through the alternative mechanism of congressional initiative and state ratification.) Gordon Wood has argued that, viewed as the product of a social contract *among the people* (rather than as a compact between people and rulers,) the Constitution was widely seen as obviating the need for any future revolution, for a people cannot revolt against itself.[44] The attempt by the Southern slave states to make a unilateral break with the Union was justified by appealing to the spirit of the Jeffersonian revolutionary principle and to a strained interpretation of the popular sovereignty principle underlying the Constitution (i.e. the argument, recently revived in a minority opinion by Supreme Court Justice Clarence Thomas, that the phrase "we the people" refers to the individual peoples of the states, each of whom delegated rather than surrendered aspects of their sovereignty to the federal government).[45] It was successfully quashed by President Lincoln in the Civil War on the grounds that the original covenant was made among the members of the sovereign American nation as a whole, and could therefore be altered only through the legal mechanisms provided for in the Constitution itself.[46]

In short order, then, the Constitution became not just a framework of government but a constitutive element of American national identity. It is true that some of the original framers and advocates of the Constitution such as James Madison stressed the ambiguous nature of the proposed governmental structure as at once federal and national in character.[47] But at the same time, in urging the document's ratification, Madison called on his readers to recognize that "the kindred blood which flows in the veins of American citizens, the mingled blood which they have shed in defense of their sacred rights, consecrate their Union and excite horror at the idea of their becoming aliens, rivals, enemies."[48] Indeed, the Constitution famously opened with the phrase "we the people of the

United States," which presupposed the existence of a unified nation while invoking its authority on behalf of the very document designed to give that nation legal and institutional form.[49] Justified by the ideal of a transcendent national unity, the Constitution itself became emblematic of the nation's identity. As Michael Kammen has noted, within a decade or two of the Constitution's ratification, both sides of every political division were already in the habit of wrapping themselves in the revered document while accusing their rivals of undermining its principles. Its symbolic power grew steadily following the great test of the Civil War, especially in the aftermath of the celebrations of the Constitution's centennial.[50] To this day, it continues to be one's acceptance of, and commitment to, the Constitution that defines one as an American; the version of the American citizenship oath in place since the 1950s commits newly naturalized members of the nation to "support and defend the Constitution and laws of the United States of America against all enemies foreign and domestic . . . " and to "bear true faith and allegiance to the same."[51]

The central role played by the Constitution in constituting American identity has arguably contributed to the highly conservative nature of American politics. In the name of the principles that inspired their revolution, Americans have been extremely reluctant to reform, let alone do away with, some of the most archaic institutions of their ancien-regime-like republic. (Of course, the Constitution is itself designed to be highly resistant to far-reaching modification.) The selection of the president of the United States through indirect elections, for instance, remains as immutable a feature of the American landscape as Mount Rushmore (perhaps even more immutable, given recent proposals to add the late Ronald Reagan's features to the national monument in the Black Hills). Intermittent proposals to reform the way in which the Electoral College functions so as to ensure that no one can be elected president without having secured a majority of the popular vote garner little support and quickly stall. To be sure, other constitutional archaisms, such as the election of senators by state legislatures, have been eliminated through the intricate and difficult amendment process. But the impression remains that – procedural hurdles aside – Americans are fundamentally loath to tamper with a document that defines who they are as a national community. As Daniel Lazare has put it:

America is a religious society caught up in a painful contradiction. On one hand, its politics rest on faith in the Founding Fathers . . . and the document they produced ... the Constitution .... On the other hand, the faith isn't working .... The more the roof leaks and the beams sag, the more fervent the odes to the original architects and builders seem to grow.[52]

By the same token, some of the most divisive political and ideological controversies revolve around the issue of what exactly is entailed by adherence to the Constitution.[53] Like the Karaites who reject rabbinical Judaism's Talmudic tradition, insisting instead on an exclusively literal application of the Torah's laws, an increasingly influential branch of American conservatism claims that the "original intent" of the Constitution's drafters represents the only legitimate standard by which to interpret the document. The most influential advocate of this position, Robert H. Bork, represents the constitution as a "social compact"[54] whose terms should be applied strictly in consonance with the way in which they would have been understood by the public at the time they were first formulated. In his view, the notion that each generation is entitled to reinterpret the Constitution serves to "teach disrespect for the actual institutions of the American nation ..." He goes on to assert that "our freedoms do not ultimately depend upon the pronouncements of judges sitting in a row. They depend upon their acceptance by the American people, and a major factor in that acceptance is the belief that these liberties are inseparable from the founding of the nation."[55] In other words, once ratified, the national covenant became as timeless as the chosen nation to which it gave birth. To depart in any respect from the original intent of the document's framers (other than by formally amending the constitution as provided for by its own terms) is seen by this school of thought as violating the essence of what it means to be an American.

Liberals reject these views as absurd, as well as ahistorical, given the diversity of meanings many of the drafters of the Constitution themselves attributed to various aspects of what was, after all, the product of an intricate series of political debates and compromises. But this is not to say that American liberals do not regard the Constitution as a sacred covenant. It is just that, in their eyes, its unique ability to serve as the eternal framework for American identity stems from its infinite adaptability to changing conditions and evolving moral standards.[56] Indeed, beyond that, the American progressive tradition has organized itself around the belief that the Constitution and the revolution that gave rise to it embody a perfect democratic ideal, and that it is the nation's mission to evolve towards an ever closer approximation of that ideal.[57]

The mainstreams of American liberalism and conservatism thus share a common reverence for the covenantal framework of the nation's history and identity. Both sides of the political spectrum view the Constitution as an inspired blueprint for a uniquely just, balanced, and enduring democratic society. They both recognize its authority as a binding document, outside of which the American nation must not stray, lest it violate the very covenant to which it owes its existence. By the same token, they compete for the role of correct interpreters of the founders' vision. In a sense, they both claim special understanding of the framers' original intent. Conservatives claim to understand it literally, as though they were in a position to consult Madison and Hamilton directly about the ins and outs of every contemporary judicial issue (and as though Madison and Hamilton would have seen eye-to-eye on every such question). The mainstream of liberal thought[58] holds to what might be understood as a more flexible conception of original intent, according to which certain transcendent principles and core qualities of the Constitution (including its very susceptibility to evolving interpretation[59]) are to guide the nation through the unpredictable twists and turns of history towards the creation of an ever more nearly perfect union.[60] Given the cultural blinkers of their times, for instance, the Founding Fathers would never have countenanced gay marriage. But, liberals insist, the egalitarian ideal that underlay the framers' efforts leaves today's courts with no legitimate option but to recognize same-sex unions, given that changed social and cultural conditions have opened our eyes to the injustices long suffered by homosexuals.

France's covenantal conflicts

These profound interpretive differences notwithstanding, the agreement across political divisions on the text of the Constitution as the binding version of the national covenant and the lasting vision of an ideal society has lent a relatively high degree of stability to the post-Civil War American political system. In France, for much of that nation's modern history, the politics of chosenness and covenant have played out in a more intricate and convoluted manner. The legacy of the country's Great Revolution has served as the covenantal framework for most of the regimes that have ruled France since 1789. But those social and political factions that opposed the revolution were never irreversibly expunged from the body politic. In the Jewish tradition, the followers of Korach who challenged the legitimacy of Moses' leadership were swallowed up by the earth.[61] In the American case, Loyalists fled in their thousands to British-controlled Canada.[62] But in France, the royalist exiles made a triumphant return following Napoleon's defeat in 1814. While the restored Bourbon regime only lasted till 1830 before again being unseated, the nation long thereafter remained split between those who looked to 1789 as a seminal covenantal moment and those who abhorred the revolution as itself a violation of the covenant between France – "first daughter of the Church" – and God.[63] The only thing the two sides shared was the conviction that France had a unique role to spread its vision to all humanity.[64]

Even among those who accepted the revolutionary legacy as the essential framework for French national identity, disagreements long raged over what the nature of that legacy was. The era of the Great Revolution did not produce any one constitutional order that gained general acceptance and went on to stand the test of time. One political manifesto of that era can be said to have reflected a broad revolutionary consensus – the Declaration of the Rights of Man and Citizen. This was the document issued by the revolutionary National Assembly on 26 August 1789, three weeks after its abolition of feudalism. The Declaration established the principles of political equality and popular sovereignty as the country's operative norms.[65] Faith in these principles became a cornerstone of national identity and political consciousness for a broad swath of the French political spectrum and remained so in the decades and centuries that followed. But the question of how to implement them was a source of bitter and often violent division both among the revolutionaries themselves and among succeeding generations of Frenchmen struggling to define the revolutionary legacy. For much of the following two centuries, a seemingly endless series of regimes, ranging from constitutional monarchies, to plebiscitary empires, to republics, ruled France. Most though not all of them claimed to embody the principles of the revolutionary covenant. But each regime seized on a different precedent from among the many constitutional experiments of the revolutionary era as the legitimizing paradigm for its own approach to government. Whereas the Declaration of the Rights of Man and Citizen and the celebration of Bastille Day attained an iconic status analogous to that of the American Declaration of Independence and the Fourth of July, no single French constitution gained anything remotely comparable to the hallowed role of the United States Constitution. Unable to agree on the full text of their covenant, the French were left with little option but to resort to the Jeffersonian principle of overthrowing their system of government as each successive regime failed to gain unquestioned recognition as the true heir to the revolution. The French national-revolutionary covenant is binding in principle, but for much of France's post-revolutionary history, the lack of consensus about what constituted that covenant contributed to a high turnover of regimes in practice.

The relative stability of de Gaulle's Fifth Republic (1958–) may be due in part to its ability to bridge the gap among its various eighteenth- to twentieth-century predecessors by combining a strong executive (a sort of republican monarch) with the plebiscitary emphasis of Napoleon and the liberal-democratic representative democracy of the moderate republican tradition. But the French remain far more ready than Americans to tinker with their political system, as suggested by the September 2000 refer-endum approving the abbreviation of the presidential term from seven years to five and the progressive devolution of various administrative powers from the central government to newly created regional authorities over the course of recent years.

* * *

As de Gaulle – ever preoccupied with the relationship between France's inner unity and its international prestige[66] – fully realized, the line separating domestic politics from foreign policy is a very thin one. It is particularly fuzzy in the case of chosen nations, whose collective sense of self is so intimately bound up with their image of their role in the world. Confronting the dilemmas of chosenness in the global arena can help transcend internal fissures over the meaning of national identity, but it can also reflect and exacerbate deep divisions about the nature of the chosen nation's burden.

CHOSEN PEOPLES' BURDENS: NATIONAL MISSIONS

The myth of national chosenness can be employed quite simply as a license to kill. Nineteenth-century Americans, regarding a great part of North America's continental expanse as part of their Promised Land, treated Indians the way certain portions of the Hebrew Bible suggested the conquering Israelites were to deal with the Canaanites. The Afrikaners saw their Great Trek of the 1830s and 1840s away from British imperial hegemony in the Cape Colony and into the Transvaal as a reenactment of Exodus – with the indigenous Africans once again consigned to the role of Canaanites.[67] British, French, Dutch, and Japanese conceptions of chosenness aggravated the self-righteous zeal and casual cruelty with which members of those nations carried out their colonial conquests.

But the idea of chosenness usually involves more complex moral dimensions alongside the potential for such straightforward abuse. The prophetic vision of Israel as "a light unto the nations"[68] is readily transposable to latter-day chosen nations – including the modern State of Israel, whose founding father, David Ben-Gurion (1886–1973), cited the line from Isaiah as an inspiration for his vision of the Jewish state.[69] Being singled out for God or History's special favor is commonly interpreted as imposing a special set of ethical constraints and obligations, upon the fulfillment of which the privileges of chosenness are conditioned. In this view, chosen nations are required to uphold elevated standards of social justice and political perfection with a view to shaping the world in their image. The idea of national chosenness is closely linked to the sense of national mission.

* * *

According to a rabbinic legend, God's offer of a covenant to the Israelites at Sinai came only after he had proposed the identical terms to all the other nations of the world. The Israelites alone chose not to turn him down.[70] In other words, it was not the Israelites who were singled out for a special privilege. Rather, it was the other nations of the world who chose not to be chosen, leaving the Israelites as the Chosen People by default.

This story addresses the tension between universalism and particularism in the covenantal principle. Chosen nations' covenants can be upheld as encapsulations of universal ideals. The American constitution and the French revolutionary legacy are each depicted by their respective proponents as the distilled essence of the just and rational polity. At one and the same time, it is the covenant that marks the nation apart from all others. It is the chosen nation's unique access to the globally relevant principles of the just society that shapes its distinctive identity. To a certain extent, every modern nation confronts certain aspects of this paradox, for the idea of the nation-state is itself a globally applicable and replicable paradigm for the definition, protection, and cultivation of circumscribed, non-replicable identities. But a nation that feels chosen in the strong, covenantal sense of the term finds the boundary between the particular and the universal particularly hard to negotiate, in so far as it regards its own covenant as deriving its essential legitimacy from the very universality of its principles.

For small, relatively weak nation-states that embrace a strong sense of chosenness (perhaps in part as a form of compensation/explanation for their historical status as underdogs), this dilemma is relatively easily resolved by conceiving of the nation as an ideal example for humanity as a whole to emulate. In this approach, the chosen nation's universal role is best fulfilled precisely by maintaining a sharp boundary between itself and others, allowing it to maintain a spiritual purity that can serve as an inspiration to other peoples. In Hebrew, after all, the term "holy" (*kadosh*) is drawn from a root meaning "to separate." As Anthony Smith emphasizes, the term "holy nation" was used in the Hebrew Bible in the sense of a nation that held itself apart ("a people dwelling apart, and not reckoning itself among the nations..."[71]), consecrated to God and unsullied by the idolatrous practices and immoral customs of its neighbors.[72]

The Swiss national myth is an example of a modern variation on this theme. The notion that Switzerland constitutes an ideal paradigm of direct democracy and the sturdy defense of liberty (against such tyrannical threats as the Habsburg overlords in the thirteenth and fourteenth centuries and Napoleonic France at the turn of the eighteenth and nineteenth centuries) has long served as an operative national myth that has held the country's diverse cantons and ethno-linguistic groups together.[73] The prevailing wisdom and constitutional tradition has it that the nation's mission to the world is best fulfilled through adherence to a permanent, armed neutrality, keeping the country safe from entanglement with external forces and maintaining the integrity of its peculiar cantonal and federal institutions and plebiscitary traditions. International institutions such as the United Nations are welcome to convene conferences and even establish headquarters on Swiss soil, and the Swiss take pride in being the birthplace and home base of the International Committee of the Red Cross (ICRC). But, given their historic experience of fending off the intrusions of neighboring great powers and their sense of uniqueness as a haven of direct democracy and interethnic coexistence, the Swiss have been loath to compromise the sanctity of their national frontiers and territorial sovereignty. Their membership in the League of Nations – itself headquartered in Geneva – was qualified by their exemption from the obligation to participate in any military sanctions against aggressor states, and the Swiss did not join the United Nations until 2002, even though Geneva has served throughout as the UN's European headquarters. Although the founders of the European Union may have drawn inspiration from the Swiss example of an interethnic federation, the Swiss themselves have so far doggedly refused to join the EU. The deeper the buffer zone protecting Switzerland's quasi-isolationism, the better, for the collective, constitutionally codified *choice to be neutral* (as distinct from, say, Austria's externally imposed, treaty obligation to remain neutral) remains a cardinal, defining characteristic of Swiss national identity, lending substance to its sense of chosenness.[74] Indeed, the Swiss claim, it is precisely their identity and status as a neutral nation that allows them to play a uniquely constructive role in the promotion of global peace and human rights by ensuring that no one will question the motives or reject the good offices of Swiss-based institutions such as the ICRC.[75]

Other small and vulnerable or embattled nations have also embraced the ideas of covenant and chosenness as a framework for self-definition. Some of them have identified so closely with the biblical Children of Israel as to draw directly upon their understanding of the Hebrew Scriptures in defining their roles and charting their courses amidst hostile geopolitical environments. Donald Akenson has undertaken the study of this phenomenon in his comparative examination of the Ulster Protestants, the Afrikaners, and modern Israel.[76] Likewise, in the early Dutch republic, the political, economic, and cultural elites as well as general populace identified their nation very closely with biblical Israel, seeing their own escape from oppressive Spanish rule as a latter-day version of the Exodus from Egypt, complete with a providential flood that helped save the besieged city of Leiden from Spanish forces in 1574 (an event likened to the drowning of Pharaoh's army in the Red Sea). Dutch national iconography was suffused with references to such symbolically resonant themes from the Hebrew Bible, the Netherlands became a European center of Hebraic scholarship, and national debates about the relative merits of monarchic and republican, centralized and federal, puritanical and tolerant, government were carried on in the form of conflicting interpretations of the ancient Israelite covenantal model.[77]

But the myth of chosenness also shapes the identities of nations that are, have been, or aspire to be, global powers.[78] This is doubtless partly a result of a tendency to explain and justify one's nation's disproportionate power as a mark of special favor, but it is also conceivable that a preconceived sense of chosenness may contribute to a nation's rise to power (most notably in the case of the United States). Among small nations, feeling chosen can contribute to self-isolation from global affairs. Among great powers, a sense of chosenness can certainly promote a similarly isolationist impulse, but it is a tendency that is much harder to maintain consistently. To the extent that a great power considers itself chosen, it is almost compelled to define its relationship with the world in terms of an active mission to transform the world in its own image.[79] Such a sense of distinctive mission often lives on as a powerful element of the nation's political culture long after explicit, quasi-religious, claims of chosenness have fallen by the historical wayside.

The idea of national mission clearly begs more questions than it answers. If the nation's *raison d'être* is the salvation of humanity, how is the national interest to be differentiated, if at all, from the interests of mankind as a whole? Can the chosen nation fulfill its mission to the world chiefly through the power of example, mainly by direct action, or through a combination of the two? Does the sense of global mission merely serve as a cloak for the imposition of one's national will on others, or can it really impose constraints on the abuse of power – or at least contribute to the cultivation of an enlightened conception of national self-interest? Such issues have framed political and ideological debates about foreign policy in the preeminent world power of the past century – the United States.

A proselytizing particularism:[80] *America's sense of global mission*

With ourselves ... national selfishness is unbounded philanthropy; for we can not do a good to America but we give alms to the world.[81] (Herman Melville)

In their relations with strangers the Americans are impatient of the slightest criticism and insatiable for praise ... One cannot imagine a more obnoxious or boastful form of patriotism. Even admirers are bored.[82] (Alexis de Tocqueville)

The orientation of the American nation towards the world was ambiguous from its revolutionary start.[83] The struggle for independence began as a revolt on behalf of what the colonists considered to be their traditional political rights as Englishmen (construed as the juridical expression of natural rights).[84] As such, the revolution was rooted in a particular national tradition, and this is what led the father of modern conservatism, Edmund Burke, to defend the position of the American rebels in the British House of Commons. Burke was later to excoriate the French Revolution precisely because of its radically rationalist ideological underpinnings.[85] But, in fact, the implications and repercussions of the American Revolution were themselves more radical than Burke may have realized.[86] After all, the American example did help inspire the French Revolution that Burke was to abhor so. Having broken with the British crown, the American Founding Fathers invoked Enlightenment conceptions of universal natural law to justify their actions and saw themselves as being engaged in a political enterprise that could serve as a replicable model of republican government.[87] The fact that this did not immediately give rise to a forceful drive to export the revolution doubtless had something to do with the particularistic aspects of the revolutionaries' outlook as well as with the firm leadership of the independence movement by members of the socially conservative American agrarian and commercial establishments. But it was also a function of certain geopolitical factors. The realities of power distribution simply did not make such an idea remotely feasible. Born in the midst of war against Britain, the United States was at first barely able to maintain its independence – and that only with the assistance of France and other European powers set on humbling Albion. This, along with America's geographic separation from Europe, contributed to the idea that the new country's special role in the world was primarily to serve as an inspiring example of the just polity.[88]

This view did not represent a disavowal of the use of power. The North American continent was viewed from the start as America's "first birthright" (as Herman Melville put it[89]), a vast arena for the creation of an empire of democracy – a territorially expansive and resource-rich polity whose material success and political stability would serve as evidence of the new nation's special virtue and enhance its attractiveness as a model to be emulated by the rest of humanity. Such visions of "manifest destiny"[90] were used to justify the dispossession of the Indians and the aggressive foreign policy pursued towards Mexico, which lost some 40 percent of its post-1836 territory to the United States in the 1846–48 war launched by President Polk, who described the conquest as having "extended the dominions of peace over additional territories."[91] The country's first bid for global power status was marked by the 1898 war of imperial expansion against Spain that originated as an intervention on behalf of Cuban rebels fighting for independence against their European colonial overlords. Once in a position to do so, the nation was willing and eager to flex its muscles beyond its shores in the name of its political values. By the same token, such moves often generated strong currents of dissent.[92]

As the United States' territorial, demographic, and economic expansion led it into ever greater entanglement in world affairs, the nation confronted new dilemmas. The First World War marked the nation's full entry into the international, great-power arena, and America has struggled inconclusively and divisively over the implications of its new position ever since. Having failed to fulfill his pledge to keep the country out of the Great War, President Woodrow Wilson (1856–1924) went to great pains to justify and rationalize American involvement in the conflict by differentiating the nation's role from that of Germany's European rivals. He insisted on designating the United States as an Associated rather than an Allied power. Eschewing any expansionist or annexationist goals of his own, Wilson presented the United States' entry into the war as designed to transform what had begun as a conflict between selfish imperial powers into a struggle for universal principles of democracy, national self-determination, and collective security.[93]

In articulating these goals, Wilson was not being particularly original. He was tapping into a strong current of European opinion and encapsulating the views of left-of-center political parties and trade unions in Britain, France, Russia (after the overthrow of the tsar in early 1917), and even Germany.[94] Indeed, even the Prusso-German military-aristocratic leadership found it expedient to use the principle of national self-determination as a cloak for the pursuit of its grandiose expansionist designs against the Russian Empire.[95] But Wilson went further than any other political leader in identifying his country's wartime interests and post-war agenda so overwhelmingly and exclusively with the fulfillment of the liberal internationalist vision.[96] In his own eyes and in the perception of (soon-to-be-disenchanted) peoples throughout the world, 1919 was, as Erez Manela has put it, the "Wilsonian moment."[97] The former Princeton professor turned president firmly believed that his country had a uniquely appointed historical role to play in saving the Old World from itself and reconfiguring the international order on the model of the American City on a Hill.[98] According to his rhetorical formulations, Americans could take legitimate patriotic pride from the very convergence of their national interests and ideals with the welfare of all humanity. Elements of this approach antedated his decision to intervene in the Great War by many years. As early as the presidential election campaign of 1912, Wilson had stated that "I believe ... we are chosen and prominently chosen to show the way to the nations of the world how they shall walk in the paths of liberty."[99] As president, Wilson had enlarged upon this theme, as in his Independence Day speech of 1914:

My dream is that as the years go on and the world knows more and more of America ... it ... will turn to America for those moral inspirations which lie at the basis of all freedom; that the world will never fear America unless it feels that it is engaged in some enterprise which is inconsistent with the rights of humanity; and that America will come into the full light of the day when all shall know that she puts human rights above all other rights and that her flag is the flag not only of America but of humanity.[100]

With such words, Wilson seemed to be obliterating any distinction between national identity and global interests. Yet, he went on to argue, it was precisely its nature as the embodiment of universal human values and interests that marked America as unique: "What other great people has devoted itself to this exalted ideal? To what other nation in the world can all eyes look for an instant sympathy that thrills the whole body politic when men anywhere are fighting for their rights?"[101]

Like the spiritual father of the mid-nineteenth-century Italian national unification movement, Giuseppe Mazzini (1805–72),[102] Wilson thought that a world of democratic nation-states would be a world free of war. International conflict, he was convinced, arose from the selfish designs of autocratic governments and the corrupt elites who led them. No government that truly represented the will of a people could conceivably choose to employ its people as cannon fodder in a campaign of military aggression against another free nation. Joined together in a League of Nations, the democratic states of a post-war order would guarantee the peace in the face of aggression by any one of their number.[103] Democracy went hand-in-hand with national self-determination in the eyes of liberal internationalists, for what democratic legitimacy could a government possibly have unless it was representative of its people's identity? In Wilson's eyes, the connection between these two principles was more readily apparent than the tension. As he saw it, the United States embodied the marriage of the two ideals, with collective commitment to democratic values itself functioning as the very element that lent substance to the nation's identity and that held it together in the face of ethnic and socio-economic differences.[104] But he was vague and inconsistent in his conception of how exactly this American model was to be applied in the post-war world. His initial reluctance to call outright for the dismantling of the multinational Habsburg Empire gave way by the summer of 1918 to official recognition of exile groups lobbying for the independence of Austria-Hungary's subject nationalities. Yet he seemed only dimly aware of the potential implications of the triumph of national self-determination as the organizing principle of a multiethnic Central and Eastern Europe or of the precedent this could set for other regions of Europe and the world. He seemed to work on the assumption that the candidates for national self-determination were certain clearly defined peoples whose territorial distribution was a matter of common knowledge and who were historically predisposed to democratic values, respect for individual rights, and tolerance of minorities. Such values would, in turn, lend stability and cohesive political identities to the independent nation-states they would establish. Wilson was encouraged in these beliefs by his encounters with Czech, Polish, and other exiled leaders who were themselves a self-selected group with a strongly Western-oriented political disposition and who naturally did all they could to play up their people's natural affinities with the American way of life.[105]

What ensued did not accord well with Wilson's understanding of America's mission or of its emulators' appointed roles. Rather than guiding newly independent nation-states on the path to democratic enlightenment, Wilson found himself at the 1919 Paris Peace Conference helping to adjudicate seemingly petty territorial disputes among rival nation-states, each of which included within its borders countless ethnic minorities that were volubly, sometimes violently, opposed to the new political arrangements. Poland clashed with Czechoslovakia over Teschen, with Lithuania over Vilnius, and with Germany over Upper Silesia; Ukrainians tried to fight off Polish rule in Eastern Galicia; Magyars (ethnic Hungarians) resisted incorporation into Romania and Czechoslovakia; Jews demanded extraterritorial autonomy throughout the region. In the Middle East, where the Ottoman Empire had been occupied by British and French forces, Zionist and Arab agendas clashed, as did Armenian, Kurdish, and Greek nationalist aspirations with the Turkish national movement. In Russia, civil war between the Bolsheviks and their opponents overlapped with fighting between ethnic separatist movements on the one hand and either Bolshevik or anti-Bolshevik armies on the other.[106] In Wilson's own words:

When I gave utterance to those words ("that all nations had a right to self-determination"), I said them without the knowledge that nationalities existed, which are coming to us day after day . . . You do not know and cannot appreciate the anxieties that I have experienced as the result of many millions of people having their hopes raised by what I have said.[107]

It must be emphasized that the chaotic playing out of nationalist conflicts in East Central Europe, Russia, and the Middle East was not simply the unhappy byproduct of an ill-conceived Wilsonian conception of American global mission. A wide variety of wartime and post-war factors all converged to produce this heavily overdetermined outcome. The point is that, *in the perception of much of the American (and British) political and intellectual establishment*, it was the president's attempt to extend the American dream to the Old World that was failing disastrously.[108] This perception was deepened, of course, by the apparent failure of the Versailles Peace Treaty with Germany to conform to the Wilsonian principle of a peace with no annexations and no indemnities.[109] As the quotation above suggests, the failure of the American model of a national identity rooted in a democratic covenant to catch on overseas was a source of cognitive dissonance for the president himself, wedded as he was to the image of America as a chosen nation. Freed from the yoke of German and Habsburg tyranny, how could the peoples of Central and Eastern Europe choose not to choose the American formula? Eight-and-a-half decades later, Americans were to have a similarly alienating encounter with post-Saddam Iraq.

But what provoked the strongest domestic backlash against Wilson's conception of the United States' global mission was his greatest apparent success – the creation of the League of Nations. It was on this issue that his efforts to secure ratification of the Versailles Treaty by the Republican-controlled Senate foundered. Much of the fault for this lies with Wilson's obdurate refusal to accept even the mildest of reservations to Senate approval of the League of Nations Covenant. There is also no question but that the League Covenant was riddled with flaws and that the organization's effectiveness as a framework for global collective security would have been highly questionable even with full American participation.[110] The point is that Senate and public opposition to the League coalesced, not around the practical problems entailed in realizing its goals, but around the threat to American sovereignty allegedly posed by its central principle, as articulated in Article X of the Covenant – the commitment on the part of all its members "to respect and preserve as against external aggression the territorial integrity and existing political independence of all Members of the League."[111] The polarizing dynamics of the public debate about the League were such that even Republican proponents of an active American involvement in both the First World War and post-war European security, such as Wilson's Senate nemesis Henry Cabot Lodge, ended up presenting America's future course in terms of a simplistic either/or choice between "Americanism and Nationalism, and ... Internationalism."[112]

If his domestic critics were to be believed, to the extent that Wilson's vision of America's national mission was fulfilled, it would threaten to erode the boundaries between the United States and the rest of the world. Universal success for American democratic proselytism would spell danger for the survival of American national particularism. Committed by solemn international covenant to the common defense of the other nations of the world, the United States would (in the opinion of the

League's opponents) have signed away the key prerogative of national sovereignty provided for in its own constitutional covenant. What would handing sovereign power over to a body dominated by foreign govern-ments be other than a mortal stab in the back of American democracy? And how could the nation continue to play its appointed role as an inspiration to the rest of the world if it compromised the political independence that shielded it from external influence?[113] As Senator William Edgar Borah, one of the most uncompromising opponents of the League and the Versailles Treaty as a whole, put it: "America must, not alone for the happiness of her own people, *but for the moral guidance and greater contentment of the world*, be permitted to live her own life."[114]

The debate over the League of Nations highlighted one of the para-doxes inherent in being a chosen people – that the global triumph of one's covenantal model would put an end to one's distinctiveness as a nation. In the final analysis, rather than confronting the paradox, the country retreated from it and back into what seemed a safer form of national exceptionalism: isolationism. Seeing the United States as an island of purity in a world awash with sin, the isolationists of the interwar years strove to guard the nation against the corrupting international diplomatic, financial, and commercial influences that – they were convinced – had lured America into fruitless involvement in the First World War.[115]

Of course, the pressures of a shrinking world and the reality of America's disproportionate influence in that world, made the full reali-zation of the isolationist agenda impossible.[116] Isolationism collapsed entirely with the Japanese attack on Pearl Harbor. Involvement in the Second World War and planning for its aftermath led to Franklin Delano Roosevelt's revival and revision of Wilson's liberal-internationalist pro-gram in the form of the United Nations Organization and the various international monetary and trade agreements and institutions established or initiated at the 1944 Bretton Woods conference and designed to promote freer global trade.[117] The United States' long-term participation in these institutions was motivated in part by a recognition that the retreat from overseas commitments in the aftermath of the First World War had helped pave the path to World War II.

But beyond that, America's long-term commitment to the liberal-internationalist agenda in the aftermath of the Second World War was spurred by the Soviet Union's determined opposition to it. Communism's geopolitical and ideological challenge to democracy lent focus to the United States' sense of national purpose and global mission.[118] A failure to remain globally engaged would have been to invite the universal triumph of Communism; it would have led, many were convinced, to the ultimate eradication of American independence and nationhood. NSC-68, the seminal National Security Council document of April 1950 that was to frame American Cold War policy for many years, invoked the preamble to the American Constitution in advocating that the United States essentially abandon a now outdated distinction between national and global security. Under the novel conditions of the Cold War, NSC-68 contended, the securing of American liberty called for in the Constitution entailed the defense and eventual extension of freedom throughout the world. In this political-military strategy, massive increases in defense spending and the solidification and extension of alliance commitments would go hand-in-hand with efforts to strengthen institutions of international cooperation such as the United Nations: "It is clear that our long-range objectives require a strengthened United Nations, or a successor organization, to which the world can look for the maintenance of peace and order in a system based on freedom and justice."[119]

By the same token, the global crusade for democracy did not present the nation with the dilemmas of success while the Soviet threat still remained in place. As long as the global triumph of democracy remained a distant light at the end of a very long tunnel, the United States did not have to confront the paradox of how to remain a chosen nation in a world that has chosen to accept the premises of one's own national covenant. To be sure, strong suspicions continued to be directed, particularly by the American Right, towards the intrusive potential of international institutions such as the United Nations. But the confrontation with the Soviet Union meant that virtually any vital debate in the United Nations Security Council would in any case culminate in a deadlock, with one side or the other using its veto power to prevent meaningful action from being taken.[120] With the United Nations effectively marginalized, organizations such as NATO and the International Monetary Fund remained the most important multinational institutions with which the country was engaged.[121] As bodies that were clearly dominated by the United States, they did not present the kind of threat to national sovereignty that a truly effective League of Nations or United Nations Organization might seem to pose. Hence, American commitments to such alliances and institutions aroused only marginal domestic opposition once the Cold War was in full swing. In retrospect, notwithstanding the deep rifts associated with McCarthyism and the Vietnam War, it is the broad consensus over the nature of the country's essential global mission as champion of freedom in the face of Communist totalitarianism that strikes one as the most salient feature of Cold War America's self-image.

The end of the Cold War complicated the picture, raising fundamental questions about the nature of the nation's mission and the appropriate means of fulfilling it. On the one hand, the decision to seize the opportunity to expand NATO into the Soviet Union's former sphere of influence and to assist in the consolidation of democratic and capitalist institutions in East Central Europe enjoyed bipartisan support. The genocide, violent ethnic cleansing, and forced border changes of World War II and its aftermath had left many of the East Central European nation-states far more ethnically homogeneous than before.[122] This eased the tension between the principles of pluralistic democracy and national self-determination. (It's easier to be tolerant towards minorities when they're not there to bother you.) Along with the overall stability and prosperity of Western economic institutions and the incentive of eventual qualification for entry into the European Union, this novel ethnographic context contributed to the successful and uncontroversial realization of the Wilsonian project in much of East Central Europe some seventy years after the original version had begun so inauspiciously. (It was precisely in the ethnically most heterogeneous country in the region – Yugoslavia – that the path to democratization proved less than smooth.)

But in other geopolitical and institutional spheres, America's role was not so clearly defined. At what some prematurely hailed as "the end of history,"[123] the chosen nation once again seemed to face the paradox of success. For neo-Wilsonians, this was the long-awaited opportunity to breathe life into institutions such as the United Nations that had for so long been paralyzed by the deadlock between the US and the USSR. George Bush Sr.'s successful use of the United Nations as the framework for legitimizing and internationalizing the country's 1991 military response to Iraq's conquest of Kuwait seemed to bode well for this approach. But this was a deceptively simple introduction to the delights of liberal internationalism. In this particular instance, the UN functioned as a supportive chorus in an American-orchestrated drama that culminated in the successful reversal of a blatant act of international aggression. The broader implications of functioning within a liberal internationalist framework, as distinct from the Cold War-era struggle for the realization of such a vision, were more divisive.

The 1990s witnessed a burst of internationalist undertakings initiated largely by European governments and non-governmental organizations

(NGOs) and supported by sympathetic elements in the American political and intellectual establishments. Notable among these were the creation of an International Criminal Court (ICC)[124] with global jurisdiction over war crimes and crimes against humanity, the conclusion of the Kyoto Protocol on the control of global warming, and United Nations missions to oversee the implementation of the Cambodian political settlement and multiparty elections and to administer Kosovo after the American-led NATO intervention against the Serbian ethnic-cleansing campaign.[125] It would be a gross oversimplification to suggest that all of this flowed from an exclusively Wilsonian ideological well-spring. The idea of international law and supranational institutions also drew on European philosophical, ideological, and institutional traditions that pre-dated Wilson's entry on to the global scene; for that matter, the European Union was an ongoing experiment in supranational government that had no parallel elsewhere in the world. But for much of the twentieth century, the United States had been at the forefront of efforts to establish global frameworks for the rule of law and collective security. Washington had taken a leading role in organizing the international war crimes trials at Nuremberg; American activists had contributed disproportionately to the creation of the international environmental movement; it was the US that had pressed most ardently for the establishment of the United Nations Organization.[126] In a way, then, many of the European-led internationalist initiatives of the 1990s *can* be seen as bearing the imprint of a distinctively American vision for the world.

It would be naïve to paint a rosy picture of the utopian potential of such developments. African and European countries were as apathetic and/or ineffectual as the United States in their responses to the horrific 1994 genocidal campaign against the Tutsis in Rwanda and the brutal ethnic cleansing pursued by the Sudanese army and militias in Darfur from 2003 on. Various double standards limited the potential impact of the Kyoto Treaty. With or without unstinting American support, the effectiveness of the United Nations would have remained limited by its continued reliance on the armed forces of member states and by the difficulty of achieving and maintaining meaningful consensus among them. By the same token, in the absence of American diplomatic leadership and military power, the belated international interventions to halt atrocities in Bosnia and Kosovo would not have been undertaken at all.

My point is that, as in 1919, it was precisely the most successful or promising aspects of these developments that elicited the strongest nationalist backlash from influential sectors of the American political

Right. The most deeply committed opponents of the UN hated the organization, not just because of specific General Assembly resolutions, but because as an institution it raised the specter of an eventual world government. They detested the International Criminal Court, not because it lacked teeth, but because it might one day grow some, not because it failed to prevent human rights outrages in Sudan, but because it might one day indict American soldiers or "civilian contractors" for war crimes. While neo-Wilsonians embraced the growth of such international institutions as vehicles for the dissemination and protection of American conceptions of democratic government and human rights, conservatives saw them as threats to American values. International trade agreements and organizations, such as NAFTA and the World Trade Organization, might be necessary as instruments for the erosion of state-constructed barriers to economic growth even if they did infringe on the nation's sovereign powers.[127] But a more effective United Nations and a new International Criminal Court would be bodies representing a new level of intrusive government in the eyes of a conservative movement that defined America's global mission as the promotion of the individual's freedom *from* government power.[128] The disciples of Ronald Reagan were particularly inclined to insist that the collapse of East European and Soviet Communism was a vindication, not just of democratic values, but of American-style free-market economics. The End of History was supposed to be marked by the worldwide spread of the American principle of limited government, not by the emergence of a new form of world government. To cede new powers to international organizations and international courts would thus not only compromise American national sovereignty, it would also undermine this broader global mission that History had appointed the nation to carry out.[129] While President Clinton signed the Kyoto Protocol as well as the treaty creating the ICC, the latter decision came in the final weeks of his administration, in the wake of earlier State Department efforts – undertaken under pressure from the likes of Senator Jesse Helms, the Republican Chair of the Senate Foreign Relations Committee – to prevent other countries from signing the ICC treaty in its existing form. In any event, the US Senate did not ratify either of these accords and the Bush Jr. administration explicitly repudiated them.[130]

On the reactionary wing of American conservatism, such attitudes were associated with neo-isolationism. In 1996, Senator Helms called on the United States to withdraw altogether from the United Nations Organization by the year 2000 if the UN had failed by then to undertake radical,

American-dictated reforms aimed at undercutting what Helms perceived as the systematic threat the organization posed to American political sovereignty.[131] Patrick Buchanan called on the United States to assume the role of "the coiled rattlesnake that threatens none so long as it is not threatened and its domain is not intruded upon."[132] In 1998, Phyllis Schlafly presented Clinton's apparent embrace of international institutions as fundamentally incompatible with America's chosen status: "We Americans have a constitutional republic so unique, so precious ... that it would be total folly to put our necks in a yoke with any other nation. St Paul warns us ... 'Be ye not unequally yoked together with unbelievers, for what fellowship hath righteousness with unrighteousness?' "[133]

The neo-isolationist version of American exceptionalism manifested itself in much of the domestic political opposition to the Clinton administration's 1999 use of American military power in Kosovo. If human-rights violations were now to serve as sufficient occasions for American intervention, where would the line be drawn? Granted, the Bosnia and Kosovo interventions were conducted through the US-led North Atlantic Treaty Organization (NATO) – in the case of Kosovo, without so much as UN Security Council approval.[134] But how, Republican leaders asked, was American security furthered by such missions, and how long would it be before such precedents led to American soldiers being placed in the service of UN missions that served no discernible American national interest? Better to propagate American values by the power of example than to be drawn into the bottomless pit of nation-building around the world. The influence of such sentiments in Congressional as well as public opinion constrained the Clinton administration's ability to pursue a liberal-internationalist agenda and forced White House apologists for this orientation to cast their arguments in terms of a narrowly conceived national interest rather than a sweeping vision of national mission.[135] For his part, in his 2000 presidential campaign, George W. Bush famously distanced himself from an allegedly overly interventionist Democratic foreign policy by calling on his country to conduct itself with greater humility on the global stage.[136] It almost seemed as though the future president was distancing himself altogether from the proposition that America had a unique role to play in the world.[137]

But for neo-conservatives, who were becoming increasingly influential in defining the political agenda of the American Right, the end of the Cold War marked, not the end of American involvement overseas, but the beginning of an unprecedented historical opportunity for America to lead the world in a new direction. To propagate the American model mostly through the power of example, as some traditional conservatives advocated, would be to betray America's higher calling and to squander the unprecedented opportunities presented by the nation's strategic hegemony. To promote it through the vehicle of international organizations would emasculate the nation and undermine the single-mindedness of its mission. Convinced of the pusillanimity and hypocrisy of European governments and of the inherent ineffectiveness of the United Nations as an institution that pandered to the lowest common international denominator, neo-conservatives saw the fall of the Soviet Union as a not-to-be-missed opportunity for active American domination of the world. This would entail not a more modest Pentagon budget but, if anything, an even larger one than was needed during the Cold War, when deterrence of the Soviet Union rather than active expansion of American influence on multiple global fronts was the military's primary mission. Precisely because the United States embodied the ideal society, its projection of power throughout the world on behalf of its own security and in the furtherance of its political vision was not just legitimate but necessary. The pursuit of American national interests was, by definition, indistinguishable from the promotion of humanity's well-being. In the neo-conservative variant of the internationalist tradition, only through the unabashed embrace of state power could America fulfill its exceptional mission of reshaping the world in its own image, and only by pursuing that mission could it ensure its own long-term security.[138] As William Kristol and Robert Kagan contended in 1996:

American foreign policy should be informed by a clear moral purpose, based on the understanding that its moral goals and its fundamental national interests are almost always in harmony. The United States achieved its current position of strength not by practicing a policy of live and let live, nor by passively waiting for threats to arise, but by actively promoting American principles of governance abroad . . . [139]

Finally, prominent elements among the increasingly influential fundamentalist Christian Right sought to identify America's national mission as literally evangelical in nature. At a January 1994 conference of the Christian Coalition's political cadres-in-training attended by former Vice-President Dan Quayle, the assembled declaimed a revised pledge of allegiance before a flag bearing the image of a cross: "I pledge allegiance to the Christian flag, and to the Saviour, for whose Kingdom it stands, one Saviour, crucified, risen, and coming again, with life and liberty for all who believe."[140] This could be taken as a substitution of religious universalism for this-worldly nationalism, but it could just as readily suggest an Americanization of the Christian credo. The point is that, for fundamentalists, there was no perceived conflict between American patriotism and Christian universalism. As the future attorney-general (under the first Bush Jr. administration), John Ashcroft, put it in his 1999 commencement address at Bob Jones University: "Unique among the nations, America recognized the source of our character as being godly and eternal, not being civic and temporal. And because we have understood that our source is eternal, America has been different. We have no king but Jesus."[141] As in the Wilsonian tradition, the political theology of the Christian Right acknowledged no conflict between the true interests of the nation and the salvation of humanity. The difference was that according to the fundamentalist school of thought, an apocalyptic period of gut-wrenching Tribulation, not an enlightened era of bleeding-heart internationalism, would mark the passage to the End of Days.[142] The gateway to this passage was to be found, not at the United Nations building in New York, but on the Temple Mount in Jerusalem, which it was Christian America's special responsibility to ensure remained in the hands of the original Chosen People (for idiosyncratic theological reasons to be described below). As Pat Robertson put it in December 2003,

the entire world is being convulsed by a religious struggle. The fight is not about money or territory; it is not about poverty versus wealth; it is not about ancient customs versus modernity. No – the struggle is whether Hubal, the Moon God of Mecca, known as Allah, is supreme, or whether the Judeo-Christian Jehovah God of the Bible is Supreme.

If God's chosen people turn over to Allah control of their most sacred sites ... if they believe their claim to the Holy Land comes only from Lord Balfour of England and the ever fickle United Nations rather than the promises of Almighty God – then in that event, Islam will have won the battle.[143]

* * *

The attacks of 11 September 2001 shook up most Americans' assumptions about their nation's place in the world. On the one hand, it was a nasty shock for many to realize that American cultural influence and political power were the objects of intense hatred among significant sectors of the Islamic world. As members of a nation that regards its own society as a pluralistic microcosm of what an ideal world would look like,

Americans genuinely expect everyone to like them and emulate them. An element of cognitive dissonance arises upon the realization that this is not necessarily the case. On the other hand, the outrageousness and horror of the attack functioned like the Japanese assault on Pearl Harbor in galvanizing support for a new American engagement with world affairs. Unlike December 1941, however, the precise identity of the enemy and the appropriate form and scope of the response were far from self-evident. The consensus on the need to pursue a war against terror left open the question of how such a war should be waged and only briefly papered over the gaps among the divergent views of the United States' role in the world. Proponents of three of the major conceptions of American mission outlined above – liberal internationalists, neo-conservatives, and Christian Fundamentalists – claimed to hold the key to resolving the nation's quandary.

Neo-Wilsonians were struck by the surge of sympathy for the United States throughout much of the rest of the world in the aftermath of 9/11 as well as the broad international support for the retaliatory campaign against Afghanistan's Taliban regime. For them, this pointed to the potential for broad international cooperation in the war against terror as well as to the possibility of using such a multilateral effort as a springboard for the strengthening of the global rule of law and collective security.[144]

An influential group of neo-conservatives with access to, and presence in, the new Bush Jr. administration reached precisely the opposite conclusion. According to them, 9/11 was a historical watershed that highlighted the dangers of subjecting American freedom of action to the restraints of international institutions. The nation had to make use of this opportunity to advance its mission by taking international law in its own hands, seizing the initiative in spreading its democratic way of life to the world region that appeared most resistant to it: the Islamic Middle East. Replacement of Saddam Hussein's totalitarian, Arab pan-nationalist, pariah regime in Iraq with an American-built democracy was, members of this group had long argued, the key to achieving this goal, just as American defeat and occupation of Germany and Japan in the 1940s had planted the seeds of freedom in those former hotbeds of totalitarianism after the Second World War and consequently contributed to democracy's containment of, and ultimate triumph over, Soviet Communism. Those allies who chose to follow the United States' lead in the Iraqi enterprise were welcome to do so. But the US needed to firmly maintain its position in the cockpit of History, unimpeded by any misgivings over the unilateral use of force – misguided qualms of the sort that had impeded America's pursuit of its global mission in the years since the end of the Cold War.[145] As William Kristol and Lawrence Kaplan put it:

Absent the United States, who else could uphold decency in the world? . . . The United Nations? Far from existing as an autonomous entity, the organization is nothing more than a collection of states, many of them autocratic and few of them as public-spirited as America . . .

A humane future . . . will require an American foreign policy that is unapologetic, idealistic, assertive and well funded. America must not only be the world's policeman or its sheriff, it must be its beacon and guide.[146]

For the Christian Right, the attacks of September 11 were a reminder that, as a nation specially blessed by Providence, the US was subject to God's wrath when it strayed from its appointed path. The Reverend Jerry Falwell, appearing on the Reverend Pat Robertson's televangelical show "The 700 Club" on 13 September 2001, took a position that seemed indistinguishable from that of the Taliban when he explained the fall of the Twin Towers in New York City as divine retribution for the secular-liberal sinfulness into which undesirable elements such as the American Civil Liberties Union, feminists, and gay activists had been leading America.[147] But by the same token, for the Talibangelists[148] and their audience of Christian extremists, al-Qaeda's assault on the US could be understood as marking the beginning of a potentially apocalyptic, and ultimately redemptive, religious war in which America would have a special role to play. It might even presage the End of Days. According to the doctrine of Dispensationalist Premillennialism, which has acquired the status of quasi-orthodoxy among the mainstream of American evangelical Christians, the thousand-year kingdom of Jesus on earth will be preceded by a period of Tribulation inaugurated by the reconstruction of the Jewish Temple in Jerusalem. True believers will then be beamed up to Heaven in the much awaited Rapture. The unbelievers "left behind"[149] will suffer the horrors of the Tribulation, while an elect minority of Jews will accept Christ, win converts among others of those left behind, and fight the forces of the Anti-Christ. The culmination of this war in the Battle of Armageddon will be followed by the millennium of Jesus' this-worldly rule.[150] A cataclysmic clash between the United States and the Islamic world fits readily into this much-heralded scenario, insofar as it seems to confer upon America a unique role in reshaping the Middle East balance of power, potentially paving the way for the restoration of the Temple and the breathlessly awaited chain of events leading to the Christian millennium.[151]

* * *

The Bush Jr. administration's post-9/11 foreign policy, and its reception by the American public, reflected the intermingled yet unequal influences of these three schools of thought. Secretary of State Colin Powell's position hewed most closely to the neo-Wilsonian line, with his repeated attempts to induce the president to gain UN sanction for whatever military action he took.[152] Yet clearly the advocates of an essentially unilateral approach to the securing of American interests and the reconfiguration of the Middle East's power balance and political culture held the upper hand in George W.'s White House. The rushed and impatient attitude toward the renewed UN inspections regime in Iraq and the rapid countdown to war regardless of the Security Council's final position, reflected a dramatic if ephemeral triumph for the neo-conservative conception of the United States' role in the world.[153]

At the same time, the administration's allies among the Christian Right embraced what they perceived as a crusade pitting Christian America against the Islamic foe. Lieutenant-General William G. Boykin, a former field commander in the United States' brief 1994 Somalian intervention, newly appointed to the Pentagon in 2003, gained notoriety by informing church congregations that the United States was engaged in a war against Satan in the Islamic world and that God routinely determined the outcome of American presidential elections (citing as evidence Bush's 2000 electoral victory despite his loss of the popular vote!).[154] The Christian Broadcasting Network (CBN), run by the Reverend Pat Robertson (founder of the politically influential Christian Coalition), likewise insinuated that the war's real protagonists were Jesus and Satan. Its website alerted readers that: "Our enemy isn't merely flesh and blood, but as Ephesians 2 tells us, we war against ' . . . the prince of the power of the air, the spirit that is at work in all of those who refuse to obey God . . . '" CBN went on to reassure the faithful that: "As God's true children, we need not fear. For God has given us the power through His Son Jesus Christ to defeat every principality and power that comes against us." Using the conflict as a recruitment tool, CBN called on the devout to form "an army of prayer warriors" that would direct its devotions towards securing "divine intervention and spiritual breakthrough in Iraq" and "supernatural protection of our troops and Coalition forces."[155] Registering on-line to join "Operation Breakthrough," as this prayer offensive was dubbed, would not only hasten salvation, it would also grant devout web-surfers a this-worldly reward in the form of privileged access to free downloads on the CBN website.[156]

The president's own evolving sense of national mission, while apparently chiefly beholden to the influence of his neo-conservative advisors and their allies in his administration, was not bereft of religious overtones. (For that matter, an at least token respect for religiosity informs the writings of many neo-conservatives.) A professed born-again Christian, Bush had initially described the war against terror as a crusade, and gone on to identify Saddam Hussein's Iraq as part of an "Axis of Evil."[157] The president quickly abandoned his earlier reticence about the nation's global role, arguing that the hostility of the United States' enemies could only be understood as an expression of their hatred of the universal value that America embodied, namely freedom.[158] The unprecedented scale of the 9/11 terror attacks thus provided a sort of perverse validation of the distinctiveness of the nation's role as a global champion of liberty. In his Second Inaugural Address, Bush articulated a sort of Truman Doctrine for the new century, declaring it to be America's national mission to spread freedom throughout the world. Although he took pains to deny that the US was a chosen nation, an observer might be forgiven for thinking that he did protest too much. His perceived need to deny any claims of chosenness appeared to be a direct function of the breathtakingly universalistic scope of his new vision for the nation's foreign policy. Mixing democratic universalism with a sense of religious mission, the president declared:

America's vital interests and our deepest beliefs are now one. From the day of our Founding, we have proclaimed that every man and woman on this earth has rights, and dignity, and matchless value, because they bear the image of the Maker of Heaven and earth. Across the generations we have proclaimed the imperative of self-government, because no one is fit to be a master, and no one deserves to be a slave. Advancing these ideals is the mission that created our Nation. It is the honorable achievement of our fathers. Now it is the urgent requirement of our nation's security, and the calling of our time.[159]

As the post-invasion occupation of Iraq dragged on amidst violence and chaos, some fissures began to appear among the various elements of the administration's ideological coalition. While liberal internationalists outside the Bush government continued to decry its alienation of world opinion and NATO allies,[160] the administration's own token neo-Wilsonian, Colin Powell, announced his resignation from the State Department on the eve of the president's second term. For their part, some neo-conservatives were aghast at the alacrity with which the over-burdened US military authorities were scaling down and backing away from many of the Bush administration's more ambitious plans for the transformation of Iraq's political culture and institutions in America's image.[161] By late 2004, even elements on the Christian Right seemed to be improvising a possible exit strategy for themselves. In a CNN interview, Pat Robertson revealed that he had harbored doubts all along over the wisdom of invading Iraq and claimed that President Bush had blithely failed to heed his pre-war advice that he prepare the nation for the certain prospect of casualties.[162] The long-term outcome of the Iraq war remained unknown at the time this book went to press. But it seems safe to say that, at the beginning of the twenty-first century, as in 1919, the experience of prolonged and serious military engagement overseas was leaving the American political establishment divided and uncertain over how to bridge the gap between the sweeping nature of its conception of the nation's global mission and the tremendous economic and human costs that a systematic commitment to such a mission would necessarily entail.

* * *

In practice, of course, American foreign policy is not informed exclusively by the sense that the nation has been chosen by God or history to carry out a special mission to the world. It would be ridiculously reductionist to make such a claim. A variety of practical economic interests, pressing security concerns (nowadays including the very real, combined threats of terrorism and nuclear proliferation), long-term alliance commitments, and often unstated ethno-cultural and religious affinities have helped motivate and direct the exercise of state power in America's case as in that of other nation-states. But the sense that America is a nation with a special role to play in world history does constitute a powerful element in the rhetorical and ideological framing of the country's foreign policy, and – by virtue of that – in its substantive shaping. As we have seen, the idea of a distinctive national mission has colored critical debates among isola-tionists and interventionists, unilateralists and internationalists, about how the country should reorient itself to the world at key historical junctures. Each school of thought has invoked the nation's special his-torical status as a basis for the legitimacy of its position. It is no less true for being trite to contend that the idea of American exceptionalism has made it difficult for American statesmen to pursue relations with other countries on the basis of an avowedly Machiavellian *Realpolitik*. This has been a source of endless frustration for diplomat-commentators such as

Henry Kissinger and the late George Kennan, who have advocated a more flexible and nuanced understanding of American national interests in a complex and deceitful world.[163] Yet it is unrealistic to expect that a country whose national origins are rooted in claims of chosenness could completely disconnect its foreign policy from this tradition. Moreover, while the pitfalls of a crude and simplistic exceptionalism are legion, a foreign policy based on a purely Hobbesian understanding of international affairs would risk falling into a dangerously self-fulfilling vicious circle of its own. As for those contemporary liberal-internationalists who decry the idea of national chosenness or exceptionalism as a form of self-aggrandizement and a source of moral corruption, they certainly have a point, but they would also do well to look to the roots of their own ideological tradition; the very idea of creating an international system subject to the rule of law was promoted by Woodrow Wilson in the name of America's special mission to the world.

Responses to American exceptionalism

America is not alone in seeing itself as the bearer of a global mission.[164] It's just that, as the most powerful country of the past century, its conception of its national mission has had a disproportionate global impact. Other societies' responses to American power and cultural influence have been shaped in part by their own competing claims to exceptional world-historical status, while America's sense of national mission has been molded by such external challenges to the legitimacy of its claims. The ideological foundation of the Soviet Union was its claim to constitute the vanguard of world-wide proletarian revolution – an internationalist perspective that became heavily tinged by more traditional claims about the unique qualities of the Russian national soul.[165] The United States' definition of the singular role it claimed for itself in world affairs was molded for much of the twentieth century by the Soviet counter-claim, starting with Woodrow Wilson's delivery of his January 1918 Fourteen Points speech as an indirect response to the ideological challenge of the Bolshevik Revolution. The Cold War pitted American and Soviet claims to chosenness against one another in a global struggle that ended when one of those claims collapsed.

Resentment of the United States in the Arab and Islamic worlds is certainly linked to American support of the State of Israel, but is also rooted in a perceived clash between the universalistic claims of Islam and the global reach of America's national sense of mission. The Western

gospel of political pluralism, cultural permissiveness, and sexual equality –
of which the United States is seen as the prime exporter – clashes
directly with patriarchal socio-cultural traditions that have become closely
associated with the Islamic way of life.[166] Islam, in turn, is a proselytizing
religion that in principle regards as illegitimate any non-Islamic form of
political sovereignty and that dismisses as inferior any non-Islamic way of
life.[167] This has made the persistent humbling of Islamic states by Euro-
Atlantic powers and increasing penetration of Islamic societies by
Western mores over the course of the modern era all the more galling.
The evangelizing quality of American foreign policy – be it the liberal-
internationalist or neo-conservative version thereof – is particularly hard to
swallow for societies that regard themselves as upholders of the one true
religion. The historic failure of quasi-secular, pan-Arab nationalism to
create a viable modern framework for an economic, cultural, and political
resurgence of the Arabo-Islamic world has widely discredited it as nothing
better than a pale reflection of a morally bankrupt Western model. Significant social sectors have fallen back on a militantly fundamentalist
interpretation of Islam as the key to restoring a sense of collective honor
and global pride of place to their peoples. Jewish political sovereignty in
the midst of the realm of Islam and American cultural, political, and
military intrusion into the region in the name of its universal mission
represent the twin evils that followers of the true religion are sworn to
overcome. The more apocalyptic the final showdown, the more decisive
an end it will bring to the transitory distraction that is history.[168]

The Cold War and the confrontation between America's global mission
and Islamic universalism are fairly obvious examples of how competing
claims of chosenness (national and otherwise) can shape dramatic international confrontations and crises. But relations among allies can also be
inflected by this theme, often in more subtle and intriguing ways.

The history of Anglo-American relations is a case in point. The relative
grace with which the British ultimately came to accept the United States'
supplanting of their dominant role in world affairs may retrospectively
blind us to the historic centrality of Britain's own sense of chosenness to
its self-definition as a world power. English – and, by extension, British –
identity had crystallized in the course of the sixteenth to eighteenth
centuries around a national self-image as a Protestant New Israel fending
off the Satanic forces of Spanish and French Catholicism in an epic
struggle of world-historical significance. This identity came to be bound
up with the evolution of constitutional monarchy and parliamentary

government – institutions that guaranteed individual liberty in contrast to the tyrannical features of Continental absolutism. In the course of the eighteenth to twentieth centuries, this Protestant nationalist tradition developed into an increasingly secularized conception of Britain's role as a model to the world of how to blend a strong sense of social hierarchy and aristocratic superiority with representative institutions that placed curbs on arbitrary authority. The country's commercial success and preeminent imperial status were taken as marks of the moral superiority of its socio-political tradition and as vehicles for the diffusion of its values.[169]

The loss of the American colonies struck a temporary but sorely felt blow to the British elite's self-confident sense of its nation's chosen status. The United States' self-defined role as a freedom-loving David resisting an oppressive British Goliath cut to the core of the English sense of historical exceptionalism. If it was to contest the usurpation of its status as chosen nation, Britain would have to do more than recoup its tarnished prestige as a world power; it would have to associate itself with an uplifting moral cause.

The wars of 1793–1815 against revolutionary and Napoleonic France served both these purposes, allowing Britain to reaffirm its superpower role in the pursuit of a just cause against a hypocritical rival that was using the torch of liberty to burn down obstacles to its Continental dominion. With Napoleon defeated, it was Britain's use of its naval power to enforce its principled stand against the international slave trade that played a central role in its reconfigured sense of chosenness. The fight to suppress the global traffic in slaves served not only to lend a lofty purpose to Britain's global exercise of power, but more specifically to undercut slave-owning Americans' rival pretensions to chosen status. Britain, not America, was the world's true beacon of liberty.[170]

At the turn of the twentieth century, in the face of new challenges to their country's preeminence from rival European powers, Britain's ruling elites strove to convince themselves and others that Britain was uniquely capable of projecting its power globally in a manner that converged with the legitimate interests of humanity as a whole. In Africa, British imperial expansion had been spearheaded by missionaries seeking to eradicate the Islamic slave trade. In Europe, Britain alone of all the great powers harbored no territorial ambitions of its own. Throughout the "civilized world," Britain's interest lay in preserving the balance of power by upholding the independence and territorial integrity of existing states. Hence, there was no reason why other powers should begrudge Britain its global reach. As one influential Foreign Office official put it, in contrasting Britain's global power with Germany's growing ambitions on the eve of the First World War, Britain's foreign policy both should be and was "so directed as to harmonize with the general desires and ideals common to all mankind ..."[171]

The growing recognition on the British establishment's part from the late nineteenth century onwards of its geopolitical vulnerability induced it to seek accommodation and avoid conflict with the United States. Yet even in the context of what might have been an increasingly humiliating relationship of growing dependence on a former colony, the idea of British national chosenness was not scuttled outright; it was cultivated by proxy, as it were. The process of accommodation to American hegemony was facilitated by a sense of historic, ethno-cultural, and linguistic affinity with the American socio-political establishment. This served in the long run to ease the pain of ceding primacy of place to America in world affairs. While America's twentieth-century rise to prominence and Britain's concurrent decline were obviously galling to many Britons, it was possible to find some solace in thinking of the United States as an offshoot of Britain and in regarding its growing global influence as an extension of the United Kingdom's historic role.[172] This was the perspective adopted by Sir Winston Churchill (himself half-American by parentage), whose *History of the English-Speaking Peoples* can be seen as an attempt to root Britain's special relationship with the United States in a shared historical consciousness.[173] After all, the very ideals espoused by America's democratic evangelists were rooted in Anglo-Saxon religio-political traditions and the spread of American cultural influence ensured the global dominance of the English language. Over the generations, many prominent members of the American political and social establishments, such as Theodore Roosevelt and Henry Cabot Lodge, had consistently presented their country's Anglo-Saxon heritage as the fount of its identity and values.[174] There was considerable comfort to be found in that, even if the brash missionary style of their not-so-quiet cousins struck world-weary twentieth-century Britons as rather off-putting and dangerously naïve.[175] At worst, American ascendance could be regarded with bemused resignation. At best, American acknowledgment of a special historic and cultural relationship with Britain represented an opportunity to maintain a global role for the United Kingdom out of proportion to its reduced economic and military power.[176]

Not so for the French. True, the French monarchy's critical support of the American War of Independence and the subsequent echoing of many of the American Revolution's themes by its French counterpart, created the basis for a myth about the existence of a special link between the two nations' destinies. Both countries have traditionally applauded the Marquis de Lafayette's service on George Washington's military staff and his subsequent role in securing official French assistance during the American War of Independence. The Statue of Liberty, presented to the United States in the name of the French people several years after the centenary of the American Revolution, was intended to stand as testimony to the idea of a common ideological commitment shared by the two nations. But such clichés resonated shallowly in comparison with the sonorant linguistic and historic cords that connected American and British elites.[177] The centrality of its language to France's conception of its civilizing mission[178] made it much more difficult for French leaders than it was for their British counterparts to regard with relative equanimity the global spread of American influence in the course of the twentieth century. Resentment of growing American power was accentuated by the experience of the Second World War, in the course of which France's unhappy episode of occupation by, and collaboration with, Nazi Germany ended thanks more to American-led military action than to the heroic struggle of the country's own resistance movement. At the same time, the Roosevelt administration had displayed obvious hostility towards the exiled General de Gaulle's wartime effort to represent his London- and Algiers-based Free French movement as the embodiment of a sovereign great power. These experiences contributed to French political and intellectual elites' insecurity about their nation's place in a superpower-dominated, post-1945 world in which its own global posture was undermined by debilitating colonial wars in Indochina and Algeria. By the same token, Britain's successful cultivation of a special relationship with the United States from the Second World War on played into growing French fears that the global role of their nation's language and civilization was in danger of being engulfed by a tidal wave of Anglo-American cultural, economic, and military-political imperialism.[179]

In their struggle to withstand this Anglophone juggernaut, French intellectual and political elites could draw on a long-established tradition, dating to well before the French Revolution, of justifying their country's own aspirations to great-power status by portraying its national culture and language as the embodiment of universal values. David A. Bell has discovered vivid examples of how mid-eighteenth-century French nationalist propaganda dwelled on the contrast between France as the fount of supranational European civilization and England as a nation of barbarians who had strayed from civilized norms.[180] The "ugly American" of the

Cold War fitted readily into this prefabricated mold,[181] serving as a foil for France's national self-image as the source of illumination for the world.[182] As Richard Kuisel has shown, in such a context, every intrusion of American culture or lifestyle could be construed as posing a mortal threat to the nation's soul. Thus, the Coca-Cola Company's post-1945 marketing offensive was portrayed by the prominent newspaper *Le Monde* as threatening "the moral landscape of France."[183] More recently, the fast-food chain McDonald's has provided French protestors with a conveniently American face to place on the impersonal forces of globalization that they claim are swamping their country's economy and culture.[184] One commentator has gone so far as to ascribe unsavory motives to beef patties, calling for "resistance to the hegemonic pretenses of hamburgers."[185]

To be sure, broad segments of the French intelligentsia and masses alike continued to be fascinated and influenced by the look and feel of things American throughout this period, just as some of their eighteenth-century predecessors had admired various features of British political and intellectual culture.[186] It was precisely the attractiveness of many aspects of Anglophone civilization – combined with France's painfully obvious twentieth-century dependence on Anglo-American military power for its very survival as an independent state – that seemed so threatening to the French sense of cultural distinctiveness and civilizing mission. After the student riots of May 1968, as a broad socio-political consensus built around a supposedly American-style mixture of consumerism, materialism, and multiculturalism seemed to be supplanting France's passionate ideological divisions of yesteryear, the very unwonted stability of their society led influential members of the French intellectual and political elite to voice their disgust with the apparent demise of France's traditional role as a battleground for world-historical ideas and as a champion of beautiful, collectivist abstractions.[187] "A French Republic that will only be a democracy like the others is insignificant," harrumphed Régis Debray.[188]

For their part, Americans have readily drawn on longstanding British stereotypes about the French as a people whose pretensions are as off-putting as they are unfounded, and whose claim to represent the principles of liberty and equality is belied by their fetish for centralized government, cultural homogenization, and their history of military aggression on the European continent.[189] The fact that Charles de Gaulle, as founder and first president of the Fifth Republic (1958–), often seemed to treat Anglo-American influence as though it posed a greater threat than the Warsaw Pact to French and West European interests, cut to the core of Americans' sense of themselves as selfless saviors of a France and

Europe that had proved incapable of keeping their own houses in order. De Gaulle's tendency to conduct himself with a Napoleonic arrogance that seemed completely out of keeping with his country's sharply reduced power profile made his challenges to American dominance of NATO and to American policy in Vietnam all the more infuriating.[190]

In resisting what they regard as American hegemonic tendencies, de Gaulle and his successors have invoked the very principles of multilateralism, democratic pluralism, and international law that the United States did so much to promote, off and on, in the course of the twentieth century. Having disengaged their country from the role of colonial power, French governments have posed as champions of Third World national self-determination in the face of American neo-imperialism. They have presented their cultural protectionism as a contribution to the defense of global diversity.[191] They have promoted the cause of European integration as a counter-balance to an American-led NATO. And, most recently, they have sought to use France's position as a permanent member of the United Nations Security Council to check or curtail what they see as the United States' unilateralist and hegemonic proclivities.[192]

There is unquestionably a self-serving quality to France's neo-Wilsonianism, as there necessarily is to virtually any invocation of collective interests and universal principles by the representatives of a state. Moreover, in its general contours, this approach has a pedigree in modern French history that long antedates Wilson's appearance on the world stage. The French revolutionaries undertook their European conquests in the name of liberating their neighbors from tyranny.[193] More subtly, under the Bourbon Restoration, France's master diplomat and champion of political survival, Talleyrand, briefly and opportunistically championed small states' rights to full and equal participation in the deliberations of the Congress of Vienna in 1814 as a tactical response to the initial exclusion of post-Napoleonic France from the inner sanctum of great power decision-making.[194] In its contemporary resistance to American global power, the French government draws on its own venerable tradition of casting its national interests in universalistic terms. There is nonetheless a delicious irony in American Defense Secretary Donald Rumsfeld's notorious dismissal of France and Germany as representatives of "Old Europe" for their espousal of the principles of international accountability that were so central to Wilson's New Diplomacy.[195]

Of course, France's stance is not remotely as threatening to America's sense of security, national identity, and global mission as the existential challenges that were once posed by Soviet Communism and are now presented by Islamic fundamentalism. But it is precisely the fact that the French challenge comes from within the Western camp and is presented in terms so similar to longstanding American positions on national self-determination, international law, and collective security that makes it so galling (so to speak!). In what was possibly the most farcical episode in the history of Franco-American rivalry, the chairman of the US House of Representatives' Administration Committee, Ohio Congressman Bob Ney, retaliated against France's opposition to the American push for a war against Iraq by ordering that the item "French fries" be renamed on House cafeteria menus.[196] Ludicrous as this attempt at a snub was, the widely emulated initiative was interesting in that it did not transform "French fries" into "American fries," but rather into "freedom fries." It was as if to suggest that, whereas the French were hypocritical in their espousal of global principles, American policy truly represented the cause of human freedom rather than a narrowly national interest.

No matter how petty and childish their competition for exceptional status may sometimes seem, it clearly shapes French and American popular images of one another as well as diplomatic relations between the two nations' governments. And no matter how self-serving the invocation of global principles in the pursuit of national security and power may be, the point is that every chosen nation that is a great power defines its very notion of national security in terms of its ability to mold the world in its own image.

CARTOGRAPHIC AMBIGUITIES: THE SHIFTING SHAPES OF
MISSIONARY NATIONS[197]

Given his country's eighteenth- and nineteenth-century experience of political instability, revolution, and regime change, it is not hard to see how Ernest Renan came by his conception of the nation as the product of a daily plebiscite.[198] Renan employed this idea in two ways. At one level, he meant it to be understood *figuratively*, as a way of encapsulating the notion that a nation's existence is a manifestation of the will of the individuals who compose it – an expression of their subjective identities rather than a function of qualities that could objectively be ascribed to them. Given this conception of nationhood as a subjective quality, he also advocated the *literal* use of plebiscites as the most just mechanism for adjudicating territorial disputes between rival nation-states.[199]

Renan's 1884 lecture on nationalism came in the wake of the forceful annexation of Alsace and most of Lorraine by the newly created German

Empire thirteen years earlier on the basis of the claim that these provinces' inhabitants were objectively Germans. There was good reason to believe that, if given the chance to vote on the matter, most Alsatians and Lorrainers would have opted to remain a part of France. But the idea of the plebiscite as the ideal democratic tool for settling rival territorial claims was generally applicable, and in the twentieth century it became a frequently employed instrument for the settling of both border disputes and secessionist claims. In some instances, entire nation-states were created and/or legitimized through referendum – as early as 1860 in the case of Italy and as late as 1999 in the case of East Timor's secession from Indonesia. Each such collective choice in effect constitutes a covenant – either among the entire population of a newly created nation-state, or between the inhabitants of a province and the nation to which a majority among them have chosen to attach themselves. In its territorial manifestation, the covenant is regarded as eternally binding – on the majority who voted for it, the hapless minority who voted against it, and their descendants, to the end of time. After all, as Renan himself acknowledged, it would be a recipe for chaos to take his initial figure of speech literally and hold such plebiscites on a daily basis. These votes constitute irreversible, once-in-a-national-lifetime choices that effectively limit the options available to subsequent generations. The territorial configuration of a nation-state having once been legitimized by a covenantal act, it becomes a seamlessly integrated Promised Land that belongs to the nation as a whole and its borders may not be tampered with again (unless it's a matter of expansion at someone else's expense!).

This, of course, is precisely one of the reasons why territorial disputes among nations are so bitter in the first place. A regional population's demand for a vote on independence runs up against the claim of the ruling nation-state that said region is an integral part of its territory by virtue of an earlier covenant (mythical or real, implied or explicit). The southern states were not allowed to break away from the American Union. The Republic of Georgia's leaders vow to reassert control one day over separatist Abkhazia and South Ossetia. A shrinking proportion of the Israeli Right continues to regard a prospective withdrawal from any part of the West Bank as an illegitimate amputation of part of the nation's ancient heartland, while many Palestinians refuse to surrender their claims to any part of pre-1948 Palestine. For Serb nationalists, Kosovo is the historic core of their nation. The fact that its ethnic Serbs have long since been reduced to the status of a small minority amidst a majority Albanian population is a testament to the long suffering of the martyred Serb people, not a legitimate basis for the province's secession from Serbia.

In the final analysis, every nation feels that it has been chosen in the weak sense of having been selected by God or History to dwell securely within its own particular land. Even the most democratized version of a national covenant carries with it the implication that the Promised Land acquired under its terms is inalienable as long as the covenant and the nation to which it gave rise still exist. So powerful are such myths of the immutability of the nation-state's frontiers that, as Ian Lustick has pointed out, even the social science literature on the modern state tends to associate boundary formation with the process of state *building*, while uncritically assuming that *established* states operate within fixed and unchanging territorial frameworks.[200]

Although, in practice, irredentist claims, expansionist ambitions, and secessionist conflicts call into question existing international frontiers, such practical disputes and inconsistencies are essentially limited to the question of where exactly the nation's borders should lie. The existence of a conflict over the matter only serves to intensify the feelings of solidarity among those who contest or defend a given line in the sand. Indeed, Benedict Anderson has vividly described the nation-state's territorial outline as constituting an immediately recognizable logo, a visual representation of the nation that can be readily portrayed on postage stamps and in textbooks and seized upon as a simple, standardized symbol of its identity. The nation's map is its face.[201]

But upon close examination, the facial features of missionary peoples are not quite so readily defined (ethnic stereotypes notwithstanding). To the extent that a nation thinks of itself as having been chosen to undertake a mission towards humanity as a whole, borders that shut out the world – or that constrain the nation – may represent an anomaly. By the same token, how can a nation-state maintain its distinctive identity without establishing some way of demarcating its territorial and demographic boundaries? Such dilemmas blur the cartographic physiognomy of some chosen nations.

The United States is the case that most vividly illustrates this tension over the need to delimit the missionary nation while maintaining a sense of its limitless potential. The United States' sense of its manifest destiny was linked early on to a vision of virtually endless expansion across the spacious geography of the North American continent. In the context of traditional American historical memory and political culture, the term "frontier" refers, not to a fixed international boundary, but to the ever-advancing zone separating settled land from land-to-be-settled and – by metaphorical extension – existing accomplishments from future ambitions.[202] The institutional framework for the absorption of new territory into the republic was the federal structure whose design allowed in principle for the accommodation of an infinite number of states in the Union. In practice, the limits of this expansion appear to have been reached with the incorporation of Alaska and Hawaii as states in 1959 (although it remains possible that Puerto Rico may one day decide to apply for statehood and one can speculate over the scenario of some Canadian provinces electing to join the United States in the event of Québec's secession). Yet, fixed as its borders may seem to be, the country's resultant map does not lend itself to use as a nationalist logo, given Alaska's and Hawaii's geographic non-contiguity with the other forty-eight states. More importantly, the historical experience of seemingly unlimited expansion prevented the crystallization of a fixed geographical self-image during the nation's formative decades.

At one and the same time, the motif of unbounded potential was always a function of Americans' sense of *geographic removal* from the Old World. For much of the nineteenth century, the broad waters of the Atlantic were seen as keeping the nation apart from the world's great powers, giving Americans the luxury of thinking of their own continent as a self-contained cosmos within which the nation's frontier could potentially move ever forward. One of the beautiful attributes of this nation's Promised Land was the fact that it was not bounded by any human-imposed limits but only by the natural features of a divinely created geography: it extended "from sea to shining sea." The 1823 Monroe Doctrine set off the entire Western Hemisphere as a zone that was out of bounds for European powers (although in practice, it was the British navy that enforced the Doctrine during much of the nineteenth century).[203] Conversely, the United States' capture of Cuba, Puerto Rico, and the Philippines from Spain at the turn of the twentieth century provoked a backlash against the prospect of alien cultures and races being incorporated wholesale into the American body politic. A sharp line was drawn between territories settled (or to be settled) by Anglo-Americans and therefore fit for inclusion as states, and heavily populated, predominantly non-white and non-English-speaking lands that could be administered by Washington but not absorbed into the nation.[204] In recent years, concerns over illegal immigration from Mexico and terrorist infiltration efforts have sharpened the impulse to focus on border control and defense of the "homeland" – itself a term that is essentially new to the American national political vocabulary, as Amy Kaplan has pointed out.[205] A shrinking globe has impinged on Americans' sense of geographic removal from the rest of the world and heightened the pressure to establish impenetrable barriers between the chosen nation and the evils that threaten it from without.

The gap between the dream of the unbounded nation and the need to protect its borders has been bridged, since the early- to mid-twentieth century, by the role of the immigrant. Of course, the actual history of immigration has itself been laced with contradictions, often eliciting hostile nativist responses.[206] But as a mythologized element of the timeless American drama, the part played by the immigrant is crucial. Its self-image as a refuge for the oppressed of the earth legitimizes the chosen nation's setting itself apart from the rest of the world. By guarding its borders (from, among other things, illegal immigration!) it protects the people from the entirety of the globe who have sought freedom and prosperity on its soil. Indeed, to the extent that America succeeds in maintaining the harmonious coexistence of its multi-ethnic population, it serves as a microcosm of an ideal of global coexistence.[207] The defense of the nation's particular, bounded interests thus serves the universal interest of humanity. For their part, in voluntarily abandoning their ancient ties to blood and soil, *choosing* instead to bind themselves to the American national covenant, immigrants have lent a concrete, human dimension to the idea of the United States as the *chosen* nation.

Early in the twentieth century, the Statue of Liberty came to be seen as an evocative symbol of these themes.[208] (See Figure 9.) Its location in New York harbor marks the transition from the world without to the realm of the chosen nation within. Its torch sheds the nation's light of freedom out upon the world beyond, while serving as an inviting beacon to the "huddled masses yearning to be free . . ." who flock to the New World's shores.[209] Juxtaposed with the Statue of Liberty is Ellis Island – the late nineteenth- to early twentieth-century clearing house for immigrants now itself a national monument to the immigrant experience. The sharply contrasting images of the inspiring statue and the prosaic, not to say exhausting and often humiliating, experience of going through (or being turned back by!) immigration control at Ellis Island[210] are woven together into a coherent symbolic tapestry.[211] The ordeal of traversing America's main port of entry, as commemorated in the photographs and inscriptions of the museum that Ellis Island has become, can be viewed as a rite of passage that marked the initiation of new arrivals into the American experience. Immigrants negotiated the frontier of New York

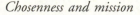

Figure 9 "Remember Your First Thrill of American Liberty." American First World War bond-issue poster advertising the Second Liberty Loan of 1917. Artist unknown. First published in New York: Sackett & Wilhelms Corp., 1917. Courtesy of the Library of Congress, Prints and Photographs Division.

harbor the way the pioneers struggled through the wastelands of the American West. Waiting endless hours in line and undergoing the scrutiny of medical staff and immigration officials, those who made it through the hazing ritual at Ellis Island went on to experience the myriad other hardships of the immigrant experience. It was precisely their willingness to endure these hardships, so goes the myth, that lent substance and meaning to their choice of America as their new national home. Rather than a product of their desperation, their submission to the ordeal of immigration is interpreted as a mark of bravery.[212] And it is one of the United States' qualities as the chosen nation that it rewards such sacrifice and suffering in this world rather than in the world to come – if not for the first generation of immigrants, then for their children.

* * *

The configuration and meaning of borders has been a complex issue for other chosen and missionary peoples as well. For the British, their natural borders long seemed central to their identity as a people marked for a special destiny, separated and distinguished by God and the English Channel from Continental Europe. (In the words of a notorious and possibly apocryphal British newspaper's weather report headline: "Fog in Channel – Continent Cut Off.") But by the same token, it was Britons' destiny to "rule the waves" and to people entire continents overseas. During Britain's heyday of global dominance, it was not immigration to, but *emigration from*, the home islands that seemed to reconcile the country's identity as an island nation with its ruling elites' aspirations to shape the destiny of the world. With English-speakers populating North America, Australia, New Zealand, and South Africa, the nation's culture seemed poised to become the basis for a global commonwealth.[213] Indeed, as suggested earlier, it was the sense of ethno-cultural affinity with the United States that helped smooth the British establishment's path to acceptance of its own empire's decline, for in some sort of broad, world-historical sense, American success could be seen as an indirect (if ironic) vindication of Britain's imperial mission.

* * *

In the case of the Soviet Union, the role of ethno-national boundaries in advancing – and ultimately undermining – the ruling party's long-term, global vision was heavily laden with contradictions and ironies. The USSR's ideological *raison d'être* was its proclaimed mission of promoting world-wide socialist revolutions that would win the class struggle, do away with the divisive, bourgeois-propagated illusion of nationalism, and replace it with proletarian internationalism. As the first Communist country in history, the Soviet Union was conceived of as a working model of the Marxist, utopian ideal of a supranational, classless society. Yet, conceding that nationality remained a focal point of popular identity during the historical interim, Lenin and his associates were determined to use it to their own advantage. Convinced that the mass-mobilizing power of separatist nationalism increased in proportion to the external suppression of ethno-national cultures, Lenin designed his revolutionary state as a federation of nominally equal national republics, replacing the Russian empire with the Union of Soviet Socialist Republics (USSR). By establishing territorially bounded republics and autonomous regions for ethnic minorities, which had composed over half of the tsarist state's population,[214] the Bolsheviks hoped to neutralize nationalism. The assumption was that, with native languages and indigenous folklores protected and enshrined in the frameworks of these republics, the motivation to break free of Moscow's control would disappear. Indeed, inspired by the precedent of nineteenth-century Russian Orthodox missionaries in Central Asia, Lenin was confident that minority languages could be employed as neutral media for the transmission of a uniform doctrine.[215] Communism's internationalist message could be propagated most effectively among the diverse peoples of the former Russian Empire if it were to be "national in form, socialist in content."[216]

Beyond providing for internal harmony, the USSR's ethno-federal structure was designed to serve as a globally attractive model of national self-determination combined with inter-national harmony. Soviet propaganda contrasted the juridical equality of European and non-European peoples in the USSR with the racist and exploitative overseas imperialism of Britain and France. As bourgeois empires fell apart, there would be no limit in principle to the number of nationalities that could join the Soviet federation as equal members of a universal socialist commonwealth. In the long run, the resultant defusing of national rivalries, erosion of cultural differences, and raising of common proletarian consciousness would lead to the unity of humanity on the model of the "Soviet man." In other words, the very establishment of bounded spaces for the expression of national identities would contribute to Communism's boundless appeal to the peoples of the world. The creation of national republics within the Soviet federation would lead dialectically to the eventual disappearance of all ethno-cultural boundaries.

In practice, this program backfired. The nominal self-rule of the Soviet republics was belied by the brutally heavy-handed centralism of the Communist Party's dictatorship. Moreover, it was a very fine line indeed that distinguished Moscow's ostensibly disinterested promotion of the Russian language as the lingua franca of the Soviet peoples from Russian chauvinist tendencies that smacked of Old Regime attitudes. The ideal of the Soviet man often seemed hard to distinguish from a Russian-national claim to a universal civilizing mission.[217] Ethno-nationalist resistance – real or perceived – to Communist policies in the non-Russian periphery provoked ruthless reprisals that culminated in collective deportations of entire ethnic groups (most notoriously the Chechens and the Crimean Tatars) during the Second World War.[218] With the decline of Communism as a supra-ethnic legitimizing system in the late 1980s, national-territorial boundaries that had long been treated as little more than propagandist formalities assumed heightened significance as frameworks of collective identity; upon the Soviet Union's collapse, they were transformed overnight into international borders.[219] Confronted with the disintegration of their universalistic empire, Russians were left uncertain whether to redefine themselves as a territorially bounded nation-state or to search for some new framework for reconstituting a more expansive form of identity.[220]

* * *

Of the cases examined in this chapter, France would seem to offer the most clear-cut example of a sharply defined cartographic self-image. The country's distinctive shape on the map is commonly referred to as though it represented a distillation of the nation's identity: the use of the term "the hexagon" to denote France in its territorial aspect is a matter of standard usage among the French.[221] Yet the implications of this linguistic convention are ambiguous. On the one hand, it suggests a starkly delimited conception of the nation's place in the world, with six neatly drawn lines setting the French off from all that lies beyond. On the other hand, the French have been known to indulge in something of a neo-Pythagorean fetish of the chosen nation's territorial outline as the manifestation of a universal ideal of geometric perfection – "symmetrical, proportional and regular," in the words of a late nineteenth-century education official.[222]

In fact, the undisputed status of "l'hexagone" as a commonly employed, positive synonym for France – virtually interchangeable with the name of the country – was only consolidated in the 1960s, as Nathaniel Smith and Eugen Weber have shown.[223] Prior to the late nineteenth century, descriptions of France as a hexagon were few and far between.[224] Leaving aside arcane disputes about whether the country's existing borders formed an octagon, a pentagon, or a hexagon,[225] there was the more fundamental question of whether France could fulfill its universal mission without expanding far beyond the confines of any geometrical form or even of the "natural frontiers" (such as the full length of the Rhine) to which eighteenth-century monarchs and revolutionaries alike laid claim.[226] Not long after Napoleon's defeat in 1814–15 had put an end to any realistic prospect of making France co-extensive with Continental Europe, expansion into Algeria (beginning in the 1830s) offered opportunities for compensation, and in 1870, the Algerian holdings were administratively integrated into France. The loss of metropolitan French territory (Alsace-Lorraine) to a newly unified Germany in 1871 did draw attention back to France's European frontiers until the land was won back in the First World War, and may have contributed to the emergence of "l'hexagone" as an image of what a now mutilated France was supposed to look like.[227]

Yet the hexagon's lines continued to come in and out of focus for decades as geopolitical circumstances changed and as conflicting conceptions of France's global mission vied for dominance. The imperial expansion of the Third Republic (1871–1940) in Indochina during the 1880s was initially derided by right-wing critics as an unwelcome diversion from the overriding necessity of regaining the lost provinces of Alsace and Lorraine. The imperial race continued anyway, and by the eve of the First World War, a broad nationalist consensus had coalesced around the importance of the country's African and Asian colonies for its standing as a great power and for its long-term prospects of regaining its lost provinces and honor in the European arena.[228] This left unanswered the question of whether overseas conquests were to be construed as integral parts of a French nation-state that opened its doors to all men and women ready to embrace French civilization, or whether firm and irrevocable cultural, racial, and geographical barriers set France proper apart from the alien lands and peoples that it ruled.[229]

In no context were the lines of the hexagon fuzzier than in relation to Algeria. The presence here of a large population of white settlers of Franco-European origin (numbering over 1 million by mid-twentieth century) led to the colony's formal, territorial integration into the French nation-state. Unlike other colonies, which fell under the jurisdiction of the Ministry of Colonies or Ministry of Foreign Affairs, Algeria was administratively incorporated into France and came under the authority of the Interior Ministry from 1870 until the country's independence in 1962.[230] The great majority of Algeria's indigenous Muslim *population* remained effectively debarred from citizenship rights, but *spatially*, as far as French law was concerned, the nation-state was not delimited by the hexagon; it straddled the Mediterranean. This incongruity between demographic and geographic frontiers was difficult to rationalize, especially for a society that defined itself as the embodiment of universal ideals. The outbreak of the Algerian war in 1954 led to profound and bitter schisms within French society over whether a France confined to the hexagon would lose its grip on the essential elements of its national identity and international prestige, or flourish as a modern democratic society, freed at last of the insoluble dilemmas and paradoxes of empire.[231]

The embrace of the hexagon was a virtue born of necessity.[232] Having finally abandoned Algeria along with the bulk of France's other overseas colonies by the early 1960s, President de Gaulle adopted the hexagon as an emblem of the nation's unity and harmony in the wake of the bitter divisions of the mid-twentieth century. He used the geometrical/geographical emblem as a way of reconciling the country to the loss of its imperial status by trying to convince it that its newly circumscribed form was the embodiment of a uniquely French rationalist-universalist mystique.[233] And, indeed, contemporary usage suggests that this symbolic association of geographical form with national-cultural content has acquired the status of a cliché in French society.[234] But even as the *location* of the country's borders was fixed, their *function* became more ambiguous than ever. The dynamics of globalization and the process of European integration have posed fundamental questions about whether national borders serve primarily to mark the nation off from its neighbors or as lines of contact with them. For de Gaulle, founder of the French Fifth Republic (1958–), there was never any question of blurring the nation's borders in the framework of a federated Europe. The only legitimate purpose of a European Economic Community, as far as he was concerned, was to serve the interests of the individual nations of which it was composed.[235] But in that capacity, European integration had an important role to play for a French political and cultural establishment that feared the prospect of Anglo-American hegemony. And the more deeply de Gaulle's successors have become engaged in building what is now the European Union, the more ambiguous its long-term implications have become for the boundaries of national identity. At times, the dynamics of the integration process seem to be eroding de Gaulle's old distinction between what he saw as the dangerously unrealistic ideal of a United States of Europe and the eminently wise alternative of a Europe of States.[236] As goods, capital, and labor have come to flow ever more freely across national borders, the lines of the hexagon have come to seem like increasingly anachronistic abstractions. Conversely, the words and actions of the most Europhile French political leaders sometimes seem to suggest to their neighbors that, rather than merging France into Europe, what they envision is the institutional and cultural assimilation of the rest of the continent into a French way of doing things that remains, after all, the foundation of European civilization.[237]

At the same time, the continued influx of large numbers of immigrants from former colonies into metropolitan France has opened new questions about the relationship between the nation's territorial and demographic boundaries. On the one hand, anti-immigrant backlashes have led to decidedly particularistic conceptions of what it means to be French, as the small but solid electoral base of Jean-Marie Le Pen's right-wing National Front party has demonstrated over recent years. On the other hand, Patrick Weil has pointed to the irony that, following Algerian independence in 1962, a child born on metropolitan France's territory to any immigrant born in pre-1962 Algeria was automatically considered a French citizen on the basis of the 1889 law conferring citizenship upon children born on French territory to aliens who had themselves been born on French territory. In other words, once Algeria had been severed from France, France retroactively addressed the disjuncture between the demographic and territorial boundaries of its pre-1962 nationhood.[238] Even more expansively, French law in principle allows immigrants from any part of the world that was once a part of the French Empire (including the territories of the Louisiana Purchase) or that is Francophone (e.g. Belgium or formerly Belgian Congo) to dispense with the normal five-year waiting period and apply immediately for naturalization. In practice, this has meant very little, since to apply for citizenship is one thing and to receive it quite another.[239] Yet this symbolic clinging to an expansive, missionary conception of Frenchness is striking. Likewise, the zeal with which the French government, alongside other Francophone countries as well as private organizations and publications, continues to defend the French language against the infiltration of English usages while promoting French language and culture around the world speaks to the continued importance of its universal mission to the Hexagon's national sense of self.[240]

CONCLUSION

This chapter has ranged over a broad array of domestic-political, diplomatic, identity, and even cartographic issues related to the concept of national chosenness and the closely linked notion of global mission. It is my contention that the wide variety of symbolic and pragmatic controversies that have been deeply colored by the ideas of chosenness and mission speaks to the power of those ideas. I would also argue that these issues are not just a random assortment; they are all interrelated. Divisions over the nature of the covenant that constitutes the chosen nation are shaped by, and shape in turn, contending notions about the role and mission of the chosen nation in the wider world. These issues are reflected in, and affected by, changing visions of where the borders that set the chosen nation apart from other nations should lie and how fixed or expansive, impermeable or porous, those borders should be. The associated debates may sometimes degenerate into absurd squabbles about the ethnicity of fried potatoes and the relative merits of rival polygons. But the very energy invested in such petty disputes is a reflection of the larger stakes involved.

It might be objected that, in practice, most people in any given society pay little heed to such world-historical concerns – that the nation as a whole does little more than pay occasional lip service to myths of chosenness or conceptions of mission. This may well be the case at most times. But I would counter that argument with two points. One is that, if only a self-selected minority of intellectuals and politicians concern themselves with, say, the strategic and geopolitical vision for a great power's foreign policy, then the prism through which members of that disproportionately influential elite perceive their nation and the world will have all the more decisive an impact on actual decisions and policies.[241] And there is no question but that conflicting conceptions of exceptionalism and chosenness have both framed and informed fundamental policy debates in such nations as the United States and France. Secondly, during times of crisis, the circle of discussion about such issues is exponentially widened, as millions of "ordinary" citizens suddenly tune in to debates about their country's role in the world that might not hold their interest in periods of humdrum, pocketbook politics. While pragmatic questions about security and material self-interest necessarily figure large in such debates, political leaders eager to garner public support for their positions in times of crisis are more likely than ever to justify their concrete policy proposals by appealing to familiar tropes about the chosen nation's unique historical mission. This was the case, for example, when President Truman won over Congressional and public support for American aid to Greece and Turkey in 1947 by framing the initially modest initiative in a "doctrine" that committed the US to come to the assistance of any country in the world whose freedom was threatened by internal or external aggression.[242] The second President Bush invoked similar themes when justifying his war in Iraq, expressing his belief that freedom is a God-given right and suggesting that the United States has a unique responsibility to promote liberty throughout the world.[243] Such phraseology may strike some as bombastic and cliché-ridden, but my point is that clichés about national chosenness are powerful forces that do in fact help shape history. By the same token, the identical cliché can be used to justify a variety of actual policies. Feeling chosen may appear to predetermine a nation's role in the world, but it really serves to frame debates about choices that each generation must make anew.

* * *

As is evident from this chapter's final section, disputes about the geographic and demographic boundaries of the nation are intimately related. The question "where is the nation?" (to paraphrase the title-line of the Czech national anthem: "Where is my home?"[244]) can only be answered by determining "who is the nation?," and vice versa. It is the vexed relationship between blood and soil in determining identity and belonging[245] that concerns us in Chapter 5.

END NOTES

1 Exodus 19:6, as translated by Bernard M. Levinson in his "Commentary" on biblical covenants in Michael Walzer, Menachem Lorberbaum, Noam J. Zohar *et al.*, eds., *The Jewish Political Tradition*, vol. 1: *Authority* (New Haven: Yale University Press, 2000), 24.

2 See the discussions in Levinson, "Commentary"; Michael Walzer, *Exodus and Revolution* (New York: Harper Collins/Basic Books, 1985), 108–113; Anthony D. Smith, *Chosen Peoples* (Oxford: Oxford University Press, 2003), 34–35.

3 Seminal works on the theme of chosenness, on which I draw in this chapter, include: Smith, *Chosen Peoples*; Steven Grosby, "The Chosen People of Ancient Israel and the Occident," *Nations and Nationalism*, vol. 5, no. 3 (1999), 357–380; Walzer, *Exodus and Revolution*; David Novak, *The Election of Israel: The Idea of the Chosen People* (Cambridge: Cambridge University Press, 1995); David Novak, *Covenantal Rights: A Study in Jewish Political Theory* (Princeton: Princeton University Press, 2000); Donald Harman Akenson, *God's Peoples: Covenant and Land in South Africa, Israel and Ulster* (Ithaca: Cornell University Press, 1992); Conor Cruise O'Brien, *Godland: Reflections on Religion and Nationalism* (Cambridge, Mass.: Harvard University Press, 1988); Clifford Longley, *Chosen People: The Big Idea that Shapes England and America* (London: Hodder & Stoughton, 2002). See also Anatol Lieven, *America Right or Wrong: An Anatomy of American Nationalism* (New York: Oxford University Press, 2004), 32–36 and *passim*.

4 This juxtaposition is highlighted in Walzer, *et al.*, eds., *Jewish Political Tradition*, vol. II: *Membership* (New Haven: Yale University Press, 2003), 16.

5 Genesis II:I. My translation.

6 Cf. Novak, *Covenantal Rights*, 84–85.

7 English translation from Walzer *et al.*, eds., *Jewish Political Tradition*, vol. II: *Membership*, 16.

8 Steven Grosby highlights the development of the biblical conception of chosenness from an unconditional to a conditional one, arguing that the latter evolved as a way of rationalizing the defeat and exile of the sixth-century BCE. In other words, by blaming their national catastrophe on their own misconduct, the Jews were able to retain their faith in God, the Covenant, and their own, conditional, chosenness. Grosby, "Chosen People."

9 Deuteronomy 16:20 (my translation).

10 Exodus 23:9 (my translation). See also Novak, *Covenantal Rights*, chs. 3–5.

11 Leviticus 19:33–34, as translated in *Tanakh: The Holy Scriptures. The New JPS Translation According to the Traditional Hebrew Text* (Philadelphia: The Jewish Publication Society, 1988).

12 Isaiah 2:3–4 (my modification of the JPS translation). The idea of a national mission was not unfamiliar to the ancient Athenians, although they conceived of it as limited to their fellow Hellenes: Thucydides has Pericles describe Athens as "an education to Greece." Thucydides, *History of the Peloponnesian War*, 2:41, trans. Rex Warner (Harmondsworth: Penguin, 1972), Penguin edn, 147.

13 Zephaniah 3:9 (cited and discussed in Novak, *Covenantal Rights*, x).

14 See A. Smith, *Chosen Peoples*, ch. 5.

15 Colette Beaune, *The Birth of an Ideology, Myths and Symbols of Nation in Late-Medieval France*, trans. Susan Ross Huston (1985; Berkeley: University of California Press, 1991), 19. See also René Rémond, "La Fille aînée de l'Église," in Pierre Nora, ed., *Les Lieux de mémoire*, vol. III: *Les France*, part 3: *De l'Archive à l'emblème* (Paris: Gallimard, 1992); Liah Greenfeld, *Nationalism. Five Roads to Modernity* (Cambridge, Mass.: Harvard University Press, 1992), ch. 2; A. Smith, *Chosen Peoples*, 106–115; Pierre Birnbaum, *The Idea of France*, trans. M. B. DeBevoise (1998; New York: Hill and Wang, 2001), 10–15.

16 A. Smith, *Chosen Peoples*, 72, 203. For an argument that questions this perspective, at least in the case of modern Greek nationalism, see Paschalis M. Kitromilides, " 'Imagined Communities' and the Origins of the National Question in the Balkans," *European History Quarterly*, vol. 19, no. 2 (April 1989), 149–192.

17 A. Smith, *Chosen Peoples*, 98–106.

18 Ivo Banac, *The National Question in Yugoslavia; Origins, History, Politics* (Ithaca: Cornell University Press, 1984), 63–65; Barbara Jelavich, *History of the Balkans*, vol. I: *Eighteenth and Nineteenth Centuries* (Cambridge: Cambridge University Press, 1983), 91–94; Rebecca West, *Black Lamb and*

Grey Falcon: A Journey through Yugoslavia (1940; New York: Penguin, 1969), 499–518.

19 A. Smith, *Chosen Peoples*, 66–73.

20 Beaune, *Birth of an Ideology*, p. 19, ch. 6, and pp. 316–317.

21 It was Voltaire who famously denied all three claims. On the rival universalist aspirations of the Habsburgs and Bourbons, as well as of Sweden's King Gustavus Adolphus, see Johannes Burkhardt, "The Summitless Pyramid: War Aims and Peace Compromises among Europe's Universalist Powers," in Klaus Bussmann and Heinz Schilling, eds., *1648: War and Peace in Europe*, vol. 1: *Politics, Religion, Law and Society*, companion publication to the 26th European Council Exhibition "1648 – War and Peace in Europe" (Veranstaltungsgesellschaft 350 Jahre Westfälischer Friede mbH: Osnabrück/Münster, 1998).

22 On the Anglican case, see J. C. D. Clark, *The Language of Liberty, 1660–1832: Political Discourse and Social Dynamics in the Anglo-American World* (Cambridge: Cambridge University Press, 1994), 48–49. Michael Keating argues that Britain did not fit the Westphalian model, insofar as it had two established religions – Anglicanism in England, Wales, and Ireland, and Presbyterianism in Scotland. Michael Keating, *Plurinational Democracy: Stateless Nations in a Post-Sovereignty Era* (Oxford: Oxford University Press, 2001), 105. But in a broadly interdenominational sense, the idea of Britain as a bastion of Protestantism certainly became crucial to the forging of its national identity, as Linda Colley has argued. Linda Colley, *Britons: Forging the Nation, 1707–1837* (New Haven: Yale University Press, 1992).

23 The now classic treatment of this theme is Benedict Anderson, *Imagined Communities: Reflections on the Origin and Spread of Nationalism*, 2nd edn (London: Verso, 1991), ch. 3. But Anderson sees the development of what he terms "print capitalism" as contributing to a decisive break with the pre-modern religious sensibility, a point which I join Anthony Smith in disputing.

24 Clifford Longley has pointed out that the script for Queen Elizabeth's 1953 coronation ceremony was so chock-full of biblical references that at times it sounded more like the anointment of an ancient Israelite monarch than of a modern British ruler. Longley, *Chosen People*, 35–41. On similar elements in pre-revolutionary French coronation ceremonies, see Rémond, "Fille aînée," 558. See also Longley's discussion of "the succession of covenants" in *Chosen People*, ch. 3.

25 Adam Sutcliffe, *Judaism and Enlightenment* (Cambridge: Cambridge University Press, 2003), ch. 2, esp. pp. 43–46. In his renowned shipboard sermon ("A Modell of Christian Charity") *en route* to Massachusetts Bay Colony in 1630, New England's founding father John Winthrop practically hit his fellow passengers over their heads with analogies between their experience and that of the Children of Israel departing from Egypt and covenanting with God on their way to the Promised Land. (It is easy to imagine some members of his seasick audience wishing the parallels were

closer, given the Israelites' crossing of the Red Sea on dry land.) See the
extended citation and discussion in Robert N. Bellah, *The Broken Covenant:
American Civil Religion in Time of Trial* (New York: The Seabury Press,
1975), 13–16. See also Anders Stephanson, *Manifest Destiny: American
Expansionism and the Empire of Right* (New York: Hill and Wang, 1995), 3–12
and *passim*; Reinhold Niebuhr, *The Irony of American History* (New York:
Charles Scribner's Sons, 1952), 23–25. Sacvan Bercovitch argues that the New
England Puritans and their ideological successors took the idea of their
people as the New Israel far more literally than did any of their European
counterparts. Sacvan Bercovitch, *The Puritan Origins of the American Self*
(New Haven: Yale University Press, 1975), ch. 3.

26 A. Smith, *Chosen Peoples*; Adrian Hastings, *The Construction of Nationhood:
Ethnicity, Religion and Nationalism* (Cambridge: Cambridge University Press,
1997); Jonathan Sheehan, "Enlightenment, Religion, and the Enigma of
Secularization," *American Historical Review*, vol. 108, no. 4 (October 2003),
1061–1080; Steven Smith, *Spinoza, Liberalism, and the Question of Jewish
Identity* (New Haven: Yale University Press, 1997), ch. 4, esp. 87–89.

27 See, for example, Adam Sutcliffe's discussion of the impact of the Jewish
covenantal model on Thomas Hobbes' thought in *Judaism and Enlightenment*, 49–51.

28 Steven Grosby, "The Biblical 'Nation' as a Problem for Philosophy," *Hebraic
Political Studies*, vol. 1, no. 1 (Fall 2005), 7–23, esp. 20–21; Daniel J. Elazar,
"Covenant as the Basis of the Jewish Political Tradition," in Daniel J. Elazar,
ed., *Kinship and Consent: The Jewish Political Tradition and Its Contemporary
Uses*, 2nd edn (New Brunswick, N.J.: Transaction, 1997), esp. 33–35.

29 See Walzer, *Exodus and Revolution*, 83. The modern, secular approach
distinguishes itself from the biblical one by making the covenant among
humans the primary source of legitimacy, but by the same token, it shares
with the Hebrew Bible a conception of society as governed by covenantal and
contractual relations. On Benedict (Baruch) Spinoza's influential role in
articulating a secularized interpretation of the Mosaic covenant and using it
as a paradigmatic example of a republican social contract, see: S. Smith,
Spinoza, ch. 6, esp. p. 148; Lea Campos Boralevi, "Classical Foundational
Myths of European Republicanism: The Jewish Commonwealth," in Martin
van Gelderen and Quentin Skinner, eds., *Republicanism: A Shared European
Heritage*, vol. 1: *Republicanism and Constitutionalism in Early Modern Europe*
(Cambridge: Cambridge University Press, 2002), 247–261. David Novak
makes the case that Spinoza's conception of the social contract retains an
essential theological element. Novak, *Election of Israel*, 31–42. On Spinoza's
ethical and political thinking more generally and on the radiation of his
intellectual influence, see Jonathan Israel, *Radical Enlightenment: Philosophy
and the Making of Modernity, 1650–1750* (Oxford: Oxford University Press,
2001), chs. 8, 11–17, and *passim*. On Spinoza as embodiment and symbol of
the tension between particularism and universalism in the Enlightenment
tradition, see Sutcliffe, *Judaism and Enlightenment*, chs. 6–7.

30 Of course, it would be foolish to disregard the stark differences that Frank
    Lambert has delineated between the Puritan theocratic tradition and the
    triumph of the principles of religious tolerance and of the religious
    "marketplace of ideas" under the Founding Fathers' constitutional
    dispensation. See Frank Lambert, *The Founding Fathers and the Place of
    Religion in America* (Princeton: Princeton University Press, 2003), Introduc-
    tion, ch. 9, pp. 183–187, and *passim*. Nonetheless, in his critique of Lambert's
    thesis, Charles Cohen contends that "the Constitution was ratified in a
    society ... certain of the perfect congruence between its fundamental law
    and Protestant moral values ... Identifying the United States as the Lord's
    favored nation increased during the nineteenth century as Americans sang
    hymns about grace being shed upon their fruited plains, declared
    proselytizing the heathen to be their manifest destiny, and invoked God
    against Yankees or Rebels with homicidal facility." Charles L. Cohen, review
    of Lambert, *Founding Fathers* in *American Historical Review*, vol. 109, no. 1
    (February 2004), 178–179. J. C. D. Clark argues that it was precisely the
    American Revolution that enshrined New England's Puritan heritage as the
    fount of the American national ideal, albeit in secularized form. Clark,
    Language of Liberty, ch. 4, Conclusion, and *passim*. In a similar vein, Sacvan
    Bercovitch contends that "early New England rhetoric provided a ready
    framework for inverting later secular values ... into the mold of sacred
    teleology." Bercovitch, *Puritan Origins of the American Self*, 136. See also
    ibid., chs. 3 and 5; William C. Widenor, *Henry Cabot Lodge and the Search for
    an American Foreign Policy* (Berkeley: University of California Press, 1980),
    63–64. On the religious inflections of American national identity, see also
    Conor Cruise O'Brien, *Godland: Reflections on Religion and Nationalism*
    (Cambridge, Mass.: Harvard University Press, 1988); Bernard Bailyn, *The
    Ideological Origins of the American Revolution* (Cambridge, Mass.: Harvard
    University Press, 1967), 32–33; Robert N. Bellah, "Religion and the
    Legitimation of the American Republic," in Robert N. Bellah and Phillip
    E. Hammond, *Varieties of Civil Religion* (San Francisco: Harper & Row,
    1980); Longley, *Chosen People*, ch. 3. On the synthesis of Greco-Roman
    political ideals and biblical covenantal themes in modern republican thought,
    see Bellah, *Broken Covenant*, ch. 1. On the influence of religious traditions,
    mentalities, and proselytizing methods on the form, content, and
    propagation of French nationalism both before and after the revolution,
    see David A. Bell, *The Cult of the Nation in France: Inventing Nationalism,
    1680–1800* (Cambridge, Mass.: Harvard University Press, 2001), Introduction,
    chs. 2, 5, 6, and *passim*.

31 Anthony D. Smith discusses the missionary form of chosenness in *Chosen
    Peoples*, chs. 3–5.

32 Since composing this heading, I have discovered that David Novak examines
    the theme of "electing to be elected" in *The Election of Israel*, 177 and *passim*.

33 For further explorations of the nuances and paradoxes of this theme, see A.
    Smith, *Chosen Peoples*, ch. 3; Walzer, *Exodus and Revolution*, ch. 3.

34 Tractate Shabbat 88a, *Babylonian Talmud*, as translated in Walzer *et al.*, eds., *Jewish Political Tradition*, vol. 1: *Authority*, 28–29; Michael J. Sandel's commentary in ibid., 30–33; Bernard Levinson's commentary in ibid., 23–27; Novak, *Covenantal Rights*, 113 and ch. 5.

35 See Michael Walzer, "Introduction: The Jewish Political Tradition" in Walzer, *et al.*, eds., *Jewish Political Tradition*, vol. 1: *Authority*.

36 Bellah, *Broken Covenant*, 33; Niebuhr, *Irony of American History*, ch. 3.

37 John Adams as quoted in Robert A. Ferguson, "The Dialectic of Liberty: Law and Religion in Anglo-American Culture," *Modern Intellectual History*, vol. 1, no. 1 (2004), 27–54.

38 See Longley, *Chosen People*, ch. 3. In his discussion of "America's Myth of Origin," Robert Bellah suggests that the American Revolution and Constitution can be seen as analogous to religious conversion and covenant, respectively. Bellah, *Broken Covenant*, ch. 1, esp. 34–35.

39 The transcript of the Declaration of Independence is available at the website of the United States National Archives and Records Administration (NARA): http://www.archives.gov/national_archives_experience/charters/declaration_transcript.html.

40 On Thomas Jefferson's endorsement of revolutions every twenty years and his disdain for the cult of constitutions, see Bellah, *Broken Covenant*, 34–35. Pauline Maier does point out that the Declaration of Independence qualifies the legitimization of revolution by emphasizing that it is justified only in cases of extreme and persistent abuse of power threatening to lead to tyranny. Pauline Maier, *American Scripture: Making the Declaration of Independence* (New York: Knopf, 1997), 136–139.

41 Ernest Renan, "What Is a Nation?," trans. Martin Thom, in Geoff Eley and Ronald Grigor Suny, eds., *Becoming National: A Reader* (New York: Oxford University Press, 1996), 53.

42 See Isaac Kramnick, "Editor's Introduction," in James Madison, Alexander Hamilton, and John Jay, *The Federalist Papers*, Isaac Kramnick, ed. (1788; London: Penguin, 1987).

43 Kramnick, "Editor's Introduction," *Federalist Papers*, 29. See also Maier, *American Scripture*, 212. Gordon Wood argues that the Federalists did not regard their undertaking as a repudiation of the spirit of 1776. Rather, their understanding of what the slogans and principles of the Revolution denoted had been transformed in the course of the intervening years. Wood also contends that the long-term impact of the Constitution and the political culture it created was more fundamentally radical than anything the original revolutionaries had conceived of, in so far as it replaced the neo-classical ideal of self-sacrificing public virtue with the novel conception of individual self-interest as the basis of a free republic. Gordon S. Wood, *The Creation of the American Republic, 1776–1787* (Chapel Hill: University of North Carolina Press, 1969), 519–524 and ch. 15. See also Gordon S. Wood, *The Radicalism of the American Revolution* (1992; New York: Random House, 1993). On the distinction between classical and modern conceptions of citizenship, see also

Judith Shklar, *American Citizenship: The Quest for Inclusion* (Cambridge: Mass.: Harvard University Press, 1991), 10–14.

44 Wood, *American Republic*, ch. 15.

45 Daniel Farber, *Lincoln's Constitution* (Chicago: University of Chicago Press, 2003), 101–102 and chs. 2–3.

46 Ibid., chs. 4–5. Of course, the disenfranchisement and dehumanization of the Southern states' slave population completely undermined the democratic legitimacy of Confederate justifications for secession.

47 James Madison, *Federalist* No. 39, *Federalist Papers*, 254–259.

48 Madison, *Federalist* No. 14, *Federalist Papers*, 144. See Chapter 5 of this book for further dissection of this image.

49 As one pair of authors has put it, "that seems a supremely confident and courageous act – to create a nation through words: words that address ... the very entity called into being by the words themselves ... " Laurence H. Tribe and Michael C. Dorf, *On Reading the Constitution* (Cambridge, Mass.: Harvard University Press, 1991), 8. See also Wood, *American Republic*, 532–536.

50 Michael Kammen, *A Machine that Would Go of Itself: The Constitution in American Culture* (New York: Knopf, 1986), 48 and chs. 4–5.

51 A recent administrative attempt to revise some of the language of the "Oath of Renunciation and Allegiance," as the US citizenship oath is known, provoked heated opposition from some members of Congress, one of whom introduced legislation (H.R. 3191) to enshrine in law the precise, existing wording of the oath. Regardless of the outcome of this controversy, the text of the oath is required by preexisting Congressional legislation to include, in one form or another, commitments to the support and defense of the Constitution. Jim Ryun, Member of Congress, Testimony before the Subcommittee on Immigration, Border Security, and Claims, House Committee on the Judiciary, House of Representatives, 1 April 2004: http://www.house.gov/judiciary/ryun040104.htm; Statement of Alfonso Aguilar (Chief, Office of Citizenship, U.S. Citizenship and Immigration Services, U.S. Department of Homeland Security) at the same hearing, 1 April 2004: http://www.house.gov/judiciary/aguilar040104.htm.

52 Daniel Lazare, *The Frozen Republic: How the Constitution Is Paralyzing Democracy* (New York: Harcourt Brace & Co., 1996), 1.

53 For a more refined analysis of this complex topic than I can hope to offer, see Robert A. Burt, *The Constitution in Conflict* (Cambridge, Mass.: Harvard University Press, 1992), ch. 1 and *passim*.

54 Robert H. Bork, *The Tempting of America: The Political Seduction of the Law* (New York: The Free Press, 1990), 19.

55 Ibid., 352–353.

56 Tribe and Dorf, *On Reading the Constitution*. On the Constitution as covenant, see Bellah, *Broken Covenant*, 32–35.

57 This basic outlook is common to late nineteenth- and early twentieth-century Progressives and to contemporary liberals, even if the former's quest for social

progress through governmental and corporate reform and the moral salvation of the individual is quite distinct from the later twentieth-century liberal emphasis on programmatic governmental engagement in social restructuring. See Robert M. Crunden, *Ministers of Reform: The Progressives' Achievement in American Civilization, 1889–1920* (New York: Basic Books, 1982), Preface and p. 51.

58 There is a more radical school of American legal thought that regards all law, including the Constitution, as nothing more than an instrument of socio-economic exploitation. See the discussion in Burt, *Constitution in Conflict*, ch. 1.

59 Cf., for example, Tribe and Dorf, who remark approvingly of Justice Oliver Wendell Holmes that "he had no doubt that the very *meaning* of the thing we call 'the Constitution'... was a reality partly reconstructed by each generation of readers. *And he had no doubt that that was as the Framers of the Constitution themselves originally intended.*" Tribe and Dorf, *On Reading the Constitution*, 9. Second emphasis added.

60 See Laurence Tribe, *Constitutional Choices* (Cambridge, Mass.: Harvard University Press, 1985), ch. 2 (esp. pp. 10–14) and Epilogue.

61 Numbers 16.

62 On the long-term identity crisis the fleeing Tories bequeathed to English Canada, see Eric Kaufmann, "Condemned to Rootlessness: The Loyalist Origins of Canada's Identity Crisis," *Nationalism and Ethnic Politics*, vol. 3, no. 1 (1997), 110–135. Kaufmann notes that by the early nineteenth century, Anglo-Canadians had started cultivating an image of themselves as the chosen elite among the chosen nation of Britain!

63 Birnbaum, *Idea of France*; René Rémond, *The Right Wing in France: From 1815 to de Gaulle*, trans. James M. Laux, 2nd American edn (1954; 1966; Philadelphia: University of Pennsylvania Press, 1969). The Vichy regime discussed in Chapter 2 of the present book was dominated by upholders of this reactionary covenantal counter-tradition.

64 Birnbaum, *Idea of France*, ch. 3 and *passim*. Michel Winock argues that part of the perennial appeal of Joan of Arc lies precisely in her embodiment, not only of the miraculous nature of the nation's destiny, but of the capacity to rise above the nation's divisions to enable it to make its mark on history. Michel Winock, "Jeanne d'Arc," in Nora, ed., *Les Lieux de mémoire*, vol. III: *Les France*, part 3: *De l'Archive à l'emblème* (Paris: Gallimard, 1992), 727.

65 The text is available at the website of the French Ministry of Justice: http://www.justice.gouv.fr/textfond/ddhc.htm.

66 Stanley Hoffmann, *Decline or Renewal? France Since the 1930s* (New York: Viking, 1974), 291.

67 See Donald Akenson, *God's Peoples*, chs. 3, 7, 10; Smith, *Chosen Peoples*, 77–85.

68 Isaiah 42:6.

69 See the discussion in Ella Belfer, *Zehut kefulah: Al ha-metach bein artsiut le-ruchaniut ba-olam ha-yehudi* [A Split Identity: The Conflict between the

Sacred and the Secular in the Jewish World] (Ramat-Gan, Israel: Bar-Ilan University, 2004), 167–172. My thanks go to Mordecai Roshwald for bringing this book to my attention. See also, A. Smith, *Chosen Peoples*, 85–94. For a sweeping critique that highlights the gap between the universalistic, socialist claims and particularistic, nationalist orientation of Ben Gurion and the Labor Zionist movement, see Zeev Sternhell, *The Founding Myths of Israel: Nationalism, Socialism, and the Making of the Jewish State*, trans. David Maisel (Princeton: Princeton University Press, 1998). Sternhell's bitter insistence that there was in fact nothing about the Zionist project to distinguish it from many other modern nationalist movements seems to reflect the author's abiding belief that Zionism *ought* to have established a uniquely just society. Thus, in discussing social policy following the establishment of the State of Israel in 1948, he writes: "Herein lay the greatness and also the weakness of Ben-Gurion and the labor elite. These people brought the state into being, and once it was created they carried out the gigantic task of immediately absorbing the great waves of immigration that followed ... However, they neither wished nor were able to provide the new state with a new society. It was a unique opportunity to innovate; the price was not out of reach, the dream did not require unattainable sums of money..." Sternhell, *Founding Myths*, 322.

70 Walzer *et al.*, eds., *Jewish Political Tradition*, vol. 1: *Authority*, 33–34.

71 Numbers 23:9, as translated in Herbert G. May and Bruce M. Metzger, eds., *The New Oxford Annotated Bible with the Apocrypha: Revised Standard Version* (New York: Oxford University Press, 1977).

72 A. Smith, *Chosen Peoples*, 58–60.

73 Oliver Zimmer, *A Contested Nation: History, Memory and Nationalism in Switzerland, 1761–1891* (Cambridge: Cambridge University Press, 2003).

74 See the 8 May 1999 report by Dr. Christoph Mörgeli, on the website of the anti-UN membership and anti-NATO membership Swiss organization, Aktion für eine unabhängige und neutrale Schweiz (Campaign for an Independent and Neutral Switzerland): http://www.cins.ch/en/meldungen/990508essence.htm.

75 Ibid.; Jürg Martin Gabriel, "The Price of Political Uniqueness: Swiss Foreign Policy in a Changing World" and Daniel Möckli, "The Long Road to Membership: Switzerland and the United Nations," in Jürg Martin Gabriel and Thomas Fischer, eds., *Swiss Foreign Policy, 1945–2002* (Basingstoke: Palgrave Macmillan, 2003); Paul Widmer, *Schweizer Aussenpolitik und Diplomatie: Von Pictet de Rochemont bis Edouard Brunner* (Zurich: Ammann, 2003), 11–36, 348–359, 402–413. For a critical examination of the moral limitations of the Swiss neutrality tradition, with specific focus on the failed role played by the ICRC in the context of the Holocaust, see Jean Claude Favez, *The Red Cross and the Holocaust*, ed. and trans. from the French by John and Beryl Fletcher (Cambridge: Cambridge University Press, 1999).

76 Akenson, *God's Peoples*. I would argue that, among Akenson's three cases, the modern Israeli secular-political mainstream actually takes the biblical model

least literally, although the country's religious Right certainly has propagated a fundamentalist perspective.

77 Simon Schama, *The Embarrassment of Riches: An Interpretation of Dutch Culture in the Golden Age* (New York: Knopf, 1988), 45, 68, 93–125; A. Smith, *Chosen Peoples*, 45–46; Steven Nadler, *Rembrandt's Jews* (Chicago: University of Chicago Press, 2003), esp. ch. 2; S. Smith, *Spinoza*, 146; Boralevi, "Classical Foundational Myths."

78 Indeed, the just-mentioned example of the seventeenth-century Netherlands could be taken as a case in point, given its global commercial and imperial reach, but the theme of a small people holding its own against superior powers and natural elements alike arguably remained predominant in the nation's self-image.

79 Anthony D. Smith (*Chosen Peoples*, chs. 3–5 – esp. pp. 49 and 95–96) makes a similar typological distinction, but he describes it as a contrast between "covenantal" and "missionary" forms of national election. (He does concede that "the ultimate purpose of the covenant is ... global salvation ... " p. 51. See also his comments on p. 95.) In my view, the "missionary" form of chosenness is *rooted* in the covenantal idea (not just "heavily influenced" by it – Smith, *Chosen Peoples*, 49), and it is precisely the dynamic tension between the principles of circumscribed covenant and universal mission that shapes debates about immigration, civil rights, cultural and educational policies, and foreign policy among many chosen nations.

80 Andrew Vincent writes about American and French "claims for the universality of their own particularity" in his *Nationalism and Particularity* (Cambridge: Cambridge University Press, 2002), 133.

81 Herman Melville, *White-Jacket* (1850; New York: Random House, 2002), 151. (For a fuller quotation of the passage from which this is excerpted see Bellah, *Broken Covenant*, 38–39.)

82 Alexis de Tocqueville, *Democracy in America*, trans. George Lawrence (1835–40; Garden City, N.Y.: Doubleday, 1969), 612.

83 For an eloquent discussion of "the ambiguities of chosenness" in the American political tradition, see Bellah, *Broken Covenant*, ch. 2, esp. p. 37.

84 Wood, *American Republic*, 10–13.

85 Edmund Burke, *Reflections on the Revolution in France* (1790; New York: Penguin, 1968).

86 See Wood, *Radicalism of the American Revolution*.

87 See, for example, Madison's *Federalist* No. 14, *Federalist Papers*, 144–145.

88 In Louis Hartz's words, "We have been able to dream of ourselves as emancipators of the world at the very moment that we have withdrawn from it ... Here, surely, is one of the great American luxuries that the twentieth century has destroyed." Louis Hartz, *The Liberal Tradition in America: An Interpretation of American Political Thought since the Revolution* (New York: Harcourt, Brace & World, 1955), 38. See also Walter A. McDougall, *Promised Land, Crusader State: The American Encounter with the World since 1776* (New York: Houghton-Mifflin, 1997), ch. 1.

89 Melville, *White-Jacket*, 151, quoted in Bellah, *Broken Covenant*, 38–39. Cf. also Bercovitch, *Puritan Origins of the American Self*, 98.

90 See Stephanson, *Manifest Destiny*.

91 As quoted in Glenn W. Price, *Origins of the War with Mexico: The Polk–Stockton Intrigue* (Austin: University of Texas Press, 1967), 13. See also Stephanson, *Manifest Destiny*, 32–38. There were, to be sure, critics who opposed the war against Mexico as inconsistent with the principles, and likely to undermine the global appeal, of the American republic. Robert W. Johannsen, *To the Halls of the Montezumas: The Mexican War in the American Imagination* (New York: Oxford University Press, 1985), ch. 10. On the expansive conception of American nationhood, see also Rachel C. St. John, "Line in the Sand: The Desert Border between the United States and Mexico, 1848–1934" (Ph.D. diss., Stanford University, 2005), ch. 1.

92 On the popularity of the Spanish–American war and the role of the Hearst press in whipping up enthusiasm for it, see Ernest R. May, *Imperial Democracy: The Emergence of America as a Great Power* (New York: Harcourt Brace Jovanovich, 1961). On the anti-imperialist movement in the United States, see Richard E. Welch, Jr., *Response to Imperialism: The United States and the Philippine–American War, 1899–1902* (Chapel Hill: University of North Carolina Press, 1979); Robert L. Beisner, *Twelve against Empire: The Anti-Imperialists, 1898–1900* (1968; Chicago: University of Chicago Press, 1985).

93 The material on Wilson is based on the following sources: Arthur S. Link, *Wilson the Diplomatist: A Look at his Major Foreign Policies* (New York: New Viewpoints, 1974); N. Gordon Levin, Jr., *Woodrow Wilson and World Politics: America's Response to War and Revolution* (London and Oxford: Oxford University Press, 1968); Lloyd E. Ambrosius, *Wilsonian Statecraft: Theory and Practice of Liberal Internationalism during World War I* (Wilmington, Del.: Scholarly Resources, 1991); Lloyd E. Ambrosius, *Woodrow Wilson and the American Diplomatic Tradition: The Treaty Fight in Perspective* (Cambridge: Cambridge University Press, 1987); Thomas J. Knock, *To End All Wars: Woodrow Wilson and the Quest for a New World Order* (Princeton: Princeton University Press, 1992); John Milton Cooper, Jr., *The Warrior and the Priest: Woodrow Wilson and Theodore Roosevelt* (Cambridge, Mass.: Harvard University Press, 1983), chs. 18–21.

94 Arno J. Mayer, *Political Origins of the New Diplomacy, 1917–1918* (1959; Cleveland: World Publishing Co., 1964).

95 See Vejas Gabriel Liulevicius, *War Land on the Eastern Front: Culture, National Identity and German Occupation in World War I* (Cambridge: Cambridge University Press, 2000); John W. Wheeler-Bennett, *Brest-Litovsk: The Forgotten Peace, March 1918* (1938; New York: Norton, 1971), 215–221; Aviel Roshwald, *Ethnic Nationalism and the Fall of Empires: Central Europe, Russia, and the Middle East, 1914–1923* (London: Routledge, 2001), 116–125.

96 It should be noted that the Bolshevik seizure of power in Russia and Lenin's indictment of the entire war effort in the name of his own universalistic,

socialist agenda, spurred Wilson to emphasize the idealistic, global vision underpinning his own diplomacy, although the fear of Bolshevik-style upheaval spreading through Europe ultimately tied Wilson's hands in his dealings with the Allied powers at the Paris Peace Conference. See Arno J. Mayer, *Politics and Diplomacy of Peacemaking: Containment and Counter-revolution at Versailles, 1918–1919* (New York: Knopf, 1967).

97 Erez Manela, "The Wilsonian Moment and the Rise of Anticolonial Nationalism: The Case of Egypt," *Diplomacy and Statecraft*, vol. 12, no. 4 (December 2001), 99–122.

98 On the influence of John Winthrop's neo-Augustinian vision on Wilson's framing of America's mission, see Crunden, *Ministers of Reform*, 233–234.

99 Woodrow Wilson, speech delivered during the campaign for the Democratic nomination for the presidency, 26 May 1912, as quoted in Knock, *To End All Wars*, 11.

100 Woodrow Wilson, "Be Worthy of the Men of 1776," Address at Independence Hall, Philadelphia, 4 July 1914, in Ray Stannard Baker and William E. Dodd, eds., *The Public Papers of Woodrow Wilson. The New Democracy: Presidential Messages, Addresses, and Other Papers (1913–1917)*, vol. 1 (New York: Harper & Brothers, 1926), 147.

101 Ibid.

102 Giuseppe Mazzini, "Faith and the Future," in Joseph [*sic*] Mazzini, *The Duties of Man and Other Essays* (London: Dent & Sons, 1907).

103 Wilson's universalism was not so sweeping as to stand in the way of double standards. He was willing to legitimize the expansion of his allies' overseas empires under the fig-leaf of League of Nations mandates that were supposed to provide for the tutelage of non-European peoples in anticipation of their eventual independence. He also rejected Japanese demands for an endorsement of the principle of racial equality by the Paris Peace Conference.

104 Lloyd Ambrosius, "Dilemmas of National Self-Determination: Woodrow Wilson's Legacy," in Christian Baechler and Carole Fink, eds., *The Establishment of European Frontiers after the Two World Wars* (Berlin: Peter Lang, 1996); Hartz, *Liberal Tradition*, 295.

105 See Roshwald, *Ethnic Nationalism*, chs. 5–6.

106 Richard Pipes, *The Formation of the Soviet Union: Communism and Nationalism, 1917–1923*, rev. edn (1954; Cambridge, Mass.: Harvard University Press, 1964), chs. 3–4; Ronald Grigor Suny, "Nationalism and Class in the Russian Revolution: A Comparative Discussion," in Edith Ragovin Frankel *et al.*, *Revolution in Russia: Reassessments of 1917* (Cambridge: Cambridge University Press, 1992). For a brief synthetic overview, see Roshwald, *Ethnic Nationalism*, 171–174.

107 As quoted in Alan Sharp, *The Versailles Settlement: Peacemaking in Paris, 1919* (New York: St. Martin's Press, 1991), 156.

108 It should be noted that the American political establishment by and large shied away from any long-term responsibilities that might be attached to the

implementation of the Wilsonian vision. Thus, Wilson's proposal to assume American responsibility for a mandate over Armenia in the wake of the Ottoman-orchestrated genocidal campaign of 1915 was rejected by the Senate in 1920. Diplomatic and rhetorical support for the principle of national self-determination was one thing; a long-term economic, administrative, and military commitment to a distant and unfamiliar corner of the world was another matter altogether. Dennis R. Papazian, "The Changing American View of the Armenian Question: An Interpretation," *Armenian Review*, vol. 39, no. 4 (Winter 1986), 47–72; Richard G. Hovannisian, "Historical Memory and Foreign Relations: The Armenian Perspective," in S. Frederick Starr, ed., *The Legacy of History in Russia and the New States of Eurasia* (Armonk, N.Y. and London: M. E. Sharpe, 1994), vol. 1 of Karen Dawisha and Bruce Parrott, series eds., *The International Politics of Eurasia.*

109 The classic indictment was penned by a disillusioned member of the British delegation to the Peace Conference: John Maynard Keynes' *The Economic Consequences of the Peace* (1920; New Brunswick, N.J.: Transaction Press, 2003) sold 100,000 copies – many of them in the US– in the first six months after its publication. Ibid., David Felix, "Transaction Introduction," xi.

110 Ambrosius, *Woodrow Wilson*, chs. 6–7 and *passim*; F. H. Hinsley, *Power and the Pursuit of Peace: Theory and Practice in the History of Relations between States* (Cambridge: Cambridge University Press, 1963), ch. 14.

111 The text of the Covenant is available online at: http://fletcher.tufts.edu/multi/www/league-covenant.html.

112 From Henry Cabot Lodge's speech to the 1920 Republican National Convention, as quoted in Widenor, *Henry Cabot Lodge*, 347–348.

113 As Robert Crunden has pointed out, the most resolute opponents of the League were themselves political progressives who drew their inspiration from the very same moralistic conception of America's role in the world that inspired Woodrow Wilson. Crunden, *Ministers of Reform*, 264–269.

114 Senator Borah, speech delivered on the floor of the US Senate, 19 November 1919, *Congressional Record*, vol. 58, part 9 (66th Congress, First Session, 14–19 November 1919) (Washington: Government Printing Office, 1919), pp. 8781–8784 (my emphasis). To be fair, one of Borah's main objections to the Versailles Treaty and League of Nations Covenant was that they consigned the greater part of the world to continued imperial rule and that by committing itself to upholding this corrupt international order, the United States would in fact be betraying the cause of global democratization. On Borah's uncompromising opposition to the League Covenant and the Treaty of Versailles as a whole (his initial, tactical support for some of Senator Lodge's proposed reservations to the Covenant notwithstanding), see Robert James Maddox, *William E. Borah and American Foreign Policy* (Baton Rouge: Louisiana State University Press, 1969), ch. 3; Marian C. McKenna, *Borah* (Ann Arbor: University of Michigan Press, 1961), ch. 10.

115 Manfred Jonas, *Isolationism in America, 1935–1941* (Ithaca: Cornell University Press, 1966), ch. 5 and *passim.*

116 On the expanding global cultural and economic influence of the United States during the interwar years, see Frank Costigliola, *Awkward Dominion: American Political, Economic, and Cultural Relations with Europe, 1919–1933* (Ithaca: Cornell University Press, 1984); Emily S. Rosenberg, *Spreading the American Dream: American Economic and Cultural Expansion, 1890–1945* (New York: Hill and Wang, 1982), chs. 5–8. On American involvement in the arbitration of Anglo-French reparations disputes with Germany and in the financing of revised reparations schedules, see Stephen A. Schuker, *The End of French Predominance in Europe: The Financial Crisis of 1924 and the Adoption of the Dawes Plan* (Chapel Hill: University of North Carolina Press, 1976); Sally Marks, *The Illusion of Peace: International Relations in Europe* (New York: St. Martin's Press, 1976), 52–54, 101–102.

117 G. John Ikenberry points out that the Bretton Woods accords actually represented a compromise between American pressure for free trade and European governments' concern to manage and protect their countries' post-war economic revitalization. G. John Ikenberry, *After Victory: Institutions, Strategic Restraint, and the Rebuilding of Order after Major Wars* (Princeton: Princeton University Press, 2001), 185–191.

118 On the role of the Cold War in providing liberal-universalist American intellectuals entrée into the policy-making establishment, see Eric P. Kaufmann, *The Rise and Fall of Anglo-America* (Cambridge, Mass.: Harvard University Press, 2004), 139, 165–166. For the more aggressive interpreters of Containment doctrine, the overarching moral imperatives of the struggle against Communism not only necessitated America's assumption of the dominant role in the Western democratic camp, but justified its pursuit of ideologically inconsistent, ethically questionable policies such as the support of brutal Third World dictatorships. See Walter Lafeber, *Inevitable Revolutions: The United States in Central America*, 2nd edn (New York: Norton, 1993), chs. 2–3.

119 "NSC-68: United States Objectives and Programs for National Security," 14 April 1950, in Thomas H. Etzold and John Lewis Gaddis, eds., *Containment: Documents on American Policy and Strategy, 1945–1950* (New York: Columbia University Press, 1978), 385–442. Quotation from page 437. For background on, and analysis of, NSC-68, see John Lewis Gaddis, *Strategies of Containment: A Critical Appraisal of Post-War American National Security Policy* (New York: Oxford University Press, 1982), ch. 4; Melvyn Leffler, *A Preponderance of Power: National Security, the Truman Administration, and the Cold War* (Stanford: Stanford University Press, 1992), 355–361.

120 One major exception was the Security Council's resolution authorizing the use of force to reverse North Korea's June 1950 invasion of South Korea. This was a historical fluke, arising from the fact that the Soviet representative was not present to exercise his veto. (The USSR happened

to be boycotting Security Council meetings in protest over the United States' refusal to allow representatives of Mao's newly established Communist regime to assume China's seat at the UN.)

121 Robert Kagan makes a similar point from a rather different perspective in his *Of Paradise and Power: America and Europe in the New World Order*, Vintage Books edn (2002; New York: Random House, 2004), 108–111.

122 Norman M. Naimark, *Fires of Hatred: Ethnic Cleansing in Twentieth-Century Europe* (Cambridge, Mass.: Harvard University Press, 2001).

123 Francis Fukuyama, *The End of History and the Last Man* (New York: The Free Press, 1992). See also Anders Stephanson's concluding speculations in *Manifest Destiny*, 129.

124 The ICC's July 1998 statute came into effect with its ratification by sixty countries as of July 2002. See the ICC's website: http://www.icc-cpi.int/ataglance/whatistheicc/history.html.

125 Stewart Patrick and Shepard Forman, eds., *Multilateralism and U.S. Foreign Policy: Ambivalent Engagement* (Boulder: Lynne Rienner Publishers, 2002); Yves Beigbeder, *Judging War Criminals: The Politics of International Justice* (London: Macmillan, 1999), ch. 10.

126 On the centrality of the U.S. government's role in creating the Nuremberg tribunal, see Gary Jonathan Bass, *Stay the Hand of Vengeance: The Politics of War Crimes Tribunals* (Princeton: Princeton University Press, 2000), ch. 5. For an analysis of how post-1945 internationalism served American national interests by creating multilateral institutional frameworks within which the exercise of U.S. power seemed less threatening to weaker states in the system, see G. John Ikenberry, "Multilateralism and U.S. Grand Strategy," in Patrick and Forman, eds., *Multilateralism*, and G. John Ikenberry, *After Victory*. Ikenberry contends that such an approach could continue to further U.S. interests in the post-Cold War era.

127 Of course, vociferous protectionist objections to economic globalization have been raised, both on the reactionary Right of American politics, by the likes of Ross Perot and Patrick Buchanan, and on the Left by trade unions, Democratic congressmen, and others concerned about the cost of free trade to American jobs and environmental protections. See Kimberly Ann Elliott and Gary Clyde Hufbauer, "Ambivalent Multilateralism and the Emerging Backlash: The IMF and WTO," in Patrick and Forman, *Multilateralism*.

128 On suspicion of state power as a formative feature of American national identity, see Seymour Martin Lipset, *American Exceptionalism: A Double-Edged Sword* (New York: Norton, 1996), 39–46.

129 Julie A. Mertus, *Bait and Switch: Human Rights and U.S. Foreign Policy* (New York: Routledge, 2004), 31–36.

130 Bartram S. Brown, "Unilateralism, Multilateralism, and the International Criminal Court," in Patrick and Forman, eds., *Multilateralism*.

131 Jesse Helms, "Saving the U.N.: A Challenge to the Next Secretary-General," *Foreign Affairs*, vol. 75, no. 5 (September/October 1996), 2–7.

132 Patrick J. Buchanan, *A Republic, Not an Empire: Reclaiming America's Destiny* (Washington, D.C.: Regnery Publishing, 1999), 364. On the increasing political isolation of Buchanan's isolationism, see Stefan Halper and Jonathan Clarke, *America Alone: The Neo-Conservatives and the Global Order* (Cambridge: Cambridge University Press, 2004), 70–72.

133 Phyllis Schlafly, as quoted in Lieven, *America*, 16.

134 Robert Tomes, "Operation Allied Force and the Legal Basis for Humanitarian Interventions," *Parameters: US Army War College Quarterly*, vol. 30, no. 1 (Spring 2000), 28–50; Richard N. Haass, *Intervention: The Use of American Military Force in the Post-Cold War World*, rev. edn (Washington, D.C.: Brookings, 1999), 37–43, 160–162, 164–167; Giovanna Bono, "NATO's War over Kosovo: The Debates, Dynamics and Consequences," in Michael C. Davis *et al.*, eds., *International Intervention in the Post-Cold War World: Moral Responsibility and Power Politics* (Armonk, N.Y.: M. E. Sharpe, 2004).

135 Sarah B. Sewall, "Multilateral Peace Operations," in Patrick and Forman, eds., *Multilateralism*; Mertus, *Bait and Switch*, 38–52. David Calleo takes a less charitable view of the Clinton administration's foreign policy. He contends that the Clinton administration's political and economic diplomacy set a fundamentally unilateralist course for the United States, with only a thin veneer of neo-Wilsonian rhetoric masking post-Cold War America's imperial pretensions. David P. Calleo, *Rethinking Europe's Future* (Princeton: A Century Foundation Book/Princeton University Press, 2003), ch. 16 and Afterword.

136 Michael Kinsley, "The Limits of Eloquence: Did Bush Mean a Word of his Speech about Democracy?" *Slate*, 13 November 2003: http://slate.msn.com/id/2091185.

137 Even later, at the height of his new-found commitment to spreading freedom throughout the world, Bush Jr. denied believing that America was a chosen nation. See Bush's Second Inaugural Address, 20 January 2005: http://www.cnn.com/2005/ALLPOLITICS/01/20/bush.transcript. Yet, as I am suggesting here, the very idea of reshaping the world along democratic lines is derived from the rhetoric and ideology of national chosenness.

138 Thomas Donnelly (principal author), Donald Kagan, and Gary Schmitt, "Rebuilding America's Defenses: Strategy, Forces and Resources for a New Century," A Report for the Project for a New American Century, September 2000 (available at http://www.newamericancentury.org/RebuildingAmericasDefenses.pdf). The Project for a New American Century is the foreign and defense policy think tank chaired by William Kristol, the intellectual dean of neo-conservatives, and editor of the neo-conservative mouthpiece, *The Daily Standard*. See also William Kristol and Robert Kagan, "Toward a Neo-Reaganite Foreign Policy," *Foreign Affairs*, vol. 75, no. 4 (July/August 1996), 18–32; Kagan, *Paradise and Power*; Lawrence F. Kaplan and William Kristol, *The War over Iraq: Saddam's Tyranny and America's Mission* (San Francisco: Encounter Books, 2003),

67–68; Charles Krauthammer, "The Unipolar Moment," *Foreign Affairs*, vol. 70, no. 1 (issue subtitled *America and the World 1990/91*), 23–33; Charles Krauthammer, "Democratic Realism: An American Foreign Policy for a Unipolar World," speech delivered before the American Enterprise Institute as the Irving Kristol Lecture, Washington, DC, February 2004 (Washington: AEI Press, 2004; also available at http://www.aei.org/docLib/ 20040227_book755text.pdf). Francis Fukuyama questions Krauthammer's approach and distances himself from the general unilateralism of the neoconservatives in "The Neoconservative Moment," *The National Interest*, no. 76 (Summer 2004), 57–68. For a sympathetic socio-intellectual history of the neo-conservative movement, see Mark Gerson, *The Neoconservative Vision: From the Cold War to the Culture Wars* (Lanham, Md.: Madison Books, 1996). A more critical assessment is offered by Peter Steinfels in *The Neoconservatives: The Men Who Are Changing America's Politics* (New York: Simon and Schuster, 1979). For a more recent dissection and critique of the neoconservatives' impact on Bush Jr.'s foreign policy, written from a self-avowed, moderately conservative perspective, see Halper and Clarke, *America Alone*.

139 Kristol and Kagan, "Neo-Reaganite Foreign Policy," 27.

140 Sidney Blumenthal, "Christian Soldiers," *The New Yorker*, 18 July 1994, 37.

141 Transcript of John Ashcroft's May 1999 Commencement Address at Bob Jones University posted on the website of *The Ethical Spectacle*, February 2001, http://www.spectacle.org/0201/ashcroft.html. See also "Bush Transition Office Releases Ashcroft's Remarks at Bob Jones University," CNN website, 12 January 2001: http://archives.cnn.com/2001/ALLPOLITICS/ stories/01/12/ashcroft.bobjones\.

142 Michael Lind, *The Next American Nation: The New Nationalism and the Fourth American Revolution* (New York: The Free Press, 1995), 245–251; William Martin, "The Christian Right and American Foreign Policy," *Foreign Policy*, no. 114 (Spring 1999), 66–80, esp. 78–79.

143 Pat Robertson, "Why Evangelical Christians Support Israel," transcript of speech delivered at The Herzliya Conference, Lauder School of Government, Diplomacy, and Strategy, 17 December 2003, posted on "The Official Site of Pat Robertson," http://www.patrobertson.com/Speeches/ IsraelLauder.asp. See also Dan Balz, "Bush Statement on Mideast Reflects Tension in GOP; President Seeks to Bridge Foreign Policy Establishment and Rising Number of Pro-Israel Conservatives," *The Washington Post*, 7 April 2002.

144 For an argument about how a judicious engagement in multilateral diplomacy can serve long-term American national interests, see Joseph S. Nye, *The Paradox of American Power: Why the World's Only Superpower Can't Go it Alone* (New York: Oxford University Press, 2002).

145 Letter addressed to President Clinton by figures associated with the neoconservative Project for the New American Century (including Paul Wolfowitz, Donald Rumsfeld, and Richard Armitage) advocating the

pursuit of regime change in Iraq without resort to further United Nations resolutions, 26 January 1998, http://www.newamericancentury.org/iraqclintonletter.htm; Kaplan and Kristol, *War over Iraq*, *passim*; Krauthammer, "Democratic Realism"; Kenneth M. Pollack, *The Threatening Storm: The Case for Invading Iraq* (New York: Random House, 2002). Stefan Halper and Jonathan Clarke argue persuasively that in the aftermath of the 9/11 attacks, neoconservative policy-makers and commentators played a critical role in blurring the distinction between Saddam Hussein and al-Qaeda, as a manipulative way of gaining public support for their aggressively interventionist plan to reshape the Middle East's political culture and balance of power. Halper and Clarke, *America Alone*, ch. 7.

146 Kaplan and Kristol, *War over Iraq*, 120.

147 Judy Mann, "Falwell's Insult Compounds Nation's Injury," *The Washington Post*, 21 September 2001, p. C8.

148 Having coined this term, I have since found I am not the only one to have done so. See, for example, Josh Lehto's website at http://bluejay.mind.net/shadowplay/handmaidstale.html.

149 Tim LaHaye's notoriously bestselling "Left Behind" series has popularized this theological doctrine in fictionalized form.

150 Gershom Gorenberg, *The End of Days: Fundamentalism and the Struggle for the Temple Mount* (Oxford: Oxford University Press, 2000). See also Martin, "The Christian Right," 73. On the nineteenth-century English roots of Evangelical Christian Zionism, see Longley, *Chosen People*, 193–200; Tony Campolo, "The Ideological Roots of Christian Zionism," *Tikkun*, vol. 20, no. 1 (January/February 2005), 19–22.

151 Lieven, *America*, 179–186.

152 Bob Woodward, *Bush at War* (New York: Simon & Schuster, 2002), 332–336, 344–349.

153 Halper and Clarke, *America Alone*.

154 Fareed Zakaria, "Rumsfeld's Crusader," *The Washington Post*, 21 October 2003, p. A25. See also Lieven, *America*, 148–149.

155 CBN website, 16 November 2004: http://www.cbn.com/special/OperationBreakthrough/index.asp. See also Max Blumenthal, "Onward Christian Soldiers," Salon.com, 15 April 2003.

156 See the "Community Login" page (as of November 2004) at: http://www.cbn.com/community/af/login.asp.

157 The other countries designated by Bush as members of the "Axis of Evil" in his January 2002 State of the Union Address were Iran and North Korea. The text of the speech is available at: http://www.whitehouse.gov/news/releases/2002/01/20020129-11.html. See also Kevin Phillips, "Crusader: Bush's Religious Passions," *Christian Century*, 13 July 2004, 8–9. For an argument that Bush's religio-political rhetoric is designed to reconcile the Christian Right with the foreign-policy strategy of the neoconservatives, see Bruce Lincoln, "Bush's God Talk," *Christian Century*, 5 October 2004, 22–29. On the Christian Right's support for the Iraq war and the Christian

fundamentalist influence on Bush's political outlook, see Lieven, *America*, 128–130, 143–144.

158 See, for instance, Bush's early remarks to reporters at the Pentagon in the aftermath of the September 11 attacks: "Bush: There's No Rules," CNN.com, 17 September 2001: http://archives.cnn.com/2001/US/09/17/gen.bush.transcript/.

159 The text of President George W. Bush's Second Inaugural Address of 20 January 2005 can be found at http://www.whitehouse.gov/news/releases/2005/01/20050120-1.html.

160 See the discussion and critique by Richard Falk in *The Declining World Order: America's Imperial Geopolitics* (New York: Routledge, 2004), chs. 8–9 and *passim*. Falk's endorsement of a Gandhian approach to the struggle with global terror places him far outside the liberal-internationalist mainstream, to be sure! Ibid., 237–238.

161 John Tierney, "The Hawks Loudly Express their Second Thoughts," *The New York Times*, 16 May 2004.

162 "No Casualties? White House Disputes Robertson Comment," CNN website, 21 October 2004: http://www.cnn.com/2004/ALLPOLITICS/10/19/robertson.bush.iraq.

163 It is worth noting that both Kennan and Kissinger look to doomed and disastrous European historical precedents for inspiration. Kennan's critique of American foreign policy – and the diplomacy of democracies more generally – was informed by a nostalgic obsession with the alleged virtues of Wilhelmine Germany's aristocratic elite. Kissinger's somewhat cynical ideas about the relationship among idealism, legitimacy, and opportunism in the formulation of foreign policy are informed by his admiring view of Metternich's supposed role in staving off the ruin of the Habsburg Empire for a few generations and by his admittedly more critical, yet still awe-struck, appraisal of Bismarck's diplomacy. George F. Kennan, *Russia and the West under Lenin and Stalin* (New York: Penguin, 1961), esp. 44–45, 344–345; George F. Kennan, *The Fateful Alliance: France, Russia, and the Coming of the First World* War (New York: Pantheon, 1984), 252–253; David Mayers, *George Kennan and the Dilemmas of US Foreign Policy* (New York: Oxford University Press, 1988), 74–78; Henry A. Kissinger, *A World Restored: Metternich, Castlereagh and the Problems of Peace, 1812–1822* (1957; Boston: Houghton Mifflin, 1973); Henry A. Kissinger, "The White Revolutionary: Reflections on Bismarck," *Daedalus*, vol. 97, no. 3 (Summer 1968), 888–924; Henry Kissinger, *Diplomacy* (New York: Simon & Schuster, 1994), chs. 4–5. Thomas J. Knock has noted that, in the 1980s, George Kennan started to adopt a more positive view of Woodrow Wilson's idealism. Knock, *To End All Wars*, 274.

164 Cf. Lind, *Next American Nation*, 227–231.

165 Steven G. Marks, *How Russia Shaped the Modern World: From Art to Anti-Semitism, Ballet to Bolshevism* (Princeton: Princeton University Press, 2003), ch. 8; Greenfeld, *Nationalism*, 260–274.

166 Hisham Sharabi, *Neopatriarchy: A Theory of Distorted Change in Arab Society* (New York: Oxford University Press, 1988). Sharabi tries to apply a neo-Marxist interpretive framework to this phenomenon, arguing that, in the contemporary context, Islamic fundamentalism and "neopatriarchalism" is largely a function of "petty bourgeois hegemony." (See chapter 9.)

167 L. Carl Brown, *Religion and State: The Muslim Approach to Politics* (New York: Columbia University Press, 2000); Bernard Lewis, *The Political Language of Islam* (Chicago: University of Chicago Press, 1988), chs. 1, 4, and 5.

168 On the historical background of Islamic modernism and Arab nationalism, see Albert Hourani, *Arabic Thought in the Liberal Age* (London: Oxford University Press, 1962); Ernest Dawn, "The Origins of Arab Nationalism" and the other essays in Rashid Khalidi *et al.*, *Origins of Arab Nationalism* (New York: Columbia University Press, 1991); James P. Jankowski and Israel Gershoni, eds., *Rethinking Nationalism in the Arab Middle East* (New York: Columbia University Press, 1997); Bassam Tibi, *Arab Nationalism: Between Islam and the Nation-State*, 3rd edn (New York: St. Martin's Press, 1997). On the contemporary Islamic fundamentalist challenge to secular Arab nationalism, see Fouad Ajami, *The Arab Predicament: Arab Political Thought and Practice Since 1967* (Cambridge: Cambridge University Press, 1981), 50–63; Bernard Lewis, *What Went Wrong? The Clash Between Islam and Modernity in the Middle East* (New York: Oxford University Press, 2002), ch. 5; Martin Kramer, *Arab Awakening and Islamic Revival: The Politics of Ideas in the Middle East* (New Brunswick, N.J.: Transaction Publishers, 1996), ch. 9; Mark Juergensmeyer, *Terror in the Mind of God: The Global Rise of Religious Violence*, 3rd edn (Berkeley: University of California Press, 2003), 62–70, 80–84.

169 Colley, *Britons*, ch. 1; Longley, *Chosen People*; Hastings, *Construction of Nationhood*, ch. 2; Smith, *Chosen Peoples*, 115–123. On the role of social hierarchy in the structuring and conceptualization of British nationhood and British Empire, see David Cannadine, *Ornamentalism: How the British Saw their Empire* (Oxford: Oxford University Press, 2001). Simon Schama contends that, in Britain, the theme of being a New Israel was essentially monopolized by the Calvinist denominations rather than embraced by the nation as a whole until the late eighteenth/early nineteenth century. Schama, *Embarrassment of Riches*, 96–97.

170 Colley, *Britons*, 351–356; Longley, *Chosen People*, ch. 6, esp. p. 159.

171 Eyre Crowe, "Memorandum on the Present State of British Relations with France and Germany", 1 January 1907, FO 371/257, in G. P. Gooch and Harold Temperley, eds., *British Documents on the Origins of the War, 1898–1914*, vol. III: *The Testing of the Entente, 1904–6* (London: His Majesty's Stationery Office, 1928), 402. See also the discussion in Zara Steiner, *The Foreign Office and Foreign Policy, 1898–1914* (1969; London: Ashfield Press, 1986), 108–118.

172 Niall Ferguson, *Empire: The Rise and Demise of the British World Order and the Lessons for Global Power* (New York: Basic Books, 2002), 369–370;

Longley, *Chosen People*, 239. Longley contends that "the phrase 'the white man's burden', used in England ironically . . . is now regarded as applicable to the United States . . ." But in fact, Rudyard Kipling's 1899 poem "The White Man's Burden" was explicitly addressed to the United States in the first place (as Ferguson points out in *Empire*, p. 369)!

173 Winston S. Churchill, *A History of the English-Speaking Peoples*, 5 vols. (New York: Dodd, Mead & Co., 1956). See his Preface in vol. 1.

174 Widenor, *Henry Cabot Lodge*, 59–61, 304; Gary Gerstle, *American Crucible: Race and Nation in the Twentieth Century* (Princeton: Princeton University Press, 2001), ch. 1.

175 See Graham Greene's classic novel, *The Quiet American* (London: William Heinemann, 1955). In the "Smiley series" of novels inaugurated by *Call for the Dead* (New York: Walker, 1962), John Le Carré's disenchanted British spies ironically refer to their intrusive American counterparts as "cousins."

176 See David Reynolds, "A Special Relationship: America, Britain and the International Order since the Second World War," *International Affairs*, vol. 62, no. 1 (Winter 1985/86), 1–20.

177 On the mixed feelings the presentation and reception of the Statue of Liberty aroused on both sides of the Atlantic, see Philippe Roger, *The American Enemy: The History of French Anti-Americanism* (Chicago: University of Chicago Press, 2005), 101–104. Roger describes the statue as "the most cumbersome gift ever offered by one nation to another." Ibid., 102.

178 On the *mission civilisatrice*, see Bell, *Cult of the Nation*, ch. 3; Alice Conklin, *Mission to Civilize: The Republican Idea of Empire in France & West Africa, 1895–1930* (Stanford: Stanford University Press, 2000); Matthew Burrows, " 'Mission Civilisatrice': French Cultural Policy in the Middle East, 1860–1914," *Historical Journal*, vol. 29, no. 1 (March 1986), 109–135.

179 On the choppy relationships between France and Britain, and France and the United States, in the context of the Second World War, see William Langer, *Our Vichy Gamble* (New York: Knopf, 1947); R. T. Thomas, *Britain and Vichy: The Dilemma of Anglo-French Relations, 1940–42* (New York: St. Martin's Press, 1979); Jean-Baptiste Duroselle, *L'Abîme: 1939–1945* (Paris: Imprimerie Nationale, 1982), 488–499 and *passim*; François Kersaudy, *Churchill and De Gaulle* (1981; New York: Atheneum, 1983); Aviel Roshwald, *Estranged Bedfellows: Britain and France in the Middle East during the Second World War* (New York: Oxford University Press, 1990).

180 Bell, *Cult of the Nation*, ch. 3 and p. 149.

181 David Bell notes that none other than George Washington had figured as the embodiment of the brutal Briton in French propaganda of the 1750s, in his capacity as a junior officer in the British army whose unit was alleged to have murdered a French officer traveling under flag of truce near present-day Pittsburgh. Bell, *Cult of the Nation*, 78–85.

182 Richard Kuisel, *Seducing the French: The Dilemma of Americanization* (Berkeley: University of California Press, 1993), 119–121, 126–127, 235–236

and *passim*; Richard Pells, *Not Like Us: How Europeans Have Loved, Hated, and Transformed American Culture since World War II* (New York: Basic Books, 1997), 160 and *passim*.

183 As quoted in Kuisel, *Seducing the French*, 65. See also Niebuhr, *Irony of American History*, 58.

184 See Charlotte Rotman, "Tilting at Golden Arches," *Civilization*, vol. 7, no. 2 (April/May 2000), p. 29. On French responses to cultural globalization, see Suzanne Berger, "French Democracy Without Borders?," MIT Industrial Performance Center Working Paper 01–009 (available at http://web.mit.edu/ipc/www/pubs/articles/01-009.pdf); Philip H. Gordon and Sophie Meunier, *The French Challenge: Adapting to Globalization* (Washington, D.C.: Brookings Institution Press, 2001), ch. 3.

185 Alain Rollat, "Vive le Rocquefort libre!" *Le Monde*, 9 September 1999, as quoted in Gordon and Meunier, *French Challenge*, 53.

186 Pells, *Not Like Us*, chs. 8–9.

187 Birnbaum, *Idea of France*, 16–24, 229–230, 238–241.

188 Régis Debray, "Républicain ou démocrate?," *Le Nouvel Observateur*, 30 November 1989, as quoted in Birnbaum, *Idea of France*, 22. Writing in the early 1990s, Richard Kuisel argued that in the aftermath of de Gaulle's successful challenge to American geopolitical hegemony on the one hand and his effective promotion of economic Americanization on the other, French critiques of consumerism and materialism had become more inwardly focused and less explicitly anti-American. The 1980s even witnessed an efflorescence of pro-American attitudes in France. Kuisel, *Seducing the French*, 152–153 and chs. 8–9. But Kuisel warned that "an unfavorable conjuncture in the future could provoke a repetition of events in the 1950s and 1960s . . ." Ibid., 234. And indeed, since the publication of Kuisel's book, the Bush Jr. administration's war in Iraq has clearly brought Franco-American relations to their lowest point since de Gaulle's withdrawal from NATO's joint military command in 1966. Philippe Roger argues even more pessimistically that anti-Americanism has continuously remained in place as one of the defining features of modern French national identity. He points to the fact that, whereas public opinion in most West European countries turned sharply against the United States in 2002 over the Bush Jr. administration's policy toward Iraq, during the same period, the percentage of French respondents reporting a negative perception of the US actually fell a (statistically meaningless) point from 63 to 62 percent. Roger's point is not that the French were less hostile than others to American policy; it is that the majority of them had harbored a reflexive and unreflective dislike of America all along, regardless of specific policy agreements or disputes. Roger, *American Enemy*, 450–451.

189 For a recent, unflattering comparison of the traditions of inclusive American liberalism and intolerant French republicanism, see Frederic Cople Jaher, *The Jews and the Nation: Revolution, Emancipation, State Formation, and the Liberal Paradigm in America and France* (Princeton: Princeton University

Press, 2002), ch. 6 and *passim*. Jaher does acknowledge the greater tolerance for genuine diversity that has arisen in post-1945 French society.

190 Alfred Grosser, *The Western Alliance: European–American Relations since 1945*, trans. Michael Shaw (1978; New York: Random House, 1982), chs. 7–8; Hoffmann, *Decline or Renewal?*, chs. 10–11; Charles de Gaulle, *Memoirs of Hope: Renewal and Endeavor*, trans. Terence Kilmartin (New York: Simon and Schuster, 1971), 208–209, 255–256, and *passim*.

191 Gordon and Meunier, *French Challenge*, ch. 3.

192 Stanley Hoffmann, "France, the United States, and Iraq," *The Nation*, vol. 278, no. 6 (February 2004), 16–19.

193 T. C. W. Blanning, *The Origins of the French Revolutionary Wars* (London: Longman, 1986). Blanning questions whether ideological differences *per se* lay at the root of the French revolutionary wars, but documents how universalistic rhetoric came to color the French conception of what lay at stake in the wars.

194 Duff Cooper, *Talleyrand* (1932; New York: Fromm, 1986), 248–252; Andreas Osiander, *The States System of Europe, 1640–1990: Peacemaking and the Conditions of International Stability* (Oxford: Oxford University Press, 1994), 171–172; Paul W. Schroeder, *The Transformation of European Politics, 1763–1848* (Oxford: Oxford University Press, 1994), 523.

195 The editorial page of the French newspaper *Le Monde* responded to Rumsfeld's disparaging reference to Old Europe by suggesting that "old Rumsfeld" ("vieux Rumsfeld") was sadly quite right in thinking that the new, East Central European member states of the European Union wanted nothing better than to "mechanically follow" American leadership in the spheres of defense and foreign policy. *Le Monde*, 25 January 2003.

196 Chuck Martin, "How to Fry the French: Act of National Ire Small Potatoes to What Would Light France's Fire," *The Cincinnati Enquirer*, 16 March 2003.

197 On the missionary sense of chosenness, see A. Smith, *Chosen Peoples*, chs. 3–5.

198 See the earlier reference in this chapter on page 176.

199 Renan, "What Is a Nation?," 53.

200 Ian S. Lustick, *Unsettled States, Disputed Lands: Britain and Ireland, France and Algeria, Israel and the West Bank-Gaza* (Ithaca: Cornell University Press, 1993), 4.

201 Anderson, *Imagined Communities*, ch. 10. Cf. also Thongchai Winichakul, *Siam Mapped: A History of the Geo-Body of a Nation* (Honolulu: University of Hawai'i Press, 1994).

202 On the uses and abuses of Frederick Jackson Turner's famous "frontier thesis," see Kerwin Lee Klein, "Reclaiming the 'F' Word, or Being and Becoming Postwestern," *Pacific Historical Review*, vol. 65, no. 2 (May 1996), 179–215.

203 Ernest R. May, *The Making of the Monroe Doctrine* (Cambridge, Mass.: Harvard University Press, 1975).

204 Welch, *Response to Imperialism*, ch. 4; Stephanson, *Manifest Destiny*, 100–104.

205 Amy Kaplan, "Homeland Insecurities: Reflections on Language and Space," *Radical History Review*, no. 85 (Winter 2003), 82–93.

206 From 1924 to 1965, American immigration law incorporated a National Origins Quota system designed to preserve the socio-political and cultural hegemony of Anglo-Protestants by preventing a disproportionate influx of immigrants from countries outside of Northern and Western Europe. Gerstle, *American Crucible*, 82, 103–104, 108–109, 268; Lind, *Next American Nation*, ch. 1; Kaufmann, *Anglo-America*, 32–34, 78, 182–183, 207. Yet, as Eric Kaufmann has argued, the past century has also witnessed the rise to prominence of a culturally pluralistic, cosmopolitan conception of American identity that has displaced older, Anglo-American frames of reference. Kaufmann, *Anglo-America*, *passim*. On the growing post-World War II consensus around the United States' character as "a nation of immigrants," see ibid., ch. 8.

207 See Lind, *Next American Nation*, 56, 105, 227 and *passim*; Kaufmann, *Anglo-America*, ch. 5.

208 Kaufmann, *Anglo-America*, 180–181.

209 The quoted phrase is from Emma Lazarus' famous poem, inscribed on the pedestal of the Statue of Liberty. See Kaufmann, *Anglo-America*, 180–181.

210 For descriptions of immigration inspection procedures at Ellis Island, see Barbara Benton, *Ellis Island: A Pictorial History* (New York: Facts on File Publications, 1985); Thomas M. Pitkin, *Keepers of the Gate: A History of Ellis Island* (New York: New York University Press, 1975). Pitkin contends that the myth of the Ellis Island ordeal is partly the result of conflation with memories of the suffering undergone by poor immigrants during their Atlantic passage. Ibid., 67.

211 The Statue of Liberty and Ellis Island were jointly restored in the 1980s by the non-profit Statue of Liberty/Ellis Island Foundation and are jointly administered by the National Park Service as the Statue of Liberty/Ellis Island National Monument. Virginia Yans-McLaughlin and Marjorie Lightman with the Statue of Liberty/Ellis Island Foundation, *Ellis Island and the Peopling of America: The Official Guide* (New York: The New Press, 1990), 203 and 59.

212 In his introduction to the official guide to the Ellis Island Museum, Lee Iacocca – founding chairman of the foundation that raised funds for the site's restoration – describes the museum as "a monument not only to the courage of those who passed through its doors, but also to the immigrant heritage of all Americans." Lee Iacocca, "Foreword," in Yans-McLaughlin and Lightman, *Ellis Island*, 5.

213 When Charles Darwin first set foot in Sydney, Australia in January 1836, during his odyssey aboard the *Beagle*, he was immediately struck by how much more advanced this relatively new British colony seemed than the far older Latin American communities he had previously visited. As he recalled

it: "My first feeling was to congratulate myself that I was born an Englishman." Charles Darwin, *Voyage of the Beagle* (abridged edn of *Journal of Researches* [London, 1839] (London: Penguin, 1989), 318.

214 Ethnic Russians slightly outnumbered members of other nationalities within the redrawn boundaries of the Soviet Union.

215 Isabelle Kreindler, "A Neglected Source of Lenin's Nationality Policy," *Slavic Review*, vol. 36, no. 1 (March 1977), 86–100; Robert Geraci, "The Il'minskii System and the Controversy over Non-Russian Teachers and Priests in the Middle Volga," in Catherine Evtuhov, Boris Gasparov, Alexander Ospovat, and Mark Von Hagen, eds., *Kazan, Moscow, St. Petersburg: Multiple Faces of the Russian Empire* (Moscow: O.G.I., 1997).

216 This discussion of Soviet nationalities policy draws on the following sources: Walker Connor, *The National Question in Marxist–Leninist Theory and Strategy* (Princeton: Princeton University Press, 1984), chs. 2–3; Pipes, *The Formation of the Soviet Union*; Yuri Slezkine, "The USSR as a Communal Apartment, or How a Socialist State Promoted Ethnic Particularism," *Slavic Review*, vol. 53, no. 2 (Summer 1994), 414–452; Robert Kaiser, *The Geography of Nationalism in Russia and the USSR* (Princeton: Princeton University Press, 1994), ch. 3 and *passim*; Rogers Brubaker, *Nationalism Reframed: Nationhood and the National Question in the New Europe* (Cambridge: Cambridge University Press, 1996), ch. 2; Hélène Carrère d'Encausse, *The Great Challenge: Nationalities and the Bolshevik State, 1917–1930* (New York: Holmes and Meier, 1992); Andreas Kappeler, *Russland als Vielvölkerreich* (Munich: C. H. Beck, 1993), Epilogue; Ronald Grigor Suny, *The Revenge of the Past: Nationalism, Revolution and the Collapse of the Soviet Union* (Stanford: Stanford University Press, 1993); Terry Martin, *The Affirmative Action Empire: Nations and Nationalism in the Soviet Union, 1923–1939* (Ithaca: Cornell University Press, 2001); Ronald Grigor Suny and Terry Martin, eds., *A State of Nations: Empire and Nation Making in the Age of Lenin and Stalin* (New York: Oxford University Press, 2001); Jeffrey Smith, *The Bolsheviks and the National Question, 1917–1923* (London: Palgrave Macmillan, 1999).

217 David Brandenberger, *National Bolshevism: Stalinist Mass Culture and the Formation of Modern Russian National Identity, 1931–1936* (Cambridge, Mass.: Harvard University Press, 2002).

218 Naimark, *Fires of Hatred*, ch. 3; Amir Weiner, "Nature, Nurture, and Memory in a Socialist Utopia: Delineating the Soviet Socio-Ethnic Body in the Age of Socialism," *American Historical Review*, vol. 104, no. 4 (Oct. 1999), 1114–1155.

219 See Suny, *Revenge of the Past*.

220 For a historical perspective on Russia's unresolved tension between imperial and national frameworks of political development and identity see Geoffrey Hosking, *Russia and the Russians: A History* (Cambridge, Mass.: Harvard University Press, 2003). In April 2005, Russian President Putin described the collapse of the Soviet Union as "the greatest geopolitical catastrophe of

the [20th] century." Alex Nicholson (Associated Press), "Russia's Putin: Soviet Collapse a Tragedy," *The Washington Post*, 25 April 2005.

221 The equivalent for a country the shape of Russia would presumably be something rather less satisfying, like "the blob" or "the amoeba."

222 As quoted in Eugen Weber, "L'Hexagone," in Pierre Nora, ed., *Les Lieux de mémoire*, vol. II: *La Nation*, part 2 (Paris: Gallimard, 1984), 98. On the nation's geographic geometry as symbol of French rationalism, see also Ernst Robert Curtius' observations in his *Essai sur la France*, trans. Jacques Benoist-Méchin (original German edn, 1931; Paris: Bernard Grasset, 1941), 71.

223 Nathaniel B. Smith, "The Idea of the French Hexagon," *French Historical Studies*, vol. 6, no. 2 (Fall 1969), 139–155; Weber, "L'Hexagone."

224 Juan Antonio Ramírez points to the use of a hexagon as a symbol of the unity of the French Republic on the emblem of a revolutionary neighborhood council (*section*) in Bordeaux as early as 1793. He conjectures "that this is the moment of incarnation of the idea of the 'hexagon' as a symbol of France ... " However, from the image itself, it is impossible to know whether the hexagon was selected as: (a) an allusion to the republic's geographic form; (b) a reference to the honeycomb cell of the beehive – itself a widely utilized symbol of social harmony and civic virtue according to Ramírez; (c) both of the above; (d) none of the above. Juan Antonio Ramírez, *The Beehive Metaphor: From Gaudí to Le Corbusier*, trans. Alexander R. Tulloch (1998; London: Reaktion Books, 2000), 21–22. It does seem safe to interpret the similar use of the hexagon on the French versions of Euro coins as a reference to the contemporary identification of France with the geometrical form. (See note 237, below.)

225 N. Smith, "Hexagon," 140–148.

226 Weber, "L'Hexagone," 101; C. R. Whittaker, "Roman Frontiers and European Perceptions," *Journal of Historical Sociology*, vol. 13, no. 4 (December 2000), 462–482, esp. 464–465.

227 N. Smith, "Hexagon," 146–148.

228 Henri Brunschwig, *Mythes et réalités de l'impérialisme colonial français, 1871–1914* (Paris: Librairie Armand Colin, 1960); Raoul Girardet, *L'Idée coloniale en France de 1871 à 1962* (Paris: La Table Ronde, 1972); Charles-Robert Ageron, *France coloniale ou parti colonial?* (Paris: Presses Universitaires de France, 1978); Harold Weinstein, *Jean Jaurès: A Study of Patriotism in the French Socialist Movement* (New York: Columbia University Press, 1936), ch. 7.

229 Raymond Betts, *Assimilation and Association in French Colonial Theory, 1890–1914* (New York: Columbia University Press, 1961); Hue-Tam Ho Tai, "Remembered Realms: Pierre Nora and French National Memory," *American Historical Review*, vol. 106, no. 3 (June 2001), 906–922, esp. 911–912; Aviel Roshwald, "Colonial Dreams of the French Right Wing, 1881–1914," *The Historian*, vol. 52, no. 1 (Autumn 1994), 59–74.

230 Patrick Weil, *Qu'est-ce qu'un Français? Histoire de la nationalité française depuis la Révolution* (Paris: Grasset, 2002), 225–244; Christopher Andrew

and A. S. Kanya-Forstner, *The Climax of French Imperial Expansion, 1914–1924* (Stanford: Stanford University Press, 1981), 18.

231 N. Smith, "Hexagon," 150; Ian Lustick, *Unsettled States*, ch. 4; Jacques Soustelle, *Le Drame algérien et la décadence française: Répond à Raymond Aron* (Paris: Plon, 1957), 66 and *passim*; Raymond Aron, *L'Algérie et la République* (Paris: Plon, 1958). Ian Lustick argues convincingly that the claim that Algeria was an integral part of France never succeeded in gaining unquestionable hegemony in French popular culture. Even advocates of this view, such as Soustelle, discussed the relationship "between France and Algeria" as though they were two separate entities – something that would not have occurred to them to do when discussing policy towards a region within the hexagon. Lustick, *Unsettled States*, 115–116.

232 However, Laurence Wylie argued that the fact that Algeria lay outside the Hexagon had meant all along that it fell beyond the bounds of what was authentically French in the eyes of most French people. See Berger, "French Democracy without Borders?," 6–7; Laurence Wylie, "Social Change at the Grass Roots," in Stanley Hoffmann *et al.*, *In Search of France: The Economy, Society, and Political System in the Twentieth Century* (1963; New York: Harper & Row, 1965), 227.

233 Gregory Flynn, "Remaking the Hexagon," in Gregory Flynn, ed., *Remaking the Hexagon: The New France in the New Europe* (Boulder: Westview Press, 1995), 6; N. Smith, "Hexagon," 149–153.

234 See, for example, the offhand reference to the equation of the hexagon with French rationality in the course of a discussion of the symbolic significance of territory in a paper given at a 1992 Paris urban planning commission seminar. Sylvia Ostrowetsky, "De l'un lieu à l'autre," paper given at seminar organized by the Permanent Secretariat of the Paris Urban Plan on "Villes et Transports" ("Cities and Means of Transportation"), 5th session, 11 June 1992. (Available through the Centre de documentation de l'urbanisme: http://www.urbanisme.equipement.gouv.fr/cdu/datas/docs/ouvr1/seance5.htm#p5).

235 Indeed, de Gaulle's left-wing critics initially decried his cult of the hexagon as an attempt to challenge the ideal of European integration. N. Smith, "Hexagon," 150.

236 See Calleo, *Rethinking Europe's Future*, ch. 8.

237 For a particularly paranoid, neo-Burkean depiction of rationalist France's alleged designs on Christian Europe, see Larry Siedentop, *Democracy in Europe* (New York: Columbia University Press, 2001). On the dilemmas European integration poses for French national identity, see Gregory Flynn, "French Identity and Post-Cold War Europe" and Stanley Hoffmann, "Thoughts on Sovereignty and French Politics" in Flynn, *Remaking the Hexagon*; Birnbaum, *Idea of France*, 280–281; Hoffmann, *Decline or Renewal*, ch. 12. It may be an apt metaphor for this ambivalent relationship between France and Europe that the French versions of the 1 Euro and 2 Euros coins bear the image of a geometrically perfect hexagon. For images

and descriptions of the coins, see http://web.tiscali.it/naplesfantastique/NF_LEuro_et_vous.htm.

238 Weil, *Qu'est-ce qu'un Français?*, 243–244.

239 Ibid., 249–251.

240 The Organisation Internationale de la Francophonie (OIF), which included the representatives of fifty-one member states as of December 2004, is devoted to the cultivation of cultural ties among the Francophone nations of the world and to the global propagation of French language and culture. Gordon and Meunier, *French Challenge*, 57–61; website of the OIF at: http://agence.francophonie.org/agence/francophonie.cfm. See also the association Défense de la Langue Française and its quarterly publication of the same name, both devoted to the protection and propagation of the French language throughout *Francophonie* and beyond. The association's website is: http://www.langue-francaise.org/Origine.php.

241 On the American public's general ignorance of world affairs and the consequent manipulative power of informed – if self-deluded – elites, see Halper and Clarke, *America Alone*, 302–304.

242 Gaddis, *Strategies of Containment*, ch. 3.

243 For instance: "I ... have this belief, strong belief, that freedom is not this country's gift to the world. Freedom is the Almighty's gift to every man and woman in this world. And as the greatest power on the face of the earth, we have an obligation to help the spread of freedom." From the transcript of President George W. Bush's 13 April 2004 White House press conference, posted online at: htttp:\\www.whitehouse.gov\news\releases\2004\04\20040413-0.html.

244 Derek Sayer, *The Coasts of Bohemia: A Czech History* (Princeton: Princeton University Press, 1998), 73.

245 See Michael Ignatieff, *Blood and Belonging: Journeys into the New Nationalism* (1993; New York: Farrar, Straus & Giroux, 1995).

CHAPTER 5

Kindred blood, mingled blood: ethnic and civic frameworks of national identity

... The *kindred blood* which flows in the veins of American citizens, the *mingled blood* which they have shed in defense of their sacred rights, consecrate their Union and excite horror at the idea of their becoming aliens, rivals, enemies.[1]

(James Madison)

That's right, you're not from Texas. Texas wants you anyway.[2]

(Lyle Lovett)

We historians and social scientists have for some years now been congratulating ourselves over our realization that all forms of identity, including national identity, are socially constructed. That is to say, no particular form of identity is innate or genetically inherited, although the capacity to have an identity may be. The ways in which people define who they are, both individually and in relation to one another, are – as we compulsively remind one another – shaped by highly contingent and variable historical, cultural, social, psychological, material, institutional, and political factors. So far, so good; we can all agree with the ultimately banal observation that nurture and nature interact in the formation of social organisms.[3] But this insight merely begs some fundamental questions. What sorts of building blocks make for the most enduring forms of social construction? More specifically to our particular area of inquiry, why do some formulations of national identity (e.g. Serb or Croat identity) seem deeply rooted in popular consciousness while others (e.g. Yugoslav) appear to lack widespread or long-lasting emotional resonance? Furthermore, is there a distinct set of independent variables that make devotees of some forms of nationalism particularly prone to outbursts of intolerance and xenophobia?

One of the most useful and influential typological distinctions used to address such questions is that between civic and ethnic forms of national identity. The former term refers to a sense of national identity manifested in a common loyalty to a territorially defined state and rooted in a set of political rights, duties, and values shared by the citizens of that state, regardless of their ancestry and of the non-political (e.g. linguistic, religious, etc.) aspects of their cultural heritage. The United States, with its shared political identity that is formally separate from the diverse origins and cultural traditions of its citizens, is often referred to as the quintessential civic nation.[4]

Among ethnic nations, as one might guess, national identity is based on shared ethnicity. That is, the kinship principle is extended to encompass and define the nation. Sharing a myth of common descent, members of the ethnic nation are bound to one another by putative ties of blood, not just by juridical categories or ideological affinities.[5] Their sense of kinship is both manifested in and reinforced by distinctive cultural attributes (such as language and/or religion) that they have in common with one another and that mark them apart from those who do not share their national identity. Membership in ethnic nations is ascriptive – that is, it is ascribed to individuals whether they like it or not and, in principle, regardless of whether they display the requisite cultural markers.[6] In other words, if their genealogy (real or attributed) places them within the fold of the ethnic nation yet they don't speak the right language or belong to the right religion, it must be because they are out of touch with their ancestral identity and are in need of reeducation.[7] Conversely, suspected aliens can, in theory, be readily identified by their failure to pass culturally.

It is hard to imagine a civic nationalism coming into being outside the context of a preexisting political-territorial unit, insofar as it is the claim to shared sovereignty over, and sentiment of common loyalty to, a state by the population that occupies its territory that constitutes the essence of the phenomenon. Indeed, this form of nationalism is commonly viewed as having arisen within long-established West European polities – whose social, political, and intellectual elites shared a common language and culture – in the course of their modernization, centralization, and transition from monarchic rule to popular sovereignty over the course of the seventeenth to twentieth centuries.

For its part, ethnic nationalism is generally considered to have originated among disaffected intelligentsias and social elites within political-territorial entities (such as the post-1815 German Confederation or the Habsburg Empire) that entered the modern era sorely lacking the administratively, economically, and/or culturally integrated features that allowed the sociopolitical establishments of countries such as Britain and France to inculcate their newly politicized masses with a sense of loyalty to the preexisting states.

Frustrated and humiliated by the relative weakness of a politically fragmented Germany, nineteenth-century German nationalists looked to cultural commonalities that transcended the borders of their petty principalities as the basis for collective empowerment and national self-determination. The territorial dimensions of a future, unified German nation-state were ideally to be defined by the geographic distribution of identifiably German people rather than by the boundaries of any existing German political entity. For their part, multi-ethnic empires like the Habsburg, Ottoman, and, arguably, Romanov[8] monarchies could not hope to infuse their subjects with a shared feeling of national identity, as their relatively abrupt, nineteenth- and early twentieth-century encounters with the phenomenon of mass politics played out against a backdrop of radical internal linguistic, religious, and institutional diversity. In the absence of a cohesive sense of popular identity coextensive with the existing polity, claims to territorially bounded popular sovereignty were made in the name of groups that were defined by shared culture rather than shared territory.[9] This quickly produced tensions among spatially overlapping ethno-cultural communities (e.g. Czechs and Germans, Poles and Ukrainians), whose claims to national self-determination (either within the bounds of reformed empires or as independent nation-states) were in conflict with one another.

In all these cases, the association of people's identities with ostensibly fixed cultural markers (i.e. hard-to-change attributes acquired in infancy, such as one's mother-tongue and native accent), rather than with their residence and membership in existing political-territorial units, arguably led directly to the sorts of ascriptive and discriminatory tendencies often associated with ethnic nationalism. These trends were reinforced by the apparent inability or unwillingness of various culturally differentiated populations (e.g. Poles and Danes in German-dominated areas; Jews, Ukrainians, and others in lands claimed by Poles) to assimilate completely into regionally dominant cultures – as well as by the growing fear that whatever assimilation did take place would provide false cover for alien infiltration of the national organism.[10] Apparently, one was either born into a national culture or one wasn't. Passed on by parents and family during childhood, a person's cultural heritage was increasingly looked upon as a mark of his/her lineage and as determinative of his/her sense of national kinship. If culture was conveyed in one's mother's milk, and culture was the basis of national identity, then national identity could readily be construed as an inherited quality. In the late nineteenth and early twentieth centuries, Social Darwinism reinforced the tendency to think of the nation as a quasi-biological organism, competing with other nations in a never-ending struggle for survival.[11]

As can be inferred from this discussion, civic nationalism is commonly associated with liberal, tolerant, inclusive values, because its criteria for membership can theoretically be met by any resident of a nation-state's territory; it's simply a matter of individually choosing to *subscribe* to a common set of principles. Civic nationalism does not in theory impose any requirements for cultural homogeneity beyond the circumscribed realm of a shared political culture. Ethnic nationalism is considered intolerant of both individual rights and cultural diversity because of its preoccupation with *ascriptive* qualities that can neither be freely acquired nor voluntarily relinquished, its conception of the nation as an organically cohesive collective entity, and its understanding of national-cultural identity as an integrated package in which there can be no distinction between a public, political-legal arena and a private or associational, cultural-communal sphere.[12]

These typologies are potentially powerful tools of analysis. But if used simplistically to place each nation and/or nation-state into one category or another, they can stand in the way of nuanced insight. Even in the abstract, these definitions prove self-contradictory, and the examination of flesh-and-blood examples causes the lines between them to grow blurry. Yet it is not my intention to try and discard them altogether. The notions of civic and ethnic nationalism can be used productively if understood as conceptions that both vie with one another and interact synergistically in the shaping and evolution of national identities.[13] These interactions contribute to the production of a variety of ever-shifting nationalist syntheses that range from the xenophobic and intolerant to the accommodating and inclusive ends of the political spectrum.

Let us explore the elements of this argument one by one.

BLURRY THEORETICAL DISTINCTIONS

Even at the theoretical level, a purely ethnic or purely civic nationalism is a contradiction in terms. Given that nationalism aspires to create or maintain a state (or sub-state unit) that embodies the identity of a nation, the institutions and characteristics of statehood are intrinsically important to any manifestation of nationalism. Therefore, even a nationalism that emphasizes ethnicity as the basis of the nation's identity is – if successful in its goal of achieving national self-determination – bound to attach some importance to at least the façade of public law and the formality of citizenship and naturalization procedures, insofar as these constitute standard attributes of a modern state. Some degree of tension will inevitably arise between the idea of a state-governed public domain and the conception of ethno-national identity as an elemental force, shaped by inherited characteristics and unmediated by rule-bound institutions.[14] Even more fundamentally, the stereotypical ethnic-nationalist conflation of culture with kinship is fraught with contradictions.[15] Stressing the importance of shared culture and tradition as the source of collective identity opens the door to the assimilation of non-kinfolk into the ethnic community, while insisting that shared ancestry alone determines national identity obliges the ethnic nation to include in its fold "blood relatives" who have become assimilated into alien cultures.

For its part, a purely civic nationalism would, arguably, not be an example of nationalism at all. As Yael Tamir and others have argued, if the only forces that held a nation-state together were a legal or constitutional apparatus and a set of shared political loyalties and values, then in theory the nation would have to be open to universal membership. The territorial dimension of national identity would melt away as the polity admitted into its ranks all those willing to subscribe to the laws and principles that defined it and as it erased the borders separating it from other nations sharing the same civic principles. As it lost any sense of demographic and territorial specificity, it would cease to be a nation-state.[16] By the same token, to the extent that a civic nationalism did limit the applicability of its principles to the residents of the nation-state's original bounded space, it would be cultivating an element of cultural-historical specificity and would even be introducing a quasi-ascriptive factor into the picture. Highlighting a common connection, hence presumably attachment, to a specific land would usher in the forces of irrational emotion and particularistic tradition that civic nationalism is supposed to abjure. Moreover, a person born in the national homeland would likely be considered more unambiguously attached to it and therefore more sincerely devoted to the nation than an immigrant secretly longing for his or her native country; hence the entry through the back door of the ascriptive element supposedly unique to ethnic nationalism.[17]

In any case, it is difficult to imagine how a purely civic nation-state could retain its social and political cohesion in practice, particularly if its political culture was informed exclusively by principles of liberal individualism. A number of political theorists and philosophers have, in recent years, pointed out that liberal democracies are fooling themselves if they think that the free interplay of rationally self-interested individual citizens

is their sole source of cohesion. For any democratic polity to function –
particularly at times when it demands personal sacrifices of its citizens – its
members must have some sense that they are bound together as a community of fate, not just a club of like-minded individuals. People have died
for God and country; no one to my knowledge has ever flung himself into a
hail of bullets on behalf of the American Dental Association. The citizens
of a polity based on the popular sovereignty principle must feel that the
state is the public expression of who they are. In other words, even the civic
nation-state must straddle the line distinguishing the sphere of public,
political culture from the zone of personal and communal identity if it is to
be regarded as legitimate by the individuals who are its citizens. And in so
doing, it ceases to be a purely civic nation-state.[18]

Once again, pointing to the contradictions inherent in these analytical
categories is not intended to suggest that they have no utility. On the
contrary, exploring such paradoxes is one way of illuminating some of the
existential dilemmas that are intrinsic to nationalism in all its forms. In
practice, one can reasonably distinguish among versions of nationalism
that are closer to the ethnic end of the spectrum (e.g. Serbian nationalism) and those that more nearly approximate the civic model (such as
American nationalism). More interesting, perhaps, are the ways in which
ethnic and civic elements interact with one another in shaping political
debates and agendas within the great majority of nationalist movements
and nation-states on either end of this spectrum.

THE CIVIC ELEMENT IN ETHNIC-LEANING NATIONS

The myth of sharing a distinctive set of common ancestors is regarded
as a salient characteristic of ethnic nationalism. To the extent that
endogamous marriage is practiced by members of an ethnic group, such
self-perceptions may become self-fulfilling over time.[19] Yet, as Donald
Horowitz has pointed out, even among cases regarded as prototypical
examples of ethnicity, the nature of the group's claims about the relationship between lineage and identity proves more complex upon closer
inspection.[20]

At the level of the most basic human kinship unit – the family –
common parentage is not the exclusive criterion for membership. In most
if not all cultures, adoption of orphaned or abandoned children into the
family is an accepted institution. Marriage outside the boundaries of
the extended family or clan – common in many societies – also stands in
the way of any purely biological definition of what constitutes kinship,

insofar as the marriage partner comes to be accepted as part of his or her spouse's family. Analogous exceptions and intricacies complicate the self-definition of ethnic groups and ethnic nations.

The biblical story of their common origins is central to Jews' sense of common ethno-national identity and unique destiny. Their religious tradition literally defines them as the descendants of Abraham, Isaac, and Jacob (Israel), and therefore as heirs to the Covenant that God first concluded with those forefathers and later renewed and elaborated upon with the Children of Israel in Sinai. (See the discussion in Chapter 4.) Yet even as it defines the national-religious implications of Jewish kinship, the idea of the Covenant is in tension with the kinship principle.[21] In so far as the Covenant is regarded as the legitimizing basis for a national-territorial state, does it or does it not encompass residents of the state's territory who are not descended from Abraham, Isaac, and Jacob? And what should be the status of aliens who volunteer to sign on to the Covenant, so to speak?

With regard to the former category, the traditional approach is ambiguous. In commanding the Israelites to treat the aliens in their midst kindly, on the grounds that the Israelites themselves had experienced the hardship of alien status in Egypt (see Chapter 3), the Torah seems to recognize the permanence of the line separating members of the Israelite descent community from those falling outside it while at the same time insisting that the boundaries of ethno-national identity do not define the limits of moral obligation. On the other hand, biblical texts emphasizing the sacredness of "all the land" of Israel might be interpreted to mean that the law of the land was considered uniformly binding on all who dwelled within the national kingdom's territorial boundaries.[22]

As to those ethnic aliens volunteering to subscribe in full to the Israelite Covenant, Jewish tradition evolved to provide for a form of religious conversion designed to erase any lines of ethnic differentiation between those who have inherited their Covenantal obligations and those who choose to assume their burden. Whereas a "native-born" Jew is referred to on legal documents and ceremonial occasions by his/her Hebrew name and his/her father's Hebrew name (e.g. "Joseph son of Gabriel"), a convert is customarily referred to by a newly conferred Hebrew name and as son or daughter of "our father Abraham" (or "of our father Abraham and our mother Sarah"). In other words, the convert is adopted not only into the civic fold of the Covenant but also into the associated ethnic-kinship circle, becoming notionally the offspring of all Jews' common ancestors.[23]

Edward Cohen has convincingly argued that ancient Athens was also not as literal in its application of an ethnicized conception of national identity as is often supposed. It is true that the Athenians claimed to be an autochthonous people, rooted in their native Attic soil since time immemorial. But the very attractiveness of this tradition was the illusion of organic cohesiveness and historical continuity that it maintained for an Athenian nation that was undergoing rapid and far-reaching demographic, economic and political transformations in the course of the fifth and fourth centuries BCE. As a major commercial emporium and a Mediterranean economic, military, and quasi-imperial power with a huge (in the hundreds of thousands) urban population, fifth-century Athens had to adapt to the presence in its midst of tens of thousands of immigrants and their descendants. Through a process of acculturation and socialization, many of Athens' resident aliens (*metics*) came to be regarded as locals (*astoi*) rather than strangers (*xenoi*). The Periclean legislation of 451/450 BCE which limited enfranchisement to men both of whose parents were considered *astoi*, was therefore itself more inclusive of people of non-Athenian origin than has generally been recognized. In any event, it represented an unsustainable nativist backlash against ultimately irreversible trends; following an initial wave of zealous enforcement, Pericles' citizenship law was largely ignored and ultimately gutted. The most important function of Athens' ethno-national myths was to serve as cultural props for its civic-national realities.[24]

Turning our attention from classical antiquity to the nineteenth and twentieth centuries, it has been the standard view – as noted above – that modern ethnic nationalism was born in Central and Eastern Europe and that it became established as the characteristic form of nationalism in this part of the world. While there is certainly a great deal of truth to this, the story is more complicated than overly simplistic pigeon-holing might suggest. Many of the intellectuals, publicists, and activists whose dreams and visions laid the ideological groundwork for the nation-states that eventually arose in the lands of the Rhine, Danube, Vltava, and Vistula originally sought to create structures of identity that incorporated both ethnic and civic elements. Most obviously, countries such as Czechoslovakia and Yugoslavia were, by definition, conceived of as polities that encompassed more than one ethnic group within their nationalizing frameworks.[25]

The founding father of Czechoslovakia, Tomáš Masaryk, himself half-Czech and half-Slovak by parentage, certainly saw the linguistic affinity and geographical propinquity of Czechs and Slovaks as providing a common ethno-cultural foundation for the forging of a union between the two peoples. But at the same time, this new nation-state was not supposed to serve merely as a protective sphere for the cultivation of unchanging ethnic traditions passed on from one generation to the next. It was intended to function as the mold for a new and improved national identity that would both transcend the ethnic distinction between Czechs and Slovaks and shift the cultural and ideological orientation of Czechs and Slovaks alike away from the Russophile tradition of pan-Slavism and towards the liberal-democratic values of the West. Masaryk and his disciples hoped to legitimize this civic-nationalist aspect of their program by linking it to what they depicted as a long-suppressed tradition of early modern Czech humanism and by presenting the Czech language as a historically favored vehicle for the articulation and propagation of enlightened ideals. This approach soon backfired, as we shall see below, but the point is that the very existence of the state in the first place was predicated on a vision of national identity that was far more complex than the label "ethnic nationalism" would lead one to expect.[26]

Among the South Slavs as well, in the years leading up to the First World War, it was the interplay of ethnic and civic visions of self-determination that shaped the development of nationalist ideologies and movements. In Habsburg-ruled Croatia, advocates of a chauvinistic Croat ethnic nationalism that looked upon Serbs as little better than Croats suffering from false consciousness were challenged by liberal-democratic opponents who forged a Serb-Croat political coalition in the last years before the outbreak of the First World War. The members of the Croat urban intelligentsia who embraced the Yugoslav vision saw themselves as bearers of a Western, liberal-democratic, humanistic tradition that could both draw strength from and offset what they saw as the tradition of Serb peasant-warrior brawn in a political marriage of the two, linguistically almost identical, peoples. The two groups, alongside the Slovenes, would forge a new national and political identity that would draw inspiration from their respective cultural and historic legacies without completely displacing them.[27]

Likewise, at the beginning of the twentieth century, the Polish nationalist movement was riven by conflict between the left-leaning ideological heirs to the proto-civic-nationalist tradition of the early modern, multi-ethnic Polish Commonwealth (partitioned by its avaricious neighbors in the late eighteenth century) and the advocates of a new form of Polish identity that was focused on the alleged biological basis of national solidarity and that unabashedly espoused a virulently racial anti-Semitism as a central tenet of its creed.[28]

In these and other cases, it was the sudden, crisis-ridden transition to political independence in 1918 that decisively shaped the evolution and repercussions of such ideological battles. Born or territorially reshaped amidst the violent circumstances of World War I and its chaotic aftermath, the would-be nation-states that sought to build new political structures amidst the ruins of the Habsburg and Romanov Empires were hard pressed to find a ready-to-hand basis for mass mobilization and political legitimization as they struggled to assert their authority in the face of internal dissension and as they fought with one another and negotiated with the Allied and Associated Powers over the definition of their international boundaries.[29] As we saw in Chapter 4, elaborate and inherently fragile systems of cultural tolerance and interethnic cooperation or compromise are liable to break down under the impact of war and political disorder. The idea of shared blood is thicker than the water of common values and in times of crisis people readily fall back on their sense of ethnic kinship to protect them from the dangers and uncertainties of a violent geopolitical neighborhood. The civic-oriented nationalisms of France and Britain had taken form over many centuries within preexisting political-territorial molds. The East European nation-states were either brought suddenly into existence or territorially transfigured in the midst of a world crisis of epic proportions and in an epoch when (as both Wilson and Lenin insisted) the fulfillment of the national self-determination principle was a vital aspect of a state's legitimacy. There was no opportunity here for the gradual crystallization of a finely balanced ethno-civic synthesis rooted in a shared historical experience that transcended internal cultural differences. One regime after another in the region ended up tilting the political scales sharply in favor of the ethno-nationalist end of the ideological spectrum – even in cases such as that of Poland, where the dominant political figure of the interwar period, Józef Piłsudski, had earlier been associated with the ideal of a multi-ethnic, federative approach to nation-building.[30]

Tensions between ethnic and civic conceptions of identity are unavoidable under any circumstances, but the way they played out in this region during the interwar years was particularly conducive to instability. Civic-territorial conceptions of nationhood and arguments about early modern historical precedents were deployed to justify claims to extensive lands populated by a multiplicity of ethnic groups. Piłsudski's invocation of the sixteenth- to eighteenth-century legacy of the Polish–Lithuanian Commonwealth, for example, was used to legitimize Poland's incorporation of sizable eastern territories populated by non-Polish nationalities such as Ukrainians, Belorussians, Lithuanians, and Jews. To be sure, the presence of ethnic Polish enclaves surrounded by non-Polish rural populations – such as the city of Lwów (the present-day Ukrainian city of Lviv) in Ukrainian-majority eastern Galicia – would have led to territorial conflicts and anomalies in any event. But the aspiration to reconnect with the tradition of a Polish political-cultural identity that transcended ethnic differences militated in favor of an approach to governance that was intolerant of ethnically based claims to regional autonomy. A similar approach prevailed among other countries in the region, such as Czechoslovakia, where the idea of granting home rule to the Slovaks (as had been promised by Masaryk prior to the creation of the state) was incompatible with the project of forging a new, enlightened, Czechoslovak identity. Such states' political elites saw it as their task not just to provide for the self-determination of existing ethnic groups, but to use the language and culture of a dominant ethnic group – claimed to be the bearer of a civilizing tradition – as the instrument for integrating a diverse population into a unitary nation-state on the model of France or Britain. But because little or no tradition of interethnic coalition building existed in these just-formed polities, whose disputed borders had been determined by military force and/or Great Power fiat rather than by commonly accepted historical precedent, such programs provoked deep resistance among ethnic minorities. Ukrainians in eastern Galicia fought a low-grade guerrilla campaign against the Polish authorities for much of the interwar period. To most Slovaks, the Masarykian agenda promoted by the government in Prague smacked of Czech cultural imperialism, and the country's large ethnic-German minority was left feeling politically marginalized. The resultant tensions were readily exploited by Nazi Germany, whose divide-and-rule tactics facilitated its dismemberment of the first Czechoslovak republic in 1938–39. In Yugoslavia, erstwhile Croat proponents of South Slav cooperation felt that their enlightened ideal had been hijacked by an expansionist Belgrade regime that ran the new country more as an extension of the Serbian monarchy than as a genuine union of equals.

Again, this neo-absolutist attachment to a conception of state sovereignty as irreducible and indivisible was not a peculiarity of East European nationalism.[31] It was modeled on the example of the successful, centralized, culturally (ostensibly) homogenized West European nation-state, the French republic serving as a particularly influential model.[32] Indeed, especially in light of their fears over Bolshevism on the one hand and a possibly revanchist Germany on the other, the Allied and Associated Powers at the Paris Peace Conference encouraged the consolidation of control in Eastern Europe by powerful, centralized states. To be sure, they forced the new states to sign treaties protecting the civil rights and cultural freedom of minorities, but international enforcement mechanisms were weak and provisions for territorial autonomy – which represented the minimal demand for many nationalities – were the exception rather than the rule.[33]

The problem was that this rigid approach was ill-suited to newly formed or expanded states that encompassed such a diversity of languages and ethnic identities. Given the circumstances, it was inevitable that the ideal of supraethnic national unity would be seen by many as a tool employed cynically and hypocritically to promote the interests of one ethnic group at the expense of others. The more resistance such policies provoked, the more tempted nationalist regimes themselves were to fall back on unabashed appeals to ethnic solidarity and on the related traditions of violation and martyrdom as they struggled to mobilize their core populations against the restive peripheries. Compounded by the multiple, global and European, economic, ideological, and geopolitical stressors of the interwar period, this approach was a recipe for political instability and the rise of authoritarianism (a political phenomenon to which Czechoslovakia alone in this region remained resistant during these years).

In the course of the Second World War and its aftermath, Eastern Europe underwent horrific experiences of genocide, ethnic cleansing, and territorial reapportionment. It is a sad irony that the successful establishment of liberal democracy in many East European states following the end of the Cold War was to some extent an indirect consequence of these devastating mid-century events, which left many of these countries far more linguistically and culturally homogeneous than before.[34] It was precisely in the country with the most complex intermixture of ethnocultural identities – Yugoslavia – that the transition away from Communism turned into a violent affair. Pluralistic values, it seems, are much easier to embrace in the absence of diversity.

The dilemmas faced by the regimes and peoples of twentieth-century Eastern Europe are not unique. Many of the world's so-called nation-states gained independence as a result of the relatively sudden collapse of overarching imperial structures – whether it be the overseas empires of Britain, France, Belgium, and the Netherlands in the aftermath of World War II or the territorially contiguous Soviet empire[35] at the end of the Cold War. The populations of many of these young states are even more diverse than were those of interwar Eastern Europe. And not unlike their early twentieth-century East European counterparts, many of these

countries' ruling establishments formally espouse a civic-territorial conception of national identity that dismisses internal ethnic differences as
legacies of primitive tribalism, or of imperial divide-and-rule tactics, or
both. Yet, particularly in the case of most African states, the only tongue
common to members of the educated elites is the language of the former
colonial power and one of the sole political traditions uniting them is that
of the struggle against that power. Using English or French as the language of official business in Nigeria or Ivory Coast may be a wisely
neutral choice, but it makes it hard to present the state as the embodiment of popular identity and indigenous tradition. And indeed, in the
absence of a deeply rooted sense of shared political culture and historical
destiny, kinship bonds and ethnic ties shape the dynamics of deal-making
and power-brokering behind the supraethnic façades of many of these
polities.[36] Clifford Geertz famously argued that, in fact, the transition to
independence accelerated the politicization of ethnicity begun by imperial
regimes in many Asian and African countries. Hitherto localized kinship
groups and cultural communities found that they could wield influence
and defend their interests more effectively on the suddenly all-important
playing field of "national" politics by building territorially and demographically extensive networks of trust and cooperation based on the idea
of shared ethnicity.[37] While political establishments and opposition forces
alike in such countries pay lip service to the principles of civic nationhood, everyone knows that ethnic politics is the name of the game.

To conclude that ethnic politics is simply an evil to be suppressed at all
costs is to miss the point. It is precisely the denial of an official role for
ethnic identity that promotes the proliferation of unofficial, and potentially disruptive, roles for ethnicity in states marked by deep cultural
cleavages. As Donald Horowitz has emphasized in his magisterial comparative overview of modern ethnic conflicts, it would be foolish to
suggest that there exists one formula that can manage, let alone resolve, all
such problems.[38] But for a government to restrict itself to promoting a
civic-territorial identity that manifestly fails to strike a resonant chord
among political elites and popular masses alike seems like an empty
gesture and a recipe for political alienation and internecine conflict.
Better in such cases to concede to ethnic groups a place on the public
stage – be it in the form of a designated share of power at the central level,
a provision for territorial autonomy on a regional basis, or some combination of these and other approaches. Such flexibility, in turn, requires
a willingness to define and distribute the attributes of sovereignty in ways
that defy the classic, neo-absolutist ideal of the sovereign state as a strictly

unitary institution wielding its power in an undifferentiated manner throughout its territory.[39] Ideally, such imaginative compromises may, in turn, allow supraethnic, civic spheres of national identity to gain in substance over time. Alternatively, where ethnic groups are concentrated in clearly defined and economically viable territories, outright partition – as in the case of the peaceful Czech–Slovak split of 1993[40] – may be an acceptable outcome.

Of course, no modern nation-state, however small, is completely or permanently devoid of ethnic diversity, and no amount of subdivision and partition will eliminate for all time the need to address the tension between an institutionally dominant ethnic identity and the sentiments of minority groups. But I would argue that an avowedly ethnic nation-state that is aware of its potential alienation of minority groups and is willing to find various ways of accommodating or compensating them, while simultaneously upholding the civil rights of all individual citizens regardless of ethnicity, is preferable to a state that actively suppresses minority cultures in the name of a supraethnic ideal.

Lest it be thought that those nation-states classically seen as dominated by ethnic politics are the only ones to face such paradoxes and dilemmas, let us examine the role of kinship imagery and cultural particularism in so-called civic nations.

MINGLED BLOOD: KINSHIP IMAGERY IN CIVIC FRAMEWORKS OF NATIONHOOD

The quotation from James Madison that opens this chapter is suggestive of the ambiguities and contradictions that lie just beneath the surface of the most civic constructions of national identity. In this founding father's words, American citizens were said to be joined by kindred blood; in the early days of the republic, when people of British ancestry still formed nearly 80% of the country's non-slave population,[41] it made sense to invoke the theme of stemming from common stock as part of an appeal on behalf of a proposed constitution that would lend coherent institutional form to the nation. As with the Chosen People of Israel, kinship could form the foundation for a covenant that would lend substance, meaning, and purpose to collective identity.[42]

Yet Madison hastened to add that American blood was more than just *kindred* – it was *mingled*. By shedding their blood in common on the battlefields of the War of Independence, those wounded or killed in the struggle had concretized and added new layers of meaning to the idea of shared bloodlines. Implicit here, moreover, was the notion that those soldiers who were not literally one another's kin had become blood brothers by jointly risking and/or sacrificing their lives for their new nation.

In some ways, such a figurative form of kinship carries more emotional power than the literal one. After all, Americans of British extraction shared common bloodlines with the British themselves as well as with one another. It was through shared sacrifice in the common cause against its overseas kin that the nation had become a distinctive familial community of its own. It would be sacrilege for the bearers and beneficiaries of that sacrifice to turn their backs on the fraternal bonds that had thus been forged.

Of course, as we saw in Chapter 3, martyrdom myths play important roles in virtually all nations, not least those with a strongly ethnic sense of identity. What is noteworthy here is how significant the familial associations and implications of battlefield sacrifice and brotherhood in arms have been in fostering a sense of nationhood among the members of such a paradigmatically civic nation as the United States. Over time, America's development as a land of immigrants (intermittent nativist backlashes notwithstanding) made it harder and harder to think of the nation as being literally of common ancestry. More elastic conceptions of kinship were vital to maintaining a cohesive national consciousness in the face of such rapid ethno-demographic change. Gary Gerstle has documented how vital such variations on kinship imagery were to Theodore Roosevelt's influential form of nationalist ideology around the turn of the twentieth century. Roosevelt presented the Rough Riders cavalry regiment which he led to victory at the Battle of San Juan Hill during the Spanish–American War as a microcosm of a new American society. The Rough Riders hailed not only from both North and South of the post-Civil War United States, but included volunteers from a variety of European ethnic backgrounds – Southern and Eastern Europeans fighting alongside those of Anglo-Saxon stock. Roosevelt pointed to this as a model demonstration of how combining the offspring of diverse European peoples and races in a disciplined, common effort could produce noble and inspiring results.[43]

Like James Madison, Teddy Roosevelt linked the themes of kindred blood and mingled blood. But for Roosevelt, the mingled blood of the battlefield *anticipated* the kindred blood of future American generations; the nation's familial unity was to be found not in his generation's unrelated *ancestors* but in its common *descendants*. Nineteenth-century

America had been forged, according to Roosevelt, through the admixture of Anglo-Saxon with other Northern European races. The same formula, extended to the new immigrants from Southern and Eastern Europe, could lend the nation strength and unity in the twentieth century. His Rough Riders had shown what a voluntaristic association of Americans of diverse European origins could achieve when animated by a common ideal. In Roosevelt's vision, such brotherhood in arms could serve as a model and inspiration for the eventual establishment of *literal fraternity* among what he considered the best elements in the nation.[44] How much stronger the American people as a whole would grow if the various immigrant communities his volunteers had sprung from became culturally integrated into the nation through common schooling and other forcefully progressive programs of assimilation. This, in turn, would facilitate the creation of a new biological synthesis through intermarriage over the course of coming generations. The strength of the United States' civic union would once again be reinforced by ties of actual kinship. Moreover, this synthesis would combine the best qualities of the nation's founding group – Anglo-Americans – with those of Irish, Italian, Jewish, and other European immigrants to produce a new hybrid race that would be stronger and healthier than any single one of its components. In his words, "we are making a new race, a new type, in this country." He anticipated that white ethnic groups sharing cultural commonalities such as religious denomination would first merge with one another:

When the Catholic Germans learn to speak English as their home tongue, they intermarry more or less with the Irish; and they will doubtless intermarry with the Slavonians and Italians under like conditions, when the latter begin to move upward in the social scale.[45]

After a few generations, "complete intermixture" among white immigrant communities would result.[46] Roosevelt even encouraged the racial assimilation of American Indians into the national mainstream, having made a point of including a few Indians in the ranks of the volunteers he led in Cuba.[47]

The extent to which the mingled blood of the battlefield should be accepted as equivalent to, or a foundation for, the inherited link of kindred blood has often been a pivotal issue around which debates between advocates of ethnicized/racialized and civic definitions of national identity have revolved. In Roosevelt's case, the circle of inclusiveness was restricted to those of European descent, with the possible exception of Indians. His acknowledgment of the role of Black regiments in clinching the victory at San Juan Hill was muted. No African-Americans were allowed into the Rough Riders themselves, and Roosevelt's vision of racial hybridization had no place in it for Blacks.[48] In fact, it was not until after the Second World War that the US Army was fully and officially desegregated and not until 1965 that national origins immigration quotas dating to the 1920s and designed to prevent further shifts away from Anglo-Protestant domination of the population's ethnoreligious and racial composition were abolished as part of the broader trend towards civil-rights legislation and the de-ethnicization of American national identity.[49] American citizens of Japanese ancestry were notoriously confined in internment camps as suspected security threats during World War II even as many of their sons and brothers served in the country's armed forces. But at the same time, it was precisely the incongruity between the image of trans-ethnic, wartime brotherhood in arms and the persistence of ethnic and racial discrimination that highlighted the injustices of the latter and helped catalyze efforts at reform – first within the army itself, and then throughout civil society.[50] In this ostensibly most civic of polities, the tension between common ancestry and common bloodshed as criteria for full inclusion in the national covenant has been a defining theme of the country's history, and its legacy continues to shape national debates about public policy and political identity.

In many European countries at the turn of the twentieth century, the claim that the army should serve as "the school of the nation" was an influential idea among strategic thinkers and military planners. The processes of technological innovation, industrial modernization, and economic globalization that were transforming the international balance of power in the years leading up to the First World War were also challenging domestic political equilibria as ever-growing sectors of the popular masses became urbanized and politicized. In the eyes of military planners this presented a potential threat in the form of class conflict and challenges to social and political authority, but also a potential opportunity for forging large, cohesive and highly motivated, mass-conscription national armies. At the same time, the army could take peasants as yet unsullied by the pernicious influence of urban culture and channel their loyalties in healthy directions. The popular masses were so much raw material waiting to be forged into a disciplined fighting force that could both project the nation's power on the international stage and serve as a model for, and source of, internal socio-political cohesion.

National armies would not just defend the nation – they would shape the nation.

Such ideas caught on among the officer corps and general staffs of powers such as Germany, France, Russia, and the Ottoman Empire (dominated by Young Turk nationalists after 1908). They were linked to an even more broadly influential, Social Darwinist idealization of war as a forge of national character, reflected in Theodore Roosevelt's ideas outlined above.[51] As with Roosevelt's Rough Riders model, the implications of construing the army as the school of the nation were ambiguous. On the one hand, this approach held the potential for some strongly civic-nationalist ramifications. The modern, mass-conscription army has in fact been commonly turned to as an instrument of supraethnic, national integration. Under the French Third Republic (1871–1940), it arguably played a role second in importance only to the school system in taking peasants and workers as well as bourgeois from all corners of the country, speaking all manner of dialects or languages, and inculcating in them a common conception of, and attachment to, France.[52] In Germany, despite the country's ever stronger ethnic-nationalist leanings,[53] many assimilated Jews hoped and expected that their loyal service in the military during the First World War would help them complete the process of gaining acceptance as fully fledged members of the German nation who happened to be of "Mosaic faith."[54] Some tsarist military officers thought the army could serve as a crucible for the creation of loyalty to state and tsar that would transcend the ethno-cultural and linguistic divisions of the Romanovs' multinational empire.[55]

On the other hand, the nature of the causal relationship between the cohesiveness and motivation of a mass-conscription army and the homogeneity of the nation was the subject of obsessive chicken-and-egg debates at the highest military and political levels. Many military planners felt that the creation of a citizen-soldier ready and willing to shed his blood on behalf of the homeland was contingent on an *a priori* sense of kinship with his co-nationals. In the case of Russia, as Peter Holquist has discovered, military textbooks published in the final years before the First World War came to include doctrinaire statements such as: "The ethnic composition of the population has primary significance ... in a military sense ... An ideal population is a monoethnic population, with one language."[56] In turn-of-the-century France, the highest military officials, enjoying the backing of powerful social, religious, and political forces, for years resisted reopening the case of Captain Dreyfus, the Jewish officer framed for the passing of military secrets to the German enemy. Better to associate the stain of treachery with someone who could be portrayed as existentially alien to France than to impugn the honor of the army as a national institution. The ultimately unsuccessful anti-Dreyfusard movement became a rallying point for the diverse opponents of the liberal-democratic republic and its culturally assimilationist approach to the cultivation of French identity.[57] In the Ottoman Empire, the Young Turk officers who came to power on the eve of World War I nominally espoused a supraethnic, "Ottomanist" vision for political reform and popular empowerment. In secret, they saw the army as, above all, a school for the Turkish nation, whose ethno-cultural solidarity could be cultivated and tapped into as a new source of cohesive strength and power-projection for the declining empire.[58] In Germany during the First World War, the Prussian war ministry conducted a notorious *Judenzählung* – a "Jew count" designed to document the purported underrepresentation of the nation's Jewish population in its fighting forces, apparently with the intention of exposing German Jews as dyed-in-the-wool shirkers. When the investigation's statistical conclusions contradicted its premise, the results were duly classified.[59] In later years, as Hitler erased any lingering vestiges of German civic nationalism, decorated Jewish veterans discovered that their demonstrated willingness to shed their blood for the nation during the Great War did not exempt them from being murderously cut out of the nation's body politic under the new ideological dispensation.

Such ethnic-nationalist and/or racist backlashes against the idea of mingled blood underline the usefulness of the image as a way of recasting our understanding of civic nationalism and of exploring its intersections and tensions with ethnic nationalism. To recapitulate, civic nationalism can be said to emphasize figurative notions of kinship as a way of binding together people of diverse lineages. This tendency manifests itself very obviously in the widespread American use of stock phrases such as "Founding Fathers" to describe the ideological ancestors that all citizens are said to have in common regardless of their actual ancestry. Metaphorical kinship trumps literal kinship in the civic-nationalist worldview; Washington, Jefferson, and Madison are deemed the forefathers of all Americans no less than Abraham, Isaac, and Jacob are the progenitors of all Jews, be they native-born or converts.[60] Civic nationalism's emphasis on figurative kinship finds expression in a fascination with the idea of blood ties that it shares with ethnic nationalism, but in civic nationalism's case, the focus of this fascination is on the joint shedding of blood in the nation's defense and/or the convergence of the nation's heterogeneous blood lines in the veins of future generations.

In any concrete example, civic images of mingled blood are both intricately intertwined and in tension with ethnic esteem for kindred blood. Efforts to promote the civic approach almost invariably either generate an ethnic-nationalist backlash (e.g. the Dreyfus Affair) or reveal latent limitations to the inclusiveness of the civic ideal itself (as in the exclusion of African-Americans from Teddy Roosevelt's racial-hybridization scenario). The proponents of mingling national blood have time and again been confronted by fears over the tainting of kindred blood. Yet this is not to say that the balance of power between literal and figurative ideas of national kinship cannot shift over time, as it most certainly has in the United States.[61] By the same token, the ideal of mingled blood can itself be associated with a culturally or ideologically coercive approach to national integration that is in conflict with liberal respect for diversity.

LIMITS TO CIVIC TOLERANCE AND DILEMMAS OF LIBERAL INCLUSIVENESS

As we have noted, civic nationalism is commonly seen as open to the world and tolerant of internal diversity. Freed of the ethnic-nationalist obsession with the preservation of supposedly timeless ancestral cultures and traditions, this is a form of nationalism that can embrace humanity as a whole. Yet upon closer inspection, this distinction also proves more complicated and problematic than first impressions would lead one to believe.

An indirect insight into civic nationalism's potential for militant intolerance is offered by a recent critique of received opinion about Western Europe's liberal-nationalist tradition. Pointing to the roots of West European national identities in the bloody religious schisms, persecutions, and wars of the early modern period, Anthony Marx conflates what he terms "exclusionary" nationalism with ethnic nationalism, concluding that at their time of origin British and French nationalisms included strong ethnic elements, just as Central and East European nationalisms were to do in modern times.[62] This argument reveals the extent to which civic and ethnic nationalisms have been uncritically identified with tolerance and intolerance, respectively: Anthony Marx assumes that an intolerant nationalism cannot be civic, and is therefore, by default, to be labeled ethnic. To my mind, Marx's analysis calls into question not the civic foundations of West European nationalism, but the simplistic equation of civic nationalism with tolerance.[63] As Jonathan

Wyrtzen has observed, the early modern religious wars and persecutions can in fact more readily be seen as the original breeding grounds for the *civic* elements in British, French, Dutch, and other West European national identities.[64] After all, one of the chief objects of these campaigns was to prevent the faithful from converting to "heretical" forms of Christianity and to terrorize the misguided into returning to the fold of their polity's established faith (be it Catholic, Calvinist, Lutheran, Anglican, etc.). In the context of these conflicts, people were by and large categorized as belonging within or without the proto-national pale on the basis of their religious *beliefs and choices* rather than on the basis of their *parentage*. (To be sure, there were racialized aspects to some religious persecutions, as in the Spanish Inquisition's obsessive distinction between Christians of pure blood and those of Jewish or Muslim extraction.[65]) In secularized form, the people's subscription to a common creed has remained central to the self-definition of nations such as France and Britain, and Britain's American offshoot, and this is precisely the ingredient that both lends them their civic quality and has the potential to lead them down the path of intolerance, as Yael Tamir has pointed out.[66] The centrality of political creed to national identity in the United States, and the ambiguity of its implications, is reflected in the peculiar linguistic usage of labeling ideas one does not like as "un-American"[67] – a practice that became most notoriously abusive during the McCarthyism of the early 1950s, but that has not disappeared from the nation's political vocabulary.[68]

It is important to note that the civic aspects of modern nationalisms do often revolve around shared beliefs in liberal-democratic principles of tolerance and human rights that represent the hard-learned lessons of the religious and ideological wars of earlier generations. Yet to the extent that full membership in the modern, civic polity remains contingent on subscribing to a specific set of values and loyalties linked to a figurative sense of shared kinship, radical non-conformity is bound to present a challenging problem even to the most flexible configurations of national identity.[69]

Inclusiveness vs. *tolerance: the French and Israeli cases*

The metaphorical and descendant-oriented conceptions of kinship common to civic nationalisms can clearly be conducive to a politics of inclusiveness. In principle, no one need be denied membership in the nation provided s/he is willing to conduct himself or herself *as if* s/he felt part of the national family. By the same token, it may come to be expected of people that they conform to "familial" norms of behavior and mentality if they are to enjoy the privileges associated with national membership.[70] The pressure to assimilate culturally into a civic-leaning nation-state readily comes into conflict with minority communities' drive for cultural self-preservation. This is very different from the types of pressure likely to be experienced by minorities in ethnically oriented nation-states.[71] For example, France's recent prohibition on the wearing of head-scarves by girls attending state schools would be unthinkable in the context of the Israeli school system. In the former case, the state draws on a long tradition of actively promoting the assimilation of cultural minorities into a supposedly universalistic French civilization. People can wear what they like in the private sphere, but in a secular, public institution devoted to the inculcation of civic values and national traditions among the young, there can be no tolerance for the flaunting of religious particularism and radical cultural non-conformity.[72] In Israel's case, the country's Arab citizens (i.e. those Palestinian Arabs residing within the state's pre-1967 borders) unquestionably suffer many disadvantages associated with their minority status in a polity defined as embodying the ethno-national identity of Jews. But because there is relatively little effort on the part of the state to foster a supraethnic sense of civic identity, the pressure on Muslim Arabs to abandon or constrain their public observance of customs traditional to their community is relatively minimal. Polygamous marriage as permitted by Islam is forbidden by Israeli law, but the government would not presume to go so far as to ban head-scarves in public schools. Indeed, state schools are segmented along lines of ethno-religious affiliation to begin with, allowing such groups as Orthodox Jews, secular Jews, Muslim Arabs, Druze Arabs, and Arabic-speaking Circassians to reaffirm, reinforce, and reproduce their separate communal/cultural identities within the framework of the state-administered educational system.[73]

Which system is more inclusive? Each is alternately inclusive and exclusive in very different ways. The French civic conception of national identity is, in its current form, arguably more inclusive of individuals regardless of their ethno-religious background than is the Israeli (although the outburst of violence among immigrant communities in France during November 2005 forces one to question what this theoretical inclusiveness really amounts to in practice). But full access to, and participation in, the institutions of the French nation-state (e.g. education in public schools or employment in the civil service) is contingent on citizens' willingness to circumscribe the public expression of those elements of their ethno-religious identities that do not conform to a set of government-defined norms. Those norms, of course, cannot be viewed as neutrally universalistic, for they are themselves the outgrowths of a specifically European and French cultural heritage.[74] The Israeli ethno-national system leaves more public, state-regulated space open to the cultivation of minority cultures than does the French approach, while at the same time leaving members of those minorities feeling that (leaving aside the enormous aggravating factor of the larger Israeli–Arab conflict) there is no clear path to assimilation into, and acceptance as full members of, the Israeli nation short of taking on Jewish ethnic identity through religious conversion.

The limits of American tolerance

Countries subscribing to what one might term the Anglo-Saxon tradition of civic nationalism have in recent decades evolved towards ever greater acceptance of public manifestations of ethno-cultural diversity.[75] As Will Kymlicka has pointed out, turbaned Sikhs are commonly exempted from North American laws requiring motorcyclists to wear helmets and observant Jews are excused from adhering to Sunday business restrictions.[76] Indeed, in the American case, as Yossi Shain has documented, the post-1960s embrace of ethnic heritage as something to be preserved and "celebrated" rather than discarded in favor of complete assimilation has contributed to an ever more prominent role for ethnic lobbies in the shaping of the country's foreign policy.[77]

But this most dramatic example of ethnic minorities' "coming into their own" as publicly recognized components of American national life also points to some of the limitations on diversity that inevitably come into play even in the most civic-leaning and inclusive nations. The United States' ever more expansive accommodation of ethnic political lobbies is accompanied by strong socio-political and cultural pressures to adhere to a somewhat constricting ideological and rhetorical paradigm of American patriotism. Be they Irish-, Jewish-, Greek-, or Arab-American, ethnic organizations that celebrate their communities' cultural heritages or engage in public advocacy for policies favorable to their overseas home-lands feel obliged to trumpet their unswerving loyalty to America and their unshakeable belief in the inherent superiority of the American economic system and the infinite promise of the American dream of individual self-reliance and limited government. Thus, in a July 2000 newspaper column addressing the Democratic Party's position on the Arab–Israeli conflict,

Dr. James Zogby, president of the Arab American Institute, made the seemingly irrelevant point of emphasizing Arab-Americans' "commitment to family, to free enterprise and the creative drive for excellence..."[78] And at its 2005 annual conference, in the wake of reports of an FBI investigation into its possible involvement in the passing of classified information to the Israeli government, the American Israel Public Action Committee (AIPAC) made an ostentatious, flag-waving show of its patriotic fervor, even eliminating the traditional singing of the Israeli anthem after the American one.[79] In other words, a certain degree of *pro forma* doctrinal and symbolic conformity with perceived national norms is seen as a precondition for reaping the full political benefits of American ethno-racial tolerance.[80] Any lobby, let alone an ethnic one, that openly identified itself as socialist in orientation would find it very hard to gain significant political traction on Capitol Hill.

Furthermore, one of the elements that contributes to many ethnic lobbies' large measure of acceptance as fixtures of the American political scene is precisely the fact that they tend to be concerned with the fate of overseas homelands rather than harboring any dreams of territorial secession from, or political change within, the United States. Advocates for the rights of illegal Mexican immigrants and supporters of bilingual Anglo-Spanish education face considerable hostility to their proposals inasmuch as they speak on behalf of populations whose ethno-cultural identities connect them to the Spanish-speaking world that lies just across the Rio Grande. This awakens fears over the erosion of America's cultural, linguistic, and demographic boundaries in a way that advocacy for Greek Cypriots, Israelis, or Irish Catholics fails to do. Civic associations have been formed to oppose the extension of social services to illegal aliens and to lobby against bilingual education, and even to engage in vigilante-style "protection" of the nation's southern border.[81]

This sort of backlash is not confined to the political fringe. In his 1995 call for the enshrinement of English as the United States' official language, Republican presidential candidate Senator Bob Dole warned of the dangers of "ethnic separatism."[82] And, writing in the highly respected journal *Foreign Policy*, prominent Harvard University political scientist Samuel Huntington has described the ongoing influx of Mexicans into American states whose territory had once formed part of Mexico as a demographic and socio-cultural *reconquista* (reconquest) that may one day give rise to a secessionist or regional-autonomy movement in the heavily Latino Southwest.[83] In stridently alarmist terms, he warns of the broader danger that transforming America into a bilingual country would pose to the nation's values and way of life. Drawing selectively on the phraseology of Latino advocates of Hispanic socio-cultural reform, such as Texan businessman Lionel Sosa, Huntington infuses new life into old prejudices by disparaging Hispanic culture as inherently incompatible with positive American qualities such as "initiative, self-reliance, and ambition..."[84] Huntington concludes his piece by categorically dismissing Sosa's call for the transformation of the allegedly self-defeating elements of the Hispanic ethos into a Latino-inflected variation on the American entrepreneurial dream – what Sosa calls "the Americano dream." "Sosa is wrong," writes Huntington. "There is no Americano dream. There is only the American dream created by an Anglo-Protestant society. Mexican Americans will share in that dream and in that society only if they dream in English."[85] Huntington warns that, faced with the prospect of a large, potentially unassimilable, minority culture becoming permanently established on their nation's soil, Americans may quickly find their customary tolerance and inclusiveness strained to the breaking point. Sadly, Huntington's own views are themselves a powerful illustration of how nasty the tone of a nativist backlash can be.

Canada's quandaries

On the North American continent, though, it is in Canada that a civic-leaning nationalism is most directly being forced to confront the contradictions and limitations of its inclusiveness by an internal ethno-territorial challenge. Québécois nationalism not only threatens the country's administrative homogeneity and/or political unity, but calls into question Canada's official self-image as a tolerant, multicultural nation.

Will Kymlicka has distinguished between polyethnic and multinational political systems, each of which seeks to resolve the tension between multiple ethnic identities and overarching civic nationhood in very different ways. Polyethnic systems tolerate the private, communal, and even public cultivation of diverse ethno-cultural traditions as long as these do not serve as the basis for any claims to territorial self-determination. The official national culture remains studiously neutral. By contrast, multinational countries are formally structured as ethno-territorial federations.[86] Contemporary Belgium, with its provision of regional autonomy for Flemish Flanders and Francophone Wallonia (alongside its recognition of linguistic communities whose institutions administer personal, as distinct from territorial, services) is an example of the latter approach.[87] The US, by contrast, exemplifies the polyethnic approach. Officially bilingual and multicultural Canada uneasily straddles the line between these two systems: the federal government in Ottawa espouses a poly-ethnic ideal for the country as a whole, while realizing that in practice Québec has a special role to play as the political-territorial locus for a distinctive, Francophone identity. The awkwardness of this asymmetrical reality[88] – so out of keeping with the formally symmetrical institutional structure of Canadian federalism – extends to nomenclature. Québec is Québec. But how does one refer to the rest of Canada in aggregate? To call it Anglophone Canada would be to ascribe an English identity to the other provinces that is out of keeping with the bilingualism of federal institutions and the multiculturalism that officially informs public policy throughout the country. As Michael Keating notes, the politically correct term for the rest of Canada is therefore simply – Rest of Canada (ROC).[89] The closest historical analogy is with the situation of the Austrian Empire after the 1867 Compromise (*Ausgleich*) that divided the Habsburg lands between a self-governing Hungary and a rest-of-the-empire which no one was ever quite sure what to call.[90]

Indeed, what is particularly galling to many Canadian patriots (such as the late prime minister, Pierre Elliott Trudeau, who saw no conflict between his pride in his Francophone background and his support for a united Canada) about Québécois-nationalist demands is precisely their implication that Canada's official, polyethnic approach is nothing but a fraud, a façade for an Anglophone cultural nationalism that is all the more insidious for not being openly acknowledged as the foundation of Canadian national identity. Québécois nationalists, for their part, are outraged by the other provinces' refusal to acknowledge that Québec's history as a victim of English military conquest and socio-cultural sub-jugation, and its position as an endangered cultural island awash in an Anglophone ocean, entitle it to constitutionally enshrined special pro-tections and exceptional status, if not outright independence.[91]

The result has been an anomalous political stalemate since 1982, when Canada patriated its constitution from the British Parliament and revised and extended its text (most notably, appending a Charter of Rights and Freedoms). Québec alone among the country's provinces refused to ratify the constitution, on the grounds that it failed to recognize the province as having a special, quasi-national status within the Canadian federation and because the Charter's predominant emphasis on individual rights threa-tened to undermine Québec's institutional and legislative ability to defend the collective identity of its Francophone population. While Canada's federal government and constitutional court have considered

Québec nonetheless subject to the constitution, they have allowed Québec to maximize its exercise of the wide-reaching autonomy that the constitution allows in principle to all provinces in the Canadian confederation. For instance, Québec is the only province to have its own tax-collection system, separate from the federal bureaucracy. Québec has even been able to use a constitutional loophole to temporarily violate the Charter of Rights and Freedoms (as interpreted by Canada's Supreme Court) in its passage and implementation of laws designed to protect and propagate the French language. Where the Québécois have been frustrated is not so much in their quest for functional self-determination as in their desire for symbolic recognition as a "distinct society" within Canada. Negotiated compromises that would have incorporated this wording into the Canadian constitution have been repeatedly rejected by the country's other provinces, which have been unwilling to grant one of their number a symbolic status denied to the rest.[92]

Canada thus remains at a constitutional and existential impasse. In the official Canadian view, the country is a federally bilingual, culturally neutral, safe haven for the protection of every individual's rights and each community's traditions. From this perspective, it is Québec that violates the spirit of the national covenant by going too far in its use of the power of the provincial government to institutionalize the superiority of Francophone culture within its borders. From a Québécois perspective, such criticism is hypocritical in light of the historic, demographic, and geopolitical hegemony of the English language. If the rest of Canada remains unwilling to bring the confederation's juridical and constitutional arrangements fully into line with the country's *de facto* multinationalism, then, Québec nationalists assert, outright secession may be the only acceptable alternative. Yet it would be simplistic to characterize this as a straightforward conflict between civic and ethnic forms of nationalism. Québec has been engaged in a coordinated effort since the late 1970s to assimilate immigrants to the province into the French-speaking community, lest they tip the demographic and political balance against French-speakers by adopting English as their primary language. This has obliged Québécois (especially in heavily multiethnic urban centers such as Montréal) to contemplate the evolution of their own national identity into a civic-oriented version of itself built around a common language and a shared tolerance for a variety of ethno-cultural identities.[93] At the same time, this Québécois variant of multiculturalism does nothing to allay the fears of the province's indigenous minorities, who worry over the erosion of their identities and potential for self-determination within the context of a nominally polyethnic Francophone nation no less than the Québécois have traditionally felt threatened by the pressures of Anglophone "civic" nationalism.[94]

IMAGINATIVE COMMUNITIES

At this juncture, readers may well throw their hands up in despair; if Canada's minimalist framework of national unity serves as the arena for such bitter accusations and deep-seated fears, what possible hope can there be for the rest of humanity in a world of nation-states? But my point here is not to argue that nationalism in all its forms is equally intolerant or destructive, but rather that all nationalist movements and nation-states, be they oriented towards the ethnic or civic ends of the spectrum, will always be obliged to juggle the conflicting elements of their political and cultural identities. The most multicultural, tolerant, and accommodating environments will unavoidably leave some ethno-cultural segments of a population feeling both substantively and symbolically underrepresented in their country's governing institutions. By the same token, the most integrative visions of cross-cultural and inter-racial synthesis may be employed in discriminatory and oppressive ways. The widespread Latin American ideal of *mestizaje* – the mixing of indigenous and immigrant races and cultures in distinctive national syntheses – was long used as a justification for policies employed by white and mestizo elites to exploit, marginalize, and/or forcibly assimilate indigenous peoples.[95] For that matter, the USSR's political identity can be seen as a form of civic nationalism that severely curtailed all forms of autonomy on the part of individuals as well as of the very ethno-national units whose sovereignty was formally enshrined in the Soviet constitution – all in the name of the international brotherhood of mankind.[96]

It does stand to reason that civic-leaning forms of nationhood are more likely to be accommodating of ethno-cultural pluralism than are nation-states that officially enshrine the identity of one particular ethnic group. But this is not necessarily the case.[97] Moreover, as we have seen, most if not all national polities represent complicated mixes of ethnic and civic elements. Finally, the history, ethno-demography, and geopolitical circumstances of some states and societies do not offer any realistic prospect of sudden conversion from an ethnic-leaning to a civic-oriented model of nationhood even if that were deemed desirable.

Perhaps, then, in addition to exploring the contrast between ethnic and civic forms of nationhood, we need to distinguish between rigid and flexible approaches to the representation and institutionalization of national identity.[98] Civic- and ethnic-leaning systems alike face a choice between being unbendingly doctrinaire or realistically adaptive in setting the standards for full membership in the nation as well as in dealing with those who fail to meet or refuse to accept those standards. Disaffected regional and/or ethno-cultural minorities would also do well to recognize that their legitimate grievances may be in conflict both with the right to self-determination of yet smaller minority groups within their territory and with the stability, viability, and/or security of the larger polity in which they live. Any single principle taken to its logical conclusion is likely to become a recipe for trouble. To claim that one's national identity is culturally neutral is to aggravate the resentments of minorities who don't fit in. To make either an inherited ethnicity or complete assimilation into an officially designated national culture absolute preconditions for citizenship in a nation-state is a recipe for institutionalized intolerance and political oppression. Conversely, proponents of radical multiculturalism need to recognize that some degree of shared identity that cuts across internal divisions is vital for the successful functioning of any polity based on the principle of popular sovereignty.[99] It is difficult to envisage how a functioning democracy lacking any overarching element of national identity could succeed in binding its self-interested citizens and sub-cultures together in a community of shared interest.

In brief, every polity necessarily embodies some element of cultural particularism and every state that is based on a liberal-democratic conception of popular sovereignty faces a contradiction between its role as embodiment of a particular culture and its espousal of equal rights for all.[100] To acknowledge this contradiction does not require a society or government to apologize endlessly for it. But it does carry with it the obligation to negotiate a balance between the conflicting principles that hold the nation-state together and lend it ethical and political legitimacy. The range of potentially helpful formulas varies according to local and historical circumstances. In some cases, what Michael Keating refers to as asymmetrical arrangements may work best, as in the United Kingdom's recent devolution of self-governing power to Scotland, Wales, and Northern Ireland without providing a historically, culturally, demographically, and economically dominant England with home rule of its own.[101] English identity is so closely bound up with the historical development of the monarchic and parliamentary institutions that now govern Britain as a whole that there is no perceived need for a separate arrangement for English self-determination. In other cases, such as those of Belgium or the former Czechoslovakia, symmetrical partition into autonomous or independent units may provide the smoothest path to peaceful accommodation of ethno-national differences. In yet other contexts, such as that of some multi-ethnic immigrant societies, it may be possible and desirable to maintain the deterritorialization of ethno-cultural identities while negotiating compromises over non-territorial issues such as bilingual education.

In general, contemporary Europe offers some of the most promising models for dealing with the tensions and contradictions of the nation-state, both in the form of such individual compromises and in the continent-wide progress towards integration that has made it easier to accommodate demands for regional autonomy without fear of breaking up larger economic units or precipitating all-or-nothing territorial conflicts. Yet here too there are limits, as the rejection of the proposed European Constitution by French and Dutch voters in mid-2005 reminded us. Putting the cart of the federated polity ahead of the national horse arouses the fears and resentments of people who wish to be governed by a state that they see as representing who they are, rather than by a pan-European entity that embodies the rarified ideals of a trans-national, technocratic elite.

To suggest that the nation-state will long remain an important fixture of the world scene is not to say that national identities are static and unchanging or that national conflicts are doomed to repeat themselves interminably. Under the impact of global forces of economic integration and changing theories and practices of international law, traditional notions about the irreducible and indivisible qualities of political sovereignty may be giving way to more flexible and nuanced ways of negotiating the relationship between the symbolic representation of identity and the functional exercise of authority. To the extent that the imagined community of the nation can become imaginative in its approach to the contradictions that are inherent to it, it can play a productive role in lending substantive meaning to democratic ideals and in providing people with a sense of belonging and self-determination amidst the often alienating and disorienting pressures of globalization and rapid historical change.

END NOTES

1 James Madison, *Federalist* no. 14, in James Madison, Alexander Hamilton, and John Jay, *The Federalist Papers*, Isaac Kramnick, ed. (1788; London: Penguin, 1987), 144. My emphases.

2 Lyle Lovett, "That's Right (You're Not from Texas)," Lyle Lovett, *Live in Texas* (Music Corporation of America [MCA] Records, 1999).

3 For a stimulating collection of articles that actually seek to analyze various aspects of the nature–nurture relationship, see *Daedalus*, vol. 133, no. 4 (Fall 2004), issue entitled *On Human Nature*. For a critique of social scientists' tendency to disregard the role of biological factors in the shaping of human behavior, see also Steven Pinker, *The Blank Slate: The Denial of Human Nature and Modern Intellectual Life* (New York: Viking, 2002).

4 See, for example, Liah Greenfeld, *Nationalism: Five Roads to Modernity* (Cambridge, Mass.: Harvard University Press, 1992), ch. 5.

5 On ethnic nationalism's (dangerous) tendency to propagate literal under-standings of metaphors about blood and family, see Michael Herzfeld, *Cultural Intimacy: Social Poetics in the Nation-State*, 2nd edn (New York: Routledge, 2005), ch. 5, esp. pp. 113 and 125.

6 See the discussion in Donald Horowitz, *Ethnic Groups in Conflict*, 2nd edn (Berkeley: University of California Press, 2000), 57–64.

7 The influential, late nineteenth-century German historian and publicist, Heinrich von Treitschke, argued passionately that Alsatians were objectively German even if their sympathies lay with France. Thomas D. Musgrave, *National Self-Determination and National Minorities* (Oxford: Oxford University Press, 1997), 11. Similarly, some late nineteenth-century Croat nationalists claimed that Serbs were nothing more than misguided Croats – although they made this argument on the basis of the principle of historic state right and the idea of Croatia as a political nation. Ivo Banac, *The National Question in Yugoslavia: Origins, History, Politics* (Ithaca: Cornell University Press, 1984), 86–89.

8 See Andreas Kappeler, *Russland als Vielvölkerreich: Entstehung, Geschichte, Zerfall* (Munich: C. H. Beck, 1993).

9 In practice, the picture was much more complex. One of the points of contention both between and within ethnic groups in Central and Eastern Europe was the relative merits of nationalist claims based on historic state rights and those rooted in the affirmation of popular sovereignty and ethnic identity. Robert A. Kann, *The Multinational Empire: Nationalism and National Reform in the Habsburg Monarchy, 1848–1918* (New York: Columbia University Press, 1950), vol. 1, ch. 2; Oscar Jaszi, *The Dissolution of the Habsburg Monarchy* (Chicago: University of Chicago Press, 1929), 292–294; Aviel Roshwald, *Ethnic Nationalism and the Fall of Empires: Central Europe, Russia and the Middle East, 1914–1923* (London: Routledge, 2001), 14–15. It is precisely because of such intricacies that I go on below to problematize the ethnic–civic distinction.

10 Brian Vick, *Defining Germany: The 1848 Frankfurt Parliamentarians and National Identity* (Cambridge, Mass.: Harvard University Press, 2002), ch. 4 and *passim*; Brian Porter, *When Nationalism Began to Hate: Imagining Modern Politics in Nineteenth-Century Poland* (New York: Oxford University Press, 2000), 164–167, 182–188, and ch. 8.

11 Nazism was the most radical manifestation of this mentality. But similar ideas took hold in many other countries and political movements, ranging from Roman Dmowski's militantly anti-Semitic National Democratic movement in interwar Poland to the fascistic, pan-Arab extremism of Sati' al-Husri in interwar Iraq. See Adam Bromke, *Poland's Politics: Idealism vs. Realism* (Cambridge, Mass: Harvard University Press, 1967); Alvin Marcus Fountain II, *Roman Dmowski: Party, Tactics, Ideology 1895–1907* (Boulder, Colo.: East European Monographs, 1980); William Cleveland, *The Making of an Arab Nationalist: Ottomanism and Arabism in the Life and Thought of Sati' al-Husri* (Princeton: Princeton University Press, 1971), 38–41, 62–63; Reeva S. Simon, *Iraq between the Two World Wars: The Creation and Implementation of a Nationalist Ideology* (New York: Columbia University Press, 1986), ch. 4; Adeed Dawisha, *Arab Nationalism in the Twentieth Century: From Triumph to Despair* (Princeton: Princeton University Press, 2003), ch. 3.

12 Thus, taking issue with John Stuart Mill's assertion that common nationality is the surest foundation for representative government (cf. John Stuart Mill, *Considerations on Representative Government* [first published 1861], in Mill, *Utilitarianism, Liberty, and Considerations on Representative Government* [London: J. M. Dent and New York: E. P. Dutton, 1972], 359–366), Lord Acton argued that one must distinguish between nations that are shaped by a common allegiance to the political principles of a state, and states that owe their legitimacy to the nationality principle untempered by any independent values. He also endorsed the coexistence of several nationalities within one polity (as in the case of the Habsburg Empire or of the United Kingdom) as the arrangement most likely to impose reliable curbs on the arbitrary exercise of authority. John Emerich Edward Dalberg-Acton, "Nationality" (essay first published in 1862) in Dalberg-Acton, *The History of Freedom and other Essays* (London: Macmillan, 1919). In the twentieth century, it was Hans Kohn who most famously distinguished between liberal-democratic, Euro-Atlantic political nationalisms and romantic, irrational, and intolerant, Central and East European ethno-cultural nationalisms. Hans Kohn, *The Idea of Nationalism: A Study in its Origins and Background* (1944; New York: Macmillan, 1948), 330–331 and *passim*. See also Rogers Brubaker, *Citizenship and Nationhood in France and Germany* (Cambridge, Mass: Harvard University Press, 1992); Liah Greenfeld, *Nationalism: Five Roads to Modernity* (Cambridge, Mass.: Harvard University Press, 1992); George Schöpflin, "Nationalism, Politics and the European Experience," *Survey*, vol. 28, no. 4 (1984), 67–86.

13 Friedrich Meinecke distinguished between cultural and political nations while also pointing out how intertwined these categories could be in practice. Friedrich Meinecke, *Cosmopolitanism and the National State*, trans. Robert B. Kimber (original German edn, 1907; Princeton: Princeton University Press, 1970), 10–18. Over nineteen centuries earlier, Cicero described Roman citizens hailing from once independent cities as having two fatherlands – their native town and the republic, affection for the former being contained

within the framework of loyalty to the latter. Cicero, *On the Laws* 2.5 in Cicero, *On the Commonwealth and On the Laws*, James E. G. Zetzel ed. (Cambridge: Cambridge University Press, 1999), 130–131. See also Taras Kuzio, "The Myth of the Civic State: A Critical Survey of Hans Kohn's Framework for Understanding Nationalism," *Ethnic and Racial Studies*, vol. 25, no. 1 (January 2002), 20–39; Karen Barkey, "Thinking about Consequences of Empire," in Karen Barkey and Mark von Hagen, eds., *After Empire – Multiethnic Societies and Nation-Building: The Soviet Union and the Russian, Ottoman, and Habsburg Empires* (Boulder: Westview Press, 1997); Roshwald, *Ethnic Nationalism*, 5–6. A recent publication that questions the usefulness of the traditional civic–ethnic distinction in understanding recent East Central European history is Stefan Auer, *Liberal Nationalism in Central Europe* (London: RoutledgeCurzon, 2004). Auer prefers to think in terms of a tension between liberal and illiberal forms of nationalism, rather than ethnic and civic. I move towards a similar position in this chapter.

14 To paraphrase the late A. J. P. Taylor, such generalizations can generally be taken to include the qualification: "with the exception of Nazi Germany." See A. J. P. Taylor, *The Struggle for Mastery in Europe, 1848–1918* (Oxford: Oxford University Press, 1954), p. xxiii, n. 4.

15 See Stephen Shulman, "Challenging the Civic/Ethnic and West/East Dichotomies in the Study of Nationalism," *Comparative Political Studies*, vol. 35, no. 5 (June 2002), 554–585, esp. 558–559.

16 Yael Tamir, *Liberal Nationalism* (Princeton: Princeton University Press, 1993); Kuzio, "Myth of the Civic State"; Shulman, "Challenging Civic/ Ethnic Dichotomies," 580–581. Andrew Vincent argues that the very idea of citizenship, in its liberal incarnation, is laden with contradictions of this nature. Andrew Vincent, *Nationalism and Particularity* (Cambridge: Cambridge University Press, 2002), ch. 3.

17 Stephen Shulman makes a similar point in "Challenging Civic/Ethnic Dichotomies," 567–568, as does Steven Grosby in *Biblical Ideas of Nationality: Ancient and Modern* (Winona Lake, Ind.: Eisenbrauns, 2002), 208–209.

18 The following publications are among those that have informed and stimulated my thinking about this topic: Tamir, *Liberal Nationalism*; George Schöpflin, *Nations, Identity, Power* (New York: New York University Press, 2000); David Miller, *On Nationality* (Oxford: Clarendon Press, 1995); Will Kymlicka, *Multicultural Citizenship: A Liberal Theory of Minority Rights* (Oxford: Oxford University Press, 1995); Amy Gutmann, "Introduction," Charles Taylor, "The Politics of Recognition," Michael Walzer, "Comment," and Jürgen Habermas, "Struggles for Recognition in the Democratic Constitutional State," in Amy Gutmann, ed., *Multiculturalism: Examining the Politics of Recognition* (Princeton: Princeton University Press, 1994); Edward Shils, "Nation, Nationality, Nationalism and Civil Society," in Athena S. Leoussi and Steven Grosby, eds., *Nationality and Nationalism*,

vol. 1: *Theoretical Studies* (London: I. B. Tauris, 2004); Shulman, "Challenging Civic/Ethnic Dichotomies"; Kuzio, "Myth of the Civic State"; Bernard Yack, "The Myth of the Civic Nation" and Kai Nielsen, "Cultural Nationalism, Neither Ethnic nor Civic," in Ronald Beiner, ed., *Theorizing Nationalism* (Albany: State University of New York Press, 1999); Eric P. Kaufmann, *The Rise and Fall of Anglo-America* (Cambridge, Mass.: Harvard University Press, 2004), ch. 12 and *passim*; Vincent, *Nationalism and Particularity*, ch. 4; Auer, *Liberal Nationalism in Central Europe*, chs. 1–2 and *passim*; Anatol Lieven, *America Right or Wrong: An Anatomy of American Nationalism* (New York: Oxford University Press, 2004), 208–216.

19 Luigi Luca Cavalli-Sforza, *Genes, Peoples, and Languages* (Berkeley: University of California Press, 2000), ch. 5, esp. 150–151; Richard Dawkins, *The Ancestor's Tale: A Pilgrimage to the Dawn of Evolution* (New York: Houghton Mifflin, 2004), 410–414.

20 "We like to think of birth and choice as mutually exclusive principles of membership, but all institutions are infused with components of both." Horowitz, *Ethnic Groups in Conflict*, 55. See also Fredrik Barth, "Introduction," in Barth, ed., *Ethnic Groups and Boundaries* (Boston: Little, Brown, 1969).

21 On the relationship between kinship and moral community/covenant in the Jewish tradition, see also Anthony Smith, *Chosen Peoples* (Oxford: Oxford University Press, 2003), 60–64.

22 I am extrapolating from the argument in Grosby, *Biblical Ideas of Nationality*, ch. 3.

23 This is a perfect illustration of Donald Horowitz's point to the effect that: "The meaningfulness of ethnic identity derives from its birth connection – it came first – or from acceptance by an ethnic group *as if* born into it." Horowitz, *Ethnic Groups in Conflict*, 57.

24 Edward E. Cohen, *The Athenian Nation* (Princeton: Princeton University Press, 2000), chs. 2–3.

25 On the interwar states of Eastern Europe as "nationalizing" states, see Rogers Brubaker, *Nationalism Reframed: Nationhood and the National Question in the New Europe* (Cambridge: Cambridge University Press, 1996), 63–66 and ch. 4.

26 H. Gordon Skilling, *T. G. Masaryk: Against the Current, 1882–1914* (University Park, Penn.: Pennsylvania State University Press, 1994), 6–7, 35–37, 101–103, and ch. 3; Robert Pynsent, *Questions of Identity: Czech and Slovak Ideas of Nationality and Personality* (Budapest: Central European University Press, 1994), 180–182; Joseph Kalvoda, *The Genesis of Czechoslovakia* (Boulder: East European Monographs, 1986), 17–32; Roman Szporluk, *The Political Thought of Thomas G. Masaryk* (Boulder: East European Monographs, 1981), ch. 4; Auer, *Liberal Nationalism in Central Europe*, 107–113. Eva Schmidt-Hartmann is critical of Masaryk's attempt to conflate ethno-cultural and universalist themes and of the elitist strain in his thinking. Eva Schmidt-Hartmann, "The Fallacy of Realism: Some Problems of Masaryk's Approach to Czech National Aspirations," in Stanley B. Winters, ed., *T. G. Masaryk (1850–1937)*, vol. 1 (New York: St. Martin's Press, 1990).

See also the discussion of Masaryk and Jan Hus in Chapter 2 of the present volume.

27 Banac, *The National Question in Yugoslavia*, 94–99; Nicholas J. Miller, *Between Nation and State: Serbian Politics in Croatia before the First World War* (Pittsburgh: University of Pittsburgh Press, 1997), 30–33, 46–52, and ch. 6; Hugh and Christopher Seton-Watson, *The Making of a New Europe: R. W. Seton-Watson and the Last Years of Austria-Hungary* (Seattle: University of Washington Press, 1981), ch. 3; Barbara Jelavich, *History of the Balkans*, vol. 1: *Eighteenth and Nineteenth Centuries* (Cambridge: Cambridge University Press, 1983), 98–99; John R. Lampe, *Yugoslavia as History: Twice There Was a Country* (Cambridge: Cambridge University Press, 1996), 77–79.

28 Porter, *When Nationalism Began to Hate*, chs. 5–8; Bromke, *Poland's Politics*. On the enlightened republicanism of early Polish political nationalism, see also Andrzej Walicki, *The Enlightenment and the Birth of Modern Nationhood: Polish Political Thought from Noble Republicanism to Tadeusz Kościuszko*, trans. Emma Harris (Notre Dame: University of Notre Dame Press, 1989).

29 I develop these ideas more fully in Roshwald, *Ethnic Nationalism*.

30 Andrzej Garlicki, *Józef Piłsudski, 1867–1935*, ed., trans., and abridged by John Coutouvidis (Aldershot: Scolar Press, 1995); Piotr S. Wandycz, "Poland's Place in Europe in the Concepts of Piłsudski and Dmowski," *East European Politics and Societies*, vol. 4, no. 3 (1990), 451–468.

31 On the link between early modern, absolutist and modern, nationalist-democratic conceptions of sovereignty, see Vincent, *Nationalism and Particularity*, ch. 1, esp. pp. 30–34.

32 On the historic use of ethnic core cultures as the basis for state-promoted national homogenization programs in Western Europe and North America, see Kymlicka, *Multicultural Citizenship*; Kaufmann, *Anglo-America*; Kuzio, "Myth of the Civic State," esp. 31–32.

33 Carole Fink, *Defending the Rights of Others: The Great Powers, the Jews, and International Minority Protection, 1878–1938* (Cambridge: Cambridge University Press, 2004), chs. 8–9; Carole Fink, "The League of Nations and the Minorities Question," *World Affairs*, vol. 157, no. 4 (Spring 1995), 197–205; C. A. Macartney, *National States and National Minorities* (Oxford: Oxford University Press, 1934), ch. 7; Patrick B. Finney, "'An Evil for All Concerned': Great Britain and Minority Protection after 1919," *Journal of Contemporary History*, vol. 30, no. 3 (July 1995), 533–551; D. R. Gadgil, "The Protection of Minorities," in William F. Mackey and Albert Verdoort, eds., *The Multinational Society: Papers of the Ljubljana Seminar* (Rowley, Mass.: Newbury House Publishers, 1975), 71–72.

34 In the Baltic states, though, a new element of complexity was added during their period of incorporation in the USSR, in the form of ethnic Russian immigrants whose status and cultural rights remain a sticky issue in Latvia and Estonia. Moreover, the Roma (Gypsy) minority remains the object of widespread social and institutional prejudice in much of Central and Eastern Europe. See Auer, *Liberal Nationalism in Central Europe*, 43–45.

35 On the debate over whether or not the Soviet Union should be thought of as an empire, see Ronald Grigor Suny, "The Empire Strikes Out: Imperial Russia, 'National Identity,' and Theories of Empire," in Ronald Grigor Suny and Terry Martin, eds., *A State of Nations: Empire and Nation-Making in the Age of Lenin and Stalin* (New York: Oxford University Press, 2001).

36 See Benyamin Neuberger, *National Self-Determination in Postcolonial Africa* (Boulder: Lynne Rienner Publishers, 1986); Basil Davidson, *The Black Man's Burden: Africa and the Curse of the Nation-State* (New York: Random House, 1992).

37 Clifford Geertz, "The Integrative Revolution: Primordial Sentiments and Civil Politics in the New States," in Clifford Geertz, ed., *Old Societies and New States: The Quest for Modernity in Asia and Africa* (London: Collier Macmillan, 1963). See also Donald Horowitz, *Ethnic Groups in Conflict*, 2nd edn (Berkeley: University of California Press, 2000), 64–82.

38 Horowitz, *Ethnic Groups in Conflict*, chs. 14–16.

39 See Michael Keating, *Plurinational Democracy: Stateless Nations in a Post-Sovereignty Era* (Oxford: Oxford University Press, 2001); Gidon Gottlieb, *Nation against State* (New York: Council on Foreign Relations Press, 1993); Tamir, *Liberal Nationalism*.

40 See Carol Skalnik Leff, *The Czech and Slovak Republics: Nation Versus State* (Boulder: Westview Press, 1996).

41 Kaufmann, *Anglo-America*, 13.

42 See also Steven Grosby, "The Nation of the United States and the Vision of Ancient Israel," in R. Michener, ed., *Nationality, Patriotism, and Nationalism* (St. Paul: Paragon, 1993). Eric P. Kaufmann argues that the United States, along with the classic West European models of civic nationhood, came into being as an ethnic nation and only gradually evolved into a truly civic nation. Kaufmann, *Anglo-America, passim*. On the dualistic tension between Anglo-Saxon identity and cosmopolitanism in early American history, see ibid., ch. 3. Of course, the perception of America as in essence a hybrid nation was articulated as early as the 1780s by Crèvecoeur, who wrote: "Here individuals of all nations are melted into a new race of men, whose labours and posterity will one day cause great changes in the world." J. Hector St. John de Crèvecoeur, *Letters from An American Farmer and Sketches of Eighteenth-Century America* (1782; New York: Penguin, 1981), 70. On the other hand, Gordon Wood notes that as early as 1788, an ethnic minority was flexing its collective political muscle: in that year's electoral campaign, Pennsylvania Germans (one-third of the state's population), demanded proportional representation on the state's congressional delegation and electoral-college slate. Many of them subsequently cast their votes along ethnic rather than party lines. Gordon S. Wood, *The Radicalism of the American Revolution* (1992; New York: Random House, 1993), 260.

43 Gary Gerstle, *American Crucible: Race and Nation in the Twentieth Century* (Princeton: Princeton University Press, 2001), chs. 1–2.

44 Ibid.; Thomas G. Dyer, *Theodore Roosevelt and the Idea of Race* (Baton Rouge: Louisiana State University Press, 1980), 130–135; James R. Barrett and David Roediger, "Inbetween Peoples: Race, Nationality and the 'New Immigrant' Working Class," *Journal of American Ethnic History*, vol. 16, no. 3 (Spring 1997), 3–44. For earlier, mid-nineteenth-century articulations of the idea that America is a nation whose greatness is derived from the hybridization of European peoples, see Reginald Horsman, *Race and Manifest Destiny: The Origins of American Racial Anglo-Saxonism* (Cambridge, Mass.: Harvard University Press, 1981), 251–255.

45 As quoted in Dyer, *Theodore Roosevelt*, 132.

46 Ibid.

47 Ibid., 83–88.

48 Gerstle, *American Crucible*, chs. 1–2.

49 Ibid., chs. 5–6; Kaufmann, *Anglo-America*, 32–34, 207–212.

50 On the impact of World War II on popular-cultural conceptions of inter-racial and interethnic relations in America, see Gerstle, *American Crucible*, 220–239; Kaufmann, *Anglo-America*, 213–214.

51 Cf. Daniel Pick, *War Machine: The Rationalisation of Slaughter in the Modern Age* (New Haven: Yale University Press, 1993), ch. 8.

52 Eugen Weber, *Peasants into Frenchmen: The Modernization of Rural France, 1870–1914* (Stanford: Stanford University Press, 1976), ch. 17.

53 The strongest case for classifying pre-1914 Germany unambiguously in the ethnic-nationalist category, in sharp contrast to the French civic-nationalist model, is made by Rogers Brubaker in his *Citizenship and Nationhood in France and Germany* (Cambridge, Mass.: Harvard University Press, 1992). Other scholars have taken issue with Brubaker's approach, depicting nineteenth- and twentieth-century Germany (apart from the Nazi period) as torn between ethnic and civic conceptions of identity. See Brian Vick, *Defining Germany: The 1848 Frankfurt Parliamentarians and National Identity* (Cambridge, Mass.: Harvard University Press, 2002); Dieter Gosewinkel, *Einbürgern und Ausschliessen: die Nationalisierung der Staatsangehörigkeit vom Deutschen Bund bis zur Bundesrepublik Deutschland* (Göttingen: Vanden-hoeck & Ruprecht, 2001), esp. 421–433. (My thanks to Björn Hofmeister for the Gosewinkel reference.) Patrick Weil has reexamined the Brubaker paradigm from the perspective of French legal history, showing that French citizenship and naturalization law has historically incorporated elements of both *jus soli* and *jus sanguinis* (i.e. territorial and lineage criteria), and that nineteenth-century German citizenship law was strongly influenced by the French example rather than standing in stark contrast to it. Patrick Weil, *Qu'est-ce qu'un Français? Histoire de la nationalité française depuis la Révolution* (Paris: Grasset, 2002). (My thanks to Aron Rodrigue for this reference.)

54 Eva G. Reichmann, "Der Bewusstseinswandel der deutschen Juden," in Werner Mosse, ed., *Deutsches Judentum in Krieg und Revolution, 1916–1923* (Tübingen: J. C. B. Mohr, 1971); Howard M. Sachar, *Dreamland: Europeans*

and Jews in the Aftermath of the Great War (2002; New York: Vintage Books/ Random House, 2003), 218–219. In Central Europe, the connection between military service and Jewish emancipation was made as early as the 1780s, during Joseph II's short-lived liberal reform efforts in Habsburg Austria. Michael K. Silber, "From Tolerated Aliens to Citizen-Soldiers: Jewish Military Service in the Era of Joseph II," in Pieter M. Judson and Marsha L. Rozenblit, eds., *Constructing Nationalities in East Central Europe* (New York: Berghahn, 2005).

55 Joshua Sanborn, "Family, Fraternity, and Nation-Building in Russia, 1905– 1925," in Suny and Martin, eds., *A State of Nations*.

56 Peter Holquist, "To Count, to Extract, and to Exterminate: Population Statistics and Population Politics in Late Imperial and Soviet Russia," in Suny and Martin, eds., *A State of Nations*, 115. See also Sanborn, "Family, Fraternity, and Nation-Building in Russia."

57 See Jean-Denis Bredin, *The Affair: The Case of Alfred Dreyfus*, trans. Jeffrey Mehlman (New York: George Braziller, 1986).

58 Masami Arai, *Turkish Nationalism in the Young Turk Era* (Leiden: Brill, 1992), chs. 1, 3–4, and Conclusion; Erik Zürcher, *The Unionist Factor: The Role of the Committee of Union and Progress in the Turkish National Movement, 1905–1926* (Leiden: Brill, 1984), 49–51; Simon, *Iraq between the Two World Wars*, ch. 2.

59 Saul Friedländer, "Die politischen Veränderungen der Kriegszeit und ihre Auswirkungen auf die Judenfrage" and Werner Jochmann, "Die Ausbreitung des Antisemitismus," in Mosse, ed., *Deutsches Judentum*; Omer Bartov, "Defining Enemies, Making Victims: Germans, Jews, and the Holocaust," *American Historical Review*, vol. 103, no. 3 (June 1998), 771–816, esp. 776–777.

60 Michael Lind puts this nicely: "Americans share common national ancestors, whatever their genetic ancestors. Even if our genetic grandparents came from Finland or Indonesia, as Americans, we are all descendants of George Washington – *and* his slaves." Michael Lind, *The Next American Nation: The New Nationalism and the Fourth American Revolution* (New York: The Free Press, 1995), 288. Eric Kaufmann, drawing on Anthony Smith's terminology, distinguishes between Anglo-American ethno-nationalists' focus on "genealogical pedigree ..." and civic nationalists' preoccupation with "an *ideological* myth of descent ..." Kaufmann, *Anglo-America*, 278 (italics in original).

61 Kaufmann, *Anglo-America*, ch. 9 and *passim*.

62 Anthony Marx, *Faith in Nation: Exclusionary Origins of Nationalism* (New York: Oxford University Press, 2003), 115–117.

63 As a separate matter, a strong case can certainly be made for the claim that West European nationalisms not only included ethnic elements at their origins, but retain strong ethno-cultural undercurrents to this day. But this has little to do with these countries' histories of religious intolerance, which form the focal point of Anthony Marx's discussion.

64 Classroom discussion, graduate colloquium on "Nationalism in Modern History," Georgetown University, Spring 2004.

65 Perez Zagorin points out that so-called heretics were also commonly dehumanized in medieval and early modern religious propaganda. Perez Zagorin, *How the Idea of Religious Toleration Came to the West* (Princeton: Princeton University Press, 2003), 43–44. See also A. Marx, *Faith in Nation*, ch. 3.

66 Tamir, *Liberal Nationalism*, 90. Bernard Yack makes a similar point in "Myth of the Civic Nation," 115–116. See also Auer, *Liberal Nationalism in Central Europe*, 5–6.

67 Cecilia O'Leary has dated the common use of this term to the 1870s or 1880s, when it was directed against trade unions and striking industrial workers. Cecilia O'Leary, *To Die For: The Paradox of American Patriotism* (Princeton: Princeton University Press, 1999), 61. See also Clifford Longley, *Chosen People: The Big Idea that Shapes England and America* (London: Hodder & Stoughton, 2002), 2.

68 In December 2003, for example, a Republican political consultant dismissed Senator Hillary Rodham Clinton's criticisms of the Bush Jr. administration's handling of the military situation in Iraq as "un-American." James G. Lakely, "Home Again, Hillary Bashes Bush," *The Washington Times*, 2 December 2003.

69 For an intellectually engaging treatment of such dilemmas and an articulate critique of radical multiculturalism as a viable alternative to liberal nationalism, see D. Miller, *On Nationality*.

70 Will Kymlicka points out that: "What distinguishes 'civic' nations from 'ethnic' nations is not the absence of any cultural component to national identity, but rather the fact that anyone can integrate into the common culture, regardless of race or colour." Kymlicka, *Multicultural Citizenship*, 24. On the culturally particularistic components of civic nationalism see also Shils, "Nation, Nationality" and Nielsen, "Cultural Nationalism." On literal and metaphorical understandings of blood and family in the rhetoric of nationalism, see also Herzfeld, *Cultural Intimacy*, ch. 5.

71 Stephen Shulman points to poll results indicating that East Europeans are more inclined than West Europeans and North Americans to favor state support for the preservation of minority cultures as evidence that, in some respects, the former are more civic minded in their nationalism than the latter. Shulman, "Challenging Civic/Ethnic Dichotomies," 576–577. I would suggest a rather different conclusion, to the effect that ethnic-leaning nationalism can be more tolerant of segmented cultural pluralism than civic-oriented nationalism; precisely because they wish to see their countries' dominant ethno-cultural identities preserved intact, members of East European majority cultures prefer to subsidize the cultural autonomy of minorities rather than merge diverse traditions and identities into an amorphous supraethnic synthesis. To be sure, the line separating this form of "separate but equal" tolerance from prejudice can be very blurry.

72 The commission under the chairmanship of Bernard Stasi, charged with making recommendations regarding the long-festering headscarf issue, was itself composed of members of various cultural backgrounds, including both Jews and Muslims. Jane Kramer has reported that the commission's proposal to prohibit conspicuous religious symbols or clothes from being worn by students in public schools was part of a broader package of recommendations aimed at facilitating the integration of minority communities into French society, but it was the only one passed into law. Kramer also notes that the commission presented a nuanced justification for its proposed ban on headscarves, arguing that its main concern was the protection of the individual rights of Muslim girls who were coming under strong – occasionally even violent – familial and social pressure to cover their hair in public whether they wanted to or not. It was the role of the public school, the commission argued, to provide them with a space in which they would be protected from such pressures. No such ban was proposed or introduced at the university level, where students are considered adults with the freedom to make their own personal choices about such matters. Jane Kramer, "Taking the Veil," *The New Yorker*, vol. 80, no. 36 (22 November 2004), 58–71. However, when asked about the persistence of restrictive dress codes for state functionaries and members of the civil service, a member of the commission defended the policy by claiming that the appearance of public officials must be "neutral." Of course, what is deemed neutral by a member of the cultural mainstream may be quite loaded for a member of a minority culture. (Present author's personal conversation with former member of the Stasi commission, to be left unnamed.) For an enlightening ethical-philosophical exploration of the relationship between cultural minorities and the liberal state, see Kymlicka, *Multicultural Citizenship*.

73 Daniel J. Elazar, "Parent Control and Educational Choice: Learning from the Israeli Experience," Jerusalem Center for Public Affairs, *Daniel Elazar Papers Index*: http://www.jcpa.org/dje/articles2/parentcontrol.htm; Devorah Eden and Devorah Kalekin-Fishman, "Multi-Cultural Education in Israel as a Fulfillment of National Ethos and Political Policy," paper posted on the University of Haifa's Faculty of Education website: http://construct.haifa.ac.il/almogt/Israel%20Political%20Pokicy.htm; Nadav Safran, *Israel: The Embattled Ally* (1978; Cambridge, Mass.: Harvard University Press, 1981), ch. 13, esp. pp. 202–206. For a critique of the unequal funding of Israel's Arabic public school sector, see "Second Class: Discrimination Against Palestinian Arab Children in Israel's Schools," *Human Rights Watch Publications*, September 2001: http://www.hrw.org/reports/2001/israel2/.

74 On the dilemmas the French state is facing in its efforts to reconcile ethno-cultural pluralism with its traditional insistence on the nation's territorial unity and fraternal solidarity, see Geneviève Koubi, "The Management of Cultural Diversity in France," in Alain Dieckhoff, ed., *The Politics of Belonging: Nationalism, Liberalism, and Pluralism* (Lanham, Md.: Lexington Books, 2004).

75 For an analytical overview of twentieth-century American approaches to ethnic diversity ranging from Israel Zangwill's strongly assimilationist conception of the "melting-pot," to Horace Kallen's cultural pluralism, to latter-day multiculturalism, see Philip Gleason, *Speaking of Diversity: Language and Ethnicity in Twentieth-Century America* (Baltimore: Johns Hopkins University Press, 1992). Eric Kaufmann argues that the dynamics of contemporary American multiculturalism are actually pointing more towards a fulfillment of the melting-pot vision than the creation of a socio-culturally segmented society. Kaufmann, *Anglo-America*, ch. 12 and Conclusion. Michael Walzer argues that it is precisely the paradoxical relationship between America's embrace of ethno-cultural pluralism and its quest for civic cohesion that lends the country its distinct, indeed exceptional, character. Michael Walzer, *What it Means to Be an American* (New York: Marsilio, 1992), 44–49.

76 Kymlicka, *Multicultural Citizenship*, 97, 114–115.

77 Yossi Shain, *Marketing the American Creed Abroad: Diasporas in the U.S. and their Homelands* (Cambridge: Cambridge University Press, 1999). For a more xenophobic perspective, see Samuel P. Huntington, *Who Are We? The Challenges to America's National Identity* (New York: Simon & Schuster, 2004), 276–291.

78 Dr. James Zogby, "My Message to the Democratic Party," 3 July 2000, posted on the website of the Arab American Institute: http://www.aaiusa.org/wwatch/070300.htm.

79 Nathan Guttman, "Think Before You Sing 'Hatikva'," *Haaretz* English Edition, 27 May 2005: http://www.haaretz.com/hasen/objects/pages/PrintArticleEn.jhtml?itemNo=581104.

80 Cf. Lieven, *America*, 47 and ch. 2.

81 Kaufmann, *Anglo-America*, 263–270; Amy Argetsinger, "In Arizona, 'Minutemen' Start Border Patrols," *The Washington Post*, 5 April 2005.

82 David Broder, "Dole Backs Official Language: English Is Needed to Unify Nation, Presidential Hopeful Says," *The Washington Post*, 5 September 1995. See also Kaufmann, *Anglo-America*, 264.

83 Samuel P. Huntington, "The Hispanic Challenge," *Foreign Policy*, no. 141 (March/April 2004), 30–45. On the *reconquista*, see p. 42.

84 Ibid., 44. For the critique of Latino culture in its original context, see Lionel Sosa, *The Americano Dream: How Latinos Can Achieve Success in Business and in Life* (New York: Penguin, 1998), 7.

85 Huntington, "Hispanic Challenge," 45; see also his *Who Are We?*, ch. 9; Lieven, *America*, 91.

86 Kymlicka, *Multicultural Citizenship*, ch. 2.

87 Keating, *Plurinational Democracy*, 116.

88 On symmetrical and asymmetrical forms of federalism, see ibid., esp. ch. 4.

89 Ibid., 109.

90 In Robert Musil's words: "The Austro-Hungarian state ... did not consist of an Austrian part and a Hungarian part that, as one might expect, complemented each other, but of a whole and a part; that is, of a Hungarian

and an Austro-Hungarian sense of statehood, the latter to be found in Austria, which in a sense left the Austrian sense of statehood with no country of its own." Robert Musil, *The Man Without Qualities*, trans. Sophie Wilkins (1930–43; New York: Alfred A. Knopf, 1995), vol. 1, p. 180.

91 This treatment of Canada's identity crisis draws on the following: Taylor, "The Politics of Recognition, " in Gutmann, ed., *Multiculturalism*, 52–61; Keating, *Plurinational Democracy, passim*; Michael Ignatieff, *Blood and Belonging: Journeys into the New Nationalism* (1993; New York: Farrar, Straus & Giroux, 1995), ch. 4; John F. Stack, Jr. and Lui Hebron, "Canada's Ethnic Dilemma: Primordial Ethnonationalism in Quebec," in David Carment, John F. Stack, Jr., and Frank Harvey, eds., *The International Politics of Quebec Secession: State Making and State Breaking in North America* (Westport: Praeger, 2001); Ramsay Cook, "Canada: A Post-Nationalist Nation?," in Sima Godfrey and Frank Unger, eds., *The Shifting Foundations of Modern Nation-States: Realignments of Belonging* (Toronto: University of Toronto Press, 2004); Augie Fleras and Jean Leonard Elliott, *Multiculturalism in Canada: The Challenge of Diversity* (Scarborough, Ont.: Nelson Canada, 1992); Jocelyn Létourneau, *A History for the Future: Rewriting Memory and Identity in Quebec*, trans. Phyllis Aronoff and Howard Scott (Montreal: McGill-Queen's University Press, 2004).

92 Taylor, *Politics of Recognition*, 52–61; Fleras and Elliott, *Multiculturalism in Canada*, ch. 8.

93 Pierre Anctil, "La trajectoire interculturelle du Québec: la société distincte vue à travers le prisme de l'immigration," in André Lapierre, Patricia Smart, and Pierre Savard, eds., *Language, Culture and Values in Canada at the Dawn of the 21st Century/Langues, cultures et valeurs au Canada à l'aube du XXIe siècle* (Dalhousie and Ottawa: International Council for Canadian Studies/ Conseil international d'études canadiennes and Ottawa: Carleton University Press, 1996).

94 Ignatieff, *Blood and Belonging*, 163–167.

95 Marilyn Grace Miller, *Rise and Fall of the Cosmic Race: The Cult of Mestizaje in Latin America* (Austin: University of Texas Press, 2004), Introduction; Waskar T. Ari, "Race and Subaltern Nationalism: AMP Activist-Intellectuals in Bolivia, 1921–1964" (Ph.D. dissertation, Georgetown University, 2004), chs. 2–3; Benedict Anderson, *Imagined Communities: Reflections on the Origin and Spread of Nationalism*, 2nd edn (London: Verso, 1991), 49–50.

96 See the discussion in Sanborn, "Family, Fraternity, and Nation-Building in Russia."

97 Andrew Vincent also makes this point in *Nationalism and Particularity*, 106.

98 Stefan Auer similarly suggests that the distinction between liberal and illiberal forms of nationalism (as competing forces within each society) is more meaningful than that between ethnic and civic identities. Auer, *Liberal Nationalism in Central Europe*, 5.

99 On the possibilities and limitations of multiculturalism, see the essays in Gutmann, ed., *Multiculturalism*.

100 As Stefan Auer puts it, "ethnic diversity can generate situations which cannot be resolved to the satisfaction of all competing demands. In many cases, the best one can hope for is the amelioration of conflicts, rather than their elimination ... Liberal nationalists have to accept that what is morally desirable is not always feasible in the political realm." Auer, *Liberal Nationalism in Central Europe*, 171.

101 Keating, *Plurinational Democracy*, ch. 4.

Conclusion

The contradictions and dilemmas that lie at the heart of nationalism make it notoriously difficult to analyze or even define. Yet it is precisely its paradoxical nature that lends nationalism much of its endurance. Lying at the intersection of the ancient and the modern, the religious and the secular, the personal and the political, the individual and the collective, the particular and the universal, nationalism plays a vital role in mediating between such apparently opposite, yet inextricably intertwined, categories of human experience.

Nationalism becomes destructive when its exponents convince themselves that they hold the key to doing away with the existential tensions that lie at its heart, rather than accepting and embracing its paradoxical qualities. Innumerable atrocities and crimes against humanity have been committed in the name of simplistic and one-sided visions of nationalism – fanatically crusading or xenophobically autarchic, mono-maniacally modernizing or crudely reactionary, zealously religious or militantly anticlerical, brutally racist or intolerantly ideological. The propensity of some nationalists to claim that loyalty to the nation transcends all ethical principles and moral considerations has unquestionably played a nefarious role in human history, and it is understandable that this should have earned nationalism in all its forms a terrible reputation. But the fact is that – as Isaiah Berlin pointed out – any principle interpreted in a simplistic manner or implemented in utter disregard of all conflicting considerations will lead to abusive behavior.[1] Single-minded devotion to the principle of economic equality has come at the cost of human liberty. A blinkered fixation on individual freedom and on the sanctity of private property and the supernatural quality of market forces will lead to untrammeled socio-economic exploitation and environmental degradation. The democratic principle of majority rule threatens the rights of minorities. This does not mean that equality, liberty, property, and democracy are intrinsically destructive concepts. It's just that they must be reconciled with conflicting principles. It is the refusal to engage with such ethical complexities that leads to serious trouble. Likewise, nationalism's twin propositions – that the state should embody the identity of its population, and that a population with a distinct identity and territorial attachment is entitled to its own state – are not inherently evil. It's just that these claims beg as many questions as they answer and are frequently in conflict with one another as well as with other values and principles. A responsible politics of nationalism accepts the need to make adaptive compromises in light of such complications. And a responsible and effective politics of liberalism does not allow reactionaries and chauvinists, with their one-sided responses to such dilemmas, to monopolize the ideology and imagery of nationalism.

In this book, I have argued that nationalism first manifested itself in the ancient world. I think grasping this is critical to understanding that it is not a transitory epiphenomenon but rather something very likely to arise from the interplay of popular identity and state authority, especially in societies where the idea of popular sovereignty, or some approximation of it, is influential. I would go so far as to say that it helps fulfill primordial human needs for a sense of connection and belonging in the context of impersonal structures of territorial authority and law. But it has never been the only means of fulfilling such needs. Theocratic ideals, universalistic conceptions of religious community, and patriarchal images and ideals are among the sources of cohesion and authority that have, singly or jointly, held together a variety of states through the ages. In many regions and periods, such as much of Europe during the early Middle Ages, the state was either non-existent or extremely weak; in the absence of substantive statehood, there simply was no framework available for the crystallization of national identities.

Conversely, to the extent that states did succeed in consolidating their authority, centralizing their rule, and thus intruding into the daily lives of their populations, the likelihood increased that the governed would either come to perceive the territorially bounded polity as some sort of extension of themselves or resist it because they failed to see their image reflected in it. Such sentiments may at first have been confined to the thin social stratum of the educated and/or well-born, as in early modern France and Poland.[2] But to the extent that such people came to see the state as an entity that either was or ought to be the embodiment of its subjects' distinctive, collective identity, they were already espousing a nationalist position. And as the idea and practice of popular sovereignty became more influential, it became ever likelier that political legitimacy would be closely associated with national identity. For when revolution or reform transfers sovereignty from the biologically singular person of the monarch to the multitude of the populace, a question is posed: what is it that gives these thousands or millions of people the transcendent unity necessary to jointly exercise the indivisible power of sovereignty?[3] The source of that unity might be found in universalistic religious beliefs or class solidarity. But these are conceptions of identity that are not readily confined territorially. (True, as we have seen, a religious faith can be defined as coextensive with, or uniquely embodied by, a specific ethnic group or territory, but then it functions politically as a source of national identity.) To the extent that the territorially bounded nature of statehood is accepted as a given, the assertion of popular sovereignty is almost unavoidably accompanied by claims that national identity is the source of the sovereign people's unity and solidarity, and by efforts to translate such claims into reality.

Hence nationalism's rise to dominance in the modern world, where the idea of popular sovereignty (be it in its pluralistic or totalitarian forms) reigns supreme. The attraction of the nationalist ideal was enhanced by its association with the power of nation-states such as France, Britain, and (after 1871) Germany. It offered societies the prospect of equipping themselves with the instruments of mass mobilization and political consolidation that seemed to go hand-in-hand with the development of modern industrial, technological, and military power. Yet it was a vehicle for *selective* assimilation into this new global political culture – a means of adopting the mechanisms of economic and political modernization without altogether abandoning the very identity of the society whose place in the world one was seeking to secure. Or perhaps in some cases it would be more accurate to say that nationalism provided a cover for the adoption of foreign ways and the jettisoning of cumbersome traditions – as in Turkey of the 1920s, where Kemal Atatürk imposed radical linguistic and dress-code reforms and secularized politics and law in the name of a distinctive Turkish identity.[4] Such inherent tensions between nationalism's assimilationist and preservationist aspects contribute to the energy and urgency of the debates and divisions we have been examining in this volume. The point is that such inner conflicts can never be definitively resolved in a world where the nature of so-called global culture is itself constantly in flux, and that globalization therefore should not be seen as superseding nationalism. On the contrary, the successive waves of globalization that have swept across the planet since the sixteenth century have been critical to the spread of nationalism as a pervasive political, social, and cultural force.[5]

To be sure, there are a variety of organizations, alliances, interests, ideologies, loyalties, and identities that either diminish the power of nationalism and the nation-state or simply function on planes that are separate from it. But this does not mean that nationalism is becoming irrelevant in a world of kaleidoscopic, post-modern identities. The fact is that people's identities have never been exclusively defined by nationalism. Nationalist extremists may periodically claim to have achieved the total homogenization and monopolization of a population's identity, but such claims are greatly exaggerated.[6] Yet the concept of national identity does remain the standard basis for the legitimization of independent statehood in the contemporary world. Therefore, the problem of how to reconcile the idea of the singular nation with the multiplicity of human affiliations continues to shape cultural and political debates and conflicts across much of the globe. In this sense, nationhood and nationalism have been and remain dominant aspects of the modern experience.

Supranational institutions and international law do have important roles to play in containing nationalism's abusive potential. European integration is rightly pointed to by many analysts as an example of the productive role that institutions transcending the nation-state can play in the contemporary world. Yet a European Union (EU) that is perceived as threatening to supplant the nation-state altogether runs the risk of alienating public support. Perhaps, over the long run, the EU will succeed in establishing itself as a more cohesive federation with a common foreign and defense policy and a sharply defined persona on the world stage. But such a development would almost by definition imply that a new, European national identity was crystallizing, taking its place in a multi-tiered structure that continued to accommodate British and Scottish, Spanish and Catalan, French and Corsican "sub-national" identities. Otherwise, it is difficult to conceive how a federal Europe would succeed in gaining acceptance and commanding loyalty among its population. A liberal-democratic Europe that sought inspiration in the historical model of the Habsburg empire would be barking up the wrong tree, for that was a patriarchal monarchy that began to fray at its ethno-national seams precisely under the pressure of modern democratic and populist politics.[7] It is from the Habsburgs' failure to cultivate a supra-ethnic, civic-style nationalism capable of accommodating the transition to democratic politics that today's multinational European Union might draw fruitful lessons.[8]

Again, having said all that, it would be mistaken to conclude that nationalism has succeeded in establishing itself as the unchallenged source of personal and collective identity and political legitimacy in the modern world. On the contrary, nationalism succeeds only to the extent that it manages to link itself to, co-opt, or coexist with, other loyalties and affiliations, ranging from the religious to the familial. Often, it fails to achieve such syntheses; many countries in the contemporary world are afflicted, not so much by the power of nationalism as by its weakness. Twentieth-century secular Arab nationalism failed to establish a stable foundation for democratic politics or a legitimizing basis for the division of the Arab world into multiple polities; conversely, it failed to unite the Arab world, to achieve a lasting synthesis with Islam, or to reach a popularly accepted *modus vivendi* with its archenemy, Israel. These failures have opened the door to a radical, transnational Islamic fundamentalism that openly challenges the very idea of the bounded nation-state as antithetical to the Islamic ideal of a universal caliphate.[9] Unconstrained by the geo-political and security interests of any existing, territorially delimited state, this brand of militant zealotry enjoys the dubious luxury of feeling free to pursue its dystopian ends with utter disregard for the human, economic, and political costs of its methods.[10]

The dangers of an overly weak national identity can afflict Western societies as well. Many Canadian commentators fear that the failure of the socially progressive brand of 1970s-era Canadian nationalism to engage the sympathies of their country's youth may leave the young generation vulnerable to exploitation by various brands of political extremism. As Robert Wright argues, a country in which Molson Beer's popular television advertisements are more successful than the political leadership and educational system in lending expression to the national spirit is a country in which the symbols of collective identity have become dangerously detached from any substantive vision of, or debate about, the just society.[11]

Analogous problems afflict the United States. Although much of the world regards the spread of globalized consumer culture as a form of American cultural imperialism, the substance of American national identity and patriotic solidarity is itself being transformed by an entire generation's monomaniacal obsession with the acquisition of Hummers, Nikes, and iPods.[12] As Robert Reich among others has pointed out, the inauguration of the Bush Jr. administration's War on Terror was marked by a call on the nation's citizenry to contribute its share to the struggle, not, as in previous conflicts, by making sacrifices, but by girding its loins and marching to the shopping malls to help boost the economy.[13]

And while progressive activists have enjoyed mocking the political establishment for its flagrantly materialistic conception of civic courage, the "post-national" ideal of the Politically Correct is not as far removed from the consumer-culture ethos as its advocates may imagine. The development of a society in which individuals are entirely free to "construct" their multifaceted identities out of whatever cultural materials they happen to find in their attics or on their international travels has great appeal in principle. Yet in practice, many people may find their attics barren and the tourist shops crammed with "Hard Rock Café Fill-in-the-City's-Name" T-shirts. Shopping around for a cause or sub-culture that will tell them who they are and how they fit into the greater scheme of things, they may prove malleable material in the hands of xenophobic militias, abusive cults, or Christian fundamentalists. Alternatively, simply by remaining alienated and apathetic non-voters, they may leave the national political arena wide open to corruption by moneyed interests and manipulation by well-organized fanatics.[14]

In light of some of these radically universalistic and alienatingly postmodern alternatives, a liberal-democratic nationalism that links itself to other aspects of human identity without swallowing them up, that accommodates spheres of cultural and/or ethno-territorial autonomy without dissipating into thin air, that consciously and deliberately straddles the divide between the defense of/respect for borders and the commitment to humanity, does not look so bad. As Yael Tamir has argued, the ascriptive elements that play some role in all forms of national identity can and do give rise to nasty prejudices and abuses, but can also constrain members of the nation to accommodate internal diversity and tolerate dissenting opinions.[15] The fact that one cannot choose what family one is born into leads some people to make a virtue of necessity; they learn to coexist with, and even maintain affection for, people whose manners or opinions they find offensive. There is something to be said for that. In other words, nationalism need not merely be endured as a necessary evil. It can be shaped and cultivated as a source of emotional sustenance for otherwise abstract and impersonal values of pluralism and tolerance.

END NOTES

1 Isaiah Berlin, "Two Concepts of Liberty," in Berlin, *The Proper Study of Mankind* (London: Chatto & Windus, 1997). See also Michael Ignatieff, *Isaiah Berlin: A Life* (New York: Henry Holt, 1998), 225–228.

2 David A. Bell, *The Cult of the Nation in France: Inventing Nationalism, 1680–1800* (Cambridge, Mass.: Harvard University Press, 2001); Andrzej Walicki, *The Enlightenment and the Birth of Modern Nationhood: Polish Political Thought from Noble Republicanism to Tadeusz Kościuszko*, trans. Emma Harris (Notre Dame: University of Notre Dame Press, 1989). Anthony D. Smith distinguishes between "lateral" and "vertical" forms of ethnic community in *National Identity* (London: Penguin, 1991), ch. 3.

3 Andrew Vincent, *Nationalism and Particularity* (Cambridge: Cambridge University Press, 2002), ch. 1, esp. 24 and 32–34. Vincent argues that the idea of collective, popular exercise of an indivisible sovereignty requires a leap of faith into a metaphysical politics even more irrational and dangerous than the idea of monarchic sovereignty. See also Bernard Yack, "The Myth of the Civic Nation," in Ronald Beiner, ed., *Theorizing Nationalism* (Albany: State University of New York Press, 1999), esp. 109–111.

4 Niyazi Berkes, *The Development of Secularism in Turkey* (Montreal: McGill University Press, 1964), ch. 16; Bernard Lewis, *The Emergence of Modern Turkey* (London: Oxford University Press, 1961), 101–102, 264–279.

5 James Cronin has pointed out that the more states lose their economic and social decision-making power to the contemporary forces of globalization, the more societies around the world are likely to latch on to a defensive form of identity politics as a form of compensation. James Cronin, *The World the Cold War Made: Order, Chaos and the Return of History* (New York: Routledge, 1996), ch. 8.

6 See Vincent, *Nationalism and Particularity*, 60–61.

7 For critical analyses of the late Habsburg empire's handling of its nationalities problems, see Steven Beller, *Francis Joseph* (London: Longman, 1996) and Oscar Jaszi's classic, *The Dissolution of the Habsburg Monarchy* (Chicago: University of Chicago Press, 1929). Jaszi praises Austria's pre-1914 progress towards equality among its nationalities, but sees the Hungarian hegemony in the east as dooming the Habsburg monarchy's prospects for interethnic harmony. Ibid., pp. 295–297, ch. 3, and *passim*. See also Aviel Roshwald, "Ethnicity and Democracy in Europe's Multinational Empires, 1848–1918," in André Gerrits and Dirk Jan Wolffram, eds., *Political Democracy and Ethnic Diversity in Modern European History* (Stanford: Stanford University Press, 2005). For a more optimistic view of the Habsburg empire's prospects had it not been for the outbreak of the First World War, see Alan Sked, *The Decline and Fall of the Habsburg Empire, 1815–1918* (London: Longman, 1989).

8 See Ian Reifowitz, *Imagining an Austrian Nation: Joseph Samuel Bloch and the Search for a Multiethnic Austrian Identity, 1846–1919* (Boulder: East European Monographs, 2003).

9 On the role of Muslim emigration to the West in the "deterritorialisation" of radical Islamist fundamentalism, see Olivier Roy, *Globalized Islam: The Search for a New Ummah* (New York: Columbia University Press, 2004).

10 Given the preoccupation of Osama Bin Laden and his ilk with the restoration of the Caliphate and the interests of the Islamic *ummah* (the universal

community of Muslims), I disagree with the common characterization of the Islamist terror networks as expressions of a Muslim nationalism (which, to my mind, would connote a more bounded set of objectives informed by the ideal of political self-determination for an ethnographically and/or territorially delimited group of people). See, for example, David R. Mandel, "Evil and the Instigation of Violence," *Analyses of Social Issues and Public Policy*, vol. 2, no. 1 (December 2002), 101–108. Of course, Islamic fundamentalism has fused with elements of various nationalist movements, such as those of the Chechens and Palestinians. My point is that the pan-Islamic ideal in and of itself is markedly different from nationalism.

11 Robert Wright, *Virtual Sovereignty: Nationalism, Culture and the Canadian Question* (Toronto: Canadian Scholars' Press, 2004), chapter 6 ("L'État, c'est Molson").

12 I am listening to my iTunes while writing this.

13 Robert Reich, "How Did Spending Become Our Patriotic Duty?" *The Washington Post*, 23 September 2001. See also Anatol Lieven, *America Right or Wrong: An Anatomy of American Nationalism* (New York: Oxford University Press, 2004), 24 and ch. 2.

14 On right-wing American backlashes against globalized popular culture, see Lieven, *America*, chs. 3–4. Lieven also argues that nationalism can play an important role in facilitating and sustaining modernization and democratization. Ibid., 208–216.

15 Yael Tamir, *Liberal Nationalism* (Princeton: Princeton University Press, 1993), 90.

Bibliography

Acuña, Rodolfo, *Occupied America: A History of Chicanos*, 4th edn (New York: Longman, 2000).

Ageron, Charles-Robert, *France coloniale ou parti colonial?* (Paris: Presses Universitaires de France, 1978).

Agha, Hussein and Malley, Robert, "Camp David: The Tragedy of Errors," *New York Review of Books*, vol. 48, no. 13 (9 August 2001).

Ahmad, Feroz, *The Making of Modern Turkey* (London: Routledge, 1993).

Ajami, Fouad, *The Arab Predicament: Arab Political Thought and Practice Since 1967* (Cambridge: Cambridge University Press, 1981).

Akenson, Donald Harman, *God's Peoples: Covenant and Land in South Africa, Israel and Ulster* (Ithaca: Cornell University Press, 1992).

Alings, Reinhard, *Monument und Nation: Das Bild vom Nationalstaat im Medium Denkmal – zum Verhältnis von Nation und Staat im deutschen Kaiserreich, 1871–1918* (Berlin: Walter de Gruyter, 1996).

Alpher, Yossi (Joseph), "Oslo's Lessons for Peacemaking," *The Jerusalem Report*, 23 September 2002, 54.

Ambrosius, Lloyd E., *Woodrow Wilson and the American Diplomatic Tradition: The Treaty Fight in Perspective* (Cambridge: Cambridge University Press, 1987).

Wilsonian Statecraft: Theory and Practice of Liberal Internationalism during World War I (Wilmington, Del.: Scholarly Resources, 1991).

"Dilemmas of National Self-Determination: Woodrow Wilson's Legacy," in Christian Baechler and Carole Fink, eds., *The Establishment of European Frontiers after the Two World Wars* (Berlin: Peter Lang, 1996).

Amr, Wafa, "Israeli Police Storm Holy Site after Jews Stoned," *Irish Examiner*, 30 July 2001.

Anctil, Pierre, "La trajectoire interculturelle du Québec: la société distincte vue à travers le prisme de l'immigration," in André Lapierre, Patricia Smart, and Pierre Savard, eds., *Language, Culture and Values in Canada at the Dawn of the 21st Century/Langues, cultures et valeurs au Canada à l'aube du XXIe siècle* (Dalhousie and Ottawa: International Council for Canadian Studies/ Conseil international d'études canadiennes and Ottawa: Carleton University Press, 1996).

Anderson, Benedict, *Imagined Communities: Reflections on the Origin and Spread of Nationalism*, 2nd edn. (London: Verso, 1991).

Andrew, Christopher, and Kanya-Forstner, A. S., *The Climax of French Imperial Exapnsion, 1914–1924* (Stanford: Stanford University Press, 1981).

Applegate, Celia, *A Nation of Provincials: The German Idea of Heimat* (Berkeley: University of California Press, 1990).

Arai, Masami, *Turkish Nationalism in the Young Turk Era* (Leiden: Brill, 1992).

Argetsinger, Amy, "In Arizona, 'Minutemen' Start Border Patrols," *The Washington Post*, 5 April 2005.

Ari, Waskar T., "Race and Subaltern Nationalism: AMP Activist-Intellectuals in Bolivia, 1921–1964" (Ph.D. dissertation, Georgetown University, 2004).

Armstrong, John A., *Nations Before Nationalism* (Chapel Hill: University of North Carolina Press, 1982).

Armstrong, Karen, *Jerusalem: One City, Three Faiths* (New York: HarperCollins, 1996).

Aron, Raymond, *L'Algérie et la République* (Paris: Plon, 1958).

Asad, Talal, "Religion, Nation-State, Secularism," in van der Veer and Lehmann, eds., *Nation and Religion*.

Ashcroft, John, May 1999 Commencement Address at Bob Jones University, posted on the website of *The Ethical Spectacle*, February 2001, http://www.spectacle.org/0201/ashcroft.html.

Attias, Jean-Christophe and Benbassa, Esther, *Israel, the Impossible Land*, trans. Susan Emanuel (Stanford: Stanford University Press, 2003).

Audoin-Rouzeau, Stéphane, *Men at War, 1914–1918: National Sentiment and Trench Journalism in France during the First World War*, trans. Helen McPhail (Oxford: Berg, 1992).

Audoin-Rouzeau, Stéphane and Becker, Annette, *14–18: Understanding the Great War*, trans. Catherine Temerson (New York: Hill and Wang/Farrar, Straus and Giroux, 2002).

Auer, Stefan, *Liberal Nationalism in Central Europe* (London: RoutledgeCurzon, 2004).

Bahar, Dan, "The Western Wall Tunnels," in Geva, ed., *Ancient Jerusalem Revealed*.

Bailyn, Bernard, *The Ideological Origins of the American Revolution* (Cambridge, Mass.: Harvard University Press, 1967).

Baker, Ray Stannard and Dodd, William E., eds., *The Public Papers of Woodrow Wilson. The New Democracy: Presidential Messages, Addresses, and Other Papers (1913–1917)*, vol. 1 (New York: Harper & Brothers, 1926).

Ball, Bill, "The Most Famous Rifle of Texas! Recreating Colonel Crockett's Rifle at the Battle of the Alamo," *Guns Magazine*, January 2004.

Balz, Dan, "Bush Statement on Mideast Reflects Tension in GOP: President Seeks to Bridge Foreign Policy Establishment and Rising Number of Pro-Israel Conservatives," *The Washington Post*, 7 April 2002.

Banac, Ivo, *The National Question in Yugoslavia: Origins, History, Politics* (Ithaca and London: Cornell University Press, 1984).

Barbour, Stephen and Carmichael, Cathie, eds., *Language and Nationalism in Europe* (Oxford: Oxford University Press, 2001).

Barclay, John M. G., *Jews in the Mediterranean Diaspora: From Alexander to Trajan (323 BCE–117 CE)* (Berkeley: University of California Press, 1996).

Barkay, Gabriel, "Excavations at Ketef Hinnom in Jerusalem," in Geva, ed., *Ancient Jerusalem Revealed*.

Barkey, Karen, "Thinking about Consequences of Empire," in Karen Barkey and Mark von Hagen, eds., *After Empire – Multiethnic Societies and Nation-Building: The Soviet Union and the Russian, Ottoman, and Habsburg Empires* (Boulder: Westview Press, 1997).

Barlow, George W., *The Cichlid Fishes: Nature's Grand Experiment in Evolution* (New York: Perseus, 2000).

Barrett, James R. and Roediger, David, "Inbetween Peoples: Race, Nationality and the 'New Immigrant' Working Class," *Journal of American Ethnic History*, vol. 16, no. 3 (Spring 1997), 3–44.

Barth, Fredrik, "Introduction," in Fredrik Barth, ed., *Ethnic Groups and Boundaries: The Social Organization of Culture Difference* (1969; Prospect Heights, Ill.: Waveland Press, 1998).

Barton, Allen H., *et al.*, eds., *Opinion-Making Elites in Yugoslavia* (New York: Praeger, 1973).

Bartov, Omer, "Defining Enemies, Making Victims: Germans, Jews, and the Holocaust," *American Historical Review*, vol. 103, no. 3 (June 1998), 771–816.

Bass, Gary Jonathan, *Stay the Hand of Vengeance: The Politics of War Crimes Tribunals* (Princeton: Princeton University Press, 2000).

Bastéa, Eleni, *The Creation of Modern Athens: Planning the Myth* (Cambridge: Cambridge University Press, 2000).

Bayly, C. A., *The Birth of the Modern World, 1780–1914: Global Connections and Comparisons* (Oxford: Blackwell, 2004).

Bazant, Jan, *A Concise History of Mexico from Hidalgo to Cardenas: 1805–1940* (Cambridge: Cambridge University Press, 1977).

Beaune, Colette, *The Birth of an Ideology: Myths and Symbols of Nation in Late-Medieval France* (Berkeley: University of California Press, 1991).

Becker, Carl L., *The Heavenly City of the Eighteenth-Century Philosophers* (New Haven: Yale University Press, 1932).

Beigbeder, Yves, *Judging War Criminals: The Politics of International Justice* (London: Macmillan, 1999).

Beilin, Yossi, *The Path to Geneva: The Quest for a Permanent Agreement, 1996–2004* (New York: RDV Books/Akashic Books, 2004).

Beiner, Ronald, ed., *Theorizing Nationalism* (Albany: State University of New York Press, 1999).

Beisner, Robert L., *Twelve against Empire: The Anti-Imperialists, 1898–1900* (1968; Chicago: University of Chicago Press, 1985).

Belfer, Ella, *Zehut kefulah: Al ha-metach bein artsiut le-ruchaniut ba-olam ha-yehudi* [A Split Identity: The Conflict between the Sacred and the Secular in the Jewish World] (Ramat-Gan, Israel: Bar-Ilan University, 2004).

Bell, David A., *The Cult of the Nation in France: Inventing Nationalism, 1680–1800* (Cambridge, Mass.: Harvard University Press, 2001).

Bellah, Robert N., *Beyond Belief: Essays on Religion in a Post-Traditional World* (New York: Harper & Row, 1970).

The Broken Covenant: American Civil Religion in Time of Trial (New York: The Seabury Press, 1975).

"Religion and the Legitimation of the American Republic," in Robert N. Bellah and Phillip E. Hammond, *Varieties of Civil Religion* (San Francisco: Harper & Row, 1980).

Bellamy, Alex J., *The Formation of Croatian National Identity: A Centuries-Old Dream?* (Manchester: Manchester University Press, 2003).

Beller, Steven, *Theodor Herzl* (New York: Grove Weidenfeld, 1991).

Francis Joseph (London: Longman, 1996).

Ben-Dov, Meir, *In the Shadow of the Temple: The Discovery of Ancient Jerusalem*, trans. Ina Friedman (New York: Harper & Row, 1985).

Ben-Sasson, H. H., "The Middle Ages," in Ben-Sasson *et al.*, eds., *History of the Jewish People.*

Ben-Sasson, H. H. *et al.*, eds., *A History of the Jewish People* (Cambridge, Mass.: Harvard University Press, 1976).

Benson, Nettie Lee, "Territorial Integrity in Mexican Politics, 1821–1833," in O. Rodriguez, ed., *The Independence of Mexico.*

Benton, Barbara, *Ellis Island: A Pictorial History* (New York: Facts on File Publications, 1985).

Benvenisti, Meron, *Conflicts and Contradictions* (New York: Villard Books, 1986).

City of Stone: The Hidden History of Jerusalem, trans. Maxine Kaufman Nunn (Berkeley: University of California Press, 1996).

Ben-Yehuda, Nachman, *The Masada Myth: Collective Memory and Mythmaking in Israel* (Madison: University of Wisconsin Press, 1995).

Bercovitch, Sacvan, *The Puritan Origins of the American Self* (New Haven: Yale University Press, 1975).

Berger, Suzanne, "French Democracy without Borders?" MIT Industrial Performance Center Working Paper 01-009, http://web.mit.edu/ipc/www/pubs/articles/01-009.pdf.

Berkes, Niyazi, *The Development of Secularism in Turkey* (Montreal: McGill University Press, 1964).

Berkovitz, Shmuel, *The Temple Mount and the Western Wall in Israeli Law* (Jerusalem: The Jerusalem Institute for Israel Studies and the Teddy Kollek Center for Jerusalem Studies, 2001).

Berkowitz, Michael, *Zionist Culture and West European Jewry before the First World War* (Cambridge: Cambridge University Press, 1993).

Berlin, Andrea M. and Overman, J. Andrew, eds., *The First Jewish Revolt: Archaeology, History, and Ideology* (London: Routledge, 2002).

Berlin, Isaiah, *Four Essays on Liberty* (London: Oxford University Press, 1969).
  The Crooked Timber of Humanity: Chapters in the History of Ideas, ed. Henry
  Hardy (New York: Random House, 1990).
  The Proper Study of Mankind (London: Chatto & Windus, 1997).
Betlyon, John Wilson, *The Coinage and Mints of Phoenicia: The Pre-Alexandrine
  Period* (Chico, Calif.: Scholars Press, 1980; Harvard Semitic Monographs
  No. 26).
Betts, Raymond, *Assimilation and Association in French Colonial Theory,
  1890–1914* (New York: Columbia University Press, 1961).
Billig, Michael, *Banal Nationalism* (London: Sage Publications, 1995), 55–59.
Birnbaum, Pierre, *The Idea of France*, trans. M. B. DeBevoise (1998; New York:
  Hill and Wang, 2001).
Blanning, T. C. W., *The Origins of the French Revolutionary Wars* (London:
  Longman, 1986).
Blumenthal, David R., "God at the Center: Selected Meditations on Jewish
  Spirituality," *Studies in Formative Spirituality*, vol. 19, no. 3 (November
  1988), 267–281.
Blumenthal, Max, "Onward Christian Soldiers," *Salon.com*, 15 April 2003.
Blumenthal, Sidney, "Christian Soldiers," *The New Yorker*, 18 July 1994, 37.
Bodnar, John, *Remaking America: Public Memory, Commemoration, and
  Patriotism in the Twentieth Century* (Princeton: Princeton University Press,
  1992).
Bohlman, Philip V., "The Remembrance of Things Past: Music, Race, and the
  End of History in Modern Europe," in Radano and Bohlman, eds., *Music
  and the Racial Imagination*.
Bollens, Scott A., "City and Soul: Sarajevo, Johannesburg, Jerusalem, Nicosia,"
  CITY: Analysis of Urban Trends, Culture, Theory, Policy, Action, vol. 5, no. 2
  (July 2001), 169–187.
Bono, Giovanna, "NATO's War over Kosovo: The Debates, Dynamics and
  Consequences," in Michael C. Davis *et al.*, eds., *International Intervention
  in the Post-Cold War World: Moral Responsibility and Power Politics*
  (Armonk, N.Y.: M. E. Sharpe, 2004).
Borah, William E., Speech delivered on the floor of the US Senate, 19 November
  1919, *Congressional Record*, vol. 58, part 9 (66th Congress, First Session,
  14–19 November 1919) (Washington: Government Printing Office, 1919),
  8781–8784.
Boralevi, Lea Campos, "Classical Foundational Myths of European
  Republicanism: The Jewish Commonwealth," in Martin van Gelderen and
  Quentin Skinner, eds., *Republicanism: A Shared European Heritage,* vol. 1:
  Republicanism and Constitutionalism in Early Modern Europe (Cambridge:
  Cambridge University Press, 2002).
Bork, Robert H., *The Tempting of America: The Political Seduction of the Law*
  (New York: The Free Press, 1990).
Bost, Suzanne, "Women and Chile at the Alamo: Feeding US Colonial
  Mythology," *Nepantla: Views from South*, vol. 4, no. 3 (2003), 493–522.

Brandenberger, David, *National Bolshevism: Stalinist Mass Culture and the Formation of Modern Russian National Identity, 1931–1936* (Cambridge, Mass.: Harvard University Press, 2002).

Brear, Holly Beachley, *Inherit the Alamo: Myth and Ritual at an American Shrine* (Austin: University of Texas Press, 1995).

"The Alamo's Selected Past," *Cultural Resource Management*, vol. 22, no. 8 (1999), 9–11.

"We Run the Alamo, and You Don't: Alamo Battles of Ethnicity and Gender," in Brundage, ed., *Where these Memories Grow,* 2000.

Bredin, Jean-Denis, *The Affair: The Case of Alfred Dreyfus*, trans. Jeffrey Mehlman (New York: George Braziller, 1986).

Breuilly, John, *Nationalism and the State*, 2nd edn (Chicago: University of Chicago Press, 1994).

Broder, David, "Dole Backs Official Language: English Is Needed to Unify Nation, Presidential Hopeful Says," *The Washington Post,* 5 September 1995.

Bromke, Adam, *Poland's Politics: Idealism vs. Realism* (Cambridge, Mass.: Harvard University Press, 1967).

Brown, Bartram S., "Unilateralism, Multilateralism, and the International Criminal Court," in Patrick and Forman, eds., *Multilateralism.*

Brown, L. Carl, *Religion and State: The Muslim Approach to Politics* (New York: Columbia University Press, 2000).

Brubaker, Rogers, *Citizenship and Nationhood in France and Germany* (Cambridge, Mass.: Harvard University Press, 1992).

Nationalism Reframed: Nationhood and the National Question in the New Europe (Cambridge: Cambridge University Press, 1996).

Brundage, W. Fitzhugh, ed., *Where these Memories Grow: History, Memory and Southern Identity* (Chapel Hill: University of North Carolina Press, 2000).

Brunschwig, Henri, *Mythes et réalités de l'impérialisme colonial français, 1871–1914* (Paris: Librairie Armand Colin, 1960).

Bryan, Dominic, "Drumcree and 'The Right to March': Orangeism, Ritual and Politics in Northern Ireland," in Fraser, ed., *Irish Parading Tradition,* 2000.

Orange Parades: The Politics of Ritual, Tradition and Control (London: Pluto Press, 2000).

Bryan, Dominic, Fraser, T. G., and Dunn, Seamus, *Political Rituals: Loyalist Parades in Portadown* (Coleraine, Northern Ireland: Centre for the Study of Conflict, University of Ulster, 1995).

Buchanan, Patrick J., *A Republic, Not an Empire: Reclaiming America's Destiny* (Washington, D.C.: Regnery Publishing, 1999).

Bucur, Maria and Wingfield, Nancy M., eds., *Staging the Past: The Politics of Commemoration in Habsburg Central Europe, 1848 to the Present* (West Lafayette, Ind.: Purdue University Press, 2001).

Burke, Edmund, *Reflections on the Revolution in France* (1790; New York: Penguin, 1968).

Burkhardt, Johannes, "The Summitless Pyramid: War Aims and Peace Compromises among Europe's Universalist Powers," in Klaus Bussmann and Heinz Schilling, eds., *1648: War and Peace in Europe*, vol. 1: *Politics, Religion, Law and Society*, companion publication to the 26th European Council Exhibition "1648 – War and Peace in Europe" (Veranstaltungsgesellschaft 350 Jahre Westfälischer Friede mbH: Osnabrück/Münster, 1998).

Burrin, Philippe, "Vichy," in Nora, ed., *Les Lieux*, vol. III, part 1.

Burrows, Matthew, "'Mission Civilisatrice': French Cultural Policy in the Middle East, 1860–1914," *Historical Journal*, vol. 29, no. 1 (March 1986), 109–135.

Burt, Robert A., *The Constitution in Conflict* (Cambridge, Mass.: Harvard University Press, 1992).

Bush, Geoge W., "State of the Union Address," 29 January 2002, http://www.whitehouse.gov/news/releases/2002/01/20020129-11.html.

"Second Inaugural Address," 20 January 2005, http://www.cnn.com/2005/ALLPOLITICS/01/20/bush.transcript.

Calinescu, Matei, "The 1927 Generation in Romania: Friendships and Ideological Choices (Mihail Sebastian, Mircea Eliade, Nae Ionescu, Eugène Ionesco, E. M. Cioran)," *East European Politics and Societies*, vol. 15, no. 3 (2002), 649–677.

Calleo, David P., *Rethinking Europe's Future* (Princeton: A Century Foundation Book/Princeton University Press, 2003 edn).

Campbell, Edward F., Jr., "A Land Divided: Judah and Israel from the Death of Solomon to the Fall of Samaria," in Michael Coogan, ed., *The Oxford History of the Biblical World* (New York: Oxford University Press, 1998), 309.

Campolo, Tony, "The Ideological Roots of Christian Zionism," *Tikkun*, vol. 20, no. 1 (January/February 2005), 19–22.

Cannadine, David, "The Context, Performance and Meaning of Ritual: The British Monarchy and the 'Invention of Tradition', c. 1820–1977," in Hobsbawm and Ranger, eds., *Invention of Tradition*, 1983.

Ornamentalism: How the British Saw their Empire (Oxford: Oxford University Press, 2001).

Čapek, Karel, *Talks with T. G. Masaryk*, trans. Dora Round, ed. Michael Henry Heim (North Haven, Conn.: Catbird Press, 1995).

Caratini, Roger, *Jeanne d'Arc: De Domrémy à Orléans et du bûcher à la légende* (Paris: l'Archipel, 1999).

Carrick, Robert, "Ecological Significance of Territory in the Australian Magpie, *Gymnorhina tibicen*," in Allen W. Stokes, ed., *Territory*, Benchmark Papers in Animal Behavior, vol. 11 (Stroudsburg, Penn.: Dowden, Hutchinson & Ross, 1974).

Cartwright, Gary, "Divine Secrets of the Alamo Sisterhood," *Texas Monthly*, vol. 32, no. 5 (2004), 62–68.

Cavalli-Sforza, Luigi Luca, *Genes, Peoples, and Languages* (Berkeley: University of California Press, 2000).

Chatterjee, Partha, *The Nation and its Fragments: Colonial and Postcolonial Histories* (Princeton: Princeton University Press, 1993).

Cherny, Andrei, "Sept. 11, 2002: A Time to Speak Up," *The Washington Post*, 31 August 2002, op. ed. page.

Churchill, Winston S., *A History of the English-Speaking Peoples*, 5 vols. (New York: Dodd, Mead & Co., 1956).

Cicero, *On the Laws*, in *Cicero, On the Commonwealth and On the Laws*, ed. James E. G. Zetzel (Cambridge: Cambridge University Press, 1999).

Clark, J. C. D., *The Language of Liberty, 1660–1832: Political Discourse and Social Dynamics in the Anglo-American World* (Cambridge: Cambridge University Press, 1994).

Cleveland, William, *The Making of an Arab Nationalist: Ottomanism and Arabism in the Life and Thought of Satiʿ al-Husri* (Princeton: Princeton University Press, 1971).

Cohen, Charles L., review of Lambert, *Founding Fathers* in *American Historical Review*, vol. 109, no. 1 (2004), 178–179.

Cohen, Edward E., *The Athenian Nation* (Princeton: Princeton University Press, 2000).

Cohen, Lenard, "The Social Background and Recruitment of Yugoslav Political Elites, 1918–48," in Barton *et al.*, eds., *Opinion-Making Elites in Yugoslavia*.

Cohen, Paul, *China Unbound: Evolving Perspectives on the Chinese Past* (London: RoutledgeCurzon, 2003).

Cohen, Roger, *Hearts Grown Brutal: Sagas of Sarajevo* (New York: Random House, 1998).

Coleman, John E., "Ancient Greek Ethnocentrism," in J. Coleman and C. Walz, *Greeks and Barbarians; Essays on the Interactions between Greeks and Non-Greeks in Antiquity and the Consequences for Eurocentrism*, Occasional Publications of the Department of Near Eastern Studies and Jewish Studies, Cornell University, No. 4 (Bethesda, Md.: Capital Decisions Limited, 1997), 175–220.

Colley, Linda, *Britons: Forging the Nation 1707–1837* (New Haven: Yale University Press, 1992).

Collins, David, S. J., "Latin Lives of the Saints in Germany, 1470–1520: Humanists, History, and Sainthood" (Ph.D. diss., Northwestern University, 2004).

Comerford, R. V. "Nation, Nationalism, and the Irish Language," in Thomas E. Hachey and Lawrence J. McCaffrey, eds., *Perspectives on Irish Nationalism* (Lexington: University Press of Kentucky, 1989).

Confino, Alon, *The Nation as a Local Metaphor: Württemberg, Imperial Germany, and National Memory, 1871–1918* (Chapel Hill: University of North Carolina Press, 1997).

Conklin, Alice, *Mission to Civilize: The Republican Idea of Empire in France & West Africa, 1895–1930* (Stanford: Stanford University Press, 2000).

Connor, Walker, *The National Question in Marxist-Leninist Theory and Strategy* (Princeton: Princeton University Press, 1984).

    Ethnonationalism: The Quest for Understanding (Princeton: Princeton University Press, 1994).

Contamine, Philippe, "Mourir pour la patrie: Xe–XXe siècle," in Nora, ed., *Les Lieux*, vol. 11, part 3.

Cook, Ramsay, "Canada: A Post-Nationalist Nation?" in Sima Godfrey and Frank Unger, eds., *The Shifting Foundations of Modern Nation-States: Realignments of Belonging* (Toronto: University of Toronto Press, 2004).

Cooper, Duff, *Talleyrand* (1932; New York: Fromm, 1986).

Cooper, John Milton, Jr., *The Warrior and the Priest: Woodrow Wilson and Theodore Roosevelt* (Cambridge, Mass.: Harvard University Press, 1983).

Costigliola, Frank, *Awkward Dominion: American Political, Economic, and Cultural Relations with Europe, 1919–1933* (Ithaca: Cornell University Press, 1984).

Craith, Máiréad Nic, *Culture and Identity Politics in Northern Ireland* (Basingstoke: Palgrave Macmillan, 2003).

Crisp, James E., *Sleuthing the Alamo: Davy Crockett's Last Stand and Other Mysteries* (New York: Oxford University Press, 2005).

Cronin, James, *The World the Cold War Made: Order, Chaos and the Return of History* (New York: Routledge, 1996).

Crook, J. H., "The Adaptive Significance of Avian Social Organizations," in Allen W. Stokes, ed., *Territory*, Benchmark Papers in Animal Behavior, vol. 11 (Stroudsburg, Penn.: Dowden, Hutchinson & Ross, 1974).

Crooke, Elizabeth, *Politics, Archaeology and the Creation of a National Museum in Ireland: An Expression of National Life* (Dublin: Irish Academic Press, 2000).

Crowe, Eyre, "Memorandum on the Present State of British Relations with France and Germany," 1 January 1907, FO 371/257, in G. P. Gooch and Harold Temperley, eds., *British Documents on the Origins of the War, 1898–1914*, vol. III: *The Testing of the Entente, 1904–6* (London: His Majesty's Stationery Office, 1928).

Crunden, Robert M., *Ministers of Reform: The Progressives' Achievement in American Civilization, 1889–1920* (New York: Basic Books, 1982).

Curtius, Ernst Robert, *Essai sur la France*, trans. Jacques Benoist-Méchin (original German edn, 1931; Paris: Bernard Grasset, 1941).

Dalberg-Acton, John Emerich Edward (Lord Acton), "Nationality" (essay first published in 1862) in Dalberg-Acton, *The History of Freedom and other Essays* (London: Macmillan, 1919).

Daniels, Stephen, "The Political Iconography of Woodland in Later Georgian England," in Denis Cosgrove and Stephen Daniels, eds., *The Iconography of Landscape: Essays on the Symbolic Representation, Design and Use of Past Environments* (Cambridge: Cambridge University Press, 1988).

  Fields of Vision: Landscape Imagery and National Identity in England and the United States (Princeton: Princeton University Press, 1993).

Darwin, Charles, *Voyage of the Beagle* (abridged edn of *Journal of Researches* [London, 1839]) (London: Penguin, 1989).

Davidson, Basil, *The Black Man's Burden: Africa and the Curse of the Nation-State* (New York: Random House, 1992).

Dawisha, Adeed, *Arab Nationalism in the Twentieth Century: From Triumph to Despair* (Princeton: Princeton University Press, 2003).

Dawkins, Richard, *The Ancestor's Tale: A Pilgrimage to the Dawn of Evolution* (New York: Houghton Mifflin, 2004).

Dawn, Ernest, "The Origins of Arab Nationalism," in Khalidi *et al.*, *Origins of Arab Nationalism* (New York: Columbia University Press, 1991).

De Crèvecoeur, J. Hector St. John, *Letters From an American Farmer and Sketches of Eighteenth-Century America* (1782; New York: Penguin, 1981).

De Gaulle, Charles, *Mémoires de Guerre*, vol. 1: *L'Appel, 1940–1942* (Paris: Plon, 1954).

   Memoirs of Hope: Renewal and Endeavor, trans. Terence Kilmartin (New York: Simon and Schuster, 1971).

De la Peña, José Enrique, *With Santa Anna in Texas: A Personal Narrative of the Revolution*, trans. and ed. Carmen Perry (College Station: Texas A&M University Press, 1975).

De Puymège, Gérard, "Le Soldat Chauvin," in Nora, ed., *Les Lieux*, vol. 11, part 3.

De Tocqueville, Alexis, *Democracy in America*, trans. George Lawrence (1835–40; Garden City, N.Y.: Doubleday, 1969).

Deák, István, *Beyond Nationalism: A Social and Political History of the Habsburg Officer Corps, 1848–1918* (New York: Oxford University Press, 1990).

Demosthenes, *Demosthenes, with an English Translation*, vol. 1, trans. J. H. Vince (Cambridge, Mass: Harvard University Press, 1935).

D'Encausse, Hélène Carrère, *The Great Challenge: Nationalities and the Bolshevik State, 1917–1930* (New York: Holmes and Meier, 1992).

Denitch, Bogdan, *Ethnic Nationalism: The Tragic Death of Yugoslavia* (Minneapolis: University of Minnesota Press, 1994).

Deutsch, Karl, *Nationalism and Social Communication. An Inquiry into the Foundations of Nationality* (Cambridge, Mass.: MIT Press, 1966).

Donnelly, Thomas (principal author), Kagan, Donald, and Schmitt, G., "Rebuilding America's Defenses: Strategy, Forces and Resources for a New Century," A Report for the Project for a New American Century, September 2000, http://www.newamericancentury.org/RebuildingAmericas Defenses.pdf.

Dragnich, Alex N., *The First Yugoslavia. Search for a Viable Political System* (Stanford: Hoover Institution Press, 1983).

   "The Anatomy of a Myth: Serbian Hegemony," *Slavic Review*, vol. 50, no. 3 (1991), 659–662.

Drakulić, Slavenka, *The Balkan Express: Fragments from the Other Side of War* (New York: Norton, 1993).

Duara, Prasenjit, *Rescuing History from the Nation: Questioning Narratives of Modern China* (Chicago: University of Chicago Press, 1995).

Dubois, Claude-Gilbert, "Rôle historique et fonction prophétique de Jeanne d'Arc dans *Les merveilleuses Victoires des femmes* de Guillaume Postel (1553)," in Jean Maurice et Daniel Couty, eds., *Images de Jeanne d'Arc* (Paris: Presses Universitaires de France, 2000).

Duroselle, Jean-Baptiste, *L'Abîme: 1939–1945* (Paris: Imprimerie Nationale, 1982).

Dyer, Thomas G., *Theodore Roosevelt and the Idea of Race* (Baton Rouge: Louisiana State University Press, 1980).

Eden, Devorah and Kalekin-Fishman, Devorah, "Multi-Cultural Education in Israel as a Fulfillment of National Ethos and Political Policy," paper posted on the University of Haifa's Faculty of Education website, http://construct.haifa.ac.il/~almogt/Israel%20Political%20Pokicy.htm.

Edwards, Ruth Dudley, *The Faithful Tribe: An Intimate Portrait of the Loyal Institutions* (London: HarperCollins, 1999).

Ehrlich, Paul R., *Human Natures: Genes, Cultures, and the Human Prospect* (Washington, D.C. and Covelo, Calif.: Island Press/Shearwater Books, 2000).

Elazar, Daniel J., "Covenant as the Basis of the Jewish Political Tradition," in Daniel J. Elazar, ed., *Kinship and Consent: The Jewish Political Tradition and its Contemporary Uses*, 2nd edn (New Brunswick, N.J.: Transaction, 1997).

Elazar, Daniel J., "Parent Control and Educational Choice: Learning from the Israeli Experience," Jerusalem Center for Public Affairs, *Daniel Elazar Papers Index*, http://www.jcpa.org/dje/articles2/parentcontrol.htm.

Eliade, Mircea, *The Myth of the Eternal Return: Or, Cosmos and History* (Princeton: Princeton University Press, 1954).

Elliott, Kimberly Ann and Hufbauer, Gary Clyde, "Ambivalent Multilateralism and the Emerging Backlash: The IMF and WTO," in Patrick and Forman, *Multilateralism*.

Etkin, William, "Co-operation and Competition in Social Behavior," in William Etkin, ed., *Social Behavior and Organization among Vertebrates* (Chicago: University of Chicago Press, 1964).

Falk, Richard, *The Declining World Order: America's Imperial Geopolitics* (New York: Routledge, 2004).

Farber, Daniel, *Lincoln's Constitution* (Chicago: The University of Chicago Press, 2003).

Favez, Jean Claude, *The Red Cross and the Holocaust*, edited and translated from the French by John and Beryl Fletcher (Cambridge: Cambridge University Press, 1999).

Fehrenbach, T. R., *Lone Star: A History of Texas and the Texans* (1968; New York: Collier, 1980).

Ferguson, Niall, *Empire: The Rise and Demise of the British World Order and the Lessons for Global Power* (New York: Basic Books, 2002).

Ferguson, Robert A., "The Dialectic of Liberty: Law and Religion in Anglo-American Culture," *Modern Intellectual History*, vol. 1, no. 1 (2004), 27–54.

Fink, Carole, "The League of Nations and the Minorities Question," *World Affairs*, vol. 157, no. 4 (1995), 197–205.

   Defending the Rights of Others: The Great Powers, the Jews, and International Minority Protection, 1878–1938 (Cambridge: Cambridge University Press, 2004).

Finkelstein, Israel and Silberman, Neil Asher, *The Bible Unearthed: Archaeology's New Vision of Ancient Israel and the Origins of its Sacred Texts* (New York: Free Press, 2001).

Finley, M. I., *The Use and Abuse of History* (1971; 1975; London: Penguin, 1990).

Finney, Patrick B., " 'An Evil for All Concerned': Great Britain and Minority Protection after 1919," *Journal of Contemporary History*, vol. 30, no. 3 (1995), 533–551.

Fishman, Joshua A., *Language and Nationalism: Two Integrative Essays* (Rowley, Mass.: Newbury House Publishers, 1972)

Fleras, Augie and Elliott, Jean Leonard, *Multiculturalism in Canada: The Challenge of Diversity* (Scarborough, Ont.: Nelson Canada, 1992).

Flores, Richard R., *Remembering the Alamo: Memory, Modernity, and the Master Symbol* (Austin: University of Texas Press, 2002).

Flynn, Gregory, "French Identity and Post-Cold War Europe," in Flynn, *Remaking the Hexagon.*

"Remaking the Hexagon," in Flynn, ed., *Remaking the Hexagon.*

Flynn, Gregory, ed., *Remaking the Hexagon: The New France in the New Europe* (Boulder: Westview Press, 1995).

Fountain, Alvin Marcus, II, *Roman Dmowski: Party, Tactics, Ideology 1895–1907* (Boulder: East European Monographs, 1980).

Fraser, T. G., ed., *The Irish Parading Tradition: Following the Drum* (Basingstoke: Macmillan and New York: St. Martin's Press, 2000).

Freeman, Simon, "Adams Calls on IRA to End Armed Struggle," (London) *Times Online*, 6 April 2005, http://www.timesonline.co.uk/article/0,,19809-1557645,00.html.

Friedland, Roger and Hecht, Richard, *To Rule Jerusalem* (Cambridge: Cambridge University Press, 1996).

Friedländer, Saul, "Die politischen Veränderungen der Kriegszeit und ihre Auswirkungen auf die Judenfrage," in Mosse, ed., *Deutsches Judentum.*

Fritzsche, Peter, "The Case of Modern Memory," *Journal of Modern History*, vol. 73, no. 1 (2001), 87–117.

Fukuyama, Francis, *The End of History and the Last Man* (New York: The Free Press, 1992).

"The Neoconservative Moment," *The National Interest*, no. 76 (Summer 2004), 57–68.

Fuller, J. G., *Troop Morale and Popular Culture in the British and Dominion Armies, 1914–1918* (Oxford: Oxford University Press, 1990).

Gabriel, Jürg Martin, "The Price of Political Uniqueness: Swiss Foreign Policy in a Changing World," in Gabriel and Fischer, eds., *Swiss Foreign Policy.*

Gabriel, Jürg Martin, and Fischer, Thomas, eds., *Swiss Foreign Policy, 1945–2002* (Basingstoke: Palgrave Macmillan, 2003).

Gaddis, John Lewis, *Strategies of Containment: A Critical Appraisal of Post-War American National Security Policy* (New York: Oxford University Press, 1982).

Gadgil, D. R., "The Protection of Minorities," in William F. Mackey and Albert Verdoort, eds., *The Multinational Society: Papers of the Ljubljana Seminar* (Rowley, Mass.: Newbury House Publishers, 1975).

Gagnon, V. P., Jr., *The Myth of Ethnic War: Serbia and Croatia in the 1990s* (Ithaca: Cornell University Press, 2004).

Garlicki, Andrzej, *Józef Piłsudski, 1867–1935*, edited, translated, and abridged by John Coutouvidis (Aldershot, UK: Scolar Press, 1995).

Garvin, Tom, *Mythical Thinking in Political Life: Reflections on Nationalism and Social Science* (Dublin: Maunsel & Co., 2001).

Geary, Patrick J., *The Myth of Nations: The Medieval Origins of Europe* (Princeton: Princeton University Press, 2002).

Geertz, Clifford, "The Integrative Revolution: Primordial Sentiments and Civil Politics in the New States," in Clifford Geertz, ed., *Old Societies and New States: The Quest for Modernity in Asia and Africa* (London: Collier Macmillan, 1963).

Gellner, Ernest, *Nations and Nationalism* (Ithaca: Cornell University Press, 1983).

"Do Nations Have Navels?" in Anthony D. Smith and Ernest Gellner, "The Nation: Real or Imagined?: The Warwick Debates on Nationalism," *Nations and Nationalism*, vol. 2, no. 3 (1996), 357–370.

Gelvin, James, *Divided Loyalties: Nationalism and Mass Politics in Syria at the Close of Empire* (Berkeley: University of California Press, 1998).

Geraci, Robert, "The Il'minskii System and the Controversy over non-Russian Teachers and Priests in the Middle Volga," in Catherine Evtuhov, Boris Gasparov, Alexander Ospovat, and Mark Von Hagen, eds., *Kazan, Moscow, St. Petersburg: Multiple Faces of the Russian Empire* (Moscow: O.G.I., 1997).

Gerson, Mark, *The Neoconservative Vision: From the Cold War to the Culture Wars* (Lanham, Md.: Madison Books, 1996).

Gerstle, Gary, *American Crucible: Race and Nation in the Twentieth Century* (Princeton: Princeton University Press, 2001).

Geva, Hillel, ed., *Ancient Jerusalem Revealed* (Jerusalem: Israel Exploration Society, 2000).

Jewish Quarter Excavations in the Old City of Jerusalem Conducted by Nahman Avigad, 1969–1982, vol. 1: Architecture and Stratigraphy, Areas A, W, and X-2: Final Report (Jerusalem: Israel Exploration Society/Institute of Archaeology, Hebrew University, 2000).

Gildea, Robert, *The Past in French History* (New Haven: Yale University Press, 1994).

Gillis, John R., ed., *Commemorations: The Politics of National Identity* (Princeton: Princeton University Press, 1994).

Girardet, Raoul, *L'Idée coloniale en France de 1871 à 1962* (Paris: La Table Ronde, 1972).

Gleason, Philip, *Speaking of Diversity: Language and Ethnicity in Twentieth-Century America* (Baltimore: The Johns Hopkins University Press, 1992).

Goldberger, Paul, "Down at the Mall: The New World War II Memorial Doesn't Rise to the Occasion," *The New Yorker*, 31 May 2004, 82–84.

Gonen, Rivka, *Contested Holiness: Jewish, Muslim and Christian Perspectives on the Temple Mount in Jerusalem* (Jersey City: Ktav, 2003).

Goodall, Jane, *The Chimpanzees of Gombe* (Cambridge, Mass.: Harvard University Press, 1986).

Gopnik, Blake, "Many Words, Little Eloquence," *The Washington Post*, 23 May 2004, pp. N1 and N6.

Gordon, Philip H., and Meunier, Sophie, *The French Challenge: Adapting to Globalization* (Washington, D.C.: Brookings Institution Press, 2001).

Gorenberg, Gershom, *The End of Days: Fundamentalism and the Struggle for the Temple Mount* (Oxford: Oxford University Press, 2000).

Gosewinkel, Dieter, *Einbürgern und Ausschliessen: die Nationalisierung der Staatsangehörigkeit vom Deutschen Bund bis zur Bundesrepublik Deutschland* (Göttingen: Vandenhoeck & Ruprecht, 2001).

Gottlieb, Gidon, *Nation against State* (New York: Council on Foreign Relations Press, 1993).

Greene, Graham, *The Quiet American* (London: William Heinemann, 1955).

Greenfeld, Liah, *Nationalism: Five Roads to Modernity* (Cambridge, Mass.: Harvard University Press, 1992).

Grosby, Steven, "Kinship, Territory and the Nation in the Historiography of Ancient Israel," *Zeitschrift für die alttestamentliche Wissenschaft*, vol. 105, no. 1 (1993), 1–18.

"The Nation of the United States and the Vision of Ancient Israel," in R. Michener, ed., *Nationality, Patriotism, and Nationalism* (St. Paul: Paragon, 1993).

"The Chosen People of Ancient Israel and the Occident," *Nations and Nationalism*, vol. 5, no. 3 (1999), 357–380.

"Nationality and Religion," in Montserrat Guibernau and John Hutchinson, eds., *Understanding Nationalism* (Oxford: Blackwell, 2001).

Biblical Ideas of Nationality: Ancient and Modern (Winona Lake, Ind.: Eisenbrauns, 2002).

"The Biblical 'Nation' as a Problem for Philosophy," *Hebraic Political Studies*, vol. 1, no. 1 (2005), 7–23.

Grosser, Alfred, *The Western Alliance: European–American Relations since 1945*, trans. Michael Shaw (1978; New York: Random House, 1982).

Gruen, Erich S., *Heritage and Hellenism: The Reinvention of Jewish Tradition* (Berkeley and Los Angeles: University of California Press, 1998).

Diaspora: Jews amidst Greeks and Romans (Cambridge, Mass.: Harvard University Press, 2002).

Gutmann, Amy, ed., *Multiculturalism: Examining the Politics of Recognition* (Princeton: Princeton University Press, 1994).

Guttman, Nathan, "Think Before You Sing 'Hatikva'," *Haaretz* English edn, 27 May 2005, http://www.haaretz.com/hasen/objects/pages/PrintArticleEn.jhtml?itemNo=581104.

Haass, Richard N., *Intevention: The Use of American Military Force in the Post-Cold War World*, rev. edn (Washington, D.C.: Brookings, 1999).

Habermas, Jürgen, "Struggles for Recognition in the Democratic Constitutional State," in Gutmann, ed., *Multiculturalism*.

Halbwachs, Maurice, *The Social Frameworks of Memory* (first published in 1925), in Lewis A. Coser, trans. and ed., Maurice Halbwachs, *On Collective Memory* (Chicago: University of Chicago Press, 1992).

Haley, James L., *Sam Houston* (Norman: Oklahoma University Press, 2002).

Hall, Jonathan M., *Hellenicity: Between Ethnicity and Culture* (Chicago: University of Chicago Press, 2002).

Halper, Stefan and Clarke, Jonathan, *America Alone: The Neo-Conservatives and the Global Order* (Cambridge: Cambridge University Press, 2004).

Hammond, N. G. L., *A History of Greece to 322 BC*, 3rd edn. (Oxford: Clarendon Press, 1986).

Hardin, Stephen L., *Texian Iliad: A Military History of the Texas Revolution, 1835–1836* (Austin: University of Texas Press, 1994).

Hartz, Louis, *The Liberal Tradition in America: An Interpretation of American Political Thought since the Revolution* (New York: Harcourt, Brace & World, 1955).

Hastings, Adrian, *The Construction of Nationhood: Ethnicity, Religion and Nationalism* (Cambridge: Cambridge University Press, 1997).

Hawking, Stephen, *A Brief History of Time: From the Big Bang to Black Holes* (New York: Bantam, 1988).

Heimerl, Daniela and Van Meurs, Wim, "The Balkans between Paris and Berlin," *Southeast European and Black Sea Studies*, vol. 4, no. 3 (2004), 343–360.

Helms, Jesse, "Saving the U.N.: A Challenge to the Next Secretary-General," *Foreign Affairs*, vol. 75, no. 5 (1996), 2–7.

Hennessey, Thomas, *The Northern Ireland Peace Process: Ending the Troubles?* (New York: Palgrave, 2001).

Henson, Margaret Swett, *Lorenzo de Zavala: The Pragmatic Idealist* (Fort Worth: Texas Christian University Press, 1996).

Herodotus, *The Histories*, trans. Aubrey de Sélincourt (Harmondsworth: Penguin, 1972).

Herzfeld, Michael, *Cultural Intimacy: Social Poetics in the Nation-State*, 2nd edn (New York: Routledge, 2005).

Hinsley, F. H., *Power and the Pursuit of Peace: Theory and Practice in the History of Relations between States* (Cambridge: Cambridge University Press, 1963).

Hobsbawm, Eric, *Nations and Nationalism since 1780: Programme, Myth, Reality* (Cambridge: Cambridge University Press, 1990)

Hobsbawm, Eric and Ranger, Terence, eds., *The Invention of Tradition* (Cambridge: Cambridge University Press, 1983).

Hoffmann, Stanley and Hoffmann, Inge, "The Will to Grandeur: de Gaulle as Political Artist," *Daedalus*, vol. 97, no. 3 (1968), 829–887.

Hoffmann, Stanley, "Paradoxes of the French Political Community," in Hoffmann *et al.*, *In Search of France*, 1965.

"Thoughts on Sovereignty and French Politics," in Flynn, *Remaking the Hexagon*, 1995.

Decline or Renewal? France Since the 1930s (New York: Viking, 1974).

"France, the United States, and Iraq," *The Nation*, vol. 278, no. 6 (16 February 2004), 16–19.

Hoffmann, Stanley *et al.*, *In Search of France: The Economy, Society, and Political System in the Twentieth Century* (1963; New York: Harper & Row, 1965).

Holquist, Peter, "To Count, to Extract, and to Exterminate: Population Statistics and Population Politics in Late Imperial and Soviet Russia," in Suny and Martin, eds., *A State of Nations*.

Horowitz, Donald L., *Ethnic Groups in Conflict*, 2nd edn (Berkeley: University of California Press, 2000).

Horsman, Reginald, *Race and Manifest Destiny: The Origins of American Racial Anglo-Saxonism* (Cambridge, Mass.: Harvard University Press, 1981).

Hosking, Geoffrey, *Russia and the Russians: A History* (Cambridge, Mass.: Harvard University Press, 2003).

Hourani, Albert, *Arabic Thought in the Liberal Age, 1798–1939* (1962; Cambridge: Cambridge University Press, 1983).

Hovannisian, Richard G., "Historical Memory and Foreign Relations: The Armenian Perspective," in S. Frederick Starr, ed., *The Legacy of History in Russia and the New States of Eurasia* (Armonk, N.Y. and London: M. E. Sharpe, 1994), vol. 1 of Karen Dawisha and Bruce Parrott, series eds., *The International Politics of Eurasia*.

Hroch, Miroslav, *Social Preconditions of National Revival in Europe: A Comparative Analysis of the Social Composition of Patriotic Groups among the Smaller European Nations* (New York: Cambridge University Press, 1985).

Huntington, Samuel P., "The Hispanic Challenge," *Foreign Policy*, no. 141 (March/April 2004), 30–45.

Who Are We? The Challenges to America's National Identity (New York: Simon & Schuster, 2004).

Hyde, Douglas, *The Necessity for De-Anglicising Ireland* (lecture first delivered in 1892), limited edition (Leiden: Academic Press, 1994).

Iacocca, Lee, "Foreword," in Yans-McLaughlin and Lightman, *Ellis Island*.

Ignatieff, Michael, *Blood and Belonging: Journeys into the New Nationalism* (1993; New York: Farrar, Straus & Giroux, 1995).

Isaiah Berlin: A Life (New York: Henry Holt, 1998).

Ikenberry, G. John, *After Victory: Institutions, Strategic Restraint, and the Rebuilding of Order after Major Wars* (Princeton: Princeton University Press, 2001).

"Multilateralism and U.S. Grand Strategy," in Patrick and Forman, eds., *Multilateralism*, 2002.

Isocrates, *Isocrates with an English Translation*, trans. George Norlin, 3 vols. (London: Heinemann and New York: Putnam, 1928–45).

Israel, Jonathan, *Radical Enlightenment: Philosophy and the Making of Modernity, 1650–1750* (Oxford: Oxford University Press, 2001).

Israeli, Raphael, *Jerusalem Divided: The Armistice Regime, 1947–1967* (London: Frank Cass, 2002).

Jackson, Tom, "Demonization and Defence of the Serbs: Balkanist Discourses During the Break-Up of Yugoslavia," *Slovo*, vol. 16, no. 2 (2004), 107–124.

Jaher, Frederic Cople, *The Jews and the Nation: Revolution, Emancipation, State Formation, and the Liberal Paradigm in America and France* (Princeton: Princeton University Press, 2002).

Jankowski, James P. and Gershoni, Israel, eds., *Rethinking Nationalism in the Arab Middle East* (New York: Columbia University Press, 1997).

Jarboe, Jan, "We Will Never Surrender or Retreat," *Texas Monthly*, vol. 22, no. 5 (1994), 124–128.

Jarman, Neil, "For God and Ulster: Blood and Thunder Bands and Loyalist Political Culture," in Fraser, ed., *The Irish Parading Tradition*.

Jaszi, Oscar, *The Dissolution of the Habsburg Monarchy* (Chicago: University of Chicago Press, 1929).

Jelavich, Barbara, *History of the Balkans*, vol. 1: *Eighteenth and Nineteenth Centuries* (Cambridge: Cambridge University Press, 1983).

Jochmann, Werner, "Die Ausbreitung des Antisemitismus," in Mosse, ed., *Deutsches Judentum*.

Joffe, Alexander H., "Israel in the Eyes of Historians: Some Jewish Historians of Nationalism on Zionism and Israel" (unpublished draft manuscript).

"The Rise of Secondary States in the Iron Age Levant," *Journal of the Economic and Social History of the Orient*, vol. 45, no. 4 (2002), 425–467.

Johannsen, Robert W., *To the Halls of the Montezumas: The Mexican War in the American Imagination* (New York: Oxford University Press, 1985).

Johnson, Benjamin Heber, *Revolution in Texas: How a Forgotten Rebellion and its Bloody Suppression Turned Mexicans into Americans* (New Haven: Yale University Press, 2003).

Jonas, Manfred, *Isolationism in America, 1935–1941* (Ithaca: Cornell University Press, 1966).

Judah, Tim, *The Serbs: History, Myth and the Destruction of Yugoslavia* (New Haven: Yale University Press, 1997).

Juergensmeyer, Mark, *Terror in the Mind of God: The Global Rise of Religious Violence*, 3rd edn (Berkeley: University of California Press, 2003).

Jünger, Ernst, *Storm of Steel* (1920; New York: Howard Fertig, 1996).

Kagan, Robert, *Of Paradise and Power: America and Europe in the New World Order*, Vintage Books edn (2002; New York: Random House, 2004).

Kaiser, Robert, *The Geography of Nationalism in Russia and the USSR* (Princeton: Princeton University Press, 1994).

Kalvoda, Joseph, *The Genesis of Czechoslovakia* (Boulder: East European Monographs, 1986).

Kaminsky, Howard, *A History of the Hussite Revolution* (Berkeley: University of California Press, 1967).

Kammen, Michael, *A Machine that Would Go of Itself: The Constitution in American Culture* (New York: Knopf, 1986).

Kanafani, Ghassan, "Men in the Sun," in Ghassan Kanafani, *Men in the Sun and Other Palestinian Stories*, trans. Hilary Kilpatrick (Cairo: American University of Cairo Press, 1991).

Kann, Robert A., *The Multinational Empire: Nationalism and National Reform in the Habsburg Monarchy, 1848–1918*, 2 vols. (New York: Columbia University Press, 1950).

Kantorowicz, Ernst H., *The King's Two Bodies: A Study in Mediaeval Political Theology* (Princeton: Princeton University Press, 1957).

Kaplan, Amy, "Homeland Insecurities: Reflections on Language and Space," *Radical History Review*, no. 85 (Winter 2003), 82–93.

Kaplan, Lawrence F., and Kristol, William, *The War over Iraq: Saddam's Tyranny and America's Mission* (San Francisco: Encounter Books, 2003).

Kaplan, Robert D., *Balkan Ghosts: A Journey through History* (New York: St. Martin's Press, 1993).

Kappeler, Andreas, *Russland als Vielvölkerreich* (Munich: C. H. Beck, 1993).

Karpel, Dalia, "With Thanks to Ghassan Kanafani," *Haaretz English Edition*, 15 April 2005, http://www.haaretz.com/hasen/spages/565228.html.

Kaufmann, Eric, "Condemned to Rootlessness: The Loyalist Origins of Canada's Identity Crisis," *Nationalism and Ethnic Politics*, vol. 3, no. 1 (1997), 110–135.

The Rise and Fall of Anglo-America (Cambridge, Mass.: Harvard University Press, 2004).

Keating, Michael, *Plurinational Democracy: Stateless Nations in a Post-Sovereignty Era* (Oxford: Oxford University Press, 2001).

Kedourie, Elie, *Nationalism*, 3rd edn (London: Hutchinson, 1966).

Kedward, H. R., *Resistance in Vichy France: A Study of Ideas and Motivation in the Southern Zone 1940–1942* (Oxford: Oxford University Press, 1978).

Kennan, George F., *Russia and the West under Lenin and Stalin* (New York: Penguin, 1961).

The Fateful Alliance: France, Russia, and the Coming of the First World War (New York: Pantheon, 1984).

Kersaudy, François, *Churchill and De Gaulle* (1981; New York: Atheneum, 1983).

Keynes, John Maynard, *The Economic Consequences of the Peace* (1920; New Brunswick, N.J.: Transaction: 2003).

Khalidi, Rashid, *Palestinian Identity: The Construction of Modern National Consciousness* (New York: Columbia University Press, 1997).

Khalidi, Rashid, *et al.*, *Origins of Arab Nationalism* (New York: Columbia University Press, 1991)

Kilgore, Dan, *How Did Davy Die?* (College Station: Texas A&M University Press, 1978).

King, Jeremy, *Budweisers into Czechs and Germans: A Local History of Bohemian Politics, 1848–1948* (Princeton: Princeton University Press, 2002).

Kinsley, Michael, "The Limits of Eloquence: Did Bush Mean a Word of his Speech about Democracy?" *Slate*, 13 November 2003, http://slate.msn.com/id/2091185.

Kirschbaum, Stanislav J., *A History of Slovakia: The Struggle for Survival* (New York: St. Martin's Press, 1995).

Kissinger, Henry A., "The White Revolutionary: Reflections on Bismarck," *Daedalus*, vol. 97, no. 3 (1968), 888–924.

A World Restored: Metternich, Castlereagh and the Problems of Peace, 1812–1822 (1957; Boston: Houghton Mifflin, 1973).

Diplomacy (New York: Simon & Schuster, 1994).

Kitromilides, Paschalis M., "'Imagined Communities' and the Origins of the National Question in the Balkans," *European History Quarterly*, vol. 19, no. 2 (1989), 149–192.

Klein, Kerwin Lee, "Reclaiming the 'F' Word, or Being and Becoming Postwestern," *Pacific Historical Review*, vol. 65, no. 2 (1996), 179–215.

Klein, Menachem, *The Jerusalem Problem: The Struggle for Permanent Status*, trans. Haim Watzman (Gainesville: University of Florida Press, 2003).

Knock, Thomas J., *To End All Wars: Woodrow Wilson and the Quest for a New World Order* (Princeton: Princeton University Press, 1992).

Kohn, Hans, *The Idea of Nationalism: A Study in Its Origins and Background* (1944; New York: Macmillan, 1948).

Kornberg, Jacques, *Theodor Herzl: From Assimilation to Zionism* (Bloomington and Indianapolis: Indiana University Press, 1993).

Koubi, Geneviève, "The Management of Cultural Diversity in France," in Alain Dieckhoff, ed., *The Politics of Belonging: Nationalism, Liberalism, and Pluralism* (Lanham, Md.: Lexington Books, 2004).

Kramer, Jane, "Taking the Veil," *The New Yorker*, vol. 80, no. 36 (22 November 2004), 58–71.

Kramer, Martin, *Arab Awakening and Islamic Revival: The Politics of Ideas in the Middle East* (New Brunswick, N.J.: Transaction Publishers, 1996).

Kramnick, Isaac, "Editor's Introduction," in James Madison, Alexander Hamilton, and John Jay, *The Federalist Papers*, Isaac Kramnick ed. (London: Penguin, 1987).

Krauthammer, Charles, *Democratic Realism: An American Foreign Policy for a Unipolar World,* speech delivered before the American Enterprise Institute as the Irving Kristol Lecture, Washington, D.C., February 2004 (Washington: AEI Press, 2004).

"The Unipolar Moment," *Foreign Affairs*, vol. 70, no. 1 (issue subtitled *America and the World*, 1990/91), 23–33.

Kreindler, Isabelle, "A Neglected Source of Lenin's Nationality Policy," *Slavic Review*, vol. 36, no. 1 (1977), 86–100.

Kristol, William and Kagan, Robert, "Toward a Neo-Reaganite Foreign Policy," *Foreign Affairs*, vol. 75, no. 4 (1996), 18–32.

Kuisel, Richard, *Seducing the French: The Dilemma of Americanization* (Berkeley: University of California Press, 1993).

"The France We Have Lost," in Flynn, ed., *Remaking the Hexagon*, 1995.

Kuzio, Taras, "The Myth of the Civic State: A Critical Survey of Hans Kohn's Framework for Understanding Nationalism," *Ethnic and Racial Studies*, vol. 25, no. 1 (2002), 20–39.

Kymlicka, Will, *Multicultural Citizenship: A Liberal Theory of Minority Rights* (Oxford: Oxford University Press, 1995).

Lafeber, Walter, *Inevitable Revolutions: The United States in Central America*, 2nd edn (New York: Norton, 1993).

Lakely, James G., "Home Again, Hillary Bashes Bush," *The Washington Times*, 2 December 2003.

Lambert, Frank, *The Founding Fathers and the Place of Religion in America* (Princeton: Princeton University Press, 2003).

Lampe, John, *Yugoslavia as History: Twice There Was a Country* (Cambridge: Cambridge University Press, 1996).

Langer, William, *Our Vichy Gamble* (New York: Knopf, 1947).

Laqueur, Thomas W., "Memory and Naming in the Great War," in Gillis, ed., *Commemorations*.

Laqueur, Walter, *Young Germany: A History of the German Youth Movement* (New York: Basic Books, 1962).

Lazare, Daniel, *The Frozen Republic: How the Constitution Is Paralyzing Democracy* (New York: Harcourt Brace & Co., 1996).

Lebovics, Herman, "Creating the Authentic France: Struggles over French Identity in the First Half of the Twentieth Century," in Gillis, ed., *Commemorations*.

Leff, Carol Skalnik, *The Czech and Slovak Republics: Nation Versus State* (Boulder: Westview Press, 1996).

Leffler, Melvyn, *A Preponderance of Power: National Security, the Truman Administration, and the Cold War* (Stanford: Stanford University Press, 1992).

Lekan, Thomas M., *Imagining the Nation in Nature: Landscape Preservation and German Identity, 1885–1945* (Cambridge, Mass.: Harvard University Press, 2004).

Leoussi, Athena S. and Grosby, Steven, eds., *Nationality and Nationalism*, vol. 1: *Theoretical Studies* (London: I. B. Tauris, 2004).

Létourneau, Jocelyn, *A History for the Future: Rewriting Memory and Identity in Quebec*, trans. Phyllis Aronoff and Howard Scott (Montreal: McGill–Queen's University Press, 2004).

Levin, N. Gordon, Jr., *Woodrow Wilson and World Politics: America's Response to War and Revolution* (London and Oxford: Oxford University Press, 1968).

Levy, Shlomit, "An Analysis of Israeli Jewish Opinion on the Status of Jerusalem" in Segal *et al., Negotiating Jerusalem*.

Lewis, Bernard, *The Emergence of Modern Turkey* (Oxford: Oxford University Press, 1961).

    The Political Language of Islam (Chicago: University of Chicago Press, 1988).

    What Went Wrong? The Clash Between Islam and Modernity in the Middle East (New York: Oxford University Press, 2002).

Lieven, Anatol, *America Right or Wrong: An Anatomy of American Nationalism* (New York: Oxford University Press, 2004).

Limón, José E., *Dancing with the Devil: Society and Cultural Poetics in Mexican–American South Texas* (Madison: University of Wisconsin Press, 1994).

Lincoln, Bruce, "Bush's God Talk," *Christian Century*, 5 October 2004, 22–29.

Lind, Michael, *The Next American Nation: The New Nationalism and the Fourth American Revolution* (New York: The Free Press, 1995).

Lindley, Thomas Ricks, *Alamo Traces: New Evidence and New Conclusions* (Lanham: Republic of Texas Press, 2003).

Link, Arthur S., *Wilson the Diplomatist: A Look at his Major Foreign Policies* (New York: New Viewpoints, 1974).

Lipset, Seymour Martin, *American Exceptionalism: A Double-Edged Sword* (New York: Norton, 1996).

Liulevicius, Vejas Gabriel, *War Land on the Eastern Front: Culture, National Identity and German Occupation in World War I* (Cambridge: Cambridge University Press, 2000).

Livezeanu, Irina, *Cultural Politics in Greater Romania: Regionalism, Nation Building, and Ethnic Struggle, 1918–1930* (Ithaca: Cornell University Press, 1995).

Longley, Clifford, *Chosen People: The Big Idea that Shapes England and America* (London: Hodder & Stoughton, 2002).

Lord, Walter, "Myths and Realities of the Alamo," *The American West*, vol. 5, no. 3 (May 1968), 18–25.

Loughlin, James, "Parades and Politics: Liberal Governments and the Orange Order, 1880–86," in Fraser, ed., *Irish Parading Tradition*.

Lustick, Ian, "Israel's Dangerous Fundamentalists," *Foreign Policy*, no. 68 (Fall 1987), 118–139.

Unsettled States, Disputed Lands: Britain and Ireland, France and Algeria, Israel and the West Bank–Gaza (Ithaca: Cornell University Press, 1993).

Macartney, C. A., *National States and National Minorities* (London: Oxford University Press, 1934).

Maddox, Robert James, *William E. Borah and American Foreign Policy* (Baton Rouge: Louisiana State University Press, 1969).

Madison, James, Hamilton, Alexander, and Jay, John, *The Federalist Papers*, ed. Isaac Kramnick (1st edn 1788; London: Penguin, 1987).

Maier, Pauline, *American Scripture: Making the Declaration of Independence* (New York: Knopf, 1997).

Malcolm, Noel, *Kosovo: A Short History* (New York: New York University Press, 1998).

Mallon, Florencia E., *Peasant and Nation: The Making of Postcolonial Mexico and Peru* (Berkeley: University of California Press, 1995).

Mandel, David R., "Evil and the Instigation of Violence," *Analyses of Social Issues and Public Policy*, vol. 2, no. 1 (2002).

Manela, Erez, "The Wilsonian Moment and the Rise of Anticolonial Nationalism: The Case of Egypt," *Diplomacy and Statecraft*, vol. 12, no. 4 (2001), 99–122.

Mann, Judy, "Falwell's Insult Compounds Nation's Injury," *The Washington Post*, 21 September 2001, p. C8.

Margolis, Nadia, "The 'Joan Phenomenon' and the French Right," in Bonnie Wheeler and Charles T. Wood, eds., *Fresh Verdicts on Joan of Arc* (New York: Garland, 1996).

Marks, Sally, *The Illusion of Peace: International Relations in Europe* (New York: St. Martin's Press, 1976).

Marks, Steven G., *How Russia Shaped the Modern World: From Art to Anti-Semitism, Ballet to Bolshevism* (Princeton: Princeton University Press, 2003).

Marrus, Michael R. and Paxton, Robert O., *Vichy France and the Jews* (New York: Basic Books, 1981).

Martin, Chuck, "How to Fry the French: Act of National Ire Small Potatoes to What Would Light France's Fire," *The Cincinnati Enquirer*, 16 March 2003.

Martin, Terry, *The Affirmative Action Empire: Nations and Nationalism in the Soviet Union, 1923–1939* (Ithaca: Cornell University Press, 2001).

Martin, William, "The Christian Right and American Foreign Policy," *Foreign Policy*, no. 114 (1999), 66–80.

Marx, Anthony, *Faith in Nation: Exclusionary Origins of Nationalism* (New York: Oxford University Press, 2003).

Matovina, Timothy M., *The Alamo Remembered: Tejano Accounts and Perspectives* (Austin: University of Texas Press, 1995).

Mattar, Philip, *The Mufti of Jerusalem: Al-Hajj Amin al-Husayni and the Palestinian National Movement*, rev. edn (New York: Columbia University Press, 1988).

Maurice, Jean and Couty, Daniel, eds., *Images de Jeanne d'Arc* (Paris: Presses Universitaires de France, 2000).

May, Ernest R., *Imperial Democracy: The Emergence of America as a Great Power* (New York: Harcourt Brace Jovanovich, 1961).

The Making of the Monroe Doctrine (Cambridge, Mass.: Harvard University Press, 1975).

Mayer, Arno J., *Political Origins of the New Diplomacy, 1917–1918* (1959; Cleveland: World Publishing Co., 1964).

Politics and Diplomacy of Peacemaking: Containment and Counterrevolution at Versailles, 1918–1919 (New York: Knopf, 1967).

Mayers, David, *George Kennan and the Dilemmas of US Foreign Policy* (New York: Oxford University Press, 1988).

Mazzini, Giuseppe, "Faith and the Future," in Joseph [*sic*] Mazzini, *The Duties of Man and Other Essays* (London: Dent & Sons, 1907).

McDougall, Walter A., *Promised Land, Crusader State: The American Encounter with the World since 1776* (New York: Houghton-Mifflin, 1997).

McKenna, Marian C., *Borah* (Ann Arbor: University of Michigan Press, 1961).

McLeod, Hugh, "Protestantism and British National Identity, 1815–1945," in van der Veer and Lehmann, eds., *Nation and Religion*.

McWhorter, John, *The Power of Babel: A Natural History of Language* (2001; New York: HarperCollins, 2003).

Meinecke, Friedrich, *Cosmopolitanism and the National State*, trans. Robert B. Kimber (original German edn, 1907; Princeton: Princeton University Press, 1970).

Melville, Herman, *White-Jacket* (1850; New York: Random House, 2002).

Mendels, Doron, *The Rise and Fall of Jewish Nationalism* (New York: Doubleday, 1992).

Mertus, Julie A., *Bait and Switch: Human Rights and U.S. Foreign Policy* (New York: Routledge, 2004).

Mildenberg, Leo, *The Coinage of the Bar Kokhba War* (Aarau: Verlag Sauerländer, 1984).

Mill, John Stuart, *Considerations on Representative Government* (first published 1861), in Mill, *Utilitarianism, Liberty, and Considerations on Representative Government* (London: J. M. Dent; New York: E. P. Dutton, 1972).

Miller, David, *On Nationality* (Oxford: Clarendon Press, 1995).

Miller, Marilyn Grace, *Rise and Fall of the Cosmic Race: The Cult of Mestizaje in Latin America* (Austin: University of Texas Press, 2004).

Miller, Nicholas J., *Between Nation and State: Serbian Politics in Croatia before the First World War* (Pittsburgh: University of Pittsburgh Press, 1997).

Miller, Randall M., review of Joseph Tovares' 2004 PBS television documentary, "Remember the Alamo" and John Lee Hancock's 2004 feature film, *The Alamo*, in *American Historical Review*, vol. 110, no. 2 (2005), 485–486.

Mitchell, W. J. T., "Holy Landscape: Israel, Palestine, and the American Wilderness," in W. J. T. Mitchell, ed., *Landscape and Power*, 2nd edn (Chicago: University of Chicago, 2002).

Möckli, Daniel, "The Long Road to Membership: Switzerland and the United Nations," in Gabriel and Fischer, eds., *Swiss Foreign Policy*.

Monk, Daniel Bertrand, *An Aesthetic Occupation: The Immediacy of Architecture and the Palestine Conflict* (Durham, N.C.: Duke University Press, 2002).

Mörgeli, Dr. Christoph, report of 8 May 1999 posted on the website of Aktion für eine unabhängige und neutrale Schweiz (Campaign for an Independent and Neutral Switzerland), http://www.cins.ch/en/meldungen/990508essence.htm.

Morris, Benny, *The Birth of the Palestinian Refugee Problem, 1947–1949* (Cambridge: Cambridge University Press, 1987).

Morrissey, Mike and Smyth, Marie, *Northern Ireland after the Good Friday Agreement: Victims, Grievance and Blame* (London: Pluto Press, 2002).

Mosse, George, *Fallen Soldiers: Reshaping the Memory of the World Wars* (New York: Oxford University Press, 1990).

Mosse, Werner, ed., *Deutsches Judentum in Krieg und Revolution, 1916–1923* (Tübingen: J. C. B. Mohr, 1971).

Mulholland, Marc, *The Longest War: Northern Ireland's Troubled History* (Oxford: Oxford University Press, 2002).

Musgrave, Thomas D., *National Self-Determination and National Minorities* (Oxford: Oxford University Press, 1997).

Musil, Robert, *The Man without Qualities*, trans. Sophie Wilkins (1930–1943; New York: Alfred A. Knopf, 1995), vol. 1.

Nadler, Steven, *Rembrandt's Jews* (Chicago: University of Chicago Press, 2003).

Naimark, Norman M., *Fires of Hatred: Ethnic Cleansing in Twentieth-Century Europe* (Cambridge, Mass.: Harvard University Press, 2001).

Nairn, Tom, *The Break-Up of Britain: Crisis and Neo-Nationalism* (London: Verso, 1981).

Neuberger, Benyamin, *National Self-Determination in Postcolonial Africa* (Boulder: Lynne Rienner Publishers, 1986).

Nicholson, Alex (Associated Press), "Russia's Putin: Soviet Collapse a Tragedy," *The Washington Post*, 25 April 2005.

Niebuhr, Reinhold, *The Irony of American History* (New York: Charles Scribner's Sons, 1952).

Nielsen, Kai, "Cultural Nationalism, neither Ethnic nor Civic," in Ronald Beiner, ed., *Theorizing Nationalism* (Albany: State University of New York Press, 1999).

Nora, Pierre, "Entre Mémoire et Histoire: La problématique des lieux," in Nora, ed., *Les Lieux*, vol. 1.

"Gaullistes et Communistes," in Nora, ed., *Les Lieux*, vol. iii, part 1.

Nora, Pierre, ed., *Les Lieux de mémoire*, vol. 1: *La République* (Paris: Gallimard, 1984).

Les Lieux de mémoire, vol. ii: *La Nation*, part 2 (Paris: Gallimard, 1984)

Les Lieux de mémoire, vol. ii: *La Nation*, part 3 (Paris: Gallimard, 1986).

Les Lieux de mémoire, vol. iii: *Les France*, part 1: *Conflits et Partages* (Paris: Gallimard, 1992).

Les Lieux de mémoire, vol. iii: *Les France*, part 3: *De l'Archive à l'emblème* (Paris: Gallimard, 1992).

Northrop, Douglas, "Nationalizing Backwardness: Gender, Empire, and Uzbek Identity," in Suny and Martin, eds., *State of Nations*.

Novak, David, *The Election of Israel: The Idea of the Chosen People* (Cambridge: Cambridge University Press, 1995).

Covenantal Rights: A Study in Jewish Political Theory (Princeton: Princeton University Press, 2000).

"NSC-68: United States Objectives and Programs for National Security," 14 April 1950, in Thomas H. Etzold and John Lewis Gaddis, eds., *Containment: Documents on American Policy and Strategy, 1945–1950* (New York: Columbia University Press, 1978).

Nye, Joseph S., *The Paradox of American Power: Why the World's Only Superpower Can't Go it Alone* (New York: Oxford University Press, 2002).

O'Brien, Conor Cruise, *Godland: Reflections on Religion and Nationalism* (Cambridge, Mass.: Harvard University Press, 1988).

O'Leary, Cecilia, *To Die For: The Paradox of American Patriotism* (Princeton: Princeton University Press, 1999).

Oren, Michael B., *Six Days of War: June 1967 and the Making of the Modern Middle East* (New York: Oxford University Press, 2002).

Osiander, Andreas, *The States System of Europe, 1640–1990: Peacemaking and the Conditions of International Stability* (Oxford: Oxford University Press, 1994).

Ostrowetsky, Sylvia, "De l'un lieu à l'autre," paper given at seminar organized by the Permanent Secretariat of the Paris Urban Plan on "Villes et Transports" ("Cities and Means of Transportation"), 5th session, 11 June 1992, Centre de documentation de l'urbanisme, http://www.urbanisme.equipement.gouv.fr/cdu/datas/docs/ouvr1/seance5.htm#p5.

Papazian, Dennis R., "The Changing American View of the Armenian Question: An Interpretation," *Armenian Review*, vol. 39, no. 4 (1986), 47–72.

Patrick, Stewart and Forman, Shepard, eds., *Multilateralism and U.S. Foreign Policy: Ambivalent Engagement* (Boulder: Lynne Rienner Publishers, 2002).

Paxton, Robert O., *Vichy France: Old Guard and New Order, 1940–1944* (New York: Knopf, 1972).

Pells, Richard, *Not Like Us: How Europeans Have Loved, Hated, and Transformed American Culture since World War II* (New York: Basic Books, 1997).

Pernoud, Régine and Clin, Marie Véronique, *Joan of Arc: Her Story*, trans. and revd. Jeremy du Quesnay Adams (New York: St. Martin's Press, 1998).

Pétain, Philippe, *Actes et écrits*, ed. Jacques Isorni (Paris: Flammarion, 1974).
 Discours aux Français, 17 juin 1940 – 20 août 1944, ed. Jean-Claude Barbas (Paris: Albin Michel, 1989).

Phillips, Kevin, "Crusader: Bush's Religious Passions," *Christian Century*, 13 July 2004, 8–9.

Pick, Daniel, *War Machine: The Rationalisation of Slaughter in the Modern Age* (New Haven: Yale University Press, 1993).

Pinker, Steven, *The Blank Slate: The Denial of Human Nature and Modern Intellectual Life* (New York: Viking, 2002).

Pipes, Richard, *The Formation of the Soviet Union: Communism and Nationalism, 1917–1923*, rev. edn (1954; Cambridge, Mass.: Harvard University Press, 1964).

Pitkin, Thomas M., *Keepers of the Gate: A History of Ellis Island* (New York: New York University Press, 1975).

Pollack, Kenneth M., *The Threatening Storm: The Case for Invading Iraq* (New York: Random House, 2002).

Poole, Colin, *Nation and Identity* (London: Routledge, 1999).

Porath, Yehoshua, *The Emergence of the Palestinian–Arab National Movement, 1918–1929* (London: Frank Cass, 1974).
 The Palestinian Arab National Movement: From Riots to Rebellion, 1929–1939 (London: Frank Cass, 1977).

Porter, Brian, *When Nationalism Began to Hate: Imagining Modern Politics in Nineteenth-Century Poland* (New York: Oxford University Press, 2000).

Price, Glenn W., *Origins of the War with Mexico: The Polk–Stockton Intrigue* (Austin: University of Texas Press, 1967).

Price, Martin Jessop and Trell, Bluma L., *Coins and their Cities: Architecture on the Ancient Coins of Greece, Rome, and Palestine* (London: Vecchi and Sons; Detroit: Wayne State University Press, 1977).

Pynsent, Robert, *Questions of Identity: Czech and Slovak Ideas of Nationality and Personality* (Budapest: Central European University Press, 1994).

Radano, Ronald and Bohlman, Philip V., eds., *Music and the Racial Imagination* (Chicago: University of Chicago Press, 2000).

Ramet, Sabrina P., *Nationalism and Federalism in Yugoslavia, 1962–1991*, 2nd edn (Bloomington: Indiana University Press, 1992).

Balkan Babel: The Disintegration of Yugoslavia from the Death of Tito to the Fall of Milošević (Boulder: Westview, 2002).

Ramírez, Juan Antonio, *The Beehive Metaphor: From Gaudí to Le Corbusier*, trans. Alexander R. Tulloch (1998; London: Reaktion Books, 2000).

Reich, Robert, "How Did Spending Become Our Patriotic Duty?" *The Washington Post*, 23 September 2001.

Reichmann, Eva G., "Der Bewusstseinswandel der deutschen Juden," in Mosse, ed., *Deutsches Judentum*.

Reichstein, Andreas V., *Rise of the Lone Star: The Making of Texas*, trans. Jeanne R. Willson (College Station: Texas A&M University Press, 1989).

Reifenberg, A., *Israel's History in Coins: From the Maccabees to the Roman Conquest* (London: East and West Library, 1953).

Reifowitz, Ian, *Imagining an Austrian Nation: Joseph Samuel Bloch and the Search for a Multiethnic Austrian Identity, 1846–1919* (Boulder: East European Monographs, 2003).

Rémond, René, "La Fille aînée de l'Église," in Nora, ed., *Les Lieux*, vol. III, part I.

The Right Wing in France: From 1815 to de Gaulle, trans. James M. Laux, 2nd US edn. (1954; 1966; Philadelphia: University of Pennsylvania Press, 1969).

Renan, Ernest, "What is a Nation?" trans. Martin Thom, in Geoff Eley and Ronald Grigor Suny, eds., *Becoming National: A Reader* (New York: Oxford University Press, 1996).

Reséndez, Andrés, *Changing National Identities at the Frontier: Texas and New Mexico, 1800–1850* (Cambridge: Cambridge University Press, 2005).

Reynolds, David, "A Special Relationship: America, Britain and the International Order since the Second World War," *International Affairs*, vol. 62, no. 1 (1985/86), 1–20.

Richmond, Susan, "The National WWII Memorial ... A Lasting Tribute to a Generation" (advertising supplement produced by *The Washington Post*'s Advertising Department in collaboration with the American Battle Monuments Commission), *The Washington Post Magazine*, 23 May 2004, pp. 21–55.

Roberts, Randy and Olson, James S., *A Line in the Sand: The Alamo in Blood and Memory* (New York: The Free Press, 2001).

Robertson, Pat, "Why Evangelical Christians Support Israel," transcript of speech delivered at The Herzliya Conference, Lauder School of Government, Diplomacy, and Strategy, 17 December 2003, posted on "The Official Site of Pat Robertson," http://www.patrobertson.com/Speeches/IsraelLauder.asp.

Rodriguez, O., Jaime, E., ed., *The Independence of Mexico and the Creation of the New Nation* (Los Angeles: UCLA Latin American Center Publications and Irvine: Mexico/Chicano Program, 1989).

Roger, Philippe, *The American Enemy: The History of French Anti-Americanism* (Chicago: University of Chicago Press, 2005).

Romero, Rolando J., "The Alamo, Slavery and the Politics of Memory," http://www.sip.uiuc.edu/rromero/alamo.htm (extended version of author's identically titled chapter in Arturo J. Aldama and Naomi H. Quiñonez, eds., *Decolonial Voices: Chicana and Chicano Cultural Studies in the 21st Century* [Bloomington: Indiana University Press, 2002]).

Rosenberg, Emily S., *Spreading the American Dream: American Economic and Cultural Expansion, 1890–1945* (New York: Hill and Wang, 1982).

Roshwald, Aviel, *Estranged Bedfellows: Britain and France in the Middle East during the Second World War* (New York: Oxford University Press, 1990).
   "Colonial Dreams of the French Right Wing, 1881–1914," *The Historian*, vol. 52, no. 1 (1994), 59–74.
   Ethnic Nationalism and the Fall of Empires: Central Europe, Russia and the Middle East, 1914–1923 (London: Routledge, 2001).
   "Jewish Identity and the Paradox of Nationalism," in Michael Berkowitz, ed., *Nationalism, Zionism and Ethnic Mobilization of the Jews in 1900 and Beyond* (Leiden: E. J. Brill, 2004).
   "Ethnicity and Democracy in Europe's Multinational Empires, 1848–1918," in André Gerrits and Dirk Jan Wolffram, eds., *Political Democracy and Ethnic Diversity in Modern European History* (Stanford: Stanford University Press, 2005).

Roshwald, Mordecai, *The Transient and the Absolute: An Interpretation of the Human Condition and of Human Endeavor* (Westport, Conn.: Greenwood Press, 1999).

Roskies, David G., *Against the Apocalypse: Responses to Catastrophe in Modern Jewish Culture* (Cambridge, Mass.: Harvard University Press, 1984).

Rossignol, Dominique, *Histoire de la propagande en France de 1940 à 1944: L'utopie Pétain* (Paris: Presses Universitaires de France, 1991).

Rotman, Charlotte, "Tilting at Golden Arches," *Civilization*, vol. 7, no. 2 (2000), 29.

Rousso, Henry, *The Vichy Syndrome: History and Memory in France since 1944*, trans. Arthur Goldhammer (Cambridge, Mass.: Harvard University Press: 1991).

Roy, Olivier, *Globalized Islam: The Search for a New Ummah* (New York: Columbia University Press, 2004).

Ryder, Chris and Kearney, Vincent, *Drumcree: The Orange Order's Last Stand* (London: Methuen, 2002).

Sa'id, Nader Izzat, "An Analysis of Palestinian Opinion on the Status of Jerusalem," in Segal *et al.*, *Negotiating Jerusalem*.

Sachar, Howard M., *Dreamland: Europeans and Jews in the Aftermath of the Great War* (2002; New York: Vintage Books/Random House, 2003).

Safrai, S., "The Era of the Mishnah and Talmud (70–640)," in Ben-Sasson *et al.*, eds., *History of the Jewish People*.

Safran, Nadav, *Israel: The Embattled Ally* (1978; Cambridge, Mass.: Harvard University Press, 1981).

Sahlins, Peter, *Boundaries: The Making of France and Spain in the Pyrenees* (Berkeley: University of California Press, 1989).

Saïd, Suzanne, "The Discourse of Identity in Greek Rhetoric from Isocrates to Aristides," in Irad Malkin, ed., *Ancient Perceptions of Greek Ethnicity* (Washington, D.C.: Center for Hellenic Studies/Trustees for Harvard University, 2001).

Saldarini, Anthony J., "Good from Evil: The Rabbinic Response," in Berlin and Overman, eds., *The First Jewish Revolt*.

Sanborn, Joshua, "Family, Fraternity, and Nation-Building in Russia, 1905–1925," in Suny and Martin, eds., *A State of Nations*.

Savage, Kirk, "The Politics of Memory: Black Emancipation and the Civil War Monument," in Gillis, ed. *Commemorations*.

Sayer, Derek, *The Coasts of Bohemia: A Czech History* (Princeton: Princeton University Press, 1998).

"Second Class: Discrimination Against Palestinian Arab Children in Israel's Schools," *Human Rights Watch Publications*, September 2001, http://www.hrw.org/reports/2001/israel2/.

Schama, Simon, *The Embarrassment of Riches: An Interpretation of Dutch Culture in the Golden Age* (New York: Knopf, 1988).

Landscape and Memory (New York: Knopf, 1995).

Schivelbusch, Wolfgang, *The Culture of Defeat: On National Trauma, Mourning, and Recovery*, trans. Jefferson Chase (New York: Henry Holt, 2001).

Schmidt-Hartmann, Eva, "The Fallacy of Realism: Some Problems of Masaryk's Approach to Czech National Aspirations," in Stanley B. Winters, ed., *T. G. Masaryk (1850–1937)*, vol. 1 (New York: St. Martin's Press, 1990).

Schniedewind, William M., *How the Bible Became a Book* (Cambridge: Cambridge University Press, 2004).

Schöpflin, George, "Nationalism, Politics and the European Experience," *Survey*, vol. 28, no. 4 (1984), 67–86.

Nations, Identity, Power (New York: NYU Press, 2000).

Schroeder, Paul W., *The Transformation of European Politics, 1763–1848* (Oxford: Oxford University Press, 1994).

Schuker, Stephen A., *The End of French Predominance in Europe: The Financial Crisis of 1924 and the Adoption of the Dawes Plan* (Chapel Hill: University of North Carolina Press, 1976).

Schulze, Hageny, *States, Nations and Nationalism: From the Middle Ages to the Present*, trans. William E. Yuill (Oxford: Blackwell, 1996)

Schwartz, Seth, "Language, Power and Identity in Ancient Palestine," *Past and Present*, no. 148 (1995), 3–47.

Segal, Jerome M., "Is Jerusalem Negotiable?" in Segal *et al.*, *Negotiating Jerusalem*.

Segal, Jerome M., Levy, Shlomit, Sa'id, Nader Izzat, and Katz, Elihu, eds., *Negotiating Jerusalem* (Albany: State University of New York Press, 2000).

Sela, Avraham, "The 'Wailing Wall' Riots (1929) as a Watershed in the Palestine Conflict," *The Muslim World*, vol. 84, no. 1–2 (1994), 60–94.

Seton-Watson, Hugh and Seton-Watson, Christopher, *The Making of a New Europe: R. W. Seton-Watson and the Last Years of Austria-Hungary* (Seattle: University of Washington Press, 1981).

Sewall, Sarah B., "Multilateral Peace Operations," in Patrick and Forman, eds., *Multilateralism*.

Shain, Yossi, *Marketing the American Creed Abroad: Diasporas in the U.S. and their Homelands* (Cambridge: Cambridge University Press, 1999).

Shapira, Anita, *Land and Power: The Zionist Resort to Force, 1881–1948*, trans. William Templer (New York: Oxford University Press, 1992).

Sharabi, Hisham, *Neopatriarchy: A Theory of Distorted Change in Arab Society* (New York: Oxford University Press, 1988).

Sharp, Alan, *The Versailles Settlement: Peacemaking in Paris, 1919* (New York: St. Martin's Press, 1991).

Shavit, Yaacov, *Jabotinsky and the Revisionist Movement, 1925–1948* (London: Frank Cass, 1988).

Sheehan, Jonathan, "Enlightenment, Religion, and the Enigma of Secularization," *American Historical Review*, vol. 108, no. 4 (2003), 1061–1080.

Sherman, Daniel J., "Art, Commerce, and the Production of Memory in France after World War I," in Gillis, ed., *Commemorations*.

Sherwin, Martin and Shain, Yossi, "A Nation is a Nation, is a nation, is a nation, is a . . . A Critique of the Semantic and Methodological Rigor in the Study of Nationalism," unpublished manuscript.

Shils, Edward, "Nation, Nationality, Nationalism and Civil Society," in Leoussi and Grosby, eds., *Nationality and Nationalism*, vol. 1.

Shklar, Judith, *American Citizenship: The Quest for Inclusion* (Cambridge, Mass.: Harvard University Press, 1991).

Shulman, Stephen, "Challenging the Civic/Ethnic and West/East Dichotomies in the Study of Nationalism," *Comparative Political Studies*, vol. 35, no. 5 (2002), 554–585.

Siedentop, Larry, *Democracy in Europe* (New York: Columbia University Press, 2001).

Silber, Laura and Little, Alan, *Yugoslavia: Death of a Nation*, rev. edn (New York: Penguin, 1997).

Silber, Michael K., "From Tolerated Aliens to Citizen-Soldiers: Jewish Military Service in the Era of Joseph II," in Pieter M. Judson and Marsha L. Rozenblit, eds., *Constructing Nationalities in East Central Europe* (New York: Berghahn, 2005).

Silberman, Neil Asher, *Between Past and Present: Archaeology, Ideology, and Nationalism in the Modern Middle East* (New York: Henry Holt, 1989).

"Promised Lands and Chosen Peoples: The Politics and Poetics of Archaeological Narrative," in Philip L. Kohl and Clare Fawcett, eds., *Nationalism, Politics, and the Practice of Archaeology* (Cambridge: Cambridge University Press, 1995).

"The First Revolt and its Afterlife," in Berlin and Overman, eds., *First Jewish Revolt*, 2002.

Simon, Reeva S., *Iraq between the Two World Wars: The Creation and Implementaiton of a Nationalist Ideology* (New York: Columbia University Press, 1986).

Sked, Alan, *The Decline and Fall of the Habsburg Empire, 1815–1918* (London: Longman, 1989).

Skilling, H. Gordon, *T. G. Masaryk. Against the Current, 1882–1914* (University Park, Penn.: The Pennsylvania State University Press, 1994).

Slezkine, Yuri, "The USSR as a Communal Apartment, or How a Socialist State Promoted Ethnic Particularism," *Slavic Review*, vol. 53, no. 2 (1994), 414–452.

Smith, Anthony D., *Nationalism in the Twentieth Century* (New York: New York University Press, 1979).

The Ethnic Origins of Nations (Oxford: Blackwell, 1986).

"The Origins of Nations," *Ethnic and Racial Studies*, vol. 12, no. 3 (1989), 340–367.

National Identity (London: Penguin, 1991).

"Nations and their Past," in Anthony D. Smith and Ernest Gellner, "The Nation: Real or Imagined?: The Warwick Debates on Nationalism," *Nations and Nationalism*, vol. 2, no. 3 (1996), 357–370.

Nationalism and Modernism: A Critical Survey of Recent Theories of Nations and Nationalism (London: Routledge, 1998).

"Dating the Nation," in Daniele Conversi, ed., *Ethnonationalism in the Contemporary World: Walker Connor and the Study of Nationalism* (London: Routledge, 2002).

Chosen Peoples (Oxford: Oxford University Press, 2003).

The Antiquity of Nations (Cambridge: Polity Press, 2004).

Smith, Jeffrey, *The Bolsheviks and the National Question, 1917–1923* (London: Palgrave Macmillan, 1999).

Smith, Nathaniel B., "The Idea of the French Hexagon," *French Historical Studies*, vol. 6, no. 2 (1969), 139–155.

Smith, Steven B., *Spinoza, Liberalism, and the Question of Jewish Identity* (New Haven: Yale University Press, 1997).

Sosa, Lionel, *The Americano Dream: How Latinos Can Achieve Success in Business and in Life* (New York: Penguin, 1998).

Soustelle, Jacques, *Le Drame algérien et la décadence française: Répond à Raymond Aron* (Paris: Plon, 1957).

St. John, Rachel C., "Line in the Sand: The Desert Border between the United States and Mexico, 1848–1934" (Ph.D. diss., Stanford University, 2005).

Stack, John F., Jr. and Hebron, Lui, "Canada's Ethnic Dilemma: Primordial Ethnonationalism in Quebec," in David Carment, John F. Stack Jr., and Frank Harvey, eds., *The International Politics of Quebec Secession: State Making and State Breaking in North America* (Westport: Praeger, 2001).

Stauter-Halsted, Keely, "Rural Myth and the Modern Nation: Peasant Commemorations of Polish National Holidays, 1879–1910," in Bucur and Wingfield, *Staging the Past*.

Stearns, Peter, "Nationalisms: An Invitation to Comparative Analysis," *Journal of World History*, vol. 8, no. 1 (1997), 57–74.

Steiner, Zara, *The Foreign Office and Foreign Policy, 1898–1914* (1969; London: The Ashfield Press, 1986).

Steinfels, Peter, *The Neoconservatives: The Men Who Are Changing America's Politics* (New York: Simon and Schuster, 1979).

Stephanson, Anders, *Manifest Destiny: American Expansionism and the Empire of Right* (New York: Hill and Wang, 1995).

Sternhell, Zeev, *The Founding Myths of Israel: Nationalism, Socialism, and the Making of the Jewish State*, trans. David Maisel (Princeton: Princeton University Press, 1998).

Sugar, Peter F., ed., *Eastern European Nationalism in the Twentieth Century* (Washington, D.C.: The American University Press, 1995).

Suny, Ronald Grigor, "Nationalism and Class in the Russian Revolution. A Comparative Discussion," in Edith Ragovin Frankel *et al.*, *Revolution in Russia: Reassessments of 1917* (Cambridge: Cambridge University Press, 1992).

   The Revenge of the Past: Nationalism, Revolution and the Collapse of the Soviet Union (Stanford: Stanford University Press, 1993).

   "The Empire Strikes Out: Imperial Russia, 'National Identity,' and Theories of Empire," Suny and Martin, eds., *A State of Nations*.

Suny, Ronald Grigor and Martin, Terry, eds., *A State of Nations: Empire and Nation-Making in the Age of Lenin and Stalin* (New York: Oxford University Press, 2001).

Sutcliffe, Adam, *Judaism and Enlightenment* (Cambridge: Cambridge University Press, 2003).

Szayna, Thomas S., ed., *Identifying Potential Ethnic Conflict: Application of a Process Model* (Santa Monica, Calif.: RAND, 2000).

Szporluk, Roman, *The Political Thought of Thomas G. Masaryk* (Boulder: East European Monographs, 1981).

Tai, Hue-Tam Ho, "Remembered Realms: Pierre Nora and French National Memory," *American Historical Review*, vol. 106, no. 3 (2001), 906–922.

Tamir, Yael, *Liberal Nationalism* (Princeton: Princeton University Press, 1993).

Tanner, Marcus, *Croatia: A Nation Forged in War* (New Haven: Yale University Press, 1997).

Taylor, A. J. P., *The Struggle for Mastery in Europe, 1848–1918* (Oxford: Oxford University Press, 1954).

Taylor, Charles, "The Politics of Recognition," in Gutmann, ed., *Multiculturalism*.

Thomas, Rosalind, "Ethnicity, Genealogy, and Hellenism in Herodotus," in Irad Malkin, ed., *Ancient Perceptions of Greek Ethnicity* (Washington, D.C.: Center for Hellenic Studies/Trustees for Harvard University, 2001).

Thomas, R. T., *Britain and Vichy: The Dilemma of Anglo-French Relations, 1940–42* (New York: St. Martin's Press, 1979).

Thoreau, Henry David, *Walden: Or, Life in the Woods* (1854; New York: Random House, 1991).

Thucydides, *History of the Peloponnesian War*, trans. Rex Warner (Harmondsworth: Penguin, 1972).

Tibi, Bassam, *Arab Nationalism: Between Islam and the Nation-State*, 3rd edn (New York: St. Martin's Press, 1997).

Tierney, John, "The Hawks Loudly Express Their Second Thoughts," *The New York Times*, 16 May 2004.

Tismaneanu, Vladimir, *Fantasies of Salvation: Democracy, Nationalism, and Myth in Post-Communist Europe* (Princeton: Princeton University Press, 1998).

Toameh, Khaled Abu, "Poll: Decrease in Palestinian Support of Terror," *The Jerusalem Post*, 8 December 2004.

Toma, Peter and Kovac, Dusan, *Slovakia: From Samo to Dzurinda* (Stanford: Stanford University Press, 2001).

Tomasevich, Jozo, *Peasants, Politics, and Economic Change in Yugoslavia* (Stanford: Stanford University Press, 1955).

Tomes, Robert, "Operation Allied Force and the Legal Basis for Humanitarian Interventions," *Parameters: US Army War College Quarterly*, vol. 30, no. 1 (2000), 28–50.

Too, Yun Lee, *The Rhetoric of Identity in Isocrates: Text, Power, Pedagogy* (Cambridge: Cambridge University Press, 1995).

Tribe, Laurence H. and Dorf, Michael C., *On Reading the Constitution* (Cambridge, Mass.: Harvard University Press, 1991).

Trumpener, Katie, "Béla Bartók and the Rise of Comparative Ethnomusicology: Nationalism, Race Purity, and the Legacy of the Austro-Hungarian Empire," in Radano and Bohlman, eds., *Music and the Racial Imagination*.

Tulard, Jean, "Le Retour des cendres," in Nora, ed., *Les Lieux*, vol. ii, part 3.

Van den Berghe, Pierre L., "Race and Ethnicity: A Sociobiological Perspective," *Ethnic and Racial Studies*, vol. i, no. 4 (1978), 401–411.

Van der Veer, Peter and Lehmann, Hartmut, eds., *Nation and Religion: Perspectives on Europe and Asia* (Princeton: Princeton University Press, 1999).

Vick, Brian E., *Defining Germany: The 1848 Frankfurt Parliamentarians and National Identity* (Cambridge, Mass.: Harvard University Press, 2002).

Vickers, Miranda, *Between Serb and Albanian: A History of Kosovo* (New York: Columbia University Press, 1998).

Vincent, Andrew, *Nationalism and Particularity* (Cambridge: Cambridge University Press, 2002).

Volkan, Vamik, *Bloodlines: From Ethnic Pride to Ethnic Terrorism* (New York: Farrar, Straus and Giroux, 1997).

Wachtel, Andrew Baruch, *Making a Nation, Breaking a Nation: Literature and Cultural Politics in Yugoslavia* (Stanford: Stanford University Press, 1998).

Walbank, Frank W., "The Problem of Greek Nationality," in Frank W. Walbank, *Selected Papers: Studies in Greek and Roman History and Historiography* (Cambridge: Cambridge University Press, 1985).

Walicki, Andrzej, *The Enlightenment and the Birth of Modern Nationhood: Polish Political Thought from Noble Republicanism to Tadeusz Kościuszko*, trans. Emma Harris (Notre Dame: University of Notre Dame Press, 1989).

Walzer, Michael, *Exodus and Revolution* (New York: Basic Books, 1985).

What it Means to Be an American (New York: Marsilio, 1992).

"Comment," in Gutmann, ed., *Multiculturalism*, 1994.

Walzer, Michael, Lorberbaum, Menachem, and Zohar, Noam J., *et al.*, eds., *The Jewish Political Tradition*, vol. 1: *Authority* (New Haven: Yale University Press, 2000).

The Jewish Political Tradition, vol. 11: *Membership* (New Haven: Yale University Press, 2003).

Wandycz, Piotr S., "Poland's Place in Europe in the Concepts of Piłsudski and Dmowski," *East European Politics and Societies*, vol. 4, no. 3 (1990), 451–468.

Ward, J. W. and Hart, Paul J. B., "The Effects of Kin and Familiarity on Interactions between Fish," *Fish and Fisheries*, vol. 4, no. 4 (2003), 348.

Wasserstein, Bernard, *Divided Jerusalem: The Struggle for the Holy City*, 2nd edn (New Haven: Yale University Press, 2002).

Watt, Nicholas and Chrisafis, Angelique, "Adams Urges Bill of Rights to Keep Peace Process Alive," *The Guardian*, 5 February 2004.

Weber, Eugen, "L'Hexagone," in Nora, ed., *Les Lieux*, vol. 11, part 2.

Peasants into Frenchmen: The Modernization of Rural France, 1870–1914 (Stanford: Stanford University Press, 1976).

Weil, Patrick, *Qu'est-ce qu'un Français? Histoire de la nationalité française depuis la Révolution* (Paris: Grasset, 2002).

Weiner, Amir, "Nature, Nurture, and Memory in a Socialist Utopia: Delineating the Soviet Socio-Ethnic Body in the Age of Socialism" *American Historical Review*, vol. 104, no. 4 (1999), 1114–1155.

Weinstein, Harold, *Jean Jaurès: A Study of Patriotism in the French Socialist Movement* (New York: Columbia University Press, 1936).

Weitz, Eric D., *A Century of Genocide: Utopias of Race and Nation* (Princeton: Princeton University Press, 2003).

Welch, Richard E., Jr., *Response to Imperialism: The United States and the Philippine-American War, 1899–1902* (Chapel Hill: University of North Carolina Press, 1979).

Werth, Alexander, *De Gaulle: A Political Biography*, new edn (Harmondsworth: Penguin, 1967).

West, Rebecca, *Black Lamb and Grey Falcon: A Journey through Yugoslavia* (1940; New York: Penguin, 1969).

Wheeler-Bennett, John W., *Brest-Litovsk: The Forgotten Peace, March 1918* (1938; New York: Norton, 1971).

Whittaker, C. R., "Roman Frontiers and European Perceptions," *Journal of Historical Sociology*, vol. 13, no. 4 (2000), 462–482.

Widenor, William C., *Henry Cabot Lodge and the Search for an American Foreign Policy* (Berkeley: University of California Press, 1980).

Widmer, Paul, *Schweizer Aussenpolitik und Diplomatie: Von Pictet de Rochemont bis Edouard Brunner* (Zurich: Ammann, 2003).

Wiebe, Robert, "*Imagined Communities*, Nationalist Experiences," *Journal of the Historical Society*, vol. 1, no. 1 (2000), 33–63.

Winders, Richard Bruce, "A Response to the Alamo's Selected Past," *Cultural Resource Management*, vol. 23, no. 3 (2000), 31.

Winichakul, Thongchai, *Siam Mapped: A History of the Geo-Body of a Nation* (Honolulu: University of Hawai'i Press, 1994).

Winock, Michel, "Jeanne d'Arc," in Nora, ed., *Les Lieux*, vol. III, part 3.

Winter, Jay, *Sites of Memory, Sites of Mourning: The Great War in European Cultural History* (Cambridge: Cambridge University Press, 1995).

Wonders, Karen, "Habitat Dioramas and the Issue of Nativeness," unpublished paper, n.d.

Wood, Gordon S., *The Creation of the American Republic, 1776–1787* (Chapel Hill: University of North Carolina Press, 1969).

The Radicalism of the American Revolution (1992; New York: Random House, 1993).

Woodward, Bob, *Bush at War* (New York: Simon & Schuster, 2002).

Wright, Robert, *Virtual Sovereignty: Nationalism, Culture and the Canadian Question* (Toronto: Canadian Scholars' Press, 2004).

Wylie, Laurence, "Social Change at the Grass Roots," in Hoffmann *et al.*, *In Search of France: The Economy, Society, and Political System in the Twentieth Century* (1963; New York: Harper & Row, 1965).

Yack, Bernard, "The Myth of the Civic Nation," in Ronald Beiner, ed., *Theorizing Nationalism* (Albany: State University of New York Press, 1999).

Yalman, Ahmed Emin Yalman, *Turkey in the World War* (New Haven: Yale University Press, 1930).

Yans-McLaughlin, Virginia, and Lightman, Marjorie, with the Statue of Liberty–Ellis Island Foundation, *Ellis Island and the Peopling of America: The Official Guide* (New York: The New Press, 1990).

Yerushalmi, Yosef Hayim, *Zakhor: Jewish History and Jewish Memory* (Seattle: University of Washington Press, 1982).

Yiftachel, Oren, "Territory as the Kernel of the Nation: Space, Time and Nationalism in Israel/Palestine," *Geopolitics*, vol. 7, no. 2 (2002), 215–248.

Zagorin, Perez, *How the Idea of Religious Toleration Came to the West* (Princeton: Princeton University Press, 2003).

Zakaria, Fareed, "Rumsfeld's Crusader," *The Washington Post*, 21 October 2003, p. A25.

Zerubavel, Eviatar, *Time Maps: Collective Memory and the Social Shape of the Past* (Chicago: University of Chicago Press, 2003).

Zerubavel, Yael, *Recovered Roots: Collective Memory and the Making of Israeli National Tradition* (Chicago: University of Chicago Press, 1995).

Zimmer, Oliver, *A Contested Nation: History, Memory and Nationalism in Switzerland, 1761–1891* (Cambridge: Cambridge University Press, 2003).

Nationalism in Europe, 1890–1940 (Basingstoke: Palgrave Macmillan, 2003).

Zogby, Dr. James, "My Message to the Democratic Party," 3 July 2000, posted on the website of the Arab American Institute, http://www.aaiusa.org/wwatch/070300.htm.

Zürcher, Erik, *The Unionist Factor. The Role of the Committee of Union and Progress in the Turkish National Movement, 1905–1926* (Leiden: E. J. Brill, 1984).

Turkey: A Modern History (London: I. B. Tauris, 1993).

Index

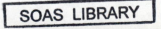